Maths Progress
Core Textbook

Series editors: Dr Naomi Norman and Katherine Pate

2

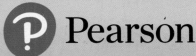

Published by Pearson Education Limited, 80 Strand, London, WC2R 0RL.

www.pearsonschoolsandfecolleges.co.uk

Text © Pearson Education Limited 2019
Project managed and edited by Just Content Ltd
Typeset by PDQ Digital Media Solutions Ltd
Original illustrations © Pearson Education Limited 2019
Cover illustration by Robert Samuel Hanson

The rights of Nick Asker, Jack Barraclough, Sharon Bolger, Gwenllian Burns, Greg Byrd, Lynn Byrd, Andrew Edmondson, Bobbie Johns, Catherine Murphy, Naomi Norman, Mary Pardoe, Katherine Pate, Harry Smith and Angela Wheeler to be identified as authors of this work have been asserted by them in accordance with the Copyright, Designs and Patents Act 1988.

First published 2019

22 21 20 19
10 9 8 7 6 5 4 3 2 1

British Library Cataloguing in Publication Data
A catalogue record for this book is available from the British Library.

ISBN 978 1 292 28004 2

Printed in Italy by Lego S.p.A.

Note from the publisher
Pearson has robust editorial processes, including answer and fact checks, to ensure the accuracy of the content in this publication, and every effort is made to ensure this publication is free of errors. We are, however, only human, and occasionally errors do occur. Pearson is not liable for any misunderstandings that arise as a result of errors in this publication, but it is our priority to ensure that the content is accurate. If you spot an error, please do contact us at resourcescorrections@pearson.com so we can make sure it is corrected.

Contents

Maths Progress Second Edition

Confidence at the heart

Maths Progress Second Edition is built around a unique pedagogy that has been created by leading mathematics educational researchers and Key Stage 3 teachers in the UK. The result is an innovative structure, based around 10 key principles designed to nurture confidence and raise achievement.

Pedagogy – our 10 key principles

- Fluency
- Problem-solving
- Reflection
- Mathematical Reasoning
- Progression
- Linking
- Multiplicative Reasoning
- Modelling
- Concrete - Pictorial - Abstract (CPA)
- Relevance

This edition of Maths Progress has been updated based on feedback from thousands of teachers and students.

The Core Curriculum

Textbooks with tried-and-tested differentation

Core Textbooks *For your whole cohort*

Based on a single, well-paced curriculum with built-in differentiation, fluency, problem-solving and reasoning so you can use them with your whole class. They follow the unique unit structure that's been shown to boost confidence and support every student's progress.

Support Books
Strengthening skills and knowledge

Provide extra scaffolding and support on key concepts for each lesson in the Core Textbook, giving students the mathematical foundations they need to progress with confidence.

Depth Books
Extending skills and knowledge

Deepen students' understanding of key concepts, and build problem-solving skills for each lesson in the Core Textbook so students can explore key concepts to their fullest.

Welcome to Maths Progress Second Edition Core Textbooks!

Building confidence

Pearson's unique unit structure has been shown to build confidence. Here's how it works.

Master

1 Students are helped to **master** fundamental knowledge and skills over a series of lessons.

Check

2 Before moving on with the rest of the unit, students **check** their understanding in a short formative assessment, and give an indication of their confidence level.

Master

Learn fundamental knowledge and skills over a series of lessons.

Unit opener
Lesson opener outlines lesson objectives, and links to the accompanying online content.

Hints
Guide students to help build problem-solving strategies throughout the course.

Warm up
Lessons begin with accessible questions designed to recap prior knowledge, and develop students' mathematical fluency in the facts and skills they will soon be using.

Challenge
Rich, problem-solving questions to help students apply what they've learned in the lesson and think differently.

Worked examples
Provide guidance around examples of key concepts with images, bar models, and other pictorial representations where needed.

Key point Explains key concepts and definitions where students need them.

Reflect Metacognitive questions that ask students to examine their thinking and understanding.

Check up
At the end of the Master lessons, students check their understanding with a short, formative Check Up test, to help decide whether to Strengthen or Extend their learning.

In areas where they have yet to develop a solid understanding or do not feel confident, they can choose to **strengthen** their learning

3 Students decide on their personalised route through the rest of the unit:

Strengthen

Extend

Test

4 Finally, students do a **test** to determine their progression across the unit.

In areas where they performed well in the assessment and also feel confident, they can choose to **extend** their learning

Strengthen

Students can choose the topics that they need more practice in. There are lots of hints and supporting questions to help.

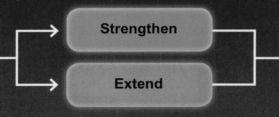

Extend

Students can apply and develop the maths they know in different situations.

Test

Students can show everything they have learned and check their progress using the end of unit test.

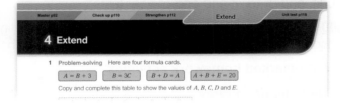

Students can use the Support and Depth Books at any point throughout the unit. They're designed to give the right level of support and additional problem-solving content to help strengthen students' understanding of key concepts.

Progress with confidence!

This innovative Key Stage 3 Mathematics course builds on the first edition KS3 Maths Progress (2014) course, drawing on input from thousands of teachers and students, and a 2-year study into the effectiveness of the course. All of this has come together with the latest cutting-edge approaches to shape Maths Progress Second Edition.

Take a look at the other parts of the series

*Active*Learn Service

The *Active*Learn service enhances the course by bringing together your planning, teaching and assessment tools, as well as giving students access to additional resources to support their learning. Use the interactive Scheme of Work, linked to all the teacher and student resources, to create a personalised learning experience both in and outside the classroom.

What's in *Active*Learn for Maths Progress?

- ☑ **Front-of-class student books** with links to PowerPoints, videos, animations and homework activities
- ☑ **96 new KS3 assessments and online markbooks,** including end-of-unit, end-of-term and end-of-year tests
- ☑ **Over 500 editable and printable homework worksheets** linked to each lesson and differentiated for Support, Core and Depth
- ☑ **Online, auto-marked homework activities**
- ☑ **Interactive Scheme of Work** makes re-ordering the course easy by bringing everything together into one curriculum for all students with links to Core, Support and Depth resources, and teacher guidance
- ☑ **Student access to videos, homework and online textbooks**

ActiveLearn Progress & Assess

The Progress & Assess service is part of the full *Active*Learn service, or can be bought as a separate subscription. It includes assessments that have been designed to ensure all students have the opportunity to show what they have learned through:

- a 2-tier assessment model
- approximately 60% common questions from Core in each tier
- separate calculator and non-calculator sections
- online markbooks for tracking and reporting
- mapped to indicative 9–1 grades

New *Assessment Builder*

Create your own classroom assessments from the bank of Maths Progress assessment questions by selecting questions on the skills and topics you have covered. Map the results of your custom assessments to indicative 9–1 grades using the custom online markbooks. *Assessment Builder* is available to purchase as an add-on to *Active*Learn Service or Progress & Assess subscriptions.

Purposeful Practice Books

Over 3,750 questions using minimal variation that:

- ☑ build in small steps to consolidate knowledge and boost confidence
- ☑ focus on strengthening skills and strategies, such as problem-solving
- ☑ help every student put their learning into practice in different ways
- ☑ give students a strong preparation for progressing to GCSE study.

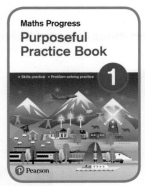

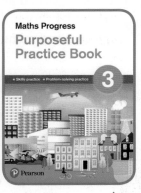

1 Number

1.1 Calculations

- Use written methods to add and subtract more than two numbers (including decimals)
- Use mental calculation for multiplication
- Estimate answers to calculations

Active Learn
Homework

Warm up

1 **Fluency** What value is ab when
   a $a = 2$ and $b = 1.5$ **b** $a = 2$ and $b = 2.5$?

2 Work out
   a 27×10 **b** 9×100 **c** 70×6 **d** 5×500 **e** 31×20

3 Use the column method to work out these calculations. Estimate the answers first.
   a $772 + 89$ **b** $1352 - 270$ **c** $22.9 + 17.87$ **d** $39.2 - 21.16$

4 Calculate
   a 64×5 **b** 32×10
   c What do you notice about the numbers you are multiplying and your answers in parts **a** and **b**?
   d 8×50 **e** 4×100
   f What do you notice about the numbers you are multiplying and your answers in parts **d** and **e**?

> **Q4c hint** Look for doubles and halves.

> **Key point**   Q4 shows a mental multiplication method called **doubling and halving**.

5 Use doubling and halving to work out these calculations. The first two are started for you.
   a 36×5 **b** 46×50 **c** 88×5
     $= 18 \times 10 = \square$ $= 23 \times 100 = \square$
   d 68×50 **e** 5×34 **f** 50×72

6 Use doubling and halving to work out these calculations. Two of them are started for you.
   a 35×8 **b** 45×6 **c** 15×12 **d** 2.5×16
     $= 70 \times 4 = \square$ $= 5 \times \square = \square$
   e 3.5×14 **f** 6×7.5 **g** 4.5×22 **h** 1.5×26

7   **Reasoning**   To work out 2.4 × 50, which number is it better to halve?
    Show working and calculate the answer.

8   **a** **i**   Double 7.5, then double the answer.

Q8a i hint Double 7.5 twice.

    ii   Halve 32, then halve the answer.
    iii   Use your answers to work out 7.5 × 32.
    b   Use doubling and halving to work out these calculations.
    i 2.5 × 48   **ii** 25 × 88   **iii** 24 × 25

9   **Problem-solving**   One ounce is approximately 28 grams.
    Work out the number of grams in 2.5 ounces.

10 Work out these calculations. They are started for you.
    a 6 × 101
    = 6 × 100 + 6 × 1
    = ☐ + ☐
    = ☐
    b 6 × 99
    = 6 × 100 − 6 × 1
    = ☐ − ☐
    = ☐

Key point   Q10 shows a mental multiplication method that involves **rounding and adjusting**.

11 Use rounding and adjusting to work out these calculations.
    a 8 × 101
    b 8 × 99
    c 7 × 102
    d 7 × 98
    e 4 × 999

Q11e hint 4 × 999 = 4 × 1000 − 4 × ☐

    f 4 × 1001
    g 3 × 499

Q11g hint 3 × 499 = 3 × 500 − 3 × ☐

    h 3 × 19

Q11h hint 3 × 19 = 3 × ☐ − 3 × 1

    i 32 × 19

12 **Problem-solving / Reasoning**
    a   An artist buys 15 pencils for 99p each.
        How much does the artist spend?
    b   How much more would the artist spend if she bought better pencils at £1.02 each?
    c   Faisal works out the answer to part **b** by calculating 15 × 3p.
        Write a sentence explaining why this method works.

13 A market stall sells T-shirts at £4.99 each.
    How much do 5 T-shirts cost?

14 Use the column method to work out these calculations.
Estimate the answers first.

Q14 hint Rounding to the nearest 10, 100 or 1000 will give an estimate.

a 1592 + 178

b 1592 + 178 − 83

c 3266 − 180

d 3266 − 180 + 34

e 5079 − 97 + 621

f 68 000 + 3250 − 19 241

15 Problem-solving Heathrow Airport has 21 075 car parking spaces altogether.
Terminal 4 has 890 short-term spaces, 1700 long-stay spaces and 330 business spaces.
Work out the total number of spaces in the other terminals.
Estimate the answer first.

16 Use the column method to calculate these.
Estimate the answers first.

a 23.7 + 1.06 + 0.88   b 96 + 8.3 − 0.47   c 9.7 − 2.58 − 0.810

17 Reasoning Sam writes three calculations using the same decimals.

 i 261.42 + 37.21 + 102.7
 ii 261.42 + 37.21 − 102.7
 iii 261.42 − 37.21 − 102.7

 a He uses the column method involving all three numbers to work out
 the answer to calculation **i** like this:

     2 6 1 . 4 2
       3 7 . 2 1
   + 1 0 2 . 7
   _____

 What is the correct answer?

 b Can you calculate parts **ii** and **iii** in the same way?
 If so, show your working.
 If not, write two separate calculations to find answers to parts **ii** and **iii**.

18 Problem-solving Lars cuts two pieces, of length 2.7 m and 1.93 m, from a 5 m length of
skirting board. What length of the skirting board is left?

19 Problem-solving A £2 coin is 2.5 mm thick; a £1 coin is 2.8 mm thick; a 10p coin is
1.85 mm thick.
Alice puts these three coins on top of each other, in a pile.
How high is the pile?

Challenge

a Substitute the values $b = 499$, $c = 21$ and $d = 7.1$ into this formula to work out the value
of a.

$a = bc - d$

b List any mental methods you used.

Reflect   Use two different methods to work out

501×18

Which method was easier? Explain.

1.2 Divisibility and division

Active Learn
Homework

* Know and use divisibility rules
* Use a written method to divide decimal numbers by integers

Warm up

1 **Fluency**   How do you know if a number divides exactly by
   a 2   **b** 10   **c** 5?

2 Copy and complete these long divisions.
   a
   ```
        2
   14)294
     28
   ```
   b
   ```
        2
   24)5088
     48
   ```

3 **Reasoning**
   a Explain why 12.0 has the same value as 12.
   b Explain why 12.00 has the same value as 12 and 12.0.
   c Explain why 12.40 has the same value as 12.4.
   d Does putting a 0 at the end of any number change its value?

> **Q3a hint** How many tenths in 12 and 12.0?

> **Q3d hint** Consider decimal numbers and whole numbers.

> **Key point**   An **integer** is a whole number. It can be positive, negative or zero.
> When you divide an integer by a second integer, if there is no remainder then the first integer is said to be **divisible by** the second integer.
> e.g. 64 ÷ 4 = 16, so 64 is divisible by 4.

4 Copy this list of numbers.
   2   3   4   5   6   7   8   9   10   11   12
   Circle those numbers that 48 is divisible by. Use your times tables to help you.

5 **a** List all the numbers between 20 and 50 that are divisible by 3.
   b Work out the sum of the digits in each number in your list.
   For example 21: 2 + 1 = 3
   If your answer has more than one digit, then sum the digits again until you get a single-digit answer.
   For example 39: 3 + 9 = 12
                   12: 1 + 2 = 3
   c What do you notice about numbers that are divisible by 3?
   d Use what you noticed in part **c** to predict if these numbers are divisible by 3.
      i 81   **ii** 123   **iii** 495   **iv** 567
      v 8310   **vi** 44442
   e Use a calculator to check your predictions from part **d**.

> **Q5e hint** Key in 81 ÷ 3. Do you get an answer with no remainder?

6 Repeat Q5, but for numbers between 20 and 100 that are divisible by 9.

7 **Reasoning** Larry says, 'A number is divisible by 6 if it is divisible by 2 *and* 3.'
Is Larry correct? Test Larry's statement with 5 numbers that are divisible by 6, and 5 numbers that are not divisible by 6.

8 **a** List all the numbers from 100 to 140 that are divisible by 4.
b Underline the last two digits in each number in your list.
c What do you notice about your answer to part **b**?
d Use what you noticed in part **c** to predict if these numbers are divisible by 4.

    i 324   **ii** 434   **iii** 1048   **iv** 5808
    v 48060   **vi** 129072   **vii** 240042   **viii** 844122

e Use a calculator to check your predictions from part **d**.

9 **Problem-solving / Reasoning** Kerry says, 'A number is divisible by 8 if the last three digits are divisible by 8.'
Check Kerry is correct by predicting if these numbers are divisible by 8.
Then check on a calculator.

    a 324   **b** 434   **c** 1048   **d** 5808
    e 48060   **f** 129072   **g** 240042   **h** 844122

10 **Reasoning** Sam says, 'All integers are divisible by 1.'
Is Sam correct? Explain.

Key point   A number is divisible by
- 3, if the sum of its digits is divisible by 3
- 4, if the last two digits are divisible by 4
- 6, if the number is divisible by 2 *and* 3
- 8, if the last three digits are divisible by 8
- 9, if the sum of its digits is divisible by 9

Worked example

Work out £28.20 ÷ 12

$$\begin{array}{r} 2.35 \\ 12\overline{)28.20} \\ -24 \\ \hline 42 \\ -36 \\ \hline 60 \\ -60 \\ \hline 0 \end{array}$$

Line up the decimal point.

Try multiples of 12: 1 × 12 = 12, 2 × 12 = 24

Try multiples of 12: 3 × 12 = 36

Try multiples of 12: 5 × 12 = 60

£28.20 ÷ 12 = £2.35

---

11 Work out
    a £68.76 ÷ 12   **b** £261.80 ÷ 11
    c £5808.60 ÷ 15   **d** £8.50 ÷ 25

Q11d hint £0.☐ ☐

12 Work out

  a 57.6 ÷ 16

  b 77.4 ÷ 12

  c 48.3 ÷ 14

  d 1028.5 ÷ 22

> **Q12b hint** 12)‾77.4
>
> The division does not end here.
> 77.4 = 77.40 so work out 12)‾77.40

13 Maurice buys a car costing £8550.

He pays a deposit of £921 and then 12 equal monthly instalments.

Copy and complete the calculations to work out Maurice's monthly instalments.

```
  8 5 5 0
−   9 2 1            12)□□□□. 00
  □□□□ ───────────↑
```

14 **Problem-solving** Helen buys a new laptop for £1015.

She pays a 10% deposit and then 18 equal monthly instalments.

What are her monthly instalments?

15 **Problem-solving / Reasoning** Alice works out 2639 ÷ 26.

She writes the answer 11.5.

  a Use estimation to show that Alice's answer is incorrect.

  b Work out the correct answer to 2639 ÷ 26.

Challenge

Here is a rule to predict if a number is divisible by 7.

Step 1 Double the last digit.

Step 2 Subtract your answer to Step 1 from the number made by the remaining digits.

Step 3 Is the answer to Step 2 in the 7 times table?
If yes, then the original number is divisible by 7.

> For example: 3 0 1
> **Step 1** Double 1 = 2
>
> **Step 2** 30 − 2 = 28
>
> **Step 3** 28 is in the 7 times table so 301 is divisible by 7.

  a Write three other 3-digit numbers that are divisible by 7. Show that the rule works for your numbers.

  b Write any three 3-digit numbers.
Use the rule to predict if they are divisible by 7.

  c Use a calculator to check your predictions from part **b**.

Reflect When might it be helpful to:

  a use a divisibility rule, rather than divide?

  b divide, rather than use a divisibility rule?

1.3 Calculating with negative integers

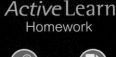

Active Learn
Homework

- Add, subtract, multiply and divide positive and negative numbers, including larger numbers and decimals

Warm up

1 Fluency
  a What is the difference between 3 and 12?   **b** Is −3 positive 3 or negative 3?

2 Work out
  a 3 − 5   **b** −2 + 5   **c** −2 − 3   **d** 0 − 7   **e** −12 + 3

3 Work out
  a 4 × 9   **b** 20 × 4   **c** 10 × 0.5   **d** 100 × 0.1

4 a Copy the tables and continue the patterns of answers to complete them.

Calculation	Answer
3 + 2	5
3 + 1	4
3 + 0	
3 + −1	
3 + −2	
3 + −3	
3 + −4	

⟩−1

Calculation	Answer
3 − 2	1
3 − 1	2
3 − 0	
3 − −1	
3 − −2	
3 − −3	
3 − −4	

⟩+1

  b Fill in the missing signs.
    i 3 + −5 is the same as 3 ☐ 5   **ii** 3 − −5 is the same as 3 ☐ 5
  c Copy and complete these rules.
    i + − is the same as ☐   **ii** − − is the same as ☐

5 Work out
  a 4 + −1   **b** 4 − −1   **c** 4 + −2   **d** 4 − −2
  e 4 + −3   **f** 4 − −3   **g** 4 + −4   **h** 4 − −4
  i 4 + −5   **j** 4 − −5   **k** 4 + −6   **l** 4 − −6

Key point   4 + −1 is 4 add negative 1. You are adding a negative number.
4 − +1 is 4 subtract positive 1. You are subtracting a positive number.
Both give the same answer.

+ − 1
− + 1

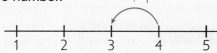

6 Work out
  a 5 + −7   **b** 5 − +7   **c** 5 − −7
  d 6 + −10   **e** 6 − +10   **f** 6 − −10

7 Work out the difference between each pair of numbers. Give your answer as a positive number.

 a 8 and 15   **b** −3 and 6   **c** −2 and 8

 d 7 and −7   **e** 1.5 and −1   **f** −6.5 and 3.5

> **Q7b hint** 6 − −3 = ☐

8 **Reasoning** Luke, Adam and Jack work out −10 − −12.
 Luke writes the answer 22.
 Adam writes the answer 2.
 Jack writes the answer −2.
 Who is correct? Explain the mistakes the other students made.

9 Work out

 a 32 − 40   **b** −40 − 32   **c** −32 + −40   **d** −40 − +32   **e** −32 − −40

> **Key point** A **bank balance** is the amount of money in a bank account.
> A **negative bank balance** (or **overdraft**) is an amount owed to the bank.
> When you put money into a bank account, this is a **deposit**.
> When you take money out, this is a **withdrawal**.

10 **Problem-solving** At the end of April, Mrs Prestwick has a bank balance of £120.
 The table shows Mrs Prestwick's bank balance each time she made a deposit (+) or
 withdrawal (−) in May.

Date in May	1	2	13	19	20	25	31
Deposit/Withdrawal (£)	−145	+20	−37	+100	−12	+55	−25
Balance (£)	−25						

 a Copy and complete the table.
 b Work out the difference in her bank balance between 1 May and 31 May.
 c Does the 31 May figure represent a balance or an overdraft?

11 **Problem-solving / Reasoning** When hydrogen gas is cooled, it becomes a liquid at
 −253 °C and freezes solid at −259 °C.
 a Hydrogen at −160 °C is cooled by 100 °C.
  After cooling, is it a gas, liquid or solid? Show your working.
 b In a science lab, hydrogen is at 20 °C.
  By how many degrees do you need to cool it for it to become liquid?

12 a Copy the tables and continue the patterns of answers to complete them.

Calculation	Answer
3 × 3	9
3 × 2	6
3 × 1	
3 × 0	
3 × −1	
3 × −2	

Calculation	Answer
3 × −3	
2 × −3	
1 × −3	
0 × −3	
−1 × −3	
−2 × −3	

 b Copy and complete the rules.
  positive × positive = positive
  negative × positive =_____

  positive × negative =_____
  negative × negative =_____

 c **Reasoning** What is an easy way to remember these rules?

13 Work out

a −2 × −4   b 8 × −3

c −6 × 6   d 5 × (−9)

e (−3) × (−3)   f −20 × 6   g −4 × (−9)

h (−12) × 5   i −10 × 0.5   j 100 × (−0.1)

Q13 hint (−9) is another way of writing the negative number −9.

14 a Copy and complete these number facts. The first one is done for you.

   i 2 × −3 = −6, so −6 ÷ 2 = −3 and −6 ÷ −3 = 2

   ii −3 × −4 = 12, so 12 ÷ −3 = ☐ and 12 ÷ −4 = ☐

   iii −2 × 5 = −10, so −10 ÷ −2 = ☐ and −10 ÷ 5 = ☐

b Copy and complete the rules.

   positive ÷ positive = positive   positive ÷ negative = _____

   negative ÷ positive = _____   negative ÷ negative = _____

15 Work out

a −8 ÷ −2   b 15 ÷ −3   c −18 ÷ 6   d (−20) ÷ 5

e 40 ÷ (−8)   f (−6) ÷ (−6)   g −1000 ÷ (−10) h 132 ÷ −11

i 200 ÷ −25   j 0.8 ÷ −2   k −12.4 ÷ 2

16 Problem-solving   Work out the missing numbers.

a 5 × ☐ = −20   b ☐ × −2 = 14   c −6 × ☐ = −24   d 16 × ☐ = 1600

e −18 ÷ ☐ = 9   f 36 ÷ ☐ = −9   g ☐ ÷ 3 = −11   h ☐ ÷ −7 = −6

17 Problem-solving   Here are some temperatures:

   −4 °C   −9 °C   −2 °C   −11 °C   1 °C   −10 °C   −7 °C

a What is the range of temperatures?

b What is the mean temperature?

18 Substitute the values into each formula and work out the answers.

a $P = -4Q$ when $Q = -8$

b $m = 2n - 1$ when $n = -7$

c $A = 3a - 4b$ when $a = -2$ and $b = -5$

d $c = -7d - 2e$ when $d = 5$ and $e = 10$

19 Work out these calculations. Use the priority of operations.

a 6 × −2 − 1   **b** 3 + −16 ÷ 4

c −5(3 − 4)   **d** −4(−3 + 5) − 2

Challenge

1 Is the answer positive or negative when you multiply these?
      Write some calculations for each.

   a positive × negative × negative

   b positive × positive × negative

2 Is the answer positive or negative when you multiply four numbers together?

Reflect   Look back at what you have learned about negative numbers in this lesson.
What is different and what is the same about positive and negative numbers?

1.4 Powers and roots

Active Learn
Homework

- Calculate using squares, square roots, cubes and cube roots
- Say which integers a square root lies between

Warm up

1. **Fluency**
   a What is the square of 9?
   b What is the square root of 9?

2. Work out the missing numbers.
   a $\sqrt{1} = \square$ b $2^2 = \square$ c $\sqrt{\square} = 4$ d $\sqrt{\square} = 5$
   e $6^2 = \square$ f $\square^2 = 64$ g $12^2 = \square$ h $100^2 = \square$

3. Work out these calculations. Use the priority of operations.
   a $3^2 + 1$ b 2×3^2 c 3×2^2 d 2×4^2 e $1 + 2 \times 5^2$

4. Work out these calculations. Use the priority of operations.
   a $\sqrt{36} \times 5$ b $\sqrt{36} + 5$ c $9 - \sqrt{9}$
   d $32 \div \sqrt{16}$ e $\sqrt{144} - 2^2$ f $4 \times \sqrt{16} + 9$

   > **Q4a hint** Work out the square root before multiplying.

5. Work out
   a 7.2^2 b 3.4^2 c 6.8^2
   d $3.9^2 \times 6$ e $10.2^2 - 100$ f $19 + 11.1^2$

   > **Q5 hint** Use the 'squared' key on your calculator.
   > Look for a key like $\boxed{x^2}$

6. Work out these calculations.
   Round your answers to 1 decimal place.
   a $\sqrt{50}$ b $\sqrt{200}$
   c $\sqrt{375}$ d $\sqrt{480}$
   e $\sqrt{468} + 73$ f $\sqrt{528} - 22$

   > **Q6 hint** Use the 'square root' key on your calculator.
   > Look for a key like $\boxed{\sqrt{}}$ $\boxed{\sqrt{x}}$ or $\boxed{\sqrt{\square}}$

Worked example

Which two integers does $\sqrt{20}$ lie between?

$\sqrt{16}$ $\sqrt{20}$ $\sqrt{25}$
$\downarrow$ $\downarrow$ $\downarrow$
4   5

> 20 lies between the square numbers 16 and 25.
> So $\sqrt{20}$ lies between $\sqrt{16}$ and $\sqrt{25}$.

$4^2 = 16$ $5^2 = 25$
$\sqrt{20}$ lies between 4 and 5.
$4 < \sqrt{20} < 5$

> This can be written with < symbols:
> 4 is less than $\sqrt{20}$, which is less than 5.

7. Which two integers does each square root lie between?
   Write your answers using <.
   a $\sqrt{6}$ b $\sqrt{15}$ c $\sqrt{40}$ d $\sqrt{55}$ e $\sqrt{92}$ f $\sqrt{175}$

8 Problem-solving 10 square tiles have a total area of 600 cm².

   a Estimate the side length of a tile.

   b Use a calculator to work out the side length to a suitable degree of accuracy.

> **Q8a hint** Find two integers that the side length lies between.

9 Problem-solving A theatre wants to arrange seats in a block that is as close to a square as possible.

There should be the same number of seats in each row. There are 420 seats.

How many should be in each row?

Key point $2^3 = 2 \times 2 \times 2$

2^3 is '2 **cubed**' or '2 **to the power** 3'

---

10 Work out these cube numbers. The first one is done for you.

   a $1^3 = 1 \times 1 \times 1 = 1$

   b $2^3 = 2 \times 2 \times 2 = \square$

   c 3^3 **d** 4^3 **e** 5^3 **f** 10^3

Key point   Finding the **cube root** is the **inverse** of finding the cube of a number.

3 cubed is 27, so the cube root of 27 is 3.

The cube root of 27 is written $\sqrt[3]{27}$.

---

11 Work out the missing numbers.

   a $\sqrt[3]{125} = \square$ **b** $\sqrt[3]{\square} = 10$ **c** $\sqrt[3]{64} = \square$

   d $\sqrt[3]{\square} = 3$ **e** $\sqrt[3]{1} = \square$ **f** $\sqrt[3]{\square} = 5$

12 Use the $\boxed{x^3}$ and $\boxed{\sqrt[3]{}}$ keys of your calculator to work out these calculations.

   a $\sqrt[3]{343}$ **b** $\sqrt[3]{729}$ **c** 11^3 **d** 16^3 **e** $\sqrt[3]{3375}$

13 Reasoning Is the cube root of an integer always an integer? Give examples.

14 Work out these calculations. Round your answers to 1 decimal place.

   a $\sqrt[3]{100}$

   b 5.5^3

   c 9.1^3

   d $\sqrt[3]{60}$

   e $\sqrt[3]{78}$

   f $\sqrt[3]{150}$

15 Work out these calculations. Use the priority of operations.

   a $4^2 - 2^3$

   b 2×2^3

   c $\sqrt{81} + \sqrt[3]{64}$

   d $3^3 - \sqrt{225}$

   e $\sqrt[3]{1000} - \sqrt{100}$

   f $64 - \sqrt{64} - \sqrt[3]{64}$

> **Q15 hint** Use BIDMAS to remember the priority of operations.
> Brackets
> Indices
> Division and Multiplication
> Addition and Subtraction

16 Work out these calculations. The first one is started for you.

   a $(-2)^2 = -2 \times -2 = \square$ **b** $(-3)^2$ **c** $(-4)^2$ **d** $(-5)^2$

   e $(-6)^2$ **f** $(-7)^2$ **g** $(-8)^2$ **h** $(-10)^2$

17 **Reasoning**

    a What do you notice about the answer when you square a negative number?

    b Is it possible to square a negative number and get an answer that is also negative? Explain.

> **Key point** $3^2 = 9$ and $(-3)^2 = 9$.
> The **positive square root** of 9 is 3.
> The **negative square root** of 9 is −3.
> The $\sqrt{\ }$ symbol is used for the principal square root, which is always a positive number.
> For example, $\sqrt{9} = 3$

18 Write the positive and negative square roots of these numbers.

    a 25   **b** 64   **c** 81   **d** 1   **e** 121   **f** 144

19 Work out these calculations. The first one is started for you.

    a $(-2)^3 = -2 \times -2 \times -2 = \square$ **b** $(-3)^3$ **c** $(-4)^3$

    d $(-5)^3$ **e** $(-10)^3$ **f** $(-1)^3$

    g Reasoning   What can you say about the cube of a negative number?

20 **Reasoning**

    a Copy and complete the Venn diagram. Write each number in its correct place.

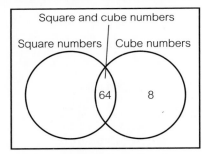 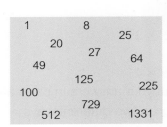

> **Q20 hint** A Venn diagram is a way of showing overlapping sets.

    b Which numbers are both square *and* cube numbers?

> **Key point**   A **counter example** is an example which proves that the statement is wrong.

> **Challenge**   Give reasons or counter examples for your answers to these questions.
>
> **a**   Is the sum of two square numbers always a square number?
>
> **b**   Is the product of two square numbers always a square number?
>
> **c**   Is the cube of a square number always a square number?

> **Reflect**   The $\sqrt{\ }$ part of the root symbol began as an old-fashioned letter r in the 16th Century. You could remember r for root!
>
> List all the mathematics notation used in this lesson, and ways you might remember it.
>
> Make sure you know what all the notation in this lesson means.
>
> **Hint** 'Notation' means symbols.

1.5 Powers, roots and brackets

- Calculate combinations of squares, square roots, cubes, cube roots and brackets

Active Learn
Homework

Warm up

1 **Fluency** Complete these sentences.
   a 9 is the square of □ .
   b 9 is the square root of □ .

2 Work out
   a $\sqrt{121}$
   b $\sqrt[3]{27}$
   c 100^2
   d 5^2
   e $\sqrt[3]{1000}$

3 Work out these calculations.
   Use the priority of operations.
   a $3^3 - 5^2$
   b $\sqrt{100} - \sqrt[3]{125}$
   c $2 \times (5^2 + 8)$
   d $(11 - 3)^2 \div 4$

> **Q3 hint** In the priority of operations, work out calculations in brackets first.

4 **Reasoning**
   a Work out
     i $(2 \times 3)^2$
     ii $2^2 \times 3^2$
   b Work out
     i $(2 \times 4)^2$
     ii $2^2 \times 4^2$
   c What do you notice about your answers in parts **a** and **b**?
   d Work out each calculation in two different ways.
     i $(2 \times 5)^2$
     ii $2^2 \times 2^2$

5 **Problem-solving / Reasoning**
   a Copy and complete the two methods to work out 20^2.

$$(2 \times 10)^2 = \square^2 \times \square^2$$
$$= \square \times \square$$
$$= \square$$

$$(4 \times 5)^2 = \square^2 \times \square^2$$
$$= \square \times \square$$
$$= \square$$

   b Do both methods give the same answer?

6 Work out
   a 15^2
   b 30^2
   c 50^2
   d 90^2
   e 200^2
   f 500^2
   g 8000^2

7 **Reasoning** Which of these are square numbers? Show your working.
   49   490   4900   49000   490000

8 **Problem-solving** At an exhibition, an image of a 12 cm square painting was projected onto a wall so that its sides were 100 times the original length.
Work out the area of the image.

9 Work out these calculations. Use the priority of operations.
Check your answers using a calculator.

a $4 \times (\sqrt{121} - 4)$ **b** $9^2 - (\sqrt{16} + 16)$

c $(3^2 + \sqrt{4})^2$ **d** $(20 - 5 \times 3)^3$

e $(3^2 + 3^3) \div 6$ **f** $5^3 - (7 - 5)^3$

Key point

For $\dfrac{\text{calculation 1}}{\text{calculation 2}}$ work out (calculation 1) ÷ (calculation 2) using the priority of operations,

e.g. $\dfrac{5 + 7}{8 - 5} = (5 + 7) \div (8 - 5)$

---

10 Work out

a $\dfrac{12 + 20}{10 - 8}$ **b** $\dfrac{13 + 8}{5 - 2}$

c $\dfrac{4^2 + 9}{5}$ **d** $\dfrac{3^2 + 7}{3 + 5}$

e $\dfrac{12 + 15}{3^2}$ **f** $\dfrac{70 - 7}{2^2 + 5}$

g $\dfrac{60}{8^2 - 7^2}$ **h** $\dfrac{3^2 + 23}{2^3}$

11 Reasoning

a Enter 12 + 20 ÷ 10 − 8 into your calculator.
Do you get the same answer as for Q10 part **a**? Explain.

b How can you enter $\dfrac{12 + 20}{10 - 8}$ into your calculator to get the correct answer?
Write down the calculator keys you would press in the order you would press them.

> **Q11b hint** Use the brackets keys on your calculator.

c Check your answers to Q10 on your calculator.

12 Work out

a $\dfrac{\sqrt{121} + 9}{10}$ **b** $\dfrac{\sqrt{144} + 3}{2 + 8}$

c $\dfrac{18 - 8}{\sqrt{25}}$ **d** $\dfrac{4^2 + 4}{\sqrt{16}}$

e $\dfrac{\sqrt[3]{64}}{3 - 1}$ **f** $\dfrac{6 + \sqrt[3]{1000}}{4}$

g $\dfrac{2^3 + 2}{\sqrt[3]{27} - 1}$ **h** $\dfrac{\sqrt[3]{1000}}{\sqrt{100} - \sqrt[3]{125}}$

Key point

For $\sqrt{\text{addition or subtraction calculation}}$ work out the calculation and then the square root,

e.g. $\sqrt{40 - 4} = \sqrt{36}$

---

13 Work out these calculations.
Check your answers using a calculator.

   a $\sqrt{40-4}$ **b** $\sqrt{20+5}$

   c $\sqrt{99+1}$ **d** $\sqrt{100-19}$

   e $\sqrt{100+41-20}$

Q13a hint When checking your answer on a calculator, use brackets to make sure you work out the correct answer: $\sqrt{40-4}$ and not $\sqrt{40}-4$

14 **Problem-solving / Reasoning** What are the missing numbers?

   a $\sqrt{52-\square}=7$ **b** $\sqrt{\square+56}=8$ **c** $\sqrt{84+\square}=12$

Q14a hint
$\sqrt{49}=7$

15 **Problem-solving / Reasoning**

   a Write three different calculations so that $\sqrt{\square+\square}=10$

   b Write a sentence describing how you decided on the missing numbers in the calculation.

16 Work out these calculations.
Check your answers using a calculator.

   a $\sqrt{40+3^2}$ **b** $\sqrt{4^2-7}$

   c $\sqrt[3]{35-8}$ **d** $\sqrt[3]{100-36}$

   e $\sqrt{3^3+9}$ **f** $\sqrt{5^2+12^2}$

17 **Reasoning**

   a Work out **i** $\sqrt{4}\times\sqrt{9}$ **ii** $\sqrt{4\times9}$

   b What do you notice about your answers in part **a**?

   c $16\times36=576$
      Use this fact to work out $\sqrt{576}$.

Q16c hint Work out $\sqrt{16\times36}$

   d $81\times121=9801$
      Use this fact to work out $\sqrt{9801}$.

   e Does the same rule work when adding or subtracting square roots?
      Explain using $\sqrt{16}+\sqrt{9}$ and 25, and $\sqrt{16}-\sqrt{9}$ and $\sqrt{7}$.

Challenge

1 **a** Find $\sqrt{5}$ using your calculator.
    b Square the answer. What do you notice?
    c Complete this sentence: If you square the square root of a number,
        _____.

2 **a** Clear your calculator display. Find $\sqrt{5}$ again. Give the answer to two decimal places.
    b Type in your answer on your calculator. Square this number.
    c What do you notice? Explain why this happens.

3 Repeat part **2** using **i** five decimal places **ii** the entire calculator display.

4 Does your calculator give the exact value of $\sqrt{5}$? Explain your answer.

Reflect   Look back at Q12g. Write down all the steps you took to work out the answer.
You may begin with, 'Step 1: I worked out 2^3.'
Now look back at each step. How did you decide what to do first, second, third ...?
Compare your decisions with others in your class.

1.6 More powers, multiples and factors

- Use index form
- Write a number as the product of its prime factors
- Use prime factor decomposition to find the highest common factor (HCF) and lowest common multiple (LCM)

*Active*Learn
Homework

Warm up

1 Fluency What are the first five prime numbers?

2 Use prime numbers to complete these multiplications.
   a $\square \times \square = 15$ **b** $\square \times \square = 21$ **c** $\square \times \square = 77$

3 a List all the factors of 8 and all the factors of 12.
   b What is the lowest common multiple of 8 and 12?
   c What is the highest common factor of 8 and 12?

> **Key point** $2^4 = 2 \times 2 \times 2 \times 2$ 2^4 is '2 to the power 4'.
> The small number is called the **index** or **power** and tells you how many 2s to multiply together.
> The power key on your calculator may look like $\boxed{y^x}$ or $\boxed{x^\square}$

4 a Work out these calculations.
   i 2^4 **ii** 2^5 **iii** 10^5 **iv** 10^6
   b Use the $\boxed{y^x}$ or $\boxed{x^\square}$ key on your calculator to check your answers.

> **Key point**   The result of multiplying numbers or letters together is called their **product**.
> For example, the product of 3 and 10 is $3 \times 10 = 30$.

5 Write each product using powers.
   a $10 \times 10 \times 10 \times 10$
   b $3 \times 3 \times 4 \times 4 \times 4$
   c $10 \times 10 \times 10 \times 2 \times 2 \times 2 \times 2 \times 2$
   d $2 \times 3 \times 3 \times 3 \times 3$
   e $2 \times 5 \times 2 \times 5 \times 2 \times 5$
   f $2 \times 3 \times 2 \times 7 \times 3 \times 3$

> **Q5b hint** $3 \times 3 \times 4 \times 4 \times 4 = 3^2 \times 4 \times 4 \times 4 =$

6 An allotment has three square vegetable-growing areas of side length 6 m and one square fruit-growing area of side length 8 m.
   a Write a calculation for the total area using powers.   **b** Calculate the total area.

> **Key point**   **Prime factors** are factors that are prime numbers.
> The factors of 36 are 1, 2, 3, 4, 6, 9, 12, 18 and 36.
> The prime factors are 2 and 3.

7 Write the prime factors of each number.
   a 12   **b** 14   **c** 18   **d** 32
   e 13   **f** 46   **g** 84   **h** 99

Unit 1 Number   1

Worked example

Write 300 as the product of its prime factors.

300

[Make a factor tree using pairs of factors.]

30   10 $300 = 30 \times 10$

$30 = 10 \times 3$ 10   ③   ⑤ ② $10 = 5 \times 2$

$10 = 5 \times 2$ ⑤ ②

[Circle the prime factors.]

[Write their product in index form.
Write the factors in size order. Put the smallest first.]

$300 = 5 \times 2 \times 3 \times 5 \times 2 = 2^2 \times 3 \times 5^2$

Key point   All positive integers can be written as a product of prime factors.
This is called **prime factor decomposition**.
The product is often written in **index form** (numbers with powers).

8   **a** Complete these factor trees for 18.
    b Write 18 as a product of its prime factors.
    c Does it matter which two factors you choose first?

    18   18
    ②   9   ③   6

9   **a** Draw factor trees and write each number as the product of
        its prime factors in index form.
        i 12   **ii** 16   **iii** 32   **iv** 36   **v** 48
        vi 60   **vii** 80   **viii** 120   **ix** 200   **x** 338
    b Look at your answers for 16 and 32. What do you notice about the product?

10 **Reasoning**   Ned finds that the prime factor decomposition of a number is $2 \times 5 \times 7$.
    What was his number?

11 **a** Write 360 as a product of its prime factors.
    b Write 24 as a product of its prime factors.
    c Does 24 divide exactly into 360? Explain your answer.
    d **Problem-solving / Reasoning**   Use prime factor decomposition to test whether these
        divisions have integer answers.
        i $336 \div 28$ **ii** $410 \div 15$ **iii** $544 \div 17$

Q11c hint How many prime
factors in the product for 24 are
also in the product for 360?

Key point   You can use prime factor decomposition to find the highest common factor
(HCF) or lowest common multiple (LCM) of two or more numbers.

12 Copy and complete the steps to use prime factor decomposition to find the highest
    common factor of 36 and 60.
    a Copy and complete to write 36 and 60 as products
        of their prime factors.
        $36 = ② \times 2 \times \square \times \square$
        $60 = ② \times 2 \times 3 \times \square$
    b Circle the common prime factors. The first one is done for you.
    c Multiply all the common prime factors together.
        $HCF = 2 \times \square \times \square$
        $= \square$

Q12a hint Do not use index form.
Write the factors in each product
calculation in order of size.

13 Use prime factor decomposition to find the highest common factor of each pair of numbers.
   a 32 and 48   **b** 12 and 30   **c** 28 and 70   **d** 90 and 100

14 Copy and complete the steps to use prime factor decomposition to find the lowest common multiple of 36 and 80.
   a Write 36 and 80 as products of their prime factors.
   $36 = 2 \times 2 \times \square \times \square$
   $80 = ②\times②\times②\times②\times \square$
   b For each different prime factor, look for the product where it appears the most times then circle them all in that product. The first one is done for you.
   c Multiply all the circled factors together.
   $LCM = 2 \times 2 \times 2 \times 2 \times \square \times \square \times \square = \square$

   > **Q14b hint** 2 occurs more times in the product for 80. Circle it all the times it occurs in that product. Now circle 3 the most times it occurs in either product.

15 Use prime factor decomposition to find the lowest common multiple of each pair of numbers in Q13.

16 **Problem-solving / Reasoning** Hotdog buns are sold in packs of 5.
   Hotdog sausages are sold in packs of 3.
   a What is the smallest number of each pack you need so that no buns are left over?
   b How many hotdogs could you make?
   c What do you notice about your answer to part **b**?

17 **Problem-solving** Two satellites cross the Greenwich meridian at 3 pm on Monday. One of them orbits the Earth every 18 hours, the other every 21 hours.
   a How many hours will pass before they next cross the Greenwich meridian at the same time?
   b At what time will this happen?

   > **Q17a hint** The number of hours must be a multiple of both 18 and 21.

18 **Problem-solving** Cassandra won seven vouchers of the same value for a department store.
   She used some vouchers to pay for a coat costing £96.
   She used some more vouchers to pay for a suit costing £72.
   She received no change for either purchase. How much was each voucher worth?

   > **Q18 hint** The voucher value must be a factor of both £96 and £72.

19 **Problem-solving** Adam and Bertie start a cross-country race at the same time.
   Adam completes the first lap in 6 minutes.
   Bertie completes the first lap in 8 minutes.
   They keep running.
   How many minutes after they start will they pass each other again?
   How many laps will they each have done?

Challenge The *unique prime factorisation property* states: every integer greater than 1 is either a prime number, or can be written as a product of prime numbers.
   a Show this is true for the numbers 2 to 20.
   b Why is each of your prime factorisations unique?

   > **Hint** 6 is the product of prime numbers 2 and 3. Does it matter if you write: 2 × 3 or 3 × 2?

Reflect Compose means to make or create something. What do you think decompose means? Write (in your own words) the meaning of 'prime factor decomposition'.

1 Check up

Calculating with positive and negative numbers

1 Work out these calculations. Show your working.
   a 5 × 18   **b** 8 × 7.5   **c** 25 × 48   **d** 12 × 19

2 Use the divisibility rule for 3 to show that 4095 is divisible by 3.

3 Samuel buys a gaming laptop for £1385 and a designer case for £67.
   He pays a deposit of £177.
   a How much does he have left to pay?
   b Samuel pays the remainder in 12 equal monthly instalments.
      How much is each instalment?

4 Work out
   a 5.35 + 13 + 6.6   **b** 20.1 − 8.88 + 19

5 Work out
   a 534.6 ÷ 11   **b** 30.1 ÷ 14

6 Work out
   a 6 − −2   **b** 7 − +8   **c** 5 + −9   **d** −50 − 64
   e 4 × −2   **f** 15 ÷ −5   **g** 12 ÷ −4 − 8   **h** −5 × (4 − 7)

Powers and roots

7 Work out
   a 4^3 **b** $\sqrt[3]{8}$ **c** $(-4)^2$
   d $\sqrt{9} \times 3$ **e** $3^3 + 2^2$ **f** $\sqrt[3]{125} - \sqrt{4}$

8 Write the two square roots of 64.

9 Write the two integers that $\sqrt{19}$ lies between.

10 Work out
   a $\sqrt{25 - 16}$ **b** $(4 + 2^3) \div 4$ **c** 60^2
   d $\sqrt{25 - 8 \times 2}$ **e** $\dfrac{36}{1 + \sqrt{64}}$ **f** $\dfrac{\sqrt[3]{1000} + 5^2}{5}$

11 9 × 36 = 324
   Use this fact to work out $\sqrt{324}$.

Factors and multiples

12 Write 40 as the product of its prime factors in index form.

13 Write the prime factor decomposition of 45.

14 **a** Work out the highest common factor of 48 and 100.
    b Work out the lowest common multiple of 35 and 55.

15 Gavin and Birdi bought some books of a small number of stamps. Gavin bought 24 stamps in total and Birdi bought 40 stamps in total.
What is the largest possible number of stamps in a book?

1 Pari says, 'A number is divisible by 11 if, when you subtract then add alternating digits in the number, the answer is divisible by 11.'
For example 2937: $2 - 9 + 3 - 7 = -11$
Write four other numbers that are divisible by 11:

a a 3-digit number   **b** a 4-digit number
c a 5-digit number   **d** a 6-digit number

2 This flow chart can help you find the highest common factor of two numbers.

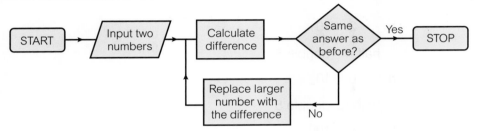

Here's what happens if you input the numbers 9 and 21:
Difference = $21 - 9 = \mathbf{12}$
Replace 21 with 12 and start again.
Difference = $12 - 9 = \mathbf{3}$
Replace 12 with 3 and start again.
Difference = $9 - 3 = \mathbf{6}$
Replace 9 with 6 and start again.
Difference = $6 - 3 = \mathbf{3}$
STOP because you have the same answer as before, 3.
Highest common factor of 9 and 21 is 3.

a i Work out the highest common factor of 8 and 20 in the usual way.
  ii Now try the flow chart. Does it work?
b Test the flow chart using other pairs of numbers. Find the highest common factor in the usual way first so that you can check if the flow chart works.
c Which pairs of numbers less than 100 take the longest time? Could you make changes to the flow chart to speed it up for these pairs of numbers?

How sure are you of your answers? Were you mostly

😞 **Just guessing**   😐 **Feeling doubtful**   🙂 **Confident**

What next? Use your results to decide whether to strengthen or extend your learning.

1 Strengthen

Calculating with positive and negative numbers

1 **a** Work out
  i $5 + 4$ **ii** $5 + 7 + 6$ **iii** $9 + 1 + 2$ **iv** $8 + 6 + 1 + 3$
  b Which of your answers to part **a** are in the 3 times table?
  c Which of these numbers are divisible by 3?
   i 54   **ii** 576
   iii 912   **iv** 8613

> **Q1c hint** Only numbers whose digits sum to a number in the 3 times table are divisible by 3.

2 Work out
  a 4×5

  b $\underset{\uparrow}{2} \times \underset{\uparrow}{10}$
     half 4   double 5

  c 12×5

  d $\underset{\uparrow}{6} \times \underset{\uparrow}{10}$
     half 12 double 5

  e 8×50

  f $\underset{\uparrow}{4} \times \underset{\uparrow}{100}$
     half 8   double 50

3 Copy and complete these calculations.
  a $6 \times 5 = \square \times 10 = \square$ **b** $16 \times 5 = \square \times \square = \square$
  c $12 \times 50 = \square \times 100 = \square$ **d** $18 \times 50 = \square \times \square = \square$
  e $5 \times 22 = 10 \times \square = \square$ **f** $50 \times 24 = 100 \times \square = \square$
     double 5 half 22   double 50 half 24

4 **a** **i** Double 2.5.
   ii Halve 12.
   iii Use doubling and halving to work out 2.5×12.
  b Use doubling and halving to work out these calculations.
   i 5×32 **ii** 26×5 **iii** 4.5×6
   iv 2.5×16 **v** 24×3.5 **vi** 12.5×28

5 Work out these calculations.
  a **i** 3×100 **ii** 3×101 **iii** 3×99
  b **i** 5×100 **ii** 5×101 **iii** 5×99
  c **i** 11×100 **ii** 11×101 **iii** 11×99

> **Q5a hint** How many more 3s in ii than i? How many fewer 3s in iii than i?

6 Copy and complete these subtractions.
  a $466 - 152 - 35$ **b** $1778 + 54 - 77$

$$\begin{array}{r} 4\,6\,6 \\ -1\,5\,2 \\ \hline \square\square\square \end{array} \rightarrow \begin{array}{r} \square\square\square \\ -\quad 3\,5 \\ \hline \square\square\square \end{array} \qquad \begin{array}{r} 1\,7\,7\,8 \\ +\quad 5\,4 \\ \hline \square\square\square\square \end{array} \rightarrow \begin{array}{r} \square\square\square\square \\ -\quad\quad 7\,7 \\ \hline \square\square\square\square \end{array}$$

7 Use the column method to work out these calculations.
  a $3784 - 625 + 1079$ **b** $22\,373 + 291 - 824$

> **Q7 hint** Line up the Ten thousands, Thousands, Hundreds, Tens and Ones.

8 **Problem-solving** In 2013, Tariq earned £18222 plus a bonus of £839.
His employer subtracted £4722 for tax, insurance and pension.
How much did Tariq receive?

9 Copy and complete these calculations.
   a 17.7 + 0.73 − 5.12

$$\begin{array}{r} 1\,7.7\,0 \\ +\ 0.7\,3 \\ \hline \square\square.\square\square \end{array} \rightarrow \begin{array}{r} \square\square.\square\square \\ -\ \ 5.1\,2 \\ \hline \square\square.\square\square \end{array}$$

   b 28.9 + 7.83 − 4.81

$$\begin{array}{r} 2\,8.9\,0 \\ +\ 7.8\,3 \\ \hline \square\square.\square\square \end{array} \rightarrow \begin{array}{r} \square\square.\square\square \\ -\ \ 4.8\,1 \\ \hline \square\square.\square\square \end{array}$$

Q10 hint Keep the decimal points in line. Fill in any empty decimal places with zeros.

10 Use the column method to work out these calculations.
   a 39.94 − 1.3 + 6.24   **b** £48.30 − £5.14 + £1.99

11 Copy and complete these divisions.

   a
$$\begin{array}{r} 3.4\square\ \ \ \\ 11\overline{)38.28} \\ 33 \\ \hline 5\,2 \\ 4\,4 \\ \hline \square\square \end{array}$$

   b
$$\begin{array}{r} 4 \\ 11\overline{)49.72} \\ 44 \end{array}$$

   c
$$\begin{array}{r} 21.6\square\ \ \ \\ 12\overline{)259.8\square} \\ 24 \\ \hline 19 \\ 12 \\ \hline 78 \\ 72 \\ \hline 6\square \end{array}$$

   d
$$\begin{array}{r} 3 \\ 12\overline{)390.6} \\ 36 \end{array}$$

Q11c hint
259.8 = 259.80

12 **Problem-solving** Dan owes his mum £75.
He agrees to pay her back in 12 equal instalments.
How much does Dan pay his mum back each month?

Q12 hint £75 = £75.00
$$\begin{array}{r} 6 \\ 12\overline{)£75.00} \\ 72 \end{array}$$

13 Work out these calculations. The first two are started for you.
   a 10 + −5   **b** 8 − −4
       = 10 − 5 = □   = 8 + 4 = □
   c −2 − −8   **d** −5 + −2

Q13 hint Replace different signs with a minus (−). Replace same signs with a plus (+).

14 Work out
   a 6 × 8

   b   ⁻6 × 8
           ↑   ↑
       different signs
       negative answer

   c 35 ÷ 7

   d   ⁻35 ÷ ⁻7
            ↑   ↑
       same signs
       positive answer

   e −12 ÷ −2   **f** −8 × −3   **g** −4 × 3

Q14 hint For multiplying and dividing, work out the calculation ignoring the signs. Now work out the sign: same signs give positive answer, different signs give negative answer.

15 Work out these calculations. Use the priority of operations.
Check your answers using a calculator. The first one is started for you.
   a 5 − 2 × 7   **b** 5 × −3 − 2   **c** −10 ÷ 2 + 3
BIDMAS: 2 × 7 = 14
        5 − 14 = □
   d 4 − 3 × −2   **e** 4 × (3 − 6)   **f** −15 ÷ (5 − 8)

Q15 hint
Brackets
Indices (powers and roots)
Division and Multiplication
Addition and Subtraction

Powers and roots

1 Copy and complete the patterns.

   a 2

     $2^2 = 2 \times 2 = \square$

     $2^3 = 2 \times 2 \times 2 = \square$

   b 3

     $3^2 = \square \times \square = \square$

     $3^3 = \square \times \square \times \square = \square$

   c 10

     $10^2 = \square \times \square = \square$

     $10^3 = \square \times \square \times \square = \square$

2 **Reasoning** Do 4^3 and 4×3 have the same answer? Explain.

> **Q2 hint** To explain:
> Work out $4^3 =$
> $4 \times 3 =$
> Write a sentence stating if they have the same answer or not.

3 Copy and complete the patterns.

   a $2^2 = \square$ so $\sqrt{4} = 2$

     $2^3 = \square$ so $\sqrt[3]{8} = 2$

   b $3^2 = \square$ so $\sqrt{\square} = 3$

     $3^3 = \square$ so $\sqrt[3]{\square} = 3$

   c $4^2 = \square$ so $\sqrt{\square} = 4$

     $4^3 = \square$ so $\sqrt[3]{\square} = 4$

   d $5^2 = \square$ so $\sqrt{\square} = 5$

     $5^3 = \square$ so $\sqrt[3]{\square} = 5$

4 What is the cube root of 1000?

> **Q4 hint** $\square^3 = 1000$ so $\sqrt[3]{1000} = \square$

5 **a** Copy and complete the diagram of square roots.
   Make your diagram as wide as possible. Label each square root on your diagram.

   $\sqrt{1}$ $\sqrt{4}$ $\sqrt{9}$ $\sqrt{\square}$ $\sqrt{\square}$ $\sqrt{\square}$ $\sqrt{\square}$ $\sqrt{\square}$ $\sqrt{\square}$ $\sqrt{\square}$

   1   2   3   4   5   6   7   8   9   10

   b Which two integers does each of these roots lie between? The first one is done for you.

    i $\sqrt{7}$ $\sqrt{7}$ lies between $\sqrt{4}$ and $\sqrt{9}$. So $\sqrt{7}$ lies between 2 and 3.

    ii $\sqrt{10}$ **iii** $\sqrt{60}$ **iv** $\sqrt{20}$ **v** $\sqrt{99}$ **vi** $\sqrt{32}$

6 **a** Work out

    i 2^2 **ii** 10^2 **iii** $2^2 \times 10^2$ **iv** 2×10 **v** $(2 \times 10)^2$

   b What do you notice about your answers to parts **a iii** and **a v**?

7 Work out these calculations. The first one is started for you.

   a $40^2 = (4 \times 10)^2$ **b** 90^2 **c** 120^2

        $= 4^2 \times 10^2$

        $= \square \times \square = \square$

   d 300^2 **e** 400^2 **f** 800^2

> **Q7d hint** $300^2 = (3 \times 100)^2$

8 **a** Work out these squares. The first one is started for you.

    i $(-2)^2$ **ii** $(-3)^2$ **iii** $(-10)^2$

       $= {-2} \times {-2} = \square$

       ↑   ↑

     same signs

     positive answer

   b Compare your answers with 2^2, 3^2, and 10^2 from Q1. What do you notice?

9 **a** Copy and complete the sentence:
    The two square roots of 9 are $\square$ and $\square$.

   b Write the two square roots of each number.

    i 16   **ii** 100   **iii** 25

    iv 49   **v** 121

10 Work out these calculations.
Use the priority of operations (BIDMAS).
The first one is started for you.

   a $\sqrt{9} \times 2$ **b** $\sqrt{16} \times 5$ **c** $\sqrt[3]{125} + 2$ **d** $10 + \sqrt[3]{8}$

BIDMAS: $\sqrt{9} = 3$
       $3 \times 2 = \square$

Q10 hint Indices are powers and roots:
$\square^{\square}$ $\sqrt{}$ or $\sqrt[3]{}$

11 Work out these calculations.
One of them is started for you.

   a $16 + 4$ **b** $9 - 4$

   c $\dfrac{16 + 4}{9 - 4} = \dfrac{\square}{\square} = \square$ **d** $\dfrac{9 \times 4}{5 + 7}$

   e $\dfrac{10^2}{13 + 7}$ **f** $\dfrac{\sqrt{81}}{10 - 7}$ **g** $\dfrac{30 + 20}{5^2}$

Q11d hint Work out the numerator and denominator separately.
$9 \times 4 = \square$
$5 + 7 = \square$
Then work out the division. $\dfrac{9 \times 4}{5 + 7}$

12 Work out these calculations.

   a $\sqrt{144}$ **b** 4^2 **c** $\sqrt{144} - 4^2$

   d $5^2 - \sqrt[3]{125}$ **e** $\sqrt{100} - 3^2$ **f** $7 + \sqrt[3]{8}$

Q12d hint Work out the power and root separately.
$5^2 = \square$
$\sqrt[3]{125} = \square$
Then work out the subtraction.
$5^2 - \sqrt[3]{125}$

13 Work out these calculations. The first one is started for you.

   a $3 \times (1 + \sqrt{16})$

BIDMAS: $1 + \sqrt{16} = 1 + 4 = 5$
       $3 \times 5 = \square$

   b $2 \times (6^2 - 20)$ **c** $5 \times (3 + \sqrt[3]{64})$

   d $(9 + 7) \div \sqrt{4}$ **e** $18 \div (\sqrt{25} + 2^2)$

14 Copy and complete these calculations.

   a $400 = 16 \times 25$ **b** $196 = 4 \times 49$
       so $\sqrt{400} = \sqrt{16 \times 25}$ so $\sqrt{196} = \sqrt{4 \times 49}$
              $= \sqrt{16} \times \sqrt{25}$ $= \sqrt{4} \times \sqrt{49}$
              $= \square \times \square$ $= \square \times \square$
              $= \square$ $= \square$

15 Eva writes    $\sqrt{36} = \sqrt{4 \times 9} = \sqrt{4} \times \sqrt{9}$

She says, 'This means $\sqrt{4 + 32}$ is $\sqrt{4} + \sqrt{32}$.'
Use a calculator to show Eva is incorrect, and that the same rule does *not* work for adding as for multiplying.

16 Work out these calculations. The first two are started for you.

   a $\sqrt{15 + 10} = \sqrt{25} = \square$
   b $\sqrt{12 + 20 \div 5} = \sqrt{12 + 4} = \sqrt{\square} = \square$
   c $\sqrt{4 \times 8 - 7}$ **d** $\sqrt{8^2 - 60}$ **e** $\sqrt[3]{7 + 4 \times 5}$

Factors and multiples

1 **a** List all the prime numbers less than 20.
    b List the prime factors of
      i 10   **ii** 21   **iii** 26
      iv 55   **v** 30

Q1b hint Which of the primes in part a are factors of the numbers in part b?

2 Write each product of prime factors in index form (powers).

   a $3 \times 3 \times 3 \times 3$

      i How many 3s are multiplied together?

      ii Copy and complete.

        $3 \times 3 \times 3 \times 3 = 3^{\square}$

   b $3 \times 3 \times 3 \times 3 \times 5 \times 5$

      i How many 3s are multiplied together?

      ii How many 5s are multiplied together?

      iii Copy and complete.

        $3 \times 3 \times 3 \times 3 \times 5 \times 5 = 3^{\square} \times 5^{\square}$

   c $3 \times 3 \times 3 \times 3 \times 5 \times 5 \times 7 = 3^{\square} \times 5^{\square} \times 7$

   d $2 \times 2 \times 2 \times 5 \times 5 \times 5$

   e $2 \times 3 \times 3 \times 5 \times 5 \times 5$

   f $2 \times 2 \times 2 \times 2 \times 3 \times 11$

   g $2 \times 3 \times 3 \times 3 \times 3 \times 3$

> **Q2c hint** There is only one 7. You don't need to write the power 1.

3 **a** Copy and complete this factor tree for 40.

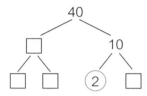

   b Circle the prime factors.

   c Write the product.

      Put the numbers in order: $\square \times \square \times \square \times \square$

   d Write the product in index form.

4 **a** Copy and complete these factor trees.

  i 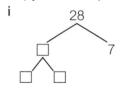   **ii** 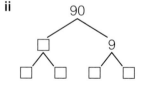   **iii**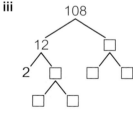

   b Write each number as a product of prime factors in index form.

5 Write the prime factor decomposition of

   a 450

   b 98

   c 216

   d 225

> **Q5a hint** Prime factor decomposition means writing a number as a product of prime factors in index form.
> Choose an easy factor pair to start with: $450 = 45 \times 10$
>
> 450
> 45   10
> $\square$ $\square$ $\square$ $\square$

a   Write 18 and 30 as products of prime factors.

$18 = 2 \times 3 \times 3$ $30 = 2 \times 3 \times 5$

b   Draw a Venn diagram of their prime factors. Use your diagram to find the highest common factor.

Prime factors of 18   3   2   5   Prime factors of 30
                                      3

These are the common prime factors.

$HCF = 2 \times 3 = 6$

> To find the HCF, multiply the common prime factors.

c   Find the lowest common multiple.

$3 \times 2 \times 3 \times 5 = 90$

> To find the LCM, multiply all the prime factors.

6   For each pair of numbers below:

   i   Write each number as the product of its prime factors.

   ii Draw a Venn diagram of their prime factors.
        Use your diagram to find the highest common factor.

   iii Find the lowest common multiple of the pair of numbers.

   a   30 and 48

   b   24 and 60

   c   42 and 70

> **Q6 hint** Use the worked example to help you.

1   a   You are trying to escape from a prison camp.
        A spotlight shines on your exit for 10 minutes, then turns off for 2 minutes.
        A guard can see your exit for 7 minutes, then cannot see it for 1 minute.
        At 8 pm the spotlight is turned on and the guard begins her patrol.
        It takes 1 minute for you to escape. When should you go?

> **Q1a hint** Draw timelines for the spotlight and guard using squared paper.

   b   After your escape, the spotlight is turned on for 9 minutes and off for 1 minute.
        How long before the next inmate can escape?

> **Q1b hint** Use the lowest common multiple.

2   Find a number between 200 and 300 whose product of primes has no repeated prime factors. For example, a suitable number between 100 and 200 is $105 = 3 \times 5 \times 7$.

   Write five different ways you used your multiplication and division skills in these Strengthen lessons. Your first two might be:

1   When doubling, I multiplied by 2.

2   When dividing a negative number by a negative number, I divided the numbers and then wrote an answer which was positive.

1 Extend

1 **a** Sally uses rounding and adjusting and then doubling and halving to work out 28×49.
   Copy and complete Sally's working.
   b Use Sally's method to work out 32×49.

$$28 \times 49 = 28 \times \square - 28 \times 1$$
$$= 14 \times \square - 28 \times 1$$
$$= \square$$

2 **a** Use doubling and halving to work out these multiplications.
   i 5×0.16 **ii** 0.24×5 **iii** 50×0.32
   iv 0.88×25 **v** 1.2×25 **vi** 25×3.6
   b Use a mental method to work out these divisions.
   i $270 \div 18$ **ii** $180 \div 12$ **iii** $700 \div 14$ **iv** $360 \div 15$

   > **Q2a hint** It is easier to multiply by 10 or 100 than by 5, 25 or 50.

3 Write the ratio $4^2 : 6^2$ in its simplest form.

4 **Problem-solving**   Square A has sides of length 14 cm.
   Square B has an area of 256 cm².
   Square C has a perimeter of 60 cm.
   a Which square has the greatest perimeter?   **b** Which square has the smallest area?

5 **Problem-solving**   The table shows a pattern of calculations.
   a Copy and complete the table.
   b Continue the pattern until the estimate is less than 1.

Pattern number	Calculation	Estimate
1	1980×198	
2	$1980 \times 198 \times 19.8$	
3	$1980 \times 198 \times 19.8 \times 1.98$	

6 Gaerwyn recorded these outside temperatures at midnight on the first day of each month.
   $11.2\,°C$ $-1.7\,°C$ $3\,°C$ $4.8\,°C$ $-7.3\,°C$ $-0.9\,°C$
   a Find the median temperature.
   b Estimate the mean temperature.
   c Work out the range.

7 **Problem-solving**   Helena did an experiment to investigate how salt affects the freezing point of water.

Salt (g)	30	60	90	120
Temperature (°C)	−1.8	−3.6	−5.4	−7.2

   She mixed different amounts of salt in a litre of water and recorded when the water started to freeze.
   a How does adding one 30 g scoop of salt affect the freezing point?
   b When six 30 g scoops of salt are added to a litre of water, what is the freezing point?

8 Substitute the values into each formula and estimate the answers.
   a $v = u + at$ when $u = 49$, $a = 6.1$ and $t = 24$
   b $x = (a + b + c) \div 3$ when $a = 347$, $b = 255$ and $c = 1233$
   c $A = \frac{1}{2} \times (a + b) \times h$ when $a = 7.1$, $b = 8.8$ and $h = 1.9$
   d **Reasoning**   Do you need to round all of the numbers when estimating a calculation?

9 Here are three numbers.   13 824   13 106   12 544
   Which one is
   a a square number?   **b** a cube number?

10 a Find the highest common factor of each set of numbers.

    i 48, 60 and 76   **ii** 28, 70 and 140

Q10a hint Write each number as the product of its prime factors.

  b Find the lowest common multiple of each set of numbers.

    i 9, 15 and 21   **ii** 6, 16 and 18

  c Mary has written two numbers as products of their prime factors:

$$2^3 \times 3^4 \text{ and } 2^2 \times 3^5$$

    Work out the highest common factor and the lowest common multiple of the two numbers.

11 Problem-solving One of the ancient Mayan calendar cycles was called the 'calendar round'. The number of days in the 'calendar round' is the lowest common multiple (LCM) of two calendars of length 260 days and 365 days.

  a Work out the number of days in a calendar round.

  b How many years are there in a calendar round?

  c The Mayans started their calendar at about 3114 BC.
Some people recently thought it predicted the end of the world on 21 December 2012!
Roughly how many calendar rounds were completed up to 21 December 2012?

Q11c hint Assume 365 days in a year. Ignore leap years.

12 Problem-solving The diagram shows an old-fashioned lift floor indicator in a block of flats.
The lift has stopped at a floor. The arrow always points to a whole number of degrees.
What is the smallest number of floors the building could have?

Ground   Penthouse

13 a $1728 = 27 \times 64$. Use this fact to work out $\sqrt[3]{1728}$.

  b $8000 = 64 \times 125$. Use this fact to work out $\sqrt[3]{8000}$.

  c Problem-solving Can you write 8000 as a product of two cubes in another way?

Challenge

a The time, t seconds, for a stone to hit the ground from a height of d m can be estimated using the formula $t = \sqrt{\dfrac{d}{5}}$

Hint For $\sqrt{\dfrac{\square}{\square}}$ work out $\dfrac{\square}{\square}$ and then square root.

Estimate the time it takes for the stone to hit the ground from a height of

  i 20 m   **ii** 30 m   **iii** 60 m

b For a stone on the Moon, the formula is $t = \sqrt{\dfrac{6d}{5}}$

Estimate the time it takes for the stone to hit the ground from a height of

  i 20 m   **ii** 30 m   **iii** 60 m

c Does the stone fall faster on the Moon or on the Earth? Suggest why.

d What height of drop on the Moon takes the same time as a 30 m drop on Earth?

Reflect Which of the questions in this Extend lesson made you think the hardest? Why?
What could you do so that questions like this don't make you think so hard in the future?

1 Unit test

1   The temperature in Moscow was −8 °C at 6 am and 2 °C at midday.
    a Work out the difference in temperature.
    b By midnight, the temperature had fallen by 14 °C compared to midday.
      i What was the temperature at midnight?
      ii What is the difference in temperature between 6 am and midnight?
    c Work out −4 − 6.

2   Use the divisibility rule for 9 to show that 783 is divisible by 9.

3   Work out these calculations.
    a $13 + \sqrt{49}$ **b** $\sqrt{4} + 9 \times 5$ **c** $\sqrt[3]{64}$

4   To make a tunnel, 17 220 tonnes of earth need removing.
    In the first week 455 tonnes were removed. In the second week 8200 tonnes were removed.
    Work out the amount of earth left to remove.

5   12 plates cost £30.60.
    How much does one plate cost?

6   Work out
    a 5×14 **b** 7×99 **c** 24×12.5 **d** 23×19

7   Work out $9 + 83.8 - 0.07$.

8   Work out $2151 \div 15$.

9   Which two integers does $\sqrt{67}$ lie between?

10 **a** Work out the highest common factor of 24 and 90.
    b Work out the lowest common multiple of 9 and 15.
    c A timer beeps every 12 seconds. Another timer beeps every 20 seconds.
        Dunstan hears the two timers beep at the same time.
        How long before they next beep at the same time?

11 12 square coasters have a total area of 960 cm².
    Estimate the side length of a coaster.

12 Write the value of each of these.
    a the two square roots of 36   **b** 70^2 **c** 2^4

13 Work out
    a $5 - {}^{-}8$ **b** $12 + {}^{-}23$
    c -3×8 **d** $16 \div -8$
    e $-10 \times (7 - 12)$ **f** $6 + 15 \div -3$
    g $(-6)^2$ **h** $3^2 \times 2^3$
    i $\sqrt[3]{1000} - \sqrt{121}$

14 **a** **i** Work out the value of $2 \times 2 \times 2 \times 3$.
        ii Write $2 \times 2 \times 2 \times 3$ in index form.
    b Write 180 as the product of its prime factors, in index form.

15 Work out

   a $5^2 - (10 - \sqrt[3]{64})$ **b** $\sqrt[3]{6^2 - 3^2}$

16 Work out $\sqrt[3]{2000}$. Give your answer correct to 1 decimal place.

17 Use your calculator to work out these calculations.

   a $1.5 \times (2^3 - \sqrt{64})$ **b** $\dfrac{\sqrt{144} + 8}{\sqrt[3]{1000}}$

18 **a** $1296 = 16 \times 81$

      Use this fact to work out $\sqrt{1296}$.

   b $3375 = 27 \times 125$

      Use this fact to work out $\sqrt[3]{3375}$.

Challenge   The aim of this puzzle is to fill in the white squares on a 5 × 5 grid with as many integers as possible.
This diagram shows how you can move from one square to the next.
The example grid starts at the number 8.

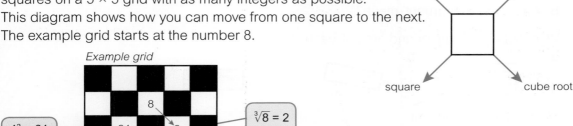

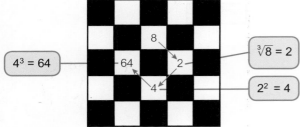

1 Draw your own copy of the grid.

2 Write any positive integer in a white square and circle it.

3 Start filling in the adjacent squares. Use arrows to show where you move to.

4 Continue until you cannot fill in any more squares.

5 Try again. Work out a strategy to fill in more squares this time.

6 Try again. This time start with a negative integer.

7 Try again. This time you can only use each operation twice.

Reflect   In this unit you have done calculations involving

- decimals
- negative numbers
- powers
- roots
- factors.

> **Hint** Look back through the unit to remind yourself of each type of calculation.

Which type of calculation did you find easiest? What made it easy?
Which type of calculation did you find hardest? What made it hard?
Write a hint, in your own words, for the type of calculation you found hardest.

2   Area and volume

Master   Check up p50   Strengthen p52   Extend p57   Unit test p59

2.1   Area of a triangle

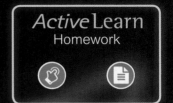

Active Learn
Homework

- Derive and use the formula for the area of a triangle
- Calculate the area of compound shapes made from rectangles and triangles

Warm up

1   **Fluency**   **a**   What does 'perpendicular' mean?
    b   What does 'congruent' mean?

2   Work out the perimeter and area of each shape.

    a   **b**   **c**

 5 cm

  2.5 cm   6 cm

l w

3   For this shape, work out
    a   the perimeter   **b**   the area.

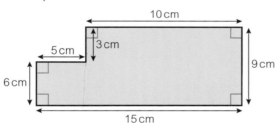

4   These triangles are drawn on
    centimetre squared paper.
    Find the areas of the triangles
    by counting squares.

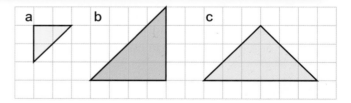

5   **a**   Each diagram shows a triangle and a rectangle.

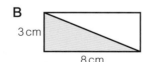

    For A and B:
      i   Work out the area of the rectangle.
      ii   How many triangles cover the same area as the rectangle?
      iii   What is the area of the triangle?

b This diagram shows A and B joined together to make another rectangle.

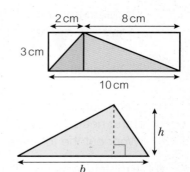

   i Work out the area of the rectangle.

   ii What fraction of the rectangle is the triangle?

c Explain in words how to find the area of a triangle.

d Write a formula connecting the area of a triangle (A), its base length (b) and its height (h).

e Use your formula to check the areas of the triangles in parts **a** and **b**.

Key point

Area of a triangle = $\frac{1}{2}$ × base length × perpendicular height
which can be written as $A = \frac{1}{2}bh$.

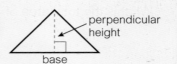

The height measurement must be perpendicular (at 90°) to the base.

Worked example

Work out the area of this triangle.

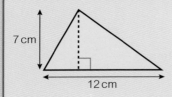

$$A = \frac{1}{2}bh$$

$$= \frac{1}{2} \times 12 \times 7$$

$$= 42 \text{ cm}^2$$

> Write the formula, then substitute the numbers into the formula.

---

6 Work out the area of each triangle.

a
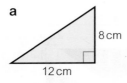

b
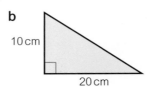

c
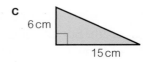

d
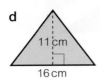

e
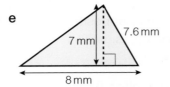

f
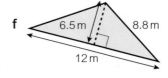

g
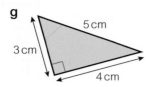

h
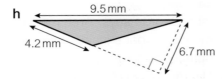

7 Problem-solving Tariq makes red, white and blue flags for bunting.

Each length of bunting has 24 flags altogether, with equal numbers of red, white and blue flags.
Each flag is a triangle of height 45 cm and base 30 cm.
Tariq needs to make five lengths of bunting.
Work out the total area of each colour material that he needs.

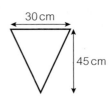

8 Problem-solving This compound shape is made from two congruent triangles and a rectangle.
What is the total area of the shape?

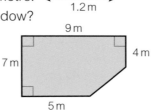

9 Problem-solving Sam makes stained glass windows like this.
   a What is the area of the window?
     Give your answer in square metres.
The stained glass costs £153 per square metre.
   b What is the cost of the glass for this window?

> **Q9a hint** Split the window into a rectangle and a triangle.

10 Problem-solving This garden is a rectangle shape with a triangle cut off.
Calculate the area of the garden.

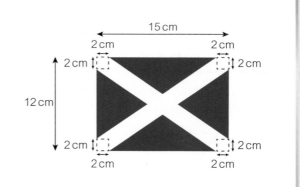

Challenge

1 Make an accurate scale drawing of the Scottish flag.
   a Draw the outer rectangle on squared paper.
   b Draw the squares at each corner, with dashed lines.
   c Join the vertices of diagonally opposite squares to make the white cross.
   d Rub out the dashed lines.

2 Show that less than half the Scottish flag is blue.

Reflect   After this lesson George says, 'Area measures the size of a shape.'
Polly says, 'Area is the amount of space inside a shape.'
Hasid says, 'Area is the number of squares a space covers.'
Which definition do you like most? Why?
Use what George, Polly and Hasid say, and your own understanding of area, to write the best possible definition. Compare your definition with others in your class.

2.2 Area of a parallelogram and a trapezium

Active Learn
Homework

- Derive and use the formula for the area of a parallelogram
- Use the formula for the area of a trapezium

Warm up

1 Fluency Which of these shapes are parallelograms? Which are trapezia?

> **Q1 hint** Trapezia is the plural of trapezium.

 A   B   C   D   E   F

2 Work out the area of each shape.

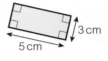
3 cm
5 cm

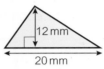
12 mm
20 mm

3 Work out the values of these expressions when $x = 5$ and $y = 9$.

a xy b $x + y$ c $4(x + y)$ d $\frac{1}{2}(x + y)$ e $\frac{1}{2}(x + y)x$

4 This parallelogram is made from two congruent triangles and a rectangle.
Work out the area of

a the rectangle   b one triangle   c the parallelogram.

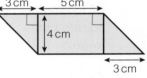
3 cm   5 cm
4 cm
3 cm

5 a Copy this parallelogram on squared paper and cut it out.

b Cut along the dashed line. Move the right-angled triangle to make a rectangle.

c Work out the area of the rectangle.

d Write a word formula for the area of a parallelogram.

e Write a formula connecting the area (A), perpendicular height (h) and base length (b) of a parallelogram.

f Check that your formula gives the area you found in part **c**.

g Check that your formula gives the area you found in Q4.

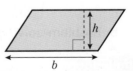
h
b

Key point

area of parallelogram = base length × perpendicular height,
$$A = bh$$

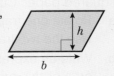
h
b

6 Work out the area of each parallelogram.

a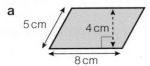
5 cm
4 cm
8 cm

b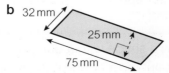
32 mm
25 mm
75 mm

c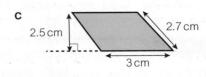
2.5 cm
2.7 cm
3 cm

d **Reasoning** In parts **a**, **b** and **c**, which lengths didn't you use? Explain why.

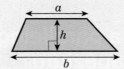
Worked example

Work out the area of this trapezium.

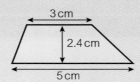

$A = \frac{1}{2}(a + b)h$

$= \frac{1}{2}(3 + 5)2.4$

$= \frac{1}{2} \times 8 \times 2.4$ ————— Work out the brackets first, then the multiplication.

$= 9.6 \text{ cm}^2$

7 Work out the area of each trapezium.

a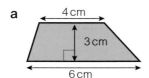

b

c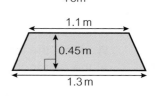

8 **Problem-solving** The glass for a car windscreen costs £315 per square metre. The shape of a car windscreen is approximately a trapezium. Work out the cost of the glass for this car windscreen.

9 **a** Match each shape to its area.

i

ii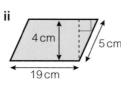

iii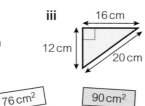

iv

| 100 cm² | 80 cm² | 76 cm² | 90 cm² | 96 cm² |

b **Problem-solving** Draw a shape to match the area that is left over.

Challenge Draw two copies of this trapezium on squared paper. Cut them out.

a Rotate one trapezium 180°.
Use the two trapezia to make a parallelogram.

b Write an expression using a, b and h for the area of this parallelogram.

c Use your expression from part **b** to write an expression for the area of the trapezium.

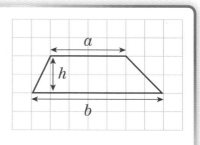

Reflect Q9b asked you to draw a shape with a particular area.
Write all the steps you took to work out the lengths of the shape.
Choose another shape. Will the steps be the same or different? Explain.

2.3 Volume of cubes and cuboids

*Active*Learn
Homework

- Calculate the volume of cubes and cuboids
- Calculate the volume of 3D solids made from cuboids
- Solve volume problems

Warm up

1 Fluency Work out the missing values.
   a $4 \times 2 \times 5 = \square$　　**b** $7 \times 2 \times \square = 70$　　**c** $\square \times 4 \times 5 = 40$

2 a Write the first five cube numbers.
   b Write the value of 10^3.

3 Work out the values of these expressions when $a = 5$, $b = 3$ and $c = 2$.
   a $a + b$　　　**b** ab　　　**c** abc　　　**d** a^2　　　**e** c^3

> **Key point**　　The **volume** of a 3D solid is the amount of 3D space
> it takes up.
> The units of volume are **cubic units** (e.g. mm³, cm³ or m³).
> A cube with sides of length 1 cm has a volume of 1 cm³.

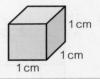

4 a Here is a layer of centimetre cubes.

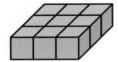

   How many cubes are in this layer?
   b Three identical layers make a cube with sides of length 3 cm.
   Work out the **volume** of the cube.

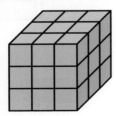

   c Work out 3^3.
   d What do you notice about your answers to parts **b** and **c**?

> **Key point**　　**volume of a cube** = side length × side length × side length
> $$V = l \times l \times l$$
> $$V = l^3$$

5 These cubes are made from centimetre cubes.
Work out the volume of each cube.

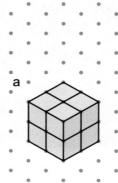
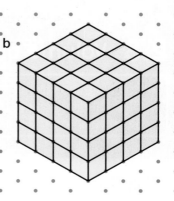

a

b

 6 Work out the volume of each cube.

a

b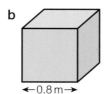

c

7 cm

←0.8 m→

32 mm

Q6a hint
Use the $\boxed{x^3}$ or the $\boxed{y^x}$ button on your calculator.

 7 Work out the volume of a cube with these side lengths.
    a 5 cm   **b** 4.2 cm   **c** 12 mm   **d** 3.5 m

8 These cuboids are made from centimetre cubes.

a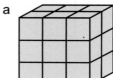

b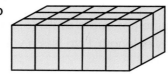

For each cuboid:
   i Count the cubes in the top layer.
  ii Count the number of layers.
 iii Work out the volume.

9 **Reasoning** This cuboid has length (l), width (w)
and height (h).
Complete these formulae.
    a area of top = length × ☐
    b volume = area of top × ☐ = length × ☐ × ☐

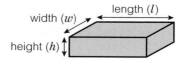
width (w)   length (l)
height (h)

Key point   **volume of a cuboid** = length × width × height
$$V = lwh$$

h
l w

Worked example

Work out the volume of this cuboid.

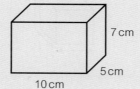

7 cm

5 cm

10 cm

Volume = lwh
      = 10 × 5 × 7
      = 50 × 7
      = 350 cm³

Write down the formula.
Substitute the values for l, w and h.

The units of length are cm so
the units of volume are cm³.

10 Calculate the volume of each cuboid.

a

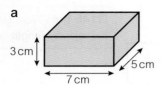

3 cm
5 cm
7 cm

b

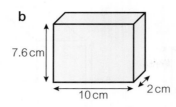

7.6 cm
10 cm
2 cm

c

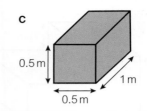

0.5 m
1 m
0.5 m

11 Problem-solving / Reasoning   A lake is estimated to be about 1.5 km long, 200 m wide and 25 m deep.

> **Q11 hint** Change 1.5 km to metres.

    a Work out an estimate of the volume of water in the lake, by modelling the lake as a cuboid.
    Give your answer in cubic metres.

    b Do you think that a cuboid is a good model for a lake? Explain your answer.

12 a Work out the volume of cube A and of cuboid B.

A

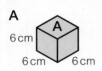

6 cm
6 cm   6 cm

B

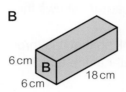

6 cm
6 cm
18 cm

    b These solid shapes are made using cube A and cuboid B.

C

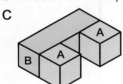

D

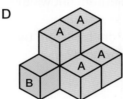

    Find the volume of each solid.

13 Reasoning   This L-shaped solid can be split into two cuboids.

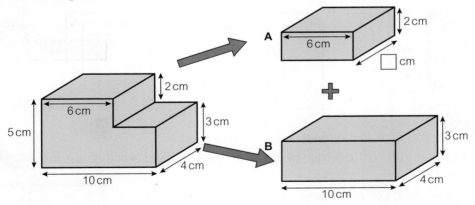

2 cm
6 cm
5 cm
3 cm
4 cm
10 cm

A
2 cm
6 cm
☐ cm

+

B
3 cm
10 cm
4 cm

    a Work out the missing length on cuboid A.
    b Calculate the volume of cuboid A.
    c Calculate the volume of cuboid B.
    d Calculate the volume of the L-shaped solid.

14 Problem-solving / Reasoning Calculate the volume of each L-shaped solid.

a

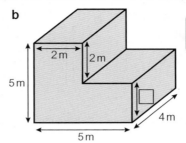

b

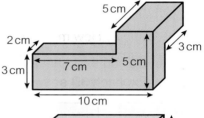

Q14b hint Work out the missing length first.

15 Problem-solving Work out the volume of this 3D solid.

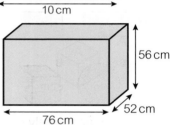

16 Problem-solving The diagram shows the dimensions of a water tank.
Alex puts water in the tank so that it is three quarters full.
What is the volume of water in the tank?

17 Problem-solving The diagram shows the dimensions of a dice.
A box has dimensions 12 cm by 10 cm by 8 cm.
How many dice will the box hold?

Q17 hint Sketch the box. Start by working out how many dice will fit along the length of the box.

Challenge Each box of Archie's Sweets needs to hold 50 cm³ of sweets. Here are three designs for the box.

A

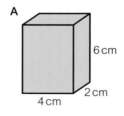

B

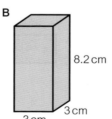

C

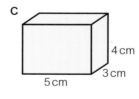

a Which design do you think is the most suitable? Why?

b Work out the side length, to 1 decimal place, of a cube-shaped box that has the correct volume.

c Work out the dimensions of two more boxes with a volume of 50 cm³.

Reflect Maths is not the only subject where you use volume. You use it in science too.
Describe when you have used volume in science.
In which ways is volume the same or different in science and in this maths lesson?
Do you think volume means the same in all subjects? Explain.

2.4 2D representations of 3D solids

*Active*Learn
Homework

- Sketch nets of 3D solids
- Draw 3D solids on isometric paper
- Draw plans and elevations of 3D solids

Warm up

1 Fluency How many vertices are there in a
   a triangle   **b** quadrilateral   **c** hexagon?

2 Match each 3D solid to its correct name.

sphere   cuboid   triangular prism   triangle-based pyramid   cylinder   cube   square-based pyramid

A   B   C   D   E   F   G

3 Draw accurately on squared paper:
   a a square of side length 5 cm   **b** a rectangle 6 cm by 4 cm.

Key point

A 3D solid has **faces**, **edges** and **vertices**.
Faces and edges can be flat or curved.

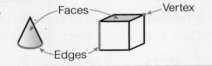

Faces — Vertex
Edges

4 The diagram shows a cuboid with the edges labelled A to L.
Write down:
   a two edges that meet at a vertex
   b a pair of parallel edges
   c two edges that do not meet and are perpendicular
     to each other
   d three edges that do not meet.

5 For each 3D solid:
   i Describe the faces.
   ii Does it have any congruent faces?
   iii Write down the number of edges and the number of vertices.

a   **b**   **c**

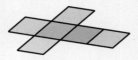 

Key point A **net** is a 2D shape that folds to make a 3D shape.

6 What 3D solid will each net make?

a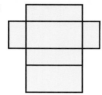

b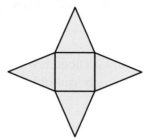

7 **Problem-solving** The diagram shows an open cube without a top. Which of these nets make an open cube?

A   B   C

D   E   F

8 **Problem-solving** Decide which of these are nets of a square-based pyramid. Give a reason for each of your answers.

A B C D E F

9 **Reasoning** Sketch a net for each of these 3D solids. Label each side with its length.

a 6 mm

b 3 cm 4 cm 1 cm

c 6 cm 2 cm

d 65 mm 30 mm

10 **Problem-solving**

a Draw an accurate net for this dice.

b The numbers on opposite faces of a dice add up to 7. Sketch the dots on the faces of your net.

 2 cm

You can draw 3D solids on **isometric paper**.
This cuboid has width 3 cm, length 5 cm and height 2 cm.

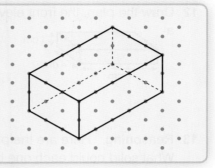

11 Here are two views of the same cuboid.

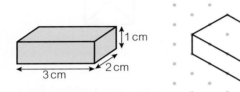

This one is drawn on isometric paper.

Draw these 3D solids on isometric paper.

a
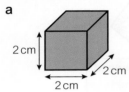

2 cm
2 cm
2 cm

b
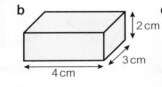

2 cm
4 cm
3 cm

c
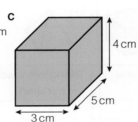

4 cm
5 cm
3 cm

Q10 hint The distance between two dots is 1 cm. Use a ruler.

The **plan** is the view from above the object.
The **front elevation** is the view of the front of the object.
The **side elevation** is the view of the side of the object.

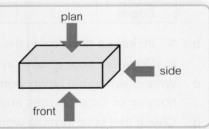

plan
side
front

Worked example

Draw the plan, the front elevation and the side elevation of this cuboid on squared paper.

2 cm
3 cm
5 cm

Use a ruler. Measure accurately. Label lengths.

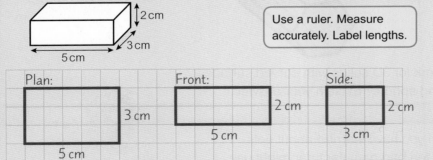

Plan:
3 cm
5 cm

Front:
2 cm
5 cm

Side:
2 cm
3 cm

12 Draw the plan, the front elevation and the side elevation of each cuboid on squared paper.

a
6 cm 4 cm 1 cm

b
8 cm 4 cm 2 cm

c
3 cm 5 cm 3 cm

13 Reasoning Here are the plan views of some 3D solids.
What solid could each one be?

a   **b**   **c**   **d**

Challenge

a Copy and complete this table showing the number of faces, edges and vertices for some 3D solids. The first one has been done for you.

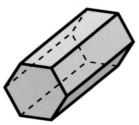

	Cube	Triangle-based pyramid	Triangular prism	Square-based pyramid
Faces	6			
Vertices	8			
Edges	12			

b **i** Include a new row in the table to show 'Faces + Vertices'.

ii Compare your answer in the new row with the number of edges. What do you notice?

c Write down a rule using words or algebra to describe the relationship between the number of faces, edges and vertices in a 3D solid.

d Check that your formula works for a hexagonal prism.

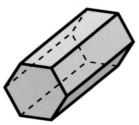

e Does your formula work for 3D solids with curved surfaces such as a cylinder and sphere? Explain your answer.

Reflect

In this lesson you have learned about nets.
Sketch all the nets that a tea bag manufacturer might use.
Beside each one, explain:
a what shape the net will make
b the advantages and disadvantages of using this shape.

2.5 Surface area of cubes and cuboids

*Active*Learn
Homework

• Calculate the surface area of cubes and cuboids

Warm up

1 Fluency What shape are the faces of

  a a cube   **b** a cuboid?

2 Work out the area of each shape. Round each area to 1 decimal place.

  a

4.6 cm

  b

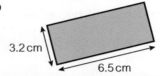

3.2 cm

6.5 cm

Key point   The **surface area** of a 3D solid is the total area of all its faces.
You can draw a net to help you find the surface area.

---

3 The diagram shows the net of a cube with edge 8 cm.

8 cm

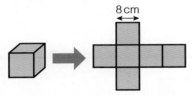

  a Work out the area of one face of the cube.

  b How many faces are there?

  c Calculate the surface area of the cube.

4 This diagram shows a cube with edges of length 7 cm.

7 cm

  a Calculate the area of one face of the cube.

  b Calculate the surface area of the whole cube.

5 A cardboard box is in the shape of an open cube with edges of length 20 cm.

  By sketching a net, work out the area of cardboard used in the box.

6 Calculate the surface area of cubes with these edge lengths.
   a 9cm   **b** 3m   **c** 25cm   **d** 13mm

7 **Reasoning** This cube has edge length x.

> **Q7a hint** Write $x \times x$ in its simplest form.

Write an expression for
  a the area of one face of the cube
  b the surface area of the cube.
  c Use your answer to part **b** to write a formula for the surface area of a cube.

8 **Problem-solving** A cube has a total surface area of $384\,cm^2$.
  a Work out the area of one face.
  b Work out the length of one edge.

9 Here is a cuboid with length 5cm, width 6cm and height 3cm.

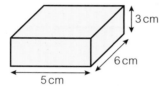

  a Sketch a net of the cuboid.
  b Label each face with its area.
  c Find the surface area of the cuboid.
  d What do you notice about the opposite faces of a cuboid?

Worked example

Calculate the surface area of this cuboid.

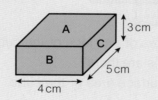

area of A = $4 \times 5 = 20\,cm^2$
area of B = $4 \times 3 = 12\,cm^2$
area of C = $5 \times 3 = 15\,cm^2$

surface area = $2 \times 20 + 2 \times 12 + 2 \times 15$
             = $40 + 24 + 30$
             = $94\,cm^2$

> There are two of each size face: top and bottom, front and back, left and right sides.

---

10 Calculate the surface area of each cuboid.

  a 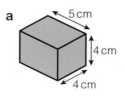   **b** 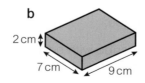   **c** 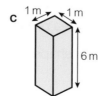   **d**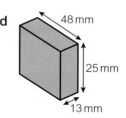

11 Problem-solving A new building is a cuboid 65 m long, 40 m wide and 220 m high.
It will be covered in glass panels on all four sides, but not the roof.
a Work out the surface area of glass needed.
The glass panels cost £128 per square metre.
b Work out the cost of the glass panels for this building.
Show how to check your answer using estimation.

12 Problem-solving Marius needs to cover the top and sides of this cake with icing.
One packet of icing covers 900 cm².

 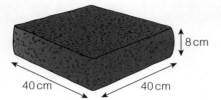

How many packets of icing will he need?

13 Reasoning Without calculating, estimate which
of these cuboids has the larger surface area.
Give a reason for your estimate.
Check your answers by calculating the actual
surface area of each cuboid.

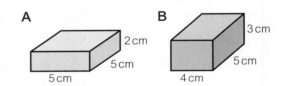

14 Problem-solving An open cardboard box has length 32 cm, width 12.5 cm and height 16.5 cm.
Work out the area of cardboard needed to make the open box.

Challenge The diagram shows a wooden shelf in the shape of a cuboid. All its faces
need to be painted with wood stain.

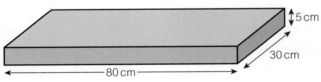

100 ml of wood stain covers an area of 4000 cm².
How many identical shelves can be stained using one 500 ml tin of wood stain?

Reflect This lesson showed you two methods for finding the surface area of a cube
or cuboid.
Method 1: draw then add
Draw a net, write the area of each face on the net, add them together (Q9).

Method 2: visualise then calculate
Visualise pairs of opposite faces, calculate 2 × area of face for each pair, add them
together (Worked example).

Which method did you prefer? Why? What are the advantages and disadvantages of your
preferred method?

2.6 Measures

- Solve problems in everyday contexts involving measures
- Convert between different measures for area, volume and capacity
- Use tonnes and hectares
- Know rough metric equivalents of imperial measures

Active Learn
Homework

Warm up

1 Fluency Copy and complete.
  a 1 m = ☐ cm   **b** 1 km = ☐ m   **c** 1 kg = ☐ g

2 Copy and complete.
  a 650 cm = ☐ m   **b** 4500 ml = ☐ litres   **c** 0.8 kg = ☐ g
  d 1.6 km = ☐ m   **e** 0.25 litres = ☐ ml   **f** 175 g = ☐ kg

3 Work out the area of a square with a side length of
  a 1 m   **b** 100 cm   **c** 1 cm   **d** 10 mm

4 Problem-solving A medicine bottle says, 'Take two 5 ml spoonfuls four times a day.'
  The bottle contains 0.15 litres. Sara has to take the medicine for 4 days.
  Is there enough medicine in the bottle? Explain your answer.

Key point

$$\times 1000 \left(\begin{array}{c} 1\ \text{ml} = 1\ \text{cm}^3 \\ 1\ \text{litre} = 1000\ \text{cm}^3 \end{array} \right) \times 1000$$

5 Work out these conversions.
  a 6000 cm³ = ☐ ml   **b** 6000 cm³ = ☐ litres
  c 2 litres = ☐ ml   **d** 2 litres = ☐ cm³
  e 3.5 litres = ☐ ml   **f** 3.5 litres = ☐ cm³
  g 4200 cm³ = ☐ litres   **h** 750 cm³ = ☐ litres
  i 0.35 litres = ☐ cm³   **j** 9.2 litres = ☐ cm³

Key point

The **capacity** of an object is the volume it can hold.

6 An Olympic swimming pool is a cuboid with length 50 m, width 25 m and depth 2 m.
  a Write the dimensions of the pool in centimetres.
  b Work out the capacity of the pool in cm³.
  c Convert your answer to part **b** to litres.

Key point

Mass: 1 **tonne** (t) = 1000 kg

7 Write the correct sign <, = or > between each pair of quantities.
  a 6 tonnes ... 600 g   **b** 4500 kg ... 0.45 tonnes
  c 1.25 tonnes ... 1250 kg   **d** 20 000 kg ... 2 tonnes

8   **Problem-solving**   The mass of a new-born elephant is 4% of the mass of an adult female elephant.
    The average mass of an adult female elephant is 3 tonnes.
    What is the average mass in kilograms of a new-born elephant?

9   **Reasoning**   Joe is using his calculator to solve some problems.
    Which value, A, B or C, should he enter for each measure?
    a 2 m 40 cm (in metres)   **A** 2.4   **B** 2.04   **C** 2.004
    b 2 m 4 cm (in metres)   **A** 2.4   **B** 2.04   **C** 2.004
    c 5 kg 250 g (in kilograms)   **A** 5.25   **B** 5.025   **C** 5.0025
    d 950 ml (in litres)   **A** 9.5   **B** 0.95   **C** 0.095

> **Key point**   You need to convert lengths into the same units before calculating areas or volumes.

> **Worked example**
>
> Work out the area of this field. Give your answer in m².
>
>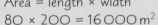
>
> 80 m   0.2 km
>
> ×1000
>
> 0.2 km = 200 m ──── Convert 0.2 km into metres.
>
> Area = length × width
> 80 × 200 = 16 000 m² ──── Write the units for your answer.

10 Work out the area of each rectangle. Include the units with your answer.

    a 300 m   b 60 cm   c 7 cm
       2 km   1.2 m   90 mm

  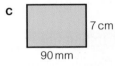

11 **Reasoning**
    a A square measures 1 cm by 1 cm. What is its area in cm²?
    b Another square measures 10 mm by 10 mm. What is its area in mm²?
    c Look at your answers to parts **a** and **b**.
       Complete this statement: $1 cm^2 = \square mm^2$
    d Complete this statement: $1 m^2 = \square cm^2$

    > **Q11d hint** Draw a diagram to show how many cm² there are in a square metre.

> **Key point** $1 cm^2 = 100 mm^2$
> $1 m^2 = 10 000 cm^2$

12 Copy and complete these area conversions.
    a $8 cm^2 = 8 \times \square = \square mm^2$ b $9.5 m^2 = 9.5 \times \square = \square cm^2$
    c $700 mm^2 = 700 \div \square = \square cm^2$ d $940 mm^2 = 940 \div \square = \square cm^2$
    e $30 000 cm^2 = \square \div \square = \square m^2$ f $420 000 cm^2 = \square \div \square = \square m^2$

13 **Problem-solving**   Work out the area of this rectangle.
    Give your answer in cm².

    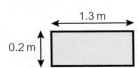

    1.3 m
    0.2 m

Key point Area: 1 **hectare** (ha) = 10 000 m²

14 Reasoning The diagram shows a plot of land.

a Work out the area of the plot in m².

Heidi works out that the area of the plot is 32.5 hectares.

b Is she correct?

Explain your answer.

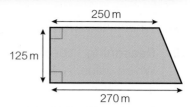

Key point You need to know these conversions between metric and imperial units.

1 **foot (ft)** ≈ 30 cm
1 **mile** ≈ 1.6 km
1 kg ≈ 2.2 **pounds (lb)**
1 litre ≈ 1.75 **pints**
1 **gallon** ≈ 4.5 litres

15 Copy and complete these metric/imperial conversions.

a 8 gallons = ☐ litres   b 7 lbs (pounds) = ☐ kg

c 4 litres = ☐ pints   d 15 litres = ☐ gallons

e 6 kg = ☐ lbs   f 8 pints = ☐ litres

Q15a hint

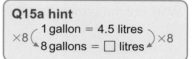

×8 (1 gallon = 4.5 litres) ×8
    8 gallons = ☐ litres

16 Problem-solving Visitors to a theme park must be taller than 1.4 m to go on a certain ride. Gemma is 5 feet tall.

Is she tall enough to go on the ride? Explain your answer.

17 Problem-solving The distance from the Earth to the Sun is approximately 93 000 000 miles. The distance from Mars to the Sun is approximately 227 000 000 km.

Which is closer to the Sun: Earth or Mars?

Challenge Here is an old recipe for marmalade.

Rewrite the recipe in metric measures to 1 decimal place.

Orange marmalade (makes about 10 lb)

3 lb Seville oranges

$4\frac{1}{2}$ –6 pints water

juice of 2 lemons

6 lb sugar

Reflect You need to remember the approximate conversions between some metric and imperial units.

Dee says, 'For feet, I remember that my ruler is 1 foot long and I know that is about 30 cm.'

Look at the other metric and imperial conversions in this lesson.

Write down a way to help you remember each of them.

Hint Use an object (like Dee), a rhyme, draw yourself a picture, make up a sentence or think of another way.

2 Check up

Areas of shapes

1 Work out the area of each triangle.

a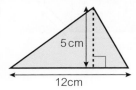
5 cm
12cm

b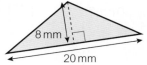
8 mm
20 mm

c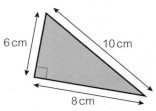
6 cm
10 cm
8 cm

2 The diagram shows the dimensions of a badge. What is the total area of the badge?

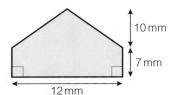
10 mm
7 mm
12 mm

3 Work out the area of this parallelogram.

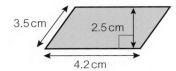
3.5 cm
2.5 cm
4.2 cm

4 Use the formula $A = \frac{1}{2}(a + b)h$ to work out the area of this trapezium.

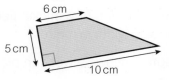
6 cm
5 cm
10 cm

Surface area and volume

5 Here is a cuboid with length 4 cm, width 8 cm and height 2 cm.
   a Sketch a net of the cuboid.
   b Draw the plan, the front elevation and the side elevation of this cuboid on squared paper.

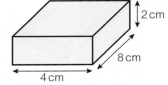
2 cm
8 cm
4 cm

6 Work out the surface area of this cube.

3 cm

7 Work out the volume of this cube.

1.5 cm

8 A biscuit tin is a cuboid of length 18 cm, width 9 cm and height 6 cm.
Work out the surface area of the tin.

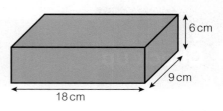

9 A cube has a side length of 15 cm.
How many cubes will fit into a box that measures 75 cm by 60 cm by 30 cm?

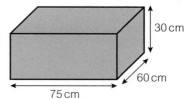

Metric and imperial measures

10 Work out these conversions.

a 5 litres = ☐ cm³   **b** 2.7 litres = ☐ cm³

c 3600 cm³ = ☐ litres   **d** 240 cm³ = ☐ litres

e 2.4 tonnes = ☐ kg   **f** 30 000 m² = ☐ ha

11 a A butcher receives an order for 10 pounds (lb) of beef mince.
Approximately how many kilograms is this?

b Sean runs 8 miles. How far is this in kilometres?

c Anna orders 900 litres of oil for her central heating oil tank.
How many gallons is this?

d One jelly mould holds 1.5 pints of jelly.
How much jelly is needed for six jelly moulds? Give your answer in litres.

e The central strip of a cricket field between the two wickets has a width of 10 feet.
What is its width in metres?

12 The diagram shows a wooden planting tray in the shape of an open cuboid.

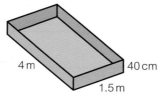

Calculate the capacity of the planting tray.

Challenge   Sketch a shape that fits each description.
Write the measurements on each shape.

a A triangle with area 32 cm²

b A parallelogram with area 32 cm²

c A trapezium with area 32 cm²

Reflect   How sure are you of your answers? Were you mostly

😞 **Just guessing**   😐 **Feeling doubtful**   😊 **Confident**

What next? Use your results to decide whether to strengthen or extend your learning.

2 Strengthen

Areas of shapes

1 For each triangle, write the base length and perpendicular height.

a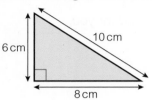

b

> **Q1 hint** The base length and the perpendicular height must be at right angles (90°) to each other.

2 Use the formula

area of a triangle = $\frac{1}{2}$ × base length × perpendicular height

to work out the area of each triangle in Q1.

> **Q2 hint** For part a, area
> $= \frac{1}{2} \times b \times h$
> $= \frac{1}{2} \times 8 \times 6$
> $= 4 \times 6 = \square \, cm^2$

3 Work out the area of this shape.
The working has been started for you.

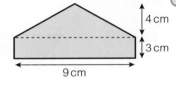

area of rectangle = length × width
$= 9 \times \square$
$= \square \, cm^2$

area of triangle = $\frac{1}{2}$ × base × height
$= \frac{1}{2} \times 9 \times \square$
$= \square \, cm^2$

total area = area of rectangle + area of triangle
$= \square + \square = \square \, cm^2$

4 Work out the area of each compound shape.

a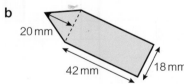

b

5 Find the area of this parallelogram.
The working has been started for you.

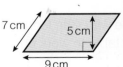

base length = $\square$ cm
perpendicular height = $\square$ cm
area = base × perpendicular height
$= \square \times \square = \square \, cm^2$

> **Q5 hint** How can you tell which is the perpendicular height?

6 Work out the area of each parallelogram.

a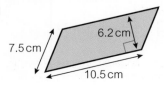

b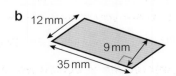

7 a Look at these two identical trapezia.

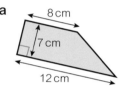

Q7 hint Trapezia is the plural of trapezium.

Copy and complete.
$a = 4\,cm$, $b = \square\,cm$, $h = \square\,cm$

b Find the area of the trapezium. The working has been started for you.

$$\text{area} = \tfrac{1}{2}(a + b)h$$

$$= \tfrac{1}{2} \times (4 + 6) \times 3$$

$$= \tfrac{1}{2} \times \square \times 3$$

$$= \square \times 3$$

$$= \square\,cm^2$$

8 Work out the area of each trapezium.

a

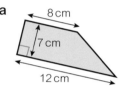

b

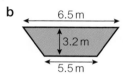

Q8b hint Enter the whole calculation into your calculator, using the bracket keys.

Surface area and volume

1 Here is a 3D solid made from four cubes.
Which of these diagrams shows
  a the plan   **b** the side elevation   **c** the front elevation?

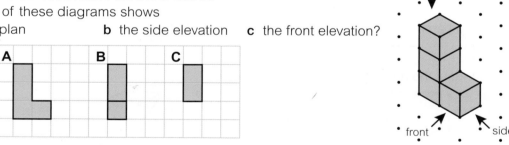

2 Here is the net of a cube with side length 2 cm.
Copy and complete the table to work out
the surface area.

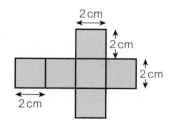

Shape of face	Area of face	Number of faces	Total area
2 cm 2 cm	$2 \times 2 = \square\,cm^2$	$\square$	$\square \times \square = \square\,cm^2$

3 The diagram shows a cube of side length 8 cm. Find the surface area of the cube.

area of one face = 8 × 8 = ☐ cm²
surface area of cube = ☐ × ☐ = ☐ cm²

8 cm

4 Calculate the surface area of a cube with side length 12 mm.

5 Copy the net for this cuboid. Label the lengths.

Q5 hint Match each face on the cuboid to a face on the net.

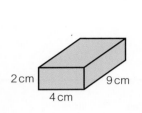

2 cm   9 cm
4 cm

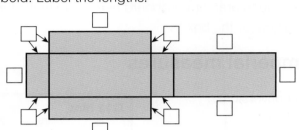

6 Find the surface area of this cuboid. The working has been started for you.

Q6 hint Altogether there are three sets of two identical faces.

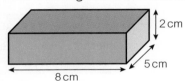

2 cm
5 cm
8 cm

area of front face = 8 × 2 = 16 cm²
area of right end face = 5 × 2 = 10 cm²
area of top face = 8 × 5 = ☐ cm²
total surface area = 16 + 16 + 10 + 10 + ☐ + ☐ = ☐ cm²

7 Work out the surface area of each cuboid.

a

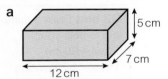

5 cm
7 cm
12 cm

b

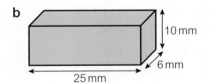

10 mm
6 mm
25 mm

8 This cuboid is made of centimetre cubes.
   a Write down
      i the length
      ii the width
      iii the height of the cuboid.
   b Work out the volume of the cuboid.

Q8b hint This cuboid is made up of two identical layers. Here is one of the layers.

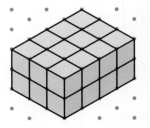

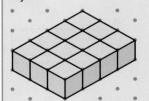

9 Work out the volume of each cuboid in Q7. The first one is started for you.
   a $l = 12$, $w = 7$, $h = 5$
      $V = lwh$
      $= 12 × ☐ × ☐$
      $= ☐ cm^3$

10 Problem-solving A box holds 12 tins of baked beans as shown.

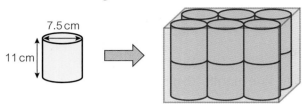

Q10 hint Use the dimensions of the tin to work out the length, width and height of the box.

a Work out the surface area of cardboard needed to make the box.

b What is the volume of the box?

Metric and imperial measures

1 Work out these conversions.
  a 3 litres $= \square \, cm^3$
  b 7 litres $= \square \, cm^3$
  c $4000 \, cm^3 = \square$ litres
  d $9000 \, cm^3 = \square$ litres
  e 4.5 litres $= \square \, cm^3$
  f 8.7 litres $= \square \, cm^3$
  g $2600 \, cm^3 = \square$ litres
  h $840 \, cm^3 = \square$ litres

Q1a hint
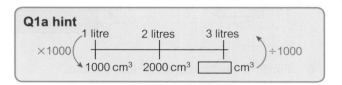

2 Work out these conversions.
  a 3 feet $\approx \square$ cm
  b 600 cm $\approx \square$ feet
  c 2.5 feet $\approx \square$ cm
  d 4 litres $\approx \square$ pints
  e 7 pints $\approx \square$ litres
  f 22.5 litres $\approx \square$ gallons
  g 6.2 gallons $\approx \square$ litres
  h 7.2 miles $\approx \square$ km
  i 22.4 km $\approx \square$ miles
  j 11 pounds $\approx \square$ kg
  k 7.2 kg $\approx \square$ lb

Q2a hint
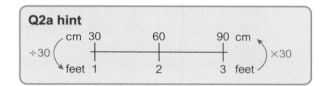

Q2 hint Draw a number line to help you.
1 foot $\approx$ 30 cm
1 litre $\approx$ 1.75 pints
1 gallon $\approx$ 4.5 litres
1 mile $\approx$ 1.6 km
1 kg $\approx$ 2.2 lb

3 Calculate the area of each rectangle in the given units.

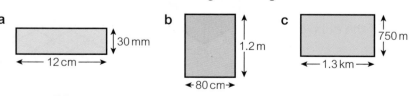

a 30 mm, 12 cm, Area = $\square \, cm^2$

b 1.2 m, 80 cm, Area = $\square \, cm^2$

c 750 m, 1.3 km, Area = $\square \, m^2$

Q3 hint For an area in cm^2 or a volume in cm^3, use lengths in cm.

4 Calculate the volume of each cuboid in the given units.

a

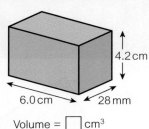

4.2 cm

6.0 cm   28 mm

Volume = ☐ cm³

b

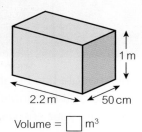

1 m

2.2 m   50 cm

Volume = ☐ m³

Challenge   Work with a partner to answer these questions.

a The diagram shows a white square and 4 yellow triangles on a 3 by 3 square grid.

   i Work out the area of the square grid.
  ii Work out the area of the triangles.
 iii Work out the area of the white square by subtracting the area of the triangles from the area of the square grid.

b Repeat part **a** for these diagrams, and for two similar diagrams of your own.

 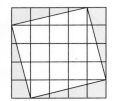

c Copy and complete this table to show all your results.

Grid size	Base of triangle	Height of triangle	Area of white square
3 × 3	2	1	

d What do you notice about the base and height of each triangle and the area of the white square?

Reflect   In this unit you have had to do lots of different things to find the answers to questions.

Write these in order, from the one you found easiest to the one you found hardest:

A Knowing which is the perpendicular height in a shape.
B Using a formula to find the area of a shape.
C Working out what the net of a 3D solid will look like.
D Finding the surface area of a cuboid.
E Knowing when to multiply and when to divide when converting measures.

Write a hint, in your own words, for the one you found the hardest.

2 Extend

1 **Reasoning**   This triangle has height 4 cm and area 16 cm².
Ellen says, 'The base of the triangle is 4 cm because 4 × 4 = 16.'
Is she correct? Explain your answer.

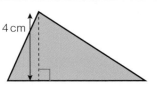

2 **Reasoning**   This parallelogram is split into two congruent triangles.
   a Write an expression for the area of each triangle.
   b Show that the area of the parallelogram $A = bh$.

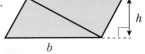

3 A cube has a total surface area of 8.64 cm².
Work out:
   a the area of one face of the cube
   b the side length of the cube.

> **Q3a hint** A cube has six identical faces.

4 **Problem-solving**   The diagram shows a square company logo.
Work out the shaded area in the logo.

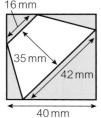

16 mm

35 mm

42 mm

40 mm

5 **Reasoning**   Caroline says, 'If I double the length of one
of the parallel sides of a trapezium, but keep the other
parallel side and the height the same, the area of the
trapezium will also be doubled.'
Draw your own trapezium to test Caroline's statement.
Show, using a counter example, that she is wrong.

> **Q5 hint** A counter example is one example that proves the statement is wrong.

6 **Problem-solving**   A water trough is in the shape of a cuboid.
It has length 1.5 m, width 0.7 m and height 0.8 m.
Water is put into the trough. The depth of the water is three quarters of the height
of the trough.
Work out the volume of the water in the trough in litres.

7 **Problem-solving**   Gareth has an oil tank that is approximately the shape of a cuboid.
It has length 1.8 m, width 80 cm and height 90 cm. It contains oil to a depth of 25 cm.
   a Can he fit 1000 litres more into his oil tank?
      Explain your answer.

> **Q7a hint** Draw a diagram to help you.

Gareth orders oil to fill his tank to 90% full.
   b How much oil does he order, to the nearest litre?

The price of oil is 69.8p per litre if you order 1000 litres or more, and 70.2p per litre if you
order less than 1000 litres.
   c How much does Gareth pay for this oil?
      Give your answer in pounds to the nearest penny.

8 **Problem-solving**   A gold bar is in the shape of a cuboid
with length 150 mm, width 45 mm and height 45 mm.
The bar is melted and made into cubes with side length 12 mm.
How many cubes of gold can be made from the cuboid?

Q8 hint The answer
must be the largest whole
number you can make.

9 **Reasoning**
  a An electric car travels 25 metres every second.
    How far will it travel in one hour?
  b Ellie's electric car can travel 140 km before the battery needs charging.
    Can her car travel 90 miles without charging the battery? Explain your answer.

10 **Problem-solving**   The diagram shows the percentage composition of whole milk.

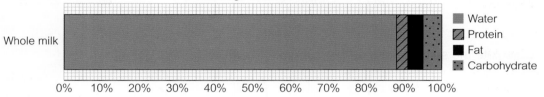

Percentage of whole milk

Whole milk
0%   10%   20%   30%   40%   50%   60%   70%   80%   90%   100%

■ Water
▨ Protein
■ Fat
▨ Carbohydrate

A farm produces 500 gallons of whole milk per day.
  a How many litres of fat are in 500 gallons of whole milk?
To make skimmed milk, 92.5% of the fat in whole milk is removed.
  b How many litres of skimmed milk can be made from 500 gallons of whole milk?

11 **Reasoning**   A cube has volume 64 cm³.
The cube is cut in half to make two cuboids.
What is the surface area of one of the cuboids?

Challenge

Khalid makes a cake and covers it on all sides in icing.
Khalid's iced cake is a cuboid 8 cm tall, 10 cm wide and 12 cm long.
The icing is 1 cm thick.
  a Copy and complete.
      volume of iced cake = ☐ cm³
      volume of cake = (8 – ☐) × (10 – ☐) × (12 – ☐) = ☐ cm³
      so volume of icing = ☐ – ☐ = ☐ cm³
  b What are the dimensions of a cube-shaped cake where the
    volume of icing is equal to the volume of cake?

Part a hint The cake is
iced on the top and bottom
so you need to subtract
2 × icing thickness from
the height of the cake.

Reflect   Look back at Q5. It asked you for a 'counter example'.
What did this counter example show about Caroline's statement?
In what sort of situation might you need to prove that a statement is untrue?
Could you use a counter example? Explain.

2 Unit test

1 Work out these conversions.
   a 9 litres = ☐ cm³
   b 0.8 litres = ☐ cm³
   c 12000 cm³ = ☐ litres
   d 950 cm³ = ☐ litres

2 The diagram shows a cube of side length 6 cm.
   Work out the surface area of the cube.

6 cm

3 Calculate the surface area of this cuboid.

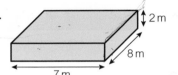

2 m
8 m
7 m

4 Work out the area of this triangle.

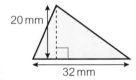

20 mm
32 mm

5 This solid is drawn on isometric dotted paper.
   Write down the number of faces, edges and vertices of this prism.

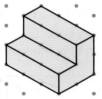

6 Work out the area of this shape.

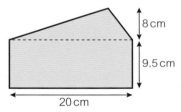

8 cm
9.5 cm
20 cm

7 Work out these conversions.
   a 8.5 cm² = ☐ mm²   b 60000 cm² = ☐ m²
   c 5000 m² = ☐ ha   d 2.5 ha = ☐ m²

8 Work out the area of each shape.

a

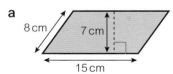

8 cm
7 cm
15 cm

b

8 mm
15 mm
20 mm

9 The diagram shows the dimensions of an eyeshadow box.
   What volume of eyeshadow does it hold?
   Give your answer in mm³.

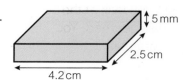

5 mm
2.5 cm
4.2 cm

10 Write these conversions.
   a 1 foot (ft) ≈ ☐ cm
   b 1 mile ≈ ☐ km
   c 1 kg ≈ ☐ pounds (lb)
   d 1 litre ≈ ☐ pints
   e 1 gallon ≈ ☐ litres

11 Rob takes part in a 12 mile charity fun run.
   How far is the fun run in kilometres?

12 A recipe for Spanish paella uses 4 pints of chicken stock.
   How much stock is this in litres?

13 Work out the volume of a cube with side length 3.6 cm.

14 An open gift box is a cuboid. It has length 18.5 cm, width 9.4 cm and height 6.2 cm.
   Work out the area of cardboard needed to make the open box.

15 A barrel of oil holds approximately 35 gallons.
   How much oil is in 50 barrels? Give your answer in litres.

16 The box for a wireless router measures 12 cm by 7.5 cm by 8 cm.
   Boxes of wireless routers are packed into a larger box.
   The larger box measures 98 cm by 32 cm by 40 cm.

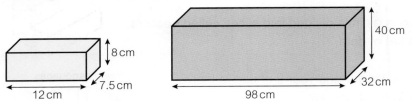

8 cm
12 cm
7.5 cm
40 cm
98 cm
32 cm

   a What is the greatest number of wireless router boxes that will fit into the larger box?
   b What volume of empty space will be left in the box?

Challenge   The diagram shows a 3D solid made up of cuboids.

Work out:
a   the volume
b   the surface area.

10 cm
2 cm
5 cm
4 cm
4 cm
8 cm

Reflect   Write a heading, 'Five important things about area and volume'.
Now look back at the work you have done in this unit, and list the five most important things
you have learned. You might include:
   • formulae
   • conversions
   • methods for working things out
   • mistakes to avoid (with tips on how to avoid them in future).

3 Statistics, graphs and charts

Master | Check up p81 | Strengthen p83 | Extend p88 | Unit test p90

3.1 Pie charts

- Interpret pie charts
- Draw pie charts

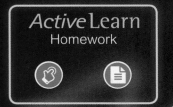
Active Learn
Homework

Warm up

1 **Fluency** How many degrees are there in a full circle?

2 Use compasses to draw a circle. Use a ruler to draw a radius (line from the centre to the edge).

3 Use a ruler and protractor to draw these angles.
   a 60°   **b** 110°

4 Work out these fractions and percentages.
   a $\frac{1}{4}$ of 360   **b** $\frac{1}{6}$ of 360   **c** 50% of 360°   **d** 20% of 360°

Key point
A **pie chart** is a circle divided into slices called **sectors**.
Each sector represents a set of data.

5 The pie chart shows the languages Year 8 chose to learn.
   a Which language was most popular?
      How do you know?
   b What fraction of the students chose
      i Spanish   **ii** German
      iii French   **iv** Mandarin?
   c There are 280 students in Year 8.
      Work out the number of students who chose each language.

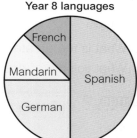
Year 8 languages

6 **Problem-solving** One week, John recorded the number of items he recycled.
   Here is a pie chart of his data.
   a He recycled 40 plastic items. How many items did he recycle altogether?
   b How many glass items did he recycle?

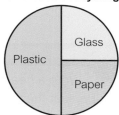
One week's recycling

7 This pie chart shows the different sources of energy used to generate electricity in a city.

   a Which is the most common energy source?

   b What percentage of the energy comes from fossil fuels (gas, coal and oil)?

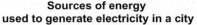
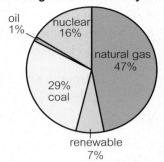

Sources of energy used to generate electricity in a city

oil 1% · nuclear 16% · natural gas 47% · 29% coal · renewable 7%

8 **Problem-solving** The pie chart shows the proportion of living species currently known.

   a Which type of species is the mode?

   b There are approximately 70 000 species of fungi.
   How many species of algae and protozoa are there?

   c How many species of insects are there?

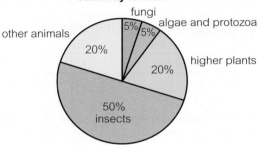

Number of living species currently known

fungi 5% · algae and protozoa 5% · higher plants 20% · other animals 20% · 50% insects

---

Worked example

Draw a pie chart to show this data about the types of cars in a car park.

Type of car	Frequency
diesel	6
petrol	2
hybrid electric	4

Work out the total number of cars.

Total number of cars = 6 + 2 + 4 = 12

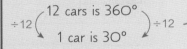

The whole pie chart (360°) represents 12 cars.
Work out the angle to represent 1 car.

÷12 (12 cars is 360° / 1 car is 30°) ÷12

Type of car	Frequency	Angle
diesel	6	6 × 30° = 180°
petrol	2	2 × 30° = 60°
hybrid electric	4	4 × 30° = 120°

Add a new column to the table with the heading 'Angle'.
Multiply the number of each type of car by 30° to work out the angle for each sector.

Check: 180° + 60° + 120° = 360°

Check that the angles add up to 360°.

Draw a circle.
Draw a radius.

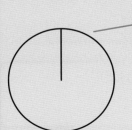

Types of cars in a car park

hybrid · diesel · petrol

Use a protractor to draw the angles. Label each sector. Give your pie chart a title.

9 The table shows students' sport choices.

    a Work out the total number of students.

    b Copy and complete to work out
       the angle for one student.

$$\div \square \left(\begin{array}{l} \square \text{ students are } 360° \\ 1 \text{ student is } \square° \end{array} \right) \div \square$$

Sport	Frequency	Angle
cricket	36	
tennis	24	
rounders	30	
Total		

    c Work out the angle for each sport.
       Check that the angles add up to 360°.

    d Draw the pie chart. Remember to give it a title and label it.

10 Problem-solving Draw a pie chart to show this data on students' lunch choices.

Lunch choice	Frequency
sandwiches	35
salad bar	15
hot meal	22

11 Problem-solving The table shows the favourite types
of films of students in class 9W.

    a Draw a pie chart to show this information.

    b What fraction of the students chose animation?

    c What is the mode?

    d What percentage of students chose
       action or drama?

Favourite type of film	Frequency
action	8
animation	6
comedy	6
drama	4

12 The table shows the percentages of
sales in a bakery in one month.

    a What angle in a whole circle represents

       i 50%   **ii** 10%   **iii** 20%?

    b Draw a pie chart of the data.

Item	Percentage
bread	50%
cakes	20%
pies	20%
pasties	10%

Challenge

a Draw a pie chart for this data on the languages spoken in a school.
    English 38%, Chinese 14%, Spanish 2%, Japanese 5%,
    Urdu 11%, Somali 4%, Other 26%

b Now move the Spanish, Japanese and Somali data to the 'Other' section.
    Draw a new pie chart.
    Which pie chart is easier to read?

c Draw a pie chart showing 'English' and 'Not English'.
    Is two sections enough for a pie chart? Explain your answer.

Reflect   Rosie says that fractions help you to interpret pie charts (as in Q5).
What other areas of mathematics help you to interpret pie charts?
What maths skills do you need to draw pie charts?

3.2 Using tables

- Calculate the mean from a frequency table
- Use two-way tables
- Use tables for grouped data

ActiveLearn
Homework

Warm up

1 **Fluency** Work out the missing numbers.
  a 25 + ☐ = 40   **b** ☐ + 18 = 30   **c** 65 + ☐ = 100

2 Find the mean, median, mode and range of these numbers.
  0, 4, 7, 4, 3, 4, 2, 1

3 The table shows the numbers of books customers
  borrowed from a library over one hour last Tuesday.
  a How many people borrowed books during that
    hour?
  b How many people borrowed fewer than four books?
  c What was the modal number of books borrowed?
  d What was the range?

Number of books	Frequency
1	7
2	10
3	8
4	6
5	1

Worked example

Jack asked students in his class how many pets they had.
Here are his results. Work out the mean.

Number of pets	Frequency	Total number of pets
0	7	0 × 7 = 0
1	8	1 × 8 = 8
2	6	2 × 6 = 12
3	3	3 × 3 = 9
4	1	4 × 1 = 4
Total	25	33

Add a column to the table.

6 people with 2 pets each.

Work out the total number of pets.

Work out the total frequency
(number of people).

$$\text{mean} = \frac{33}{25} = 1.32$$

$$\text{mean} = \frac{\text{total number of pets}}{\text{total number of people}}$$

Use a calculator.

4 The table shows the numbers of siblings
  of students in a Year 9 class.
  a How many students are in the class?
  b How many siblings were counted altogether?
  c Work out the mean number of siblings.

Siblings	Frequency
0	2
1	3
2	4
3	1
4	3

5 The table shows the numbers of goals scored in netball matches in one season.
Work out the mean number of goals scored.

Goals scored	Frequency
0	3
1	8
2	5
3	3
4	1

6 The table shows the numbers of peas in different pods.
  a What is the modal number of peas in a pod?
  b What is the range?
  c Work out the mean number of peas in a pod.

Number of peas in a pod	Frequency
0	2
1	2
2	9
3	7
4	6
5	11
6	3

7 **Problem-solving / Reasoning** The label on a matchbox says, 'Average contents 32'.
The table shows the numbers of matches in some of these matchboxes.
  a Is the label on the matchbox correct?
  b Which average should you use for 'Average contents'? Does it matter?

Number of matches	Frequency
29	5
30	21
31	21
32	22
33	14
34	12
35	2

> **Key point** A **two-way table** divides data into groups in rows across the table and in columns down the table. You can calculate the totals across and down.

8 **Reasoning** This two-way table shows the types of drinks bought by adults and children at a café. Each person bought one drink.
  a Work out the total number of children who bought a drink.
  b How many cold drinks were bought altogether?
  c How many drinks were bought altogether?

	Hot drinks	Cold drinks	Total
Adults	20	15	35
Children	25	12	
Total	45		

9 **Reasoning** This two-way table shows the numbers of tickets sold at a cinema.

	Standard seats	Luxury seats	Total
Adult	39	33	72
Child	15	9	
Total	54		

  a Work out the total number of luxury seat tickets sold.
  b How many child tickets were sold in total?
  c How many tickets were sold altogether?
  d What fraction of the tickets sold were for children?

> **Q9d hint**
> child total
> ─────────
> total

10 **Reasoning** The table shows the number of members of a salsa dance club.

	Beginners	Intermediate	Advanced	Total
Men	33	36		90
Women			38	110
Total	65			

  a Copy and complete the table.

  b How many men are in the advanced group?

  c How many men are above beginner level?

  d Which level has the greatest difference in numbers of men and women?

  e What percentage of the total membership is women at advanced level?

11 **Problem-solving / Reasoning** Tim records the food sold in his café one weekend.

  a Which food is most popular on

   i Saturday   **ii** Sunday?

  b Tim makes a profit of

   • 35p on each sandwich

   • 50p on each salad

   • £1.30 on each portion of fish and chips

   • 40p on each cake.

   What does he make the most profit on, over this weekend?

	Saturday	Sunday	Total
Sandwiches	25	21	
Salads	12	9	
Fish and chips	7	6	
Cakes	13	27	
Total			

  c Tim wants to cut a menu item on Sundays.
   Which should he cut?
   Explain why.

Q11c hint Look at the profit for each item on Sunday.

> **Key point**
>
> The class $4 \leqslant l < 6$ includes all values of length l from $l = 4$ cm up to, but not including, 6 cm.
> The **width** of this class is 2 cm. $\leqslant$ means 'less than or equal to'.

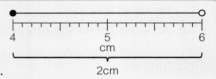

12 Some children measure the lengths of pea pods.
   Daisy starts this table for her results.

  a The first class includes all lengths up to, but not including, 2.0 cm.
   Which class contains the length 2.0 cm?

Length, l (cm)	Tally	Frequency
$0 \leqslant l < 2$		
$2 \leqslant l < 4$		
$4 \leqslant l < 6$		
$6 \leqslant l < 8$		

  b **i** Copy the table and tally these lengths in cm.

5.7	2.0	3.7	6.1	5.0	2.4	6.8	4.5
6.8	3.7	4.0	5.6	6.3	4.9	6.0	4.1

   ii Fill in the frequency column.

  c Which is the modal class?

  d Calculate the range of the data in part **b**.

  e **Reasoning** From this grouped frequency table, an estimate of the range is
   $8 - 0 = 8$ cm.
   Explain why this is not the same as your answer to part **d**.

13 Reasoning A farmer recorded the masses m of lambs when they were born.

| 3.8 | 5.2 | 4.3 | 3.8 | 3.1 | 4.5 | 4.2 |
| 5.4 | 3.9 | 4.0 | 4.1 | 3.7 | 3.5 | 4.1 |

Mass, m (kg)	Tally	Frequency
$3.0 \leqslant m < 3.5$		
$3.5 \leqslant m < 4.0$		
$4.0 \leqslant m < 4.5$		
$4.5 \leqslant m < 5.0$		
$5.0 \leqslant m < 5.5$		

a Copy and complete the grouped frequency table.

b What is the modal class?

c What is the width of each class?

14 Problem-solving A scientist measured the lengths l of some embryos in mm.

| 15.3 | 19.8 | 11.1 | 14.0 | 18.9 | 16.5 | 18.0 |
| 15.3 | 14.9 | 10.7 | 19.4 | 16.0 | 14.8 | 15.4 |

Length, l (mm)	Tally	Frequency
$10 \leqslant l < 14$		
$14 \leqslant l < \square$		
$\square \leqslant l < \square$		

a Copy and complete the table so that all the classes are the same width.

b What is the modal class?

15 Lucy asked shoppers in the town centre how far they had travelled to the shops that day.
Complete these sentences from Lucy's report.

a The modal distance travelled to the shops is _____.

b More than half the shoppers had travelled less than _____.

c An estimate for the range is _____ .

Distance travelled (d miles)	Frequency
$0 \leqslant d < 3$	6
$3 \leqslant d < 6$	9
$6 \leqslant d < 9$	4
$9 \leqslant d < 12$	5

Challenge

The data shows the times, in seconds, that some students took to type 60 words.

| 72.5 | 83.9 | 59.7 | 62.5 | 95.3 | 85.0 | 69.0 | 82.4 | 99.9 | 78.9 |
| 83.6 | 87.7 | 93.8 | 90.0 | 69.7 | 75.0 | 70.1 | 84.2 | 60.0 | 69.9 |

a For this data, create:
  i a frequency table with three class intervals of equal width
  ii a frequency table with five class intervals of equal width
  iii a frequency table with ten class intervals of equal width.

b Which frequency table do you think shows the data best? Explain.

Reflect Freddie and Claudia are talking about tables.
Freddie says, 'Tables show information in columns and rows.'
What do you think of Freddie's definition of a table? Is it true for all the tables in this lesson?
Where else do you see tables displaying information in everyday life?

3.3 Stem and leaf diagrams

ActiveLearn
Homework

- Draw stem and leaf diagrams for data
- Interpret stem and leaf diagrams

Warm up

1 Fluency Work out the median, mode and range of: 1, 2, 2, 2, 2, 3, 4, 4, 4, 5

2 Priya has written ten data values in order: 1, 1, 2, 3, 5, 7, 8, 8, 8, 9
She says, 'For ten data values in order, the median is the fifth one.'
Is she correct? Explain your answer.

Key point

In a set of 9 data values, the median is the $\dfrac{9 + 1}{2}$ = 5th one.

In a set of 10 data values, the median is the $\dfrac{10 + 1}{2} = \dfrac{11}{2}$ = 5.5th one.

In a set of n data values, the median is the $\dfrac{n + 1}{2}$th one.

3 These sets of data are written in order.
a 3, 5, 7, 7, 8, 9, 9, 10, 11   **b** 7, 9, 10, 10, 10, 12, 17   **c** −3, −2, 0, 0, 1
For each set:
  i count the number of values, n **ii** work out $\dfrac{n + 1}{2}$ to find the middle value
  iii write down the median.

4 Repeat Q3 for these sets of data.
a 0, 1, 5, 7, 9, 11, 12, 12, 12, 13   **b** 5, 5, 5, 7, 8, 10, 12, 15

Key point

A **stem and leaf diagram** shows numerical data split into a 'stem' and 'leaves'. The key shows you how to read the values.

Worked example

Here are the heights of some tomato seedlings (in cm).
    2.8   3.4   4.5   4.1   4.3   2.7   1.6   3.2   1.9   2.5
Construct a **stem and leaf** diagram for this data.

Unordered diagram

1 Decide on a stem.

```
1 | 6  9
2 | 8  7  5
3 | 4  2
4 | 5  1  3
```

2 Write in the leaves as you work along the data list. It helps to cross out the values as you write them on the diagram.

Ordered diagram

```
1 | 6  9
2 | 5  7  8
3 | 2  4
4 | 1  3  5
```

Key: 1 | 6 means 1.6 cm

3 Write out your diagram again, putting the leaves in order.

4 Give your diagram a key.

5 Here are the weights of some parcels (in kg).

1.8	2.7	5.3	4.9	2.3	3.8
1.4	2.2	3.1	5.6	4.5	5.1

Construct a stem and leaf diagram for this data. Remember the key.

6 The numbers of visitors each day to a stately home were

61	52	65	77	79	84	86	91	85	70	64
53	77	56	68	73	92	85	87	78	90	

a Construct a stem and leaf diagram for this data. Use the 'tens' digit as the stem.

b **Problem-solving** Use your diagram to answer these questions.

  i On how many days was the stately home open?

  ii On how many days were there more than 70 visitors?

  iii The manager calculates that the house needs at least 65 visitors each day to make a profit. On what percentage of days did it make a profit?

7 The stem and leaf diagram shows the heights of Year 8 students, measured to the nearest centimetre.
Find:

a the mode

b the range

c the number of values, n

d the $\dfrac{n+1}{2}$th value

e the median.

```
14 | 6 9
15 | 1 1 2 3 5 5 5 6
16 | 2 3 4 5 5 5 7 9 9
17 | 0 2 4
```

Key: 14 | 6 means 146 cm

f **Reasoning** Why didn't you need to write the data in order before finding the middle one?

g **Problem-solving** How many students are less than 160 cm?

8 **Problem-solving** From your stem and leaf diagram for Q5, find:

a the median   **b** the range.

9 **Problem-solving** Jay owns a newsagent's.
He records the amounts his customers spent one morning.

```
0 | 65 87
1 | 08 12 36 88 97
2 | 40 52 56 68 87 95
3 | 05 15 20 35 38 40 46 62 77 99
4 | 39 68
```

Key: 1 | 08 means £1.08

Jay wants to increase the 'average' spend by £1 per customer. He puts a special offer of 'Chocolate bars, 3 for a £1' by the till. He records the amounts spent the next morning.

```
0 | 92
1 | 12 18 36 52
2 | 36 40 75 99
3 | 15 19 24 36 42 49 51 60 66 85 90
4 | 04 39 78 82
```

Key: 1 | 36 means £1.36

Q9 hint Which average will you choose? Compare for the two diagrams.

Has the special offer increased the average spend by £1?

10 **Problem-solving**   The times (in minutes) for a cross country race are

107   112   105   123   131   119   100   117   134   127

a Draw a stem and leaf diagram for this data.

b Find the median race time.

11 **Problem-solving / Reasoning**   At the end of a secretarial course, students were tested on their typing speeds for
- number of words per minute typing their own text
- number of words per minute when typing words from an audio file.

This back-to-back stem and leaf diagram shows their results.

Q11 hint The circled value is 52.

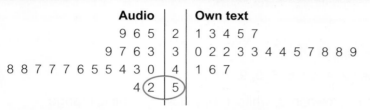

```
        Audio │ │ Own text
      9 6 5 │ 2 │ 1 3 4 5 7
    9 7 6 3 │ 3 │ 0 2 2 3 3 4 4 5 7 8 8 9
8 8 7 7 6 5 5 4 3 0 │ 4 │ 1 6 7
          4 ②  │ 5 │
```

Key: 5 | 2 | means 25 words per minute for audio
     | 2 | 1 means 21 words per minute for own text

a The course leader says, 'Most of the audio scores are between 40 and 49.'
Write a sentence like this for the own text scores.

b Work out the median and range for:

i audio   **ii** own text.

a Put the visitor data from Q6 into a grouped frequency table.
Use classes 50–59, 60–69 etc.

b Draw a bar chart for the data. Remember to label your axes and give your chart a title.

c Which of the parts in Q6 can you answer from your bar chart?
If there are any you cannot answer, explain why not.

d Can you work out a median from a bar chart?

e i Which is better, a stem and leaf diagram or a bar chart? Write your reasons in a table.

Stem and leaf is better for	Bar chart is better for
	Colourful diagrams

ii Is there anything they are equally good for?

Hannah, Sam and Tilly discuss how they use worked examples.

Sam says, 'I read the question, then the answer, then all the note boxes telling me what to do.'

Hannah says, 'I only read the note boxes and bits of the answer when I get stuck.'

Tilly says, 'I read the question, then the first part of the answer and its notes.
Then I read the next bit of the answer and its notes, and so on.'

Describe how you read the worked example for this lesson.

Try reading it again in different ways (like Sam, Hannah and Tilly).

Which way do you think is best? Why?

3.4 Comparing data

- Compare two sets of data using statistics or the shape of the graph
- Construct line graphs
- Choose the most appropriate average to use

Active Learn
Homework

Warm up

1 Fluency Here are two sets of data.

A Scores in a test: 2, 4, 12, 6, 8, 5, 9, 10, 7

B Favourite colour: brown, red, white, red, yellow, red, pink, orange

a For which of these sets of data can you *not* find the range?

b Which set of data does *not* have a mode?

2 Here are the scores of two different teams in seven rounds of a quiz.

| Team A | 12 | 20 | 24 | 25 | 25 | 25 | 26 |
| Team B | 23 | 24 | 24 | 25 | 25 | 27 | 27 |

a Work out the median score for each team.

b Work out the range of scores for each team.

c Which team's scores were more 'spread out'?

d Which team's scores were closer together?

> **Key point** A small range shows that the data items are close together.
> This means the data is more **consistent**.

3 Here are the times, in seconds, of two 100 m sprinters in one season.

| Sprinter A | 11.1 | 11.2 | 11.6 | 11.6 | 11.7 |
| Sprinter B | 11.2 | 11.3 | 11.4 | 11.1 | 11.4 |

a Calculate the range of times for each sprinter.

b Which of the sprinters was more consistent in their times?

c Which sprinter has a shorter median time?

4 Here are the scores that Nathaniel and Caitlin achieved when playing a computer game.

| Nathaniel | 20 | 15 | 8 | 14 | 13 |
| Caitlin | 16 | 16 | 17 | 16 | 15 |

a Work out the mean score for each player.

b Work out the range of scores for each player.

c **Reasoning** Write two sentences to compare the mean and the range.

5 Here are the quarterly profit figures for two businesses.

	1st quarter	2nd quarter	3rd quarter	4th quarter
Business A	£5324	£9637	£14658	£5017
Business B	£8471	£9365	£8852	£10345

Q5 hint The quarterly profits are the profits for a quarter of the year (3 months). 1st quarter is January–March, and so on.

a For each business, work out:
  i the mean quarterly profit   ii the range.
b **Reasoning** Copy and complete these sentences comparing the profits of the two businesses.
  Business ____ has a higher mean quarterly profit.
  Business ____ has a lower range than Business ____ so Business ____'s profits are more consistent.

6 The manager of a shoe shop records the women's shoes sold over a month.

Size	$3\frac{1}{2}$	4	$4\frac{1}{2}$	5	$5\frac{1}{2}$	6	$6\frac{1}{2}$	7	$7\frac{1}{2}$	8	$8\frac{1}{2}$
Pairs sold	0	12	9	11	21	24	38	22	12	5	0

a Which shoe size was the mode?
The manager calculates that the mean shoe size sold is 6.1.
She uses the averages to help her decide which size shoes to order.
b Which size should she order most of? Which average should she use?
c How useful is the mean shoe size?
d **Reasoning** How could she use the range to help her decide what sizes to order?

7 The table shows two boys' results in an Under-15 long jump competition.

	1st jump	2nd jump	3rd jump	4th jump
Alex	5.27 m	5.19 m	2.78 m	5.40 m
Dan	5.01 m	5.12 m	5.15 m	5.08 m

a From the results in the table, which boy do you think can jump the longest distance?
b Calculate the mean distance for each boy.
c Work out the median distance for each boy.
d Which average, mean or median, best represents each boy's performance?
e **Reasoning** Which value affected Alex's mean distance? Why didn't it affect the median?
f **Reasoning** Compare the two boys' performances. Who would you choose to represent the school in a long jump competition?

8 **Reasoning** The graphs show the scores of the winning and losing teams each week in the TV quiz University Challenge.

a Which line shows the winning team's scores?

b In which week was the difference between the winning and losing scores:

  i the greatest

  ii the smallest?

c Min says, 'All the winning teams' scores are higher than the losing teams' scores.'
Is she correct? Explain your answer.

d Did you need to read exact values from the graph to answer these questions?

University Challenge scores 2018 season

9 **Problem-solving / Reasoning** Here are the annual salaries of eight people working in a small company.

£27 000   £15 500   £23 750   £16 000
£18 950   £31 000   £18 200   £75 000

a Which salary do you think is the managing director's?

b Work out:

  i the mean salary

  ii the median salary.

c How many people in the company earn less than the mean?

d How many people earn less than the median?

e Which best represents the average salary for this company – the median or the mean?

f Which average would be used by

  i the managing director to attract more staff to the company

  ii the staff to show that they should get a pay rise?

10 The table gives the mean monthly temperatures (°C) in Moscow and Barbados over one year.

	Jan	Feb	Mar	Apr	May	Jun	Jul	Aug	Sept	Oct	Nov	Dec
Barbados	25	25.3	25	26.3	27	27	26.7	27	27	26.7	26.3	25
Moscow	−8	−7	−2	5	12	15	17	15	10	3	−2	−6

a Draw a line graph to show both sets of temperatures.
Start your axes like this.

b **Reasoning** Write two sentences about your graph, comparing the temperatures in Barbados and Moscow.
You could use some of these words:
warmer, colder, maximum, minimum, range.

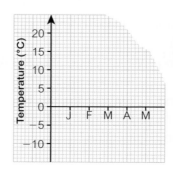

Q10a hint
Use the initial for each month.

11 Problem-solving The pie charts show the ages of patients at two different dental surgeries.

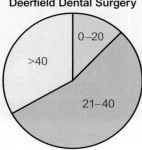

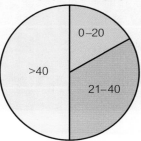

a Which surgery has:

  i the greatest proportion of patients over 40

  ii the lowest proportion of patients under 20?

Loxley Dental Surgery has 1500 patients. Deerfield Dental Surgery has 2400 patients.

b Which surgery has:

  i the greatest number of patients over 40

  ii the lowest number of patients under 20?

> **Key point**   An extreme value that doesn't fit the pattern of the other values is called an **outlier**.

12 a Look back at the data used in Q7. Which value is the outlier?

   b Look back at the data used in Q9. Which value is the outlier?

Challenge

a   For this set of data, work out:

  i the median   **ii** the mean   **iii** the mode.

         1   2   2   3   3   3   4   4   4   4   100

b   Why are the mean and the median so far apart?

c   Which average describes the data better?

The set of data without the outlier is

         1   2   2   3   3   3   4   4   4   4

d   For this set of data, work out:

  i the median   **ii** the mean   **iii** the mode.

e   Produce your own set of data where the value of the mean is 10 times the value of the median.

f   Which average is most affected by an outlier – the mode, median or mean?

Reflect   In this lesson, you compared data by comparing averages and the range, and by comparing graphs or pie charts of the data.

Which did you prefer, and why?

3.5 Scatter graphs

- Draw a scatter graph
- Draw a line of best fit on a scatter graph
- Describe types of correlation

*Active*Learn
Homework

Warm up

1 Fluency What are the coordinates of the points A, B, C and D?

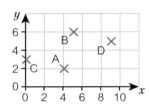

2 Look at the x and y values in these coordinates.

A (20, 9)   **B** (10, 12)   **C** (14, 20)   **D** (28, 0)   **E** (16, 22)

On squared paper, draw axes that include all these values. Plot the points with crosses.

Key point
A **scatter graph** plots two sets of data on the same graph. The shape of the graph shows if there is a relationship or **correlation** between them.

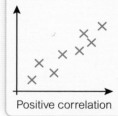

Positive correlation   Negative correlation   No correlation

3 This scatter graph shows the maths test marks of 10 students and the number of maths lessons they missed.

  a How many students missed 2 maths lessons?

  b One student missed 5 maths lessons.
    What was their mark?

  c 2 students scored 30 on their test.
    How many maths lessons did each student miss?

  d What type of correlation does this graph show?

  e Problem-solving Describe the relationship between test mark and lessons missed.

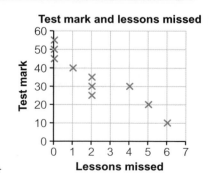

Test mark and lessons missed

4 For each graph:
  i describe the correlation shown
  ii copy and complete the sentence to describe the relationship.

a   Maths scores and class sizes around the world

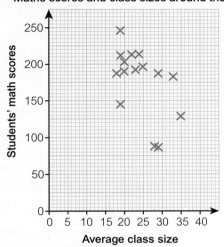

b   Second-hand laptop prices

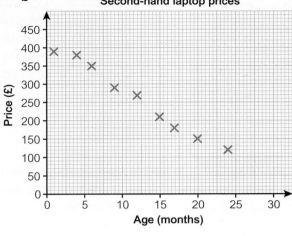

_____ and _____ do not appear to be related.

As laptops get older, their _____ _____.

5 A healthcare trust wanted to reduce the number of patients who developed an infection in hospital. They put alcohol handrub at the entrances to the wards to encourage people to clean their hands regularly.
They produced this scatter graph.
  a What type of correlation does this scatter graph show?
  b **Problem-solving**   Does the data suggest that increasing the amount of alcohol handrub used will reduce the number of infections? Explain your answer.

Patient infections and alcohol handrub use

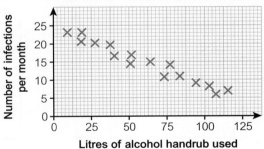

6 **Reasoning**   The table shows the size of engine and top speed of some cars.

Engine size (litres)	1.2	1.4	2	1.6	1.4	1	2.2	1.2	2
Top speed (km/h)	180	200	230	210	220	160	240	190	210

  a Copy these axes on to graph paper and draw a scatter graph to show the information.
  b Copy and complete:
  The larger the engine size, the _____ the top speed.

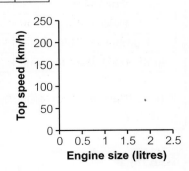

7 The table shows data from 15 countries on mothers' employment and child poverty.

% of mothers employed	63	71	77	46	85	50	44	51	57	22	61	67	65	36	56
% of children living in poverty	15	14	4	9	8	17	25	12	20	28	10	21	8	11	25

Source: Child poverty, http://www.oecd.org/els/family/, Copyright OECD

a Plot a scatter graph to show this data, with 'Percentage of mothers employed' on the horizontal axis and 'Percentage of children living in poverty' on the vertical axis. Choose a suitable scale to fit all the data on the axes.

b What type of correlation does your scatter graph show?

c Write a sentence to explain what the graph shows about the relationship between the proportion of mothers who work and child poverty.

> **Key point** A **line of best fit** shows the relationship between two sets of data. Draw a line of best fit so that there are the same number of crosses on each side of the line. There may or may not be crosses on the line.

8 **Problem-solving** Three students drew lines of best fit on their graphs. Whose line best represents the relationship between the age and price of second-hand laptops? Explain why.

Q8 hint Whose line best follows the 'shape' of the data? Check the number of crosses on each side.

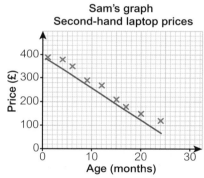

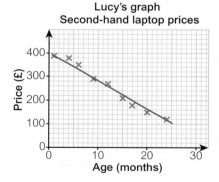

9 Draw a line of best fit on the graph you drew in
   a Q6   **b** Q7.

> **Challenge** Is there any correlation between any of these data sets taken from a group of children? You could use a spreadsheet to draw scatter graphs.
>
> | Age (years) | 6 | 7 | 8 | 9 | 10 | 11 | 12 | 13 | 14 | 15 |
> |---|---|---|---|---|---|---|---|---|---|---|
> | Height (cm) | 115 | 122 | 130 | 132 | 138 | 142 | 147 | 156 | 165 | 170 |
> | Number of siblings | 3 | 2 | 5 | 1 | 4 | 2 | 1 | 0 | 3 | 1 |
> | Number of letters in name | 5 | 5 | 9 | 3 | 7 | 4 | 3 | 3 | 6 | 3 |
>
> Where there is a correlation, do you think there is a real-life relationship between the two sets of data?

> **Reflect** Think about the different ways to display data. Think back to Year 7 too.
> - Which is the easiest to read and understand? Which is the hardest? Why?
> - Which is the easiest to draw? Which is the hardest? Why?

3.6 Misleading graphs

- Interpret graphs and charts
- Explain why a graph or chart could be misleading

Active Learn
Homework

Warm up

1 Fluency What is missing from this graph?

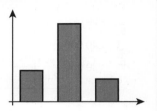

2 Naomi asked some Year 8 students their favourite type of film.
She made this pictogram to show the results.

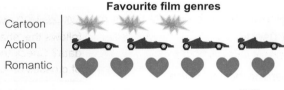

Favourite film genres

Cartoon
Action
Romantic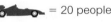

Key = 5 people   = 20 people   = 10 people

a Naomi says, 'The pictogram shows that Romantic films are the most popular.'
Is she correct? Explain.

b What is misleading about the symbols Naomi has used?

c Redraw the pictogram using only one type of symbol to represent the same quantity
in each row.

Key point

Before you read values from a graph or chart

- read the title
- read the axis labels
- read the scales.

You cannot draw accurate conclusions from an inaccurate graph.

3 Reasoning The table and the graph show the
average price of a 1 kg loaf of white bread from
1914 to 2004.

1914	1947	1958	1970	1978	1990	2000	2004
1p	2p	4p	8p	32p	64p	70p	90p

a What is unusual about the vertical scale on
the graph?

b What do you think the graph would look like
with a vertical scale, 0, 10, 20, 30, 40, ...?
Draw the graph to check your prediction.

c Which graph shows the real increase in price
from 1914 to 2004 most clearly? Explain.

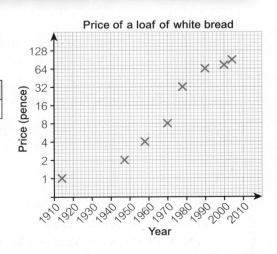

Price of a loaf of white bread

4 **Reasoning** These graphs show average house prices in 2017 and 2018.

a An estate agent says, 'The average house price was $2\frac{1}{2}$ times more in 2018 than 2017.'
Which graph has the estate agent used?

b Why is she incorrect?

c Estimate the actual increase in average house price.

5 **Reasoning** Here are two graphs showing the same sales figures for Hilary's hat shop.

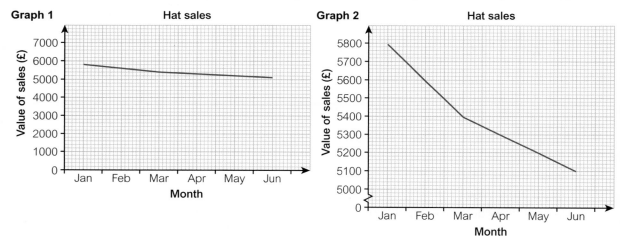

a Hilary says, 'Sales are very slightly down.' Which graph is she using?

b Her bank manager says, 'There has been a massive decrease in sales.'
Which graph is he using?

c What is the actual fall in sales?

6 **Reasoning** There are at least three reasons why this pie chart
is misleading. Write all the reasons you can find.

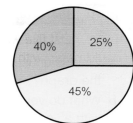

7 Reasoning These two graphs show the increase in mobile tablet use in the UK between 2012 and 2017.

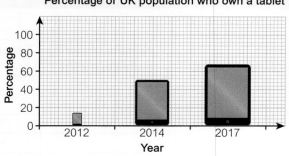

Percentage of UK population who own a tablet

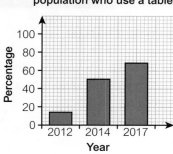

Percentage of UK population who use a tablet

a Which graph shows the increase in the percentage of people using tablets most clearly?

b Which graph appears to show the biggest increase in tablet use? How does this graph make the increase look bigger?

Challenge The bar chart shows the ages of people who visit a theatre one Saturday.

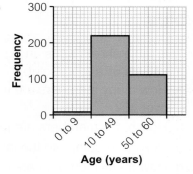

1 Which is the age group that visits the theatre most often?

2 The table shows the original theatre visitor data.

Age, a (years)	Frequency
$0 \leqslant a < 10$	10
$10 \leqslant a < 20$	30
$20 \leqslant a < 30$	40
$30 \leqslant a < 40$	50
$40 \leqslant a < 50$	100
$50 \leqslant a < 60$	110

a Draw a bar chart using the original data. Use a horizontal scale like this.

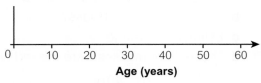

b From your bar chart, which age group visited the theatre most often?

c Why was the first bar chart misleading?

Reflect List five ways that graphs can mislead you.
You could begin with, 'It is misleading when different symbols are used on the same _____.'

3 Check up

Averages and range

Number of merit points in a week	Frequency
0	5
1	7
2	9
3	6
4	3

1 The frequency table shows the numbers of merit points Hetty won each week, in two terms.
   a Find the mode.
   b Work out the range.
   c Work out the mean number of merit points for a week.

2 Ali worked out these statistics for his merit points:
      mean 1.95, range 7
   a Write sentences to compare Ali's mean and range with Hetty's in Q1.
   b The team with most merit points wins a prize.
     Who would you rather have on your team, Ali or Hetty? Explain why.

Tables

	Under 18	18–40	Over 40	Total
Male	10		55	95
Female		38		
Total	40			200

3 This table shows ages and genders of members of a tennis club.
   a How many members are males over 40?
   b How many members are females under 18?
   c Copy and complete the table.
   d How many members are over 40?
   e What percentage of members are under 18?

4 The table shows the masses, in grams, of some newly-hatched chicks.
   a How many chicks were weighed in total?
   b Which is the modal class?
   c Estimate the range.
   d These three masses were missed out of the table:

Mass, m (g)	Frequency
$0 \leqslant m < 30$	8
$30 \leqslant m < 40$	13
$40 \leqslant m < 50$	14
$50 \leqslant m < 60$	6

      36 g 42 g 40 g

   When they are put in the table, will the modal class change? Explain your answer.

Charts and graphs

Car colours in a car park

5 This pie chart shows the colours of cars in a car park one morning.
   a Which colour is the mode?
   b Kai says, 'There are more silver cars than all the others put together.' Is he correct? Explain.
   c There were 18 black cars in the car park.
     How many cars were there altogether?

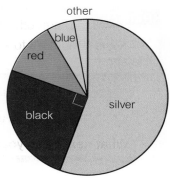

6 These are the vegetables Jane dug from her allotment one day.
Draw a pie chart to show this information.

Vegetable	potatoes	carrots	beetroot
Frequency	20	30	10

7 This stem and leaf diagram shows students' marks in a maths test.
   a What is the lowest mark?
   b Work out the range.
   c What is the modal mark?
   d Find the median mark.
   e Students who scored less than 35 had to re-sit the test.
   How many students had to do this?

```
2 | 6 7 9
3 | 0 5 7 8 8 9
4 | 1 3 6 6 9
5 | 2 4 6 8 9 9 9
6 | 0 2 4 8 8
7 | 1 5 8 8
```
Key: 2 | 6 means 26 marks

8 Ms Barber plotted her students' maths test scores against the number of homeworks they completed.
   a What type of correlation does this scatter graph show?
   b What word is missing from this sentence about the graph?

   'Students who complete more homeworks get _____ test marks.'

Maths test scores and number of homeworks

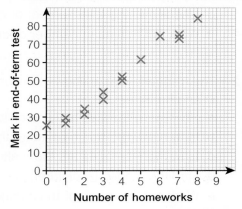

9 The graphs show the annual rainfall in Australia in 2008 and 2018.

Sam says, 'There is a huge difference in the rainfall for the two years.'
   a Which graph has Sam used?
   b Why could this graph be misleading?

Annual rainfall Australia

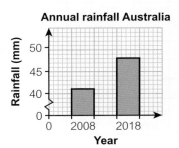

Annual rainfall Australia

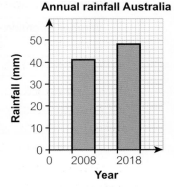

Challenge

a Design a two-way table to record any information you choose.
b In pencil, write numbers in all the cells so that the totals all add up correctly.
c Rub out some of your numbers so that you can still work out the missing values from the ones that are left. What is the smallest number of values you can keep?
d Give your table to a partner to see if they can fill in the gaps.

Reflect   How sure are you of your answers? Were you mostly

   ☹ **Just guessing**   😐 **Feeling doubtful**   🙂 **Confident**

What next? Use your results to decide whether to strengthen or extend your learning.

3 Strengthen

Averages and range

1 Ten families live in one street. Here are the number of children in those families.

1	3	5	2	3
2	0	2	2	3

a Find the mode: ☐ children

b Work out the range.

c Check that the total number of children is 23.

d Work out the mean number of children per family.

> **Q1d hint** Finding the mean is like sharing out the children equally between the families.
>
> 23 children
>
> 1 family

2 The frequency table shows the number of children in families in another street.

Number of children	Frequency
0	3
1	6
2	10
3	4
4	1

a How many families have no children?

b How many families have more than two children?

c How many families are there altogether?

d Find the mode: ☐ children

e Work out the range of the number of children.

f Copy and complete this table.

Number of children	Frequency	Total number of children
0	3	0 × 3 = 0 children
1	6	
2	10	2 × 10 = 20 children
3	4	
4	1	
Total number of families ☐		Total number of children ☐

> **Q2d hint** The mode is the number of children with the highest frequency.

> **Q2f hint** 10 families have 2 children each. This makes 20 children in those families.

g Work out the mean number of children for each family.

3 Here are two people's marks in three rounds of a quiz.

Flo: 7   7   6

Jim: 10   0   4

a Whose results are the most consistent (similar every time)?

b Work out the range for Flo and for Jim.

c Which word fits this sentence – 'smaller' or 'larger'?

'The _____ the range, the more consistent the results.'

d Who scored highest in two of the three rounds?

e Work out the mean for Flo and for Jim.
Who had the higher mean score?

f **Reasoning** Who would you like on your team – Flo or Jim? Explain why.

> **Q2g hint**
>
> mean = $\dfrac{\text{total number of children}}{\text{total number of families}}$

4 Reasoning The table shows the median mark and the range of marks that two classes scored in a test.

	Median	Range
9R	42	3
9W	43	10

Choose words from the box to complete these sentences comparing the marks of the two classes.

9W had a _____ median than 9R.
9R had a _____ range than 9W, so their results were _____ consistent.

larger
less   more
smaller

5 Cameron recorded the time, in minutes, it took him to get to school each morning for 2 weeks.

　　25　21　24　27　19　59　24　23　24　27

　　a There was an accident on the road one morning.
　　　How long did it take him to get to school on that morning?
　　b Work out:
　　　i the median
　　　ii the mean
　　　iii the range.
　　c Reasoning Which average best represents the time it takes Cameron to get to school?

Tables

1 Copy this table of instruments played by Year 8s and 9s.

	Flute	Violin	Trumpet	Total
Year 8	13	10	6	ii
Year 9	12	i	iv	iii
Total		18	v	53

　　a How many Year 8 students play the flute?
　　b How many Year 9 students play the flute?
　　c How many students in total play the flute?
　　　Write your answer in the correct space in the table.
　　d Find the number 6 in this table.
　　　Copy and complete: '6 students in Year ____ play the ____.'
　　e Find the number 18 in the table.
　　　What does this number tell you?
　　f Work out the rest of the values in the table, in the order **i, ii, iii, iv, v**, and write them in.
　　g How many Year 9s play the trumpet?
　　h How many Year 8 and 9s play the flute, violin or trumpet?

> **Q1e hint** You could begin: '18 students …'

2 This two-way table shows the number of people who went skiing or snowboarding one day.

	Skiing	Snowboarding	Total
Adults	25		37
Children		23	
Total		35	80

　　a Work out the number of adults who went snowboarding.
　　b Work out the total number of children.
　　c Work out the number of children who went skiing.
　　d Work out the total number of people who went skiing.

3 Which of these distances, d (km), are in the class $5 \leqslant d < 10$?

6 km, 3.5 km, 4 km, 6.5 km, 10 km, 9 km, 5 km, 10.5 km

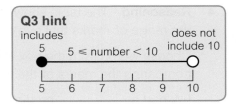

Q3 hint

includes 5 $5 \leqslant$ number < 10 does not include 10

4 Here are the masses of turkeys on sale in a butcher's shop.

10.5 kg   15.2 kg   16.0 kg   14.7 kg   11.0 kg,
10.9 kg   14.0 kg   13.2 kg   15.9 kg   17.5 kg

a What does kg 10 kg $\leqslant m <$ 12 kg mean?

b Copy the table.
Tally the masses into it.
Complete the frequency column.

c Which is the modal class?

d Estimate the range: $18 - \square = \square$

Mass, m (kg)	Tally	Frequency
$10 \leqslant m < 12$		
$12 \leqslant m < 14$		
$14 \leqslant m < 16$		
$16 \leqslant m < 18$		

Q4c hint Write the class like this:
$\square$ kg $\leqslant m < \square$ kg.

Charts and graphs

1 Tina asked some students to pick a colour.
The pie chart shows the results.

a What fraction of the students chose blue?

8 students chose blue.

b Sketch or trace the pie chart. Write 8 in the blue sector.

c How many students chose green? Write this number in the sector.

d How many chose:

  i red   **ii** yellow?

  Write these numbers in the sectors.

e How many students were asked?

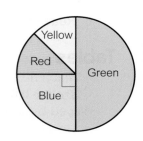

2 The table shows the number of different types of fish in a lake.

a How many fish are there in the lake in total?

b Copy and complete to work out what fraction of the fish are carp.

$$\frac{20}{\square} = \frac{10}{\square} = \frac{1}{\square}$$

c What fraction of the fish are

  i rudd

  ii tench

  iii bream?

d Divide a circle into 8 equal sections like this.

e Use the fractions you found in parts **b** and **c** to help you draw a pie chart.

Type of fish	Frequency
carp	20
rudd	10
tench	40
bream	10

3 The table shows where 180 people went on holiday.

Holiday	Frequency	Degrees
UK	100	100 × ☐°
Spain	45	45 × ☐°
India	20	20 × ☐°
USA	15	15 × ☐°
Total	180	180 × ☐°

a 360° in a circle represent 180 people. 180 × ☐° = 360°
How many degrees represent one person?

b Copy and complete the table.

4 The stem and leaf diagram shows the ages
of people using a swimming pool one day.

a What does 4 | 0 mean?

b How many values are in the 4 | … row?

c How many people in their 40s were in the pool?

d How old was the youngest person in the pool?

e Circle any repeated digits in the 'leaves'.
Which has most values in it? This is the mode.
Use the key to work out the mode of this data.

f How many people were in the swimming pool?

g Imagine all the people lined up in age order,
holding numbers 1, 2, 3, 4, 5, …
What number would the 'middle' person hold?

h Use your answer to part **f** to help you find the median
age from the stem and leaf diagram.

```
2 | 2 7 9
3 | 3 4 5 7
4 | 0 5 6 7 8
5 | 1 1 1 4 6 7
6 | 0 3 5 5 7
7 | 1 3
```

Key: 2 | 7 means 27

```
22  27  29  33
[1] [2] [3] [4]
```

5 This scatter graph shows the ages of some children and the time it took them to
complete a puzzle.

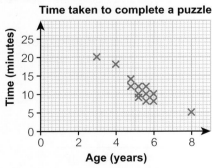

Time taken to complete a puzzle

a How long did it take a 3-year-old to complete the puzzle?
Or a 4-year-old? Or an 8-year-old?

b Copy and complete this sentence:
As the children got older, they took _____ time to complete the puzzle.

6 For each graph, decide whether it shows positive correlation negative correlation or no correlation.

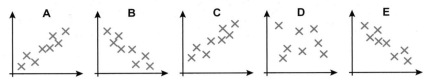

Q6 hint Positive **correlation** – looking from (0, 0), the points go 'uphill': the values are increasing. **Negative correlation** – looking from (0, 0), the points go 'downhill': the values are decreasing. **No correlation** – the points are not close to a straight line, uphill or downhill.

7 **Reasoning** These bar charts show a shop's motorbike sales over 2 years.

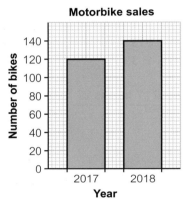

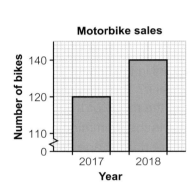

a What were the sales in 2017? What were the sales in 2018?

b The shop owner says, 'My sales nearly doubled in 2018.' Is this correct? Show working to explain.

c Which graph is misleading? Explain why.

Challenge

1 Here are the 2005 to 2018 World Record times, in seconds, to solve a Rubik's cube.

9.55   10.36   5.55   11.75   9.77   6.18   8.72   11.13   7.08   6.77   6.24
9.18   6.65   10.48   9.86   7.03   5.66   4.9   4.69   4.59   4.22

Source: http://www.recordholders.org/en/list/rubik.html

a Tally the times into a grouped frequency table. Use the classes $4 \leqslant t < 6$, $6 \leqslant t < 8$, $8 \leqslant t < 10$ and so on.

b Draw a bar chart for the times. Use a horizontal scale like this.

```
    4    6    8    10    12
        Time (seconds)
```

c How many of the World Record times are less than 8 seconds? Is it easier to work this out from the bar chart or the list of times? Explain.

Reflect For this Strengthen lesson, copy and complete these sentences.

I found questions _____ easiest. They were on _____ (List the topics.)

I found questions _____ most difficult. I still need help with _____ (List the topics.)

3 Extend

1   **Problem-solving**   Sushma is doing a survey to find out what people enjoy at the theatre.
    Here is part of her questionnaire.
    How old are you?
    under 16 ☐   16–25 ☐   26–45 ☐   over 45 ☐
    Which of these have you seen at a theatre in the past year? Tick all that apply.
    Stand up comedy ☐   Musical ☐   Drama ☐   Other ☐

    When she has collected in her questionnaires,
    Sushma wants to put all the results into a table.
    a   Design a table she could use to show all this information.
    b   Which averages can she find from her table?

2   The pie chart shows a family's Playstation use in one week.
    a   Which member of the family plays the most?
    b   Measure the angle of each sector of the
        pie chart and complete the table.

Playstation use

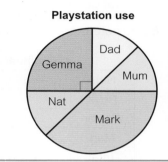

Family member	Angle	Hours
Dad		
Mum		
Mark		
Nat		
Gemma		4

Q2b hint

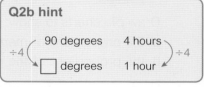

÷4 (90 degrees → ☐ degrees   4 hours → 1 hour) ÷4

3   This frequency diagram shows the numbers
    of cubs in litters of Arctic wolves.
    Work out the mean number of cubs per litter.

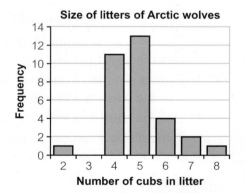

Size of litters of Arctic wolves

4   **Reasoning**   The tables show the number of wins by
    Joanne and Peter in 10 chess tournaments.

Joanne	
Wins	Frequency
1	1
2	2
3	3
4	1
5	3

Peter	
Wins	Frequency
1	0
2	1
3	4
4	4
5	1

    a   Calculate the mean and range for each player.
    b   Which player did better? Justify your answer.

5 The table shows the mean monthly rainfall, in mm, in Mumbai and London.

Month	Jan	Feb	Mar	Apr	May	Jun	Jul	Aug	Sep	Oct	Nov	Dec
Mumbai	0.6	1.5	0.1	0.6	13.2	574.1	868.3	553.0	306.4	62.9	14.9	5.6
London	82.9	60.3	64.0	58.7	58.4	61.8	62.6	69.4	69.7	91.7	88.2	87.2

a Draw two line graphs for this data, on the same axes.
Put the months on the horizontal axis.
The vertical axis for rainfall will have to go from 0 to 870 mm.
b For how many months of the year is London wetter than Mumbai?
c What happens to the rainfall in Mumbai in the monsoon season (June to September)?
d Reasoning   Compare the rainfall in the two cities using the mean monthly rainfall and the range for each.

6 Problem-solving   This table shows the number of members of a hockey club.

	Beginner	Intermediate	Advanced	Total
Girls	6	20		38
Boys			10	34
Women	2		13	25
Men		6		23
Total	21	50		

Draw pie charts to show:
a the proportions of members that are boys, girls, women and men
b the proportions of the members that are beginner, intermediate and advanced.

7 Here are the numbers of pages in the books entered for a literature prize.

125   200   316   412   517   627   196   256   358   420   464   562
446   376   137   294   327   488   534   496   382   584   367   578

a Draw a stem and leaf diagram for the data.
Use the key '1 | 25 means 125 pages'.
b Draw a grouped frequency table for this data.
Use the classes $100 \leqslant p < 200$, $200 \leqslant p < 300$, etc.
c Use the stem and leaf diagram and your frequency table to find:
  i the median number of pages   **ii** the mean number of pages
  iii the range   **iv** the modal class(es).

Challenge   Write down five numbers with:
a a median less than the mean
b a median greater than the mean
c a mode less than the mean.

Reflect   Q5 uses data that climate scientists might use. It also uses these maths topics:
line graphs, mean and range.
List all the other maths topics you have used in these Extend lessons.
How might climate scientists use these maths topics too?

3 Unit test

1   This pie chart shows the types of cake on a stall.

    a   Which type of cake is the mode?

    b   Jonah says, 'There are more brownies than all the other cakes put together.' Is he correct? Explain.

    c   There were 12 cupcakes on the stall. How many cakes were there altogether?

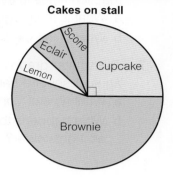

Cakes on stall

2   A survey about shopping habits asked people how many items they had bought online that week. The table shows the results.

    a   Work out the range

    b   Work out the mean. Give your answer to 1 decimal place.

    c   Draw a pie chart for this data.

    d   What is the mode?

Items bought online	Frequency
0	5
1	8
2	12
3	10
4	8
5	2

3   The table shows the amounts two families spent on their weekly food shop over one year.

	Mean	Median	Range
Smith family	£85	£82.50	£38
Jones family	£75	£81	£24

    a   Write two sentences comparing the amounts the two families spent on food.

    b   Explain why there is unlikely to be a modal value for a family's weekly food shop.

4   Here are the prices of some mobile phones in one shop.

      £129.99, £118.95, £95.99, £92.50, £329.99

    a   Work out the mean, median and mode. Give your answers to the nearest penny.

    b   Which average best represents the prices of phones in the shop?

5   A chicken farmer recorded the mass of the eggs laid one morning.

      58.5 g, 61.3 g, 55.2 g, 58.6 g, 49.1 g, 45.2 g, 64.7 g, 61.2 g, 55.0 g, 59.5 g

  Copy and complete the grouped frequency table for the data.

Mass, m (g)	Tally	Frequency
$45 \leqslant m < 50$		

6 Learner drivers take a hazard perception test as part of their driving theory exam. The stem and leaf diagram shows some learner drivers' reaction times in the test.

a What is the range?

b What is the median?

Key: 10 | 7 means 10.7 seconds

7 The scatter graph shows prices and ages of second-hand cars.

a What type of correlation does it show?

b What happens to the price of a car as it gets older?

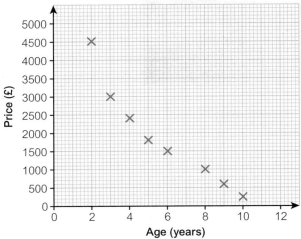

Second-hand car prices

8 An estate agent produces a bar chart to show how house prices have changed in his area between 1990 and 2010.

Explain why the graph is misleading.

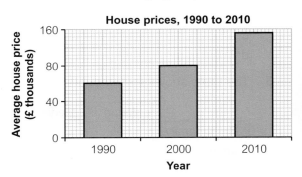

House prices, 1990 to 2010

Challenge

| 75% of 5–16 year olds get pocket money. | Average pocket money is £9.60 per week. | Approximately 12 million children aged 5–16 in the UK. |

Use these facts to estimate the total pocket money UK parents pay per week.

Reflect   Think back to when you have struggled to answer a question in a maths test.

a Write two words that describe how you felt.

b Write two things you could do when you're finding it hard to answer a question in a maths test.

c Imagine you have another maths test and you do the two things you wrote in your answer to part **b**. How do you think you might feel then?

4 Expressions and equations

Master   Check up p110   Strengthen p112   Extend p116   Unit test p118

4.1 Algebraic powers

- Understand and simplify algebraic powers
- Write and use expressions involving powers

Active Learn
Homework

Warm up

1 Fluency Work out these calculations.
  a 4^2
  b 2^3
  c 9^2
  d 3^3

2 Work out the value of each expression.
  a $4c$ when $c = 5$
  b $6t$ when $t = 3$

3 Write these products in **index form**.
  a $2 \times 2 \times 2 \times 2 \times 2$
  b 10×10
  c $3 \times 3 \times 3 \times 10$
  d $5 \times 10 \times 10 \times 10 \times 5$

> **Q3 hint Index form** means to write using a **power** or **index**. For example, 3×3 is written 3^2.

4 Write each product in index form.
  a $d \times d$
  b $m \times m \times m$
  c $c \times c \times c \times c$
  d $t \times t \times t \times t \times t \times t$

5 Write each power as a product.
  a 10^4
  b 2^6
  c n^3
  d x^2
  e w^5
  f u^{10}

Key point

In an algebraic expression, write numbers first and then letters in alphabetical order.

Worked example

Simplify these expressions.
  a $y \times 2 \times x$ $\quad y \times 2 \times x = 2 \times x \times y$ ——— [Rewrite with the number first, letters in order.]
  $\quad\quad\quad\quad\quad\quad\quad = 2xy$
  b $2m \times 5n$ $\quad 2m \times 5n = 2 \times m \times 5 \times n$
  $\quad\quad\quad\quad\quad\quad\quad\quad = 2 \times 5 \times m \times n$
  $\quad\quad\quad\quad\quad\quad\quad\quad = 10mn$

6   Simplify these expressions.

   a $s \times t \times 2$ **b** $s \times 5 \times t$ **c** $t \times s \times 3$ **d** $2a \times 3b$

   e $3b \times 3a$ **f** $3b \times 2a \times c$ **g** $3b \times 2a \times 5c$ **h** $2b \times 5c \times 4d$

Worked example

Simplify these expressions.

   a $a \times a \times b \times b \times b$

   $a \times a \times b \times b \times b = a^2 \times b^3$ ── Write using index form, then simplify.

   $\qquad\qquad\qquad\qquad = a^2 b^3$

   b $3m \times m$

   $3m \times m = 3 \times m \times m$

   $\qquad\quad = 3m^2$

   c $5g \times g \times 2h$

   $5g \times g \times 2h = 5g^2 \times 2h$

   $\qquad\qquad\quad = 5 \times 2 \times g^2 \times h$

   $\qquad\qquad\quad = 10g^2 h$

---

7   Simplify these expressions. Write each answer using powers.

   a $c \times c \times c \times d \times d$ **b** $m \times n \times n$

   c $r \times s \times r \times s \times r$ **d** $3 \times f \times f$

   e $e \times e \times 7 \times e$ **f** $e \times e \times 7 \times f$

   g $e \times f \times 7 \times f$ **h** $2n \times n$

   i $n \times 5n$ **j** $n \times 5n \times n$

   k $3n \times 2n \times 5n \times n$ **l** $3m \times 2n \times 4n \times m$

   m $2e \times 3f \times 4g \times e \times e \times g$ **n** $3a \times 5b \times 2a \times b \times b \times c$

   o $2e^2 \times -3f$ **p** $-2e^2 \times -3f$

8   Work out the value of each expression.

   a x^2 when $x = 3$ **b** y^2 when $y = 8$ **c** z^2 when $z = 0.2$

   d a^3 when $a = 2$ **e** b^3 when $b = 10$ **f** c^3 when $c = 3$

9   **Reasoning**   A square has a side of length s metres.

s

   Write your answers to these questions using powers.

   a Write an expression for the area of the square.

   b Write an expression for the total area of

      i 3 squares

$s \quad s \quad s$

      ii n squares

     iii $2n$ squares.

   c Write an expression for the total area of

      i 5 rows of 3 squares

      ii 5 rows of n squares.

10 Solar panels are squares with side s metres.

    a In a small solar panel, $s = 60\,cm$.
       Use your expression from Q9b **i** to work out the area
       of 3 panels.

    b In a large solar panel, $s = 90\,cm$.
       Use your expression from Q9c **i** to work out the area of 5 rows of 3 panels.

Q10 hint Substitute the value of s into your expression.

11 A rectangle has side lengths of $3x$ and x.

    a Write an expression for the area of this rectangle.

    b Use your expression to find the area when $x = 5\,cm$.

12 a Write an expression for the volume of each cuboid.

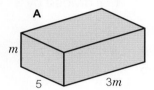

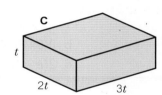

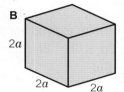

    b Work out the volume of cuboid C when $t = 4\,cm$.

13 Problem-solving The formula for the total surface area A of a cube of side d is $A = 6d^2$.
Calculate the surface area when $d = 7.5\,cm$.

Challenge

a Copy and complete this table.

n	1	3	4		9			
$2n$	$2 \times 1 = \square$						24	60
n^2	$1^2 = \square$			49		121		

b Is there a difference between $2n$ and n^2? Explain your answer.

c Are there any values for which $2n$ and n^2 are the same?

d Is there a difference between $3n$ and n^3?

Reflect   Sally says that $4 \times x \times x$ is $4 \times 2x = 8x$.

Explain why Sally is wrong.

4.2 Expressions and brackets

- Expand brackets
- Write and simplify algebraic expressions and formulae using brackets and division

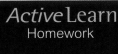

Active Learn
Homework

Warm up

1 Fluency   Work out these calculations.

a $-3 + 5$ **b** $3 - 5$ **c** 3×-5 **d** -3×5 **e** -3×-5

2   Write an algebraic expression for

a the sum of a and 2   **b** 6 more than s **c** double m

d 4 less than e **e** half of b **f** c divided by 3

3   Simplify these expressions.

a $4a + 3a + 6b - 2b$ **b** $2p + 5 - 2 + 5p$

c $2m - 5m$ **d** $3d - 4 - 7d + 6$

4   Expand and simplify

a $2(m - 7)$ **b** $3(5s + 2)$

c $4(h + 3) + 2(h - 3)$ **d** $2(e - 3) + 5(2e + 1)$

Key point   Division can be written as a fraction.

For example, $a \div 3$ can be written as $\frac{a}{3}$.

---

5   Copy and complete these divisions.

a $m \div 5 = \frac{\square}{\square}$ **b** $\frac{8}{d} = \square \div \square$ **c** $2e \div 3 = \frac{\square}{\square}$ **d** $\frac{u - 3}{3} = \square \div \square$

Key point   An **expression** uses variables (letters) to stand for numbers.

Worked example

A cup contains b grams of sugar. A teaspoon holds 5 g of sugar.
Write an expression for

a   the number of teaspoons of sugar in the cup

In 20 grams there are $20 \div 5 = 4$ teaspoons of sugar.

In b grams there are $b \div 5 = \frac{b}{5}$ teaspoons of sugar

5 g

b grams

Try using a number instead of b to help you see the maths to use.

b   the number of teaspoons of sugar in 3 cups.

3 cups hold $3b$ grams

$3b \div 5 = \frac{3b}{5}$

6 Problem-solving

  a A bottle holds x ml of anaesthetic.
    A syringe holds 100 ml.
    Write an expression for
    i the number of syringes that can be filled from a 300 ml bottle
    ii the number of syringes that can be filled from an x ml bottle
    iii the number of syringes that can be filled from three x ml bottles.
  b There are d ml of anaesthetic in a drop.
    Write an expression for the number of drops in a 600 ml bottle.

7 Write an expression for
  a the number of 25 cm ribbons you can cut from n cm of ribbon
  b the number of 25 cm ribbons you can cut from $4n$ cm of ribbon
  c the number of 125 ml glasses you can fill from one y ml bottle of juice
  d the number of 125 ml glasses you can fill from four y ml bottles of juice
  e the number of x ml glasses you can fill from a 750 ml bottle of juice.

8 Reasoning A tin weighs 20 g. It contains 150 g of tomatoes.
  a What does the calculation 20 + 150 work out?
  b What does the calculation 5(20 + 150) work out?

9 A tin weighs t g and contains f g of tomatoes.
  a Write an expression for the total weight of one tin of tomatoes.
  b Write an expression with brackets for the total weight of 4 tins.
  c Write an expression with brackets for the total weight of n tins.

10 a The usual price of a T-shirt is £m.
    In a sale, the price is reduced by £3.
    Write an expression for the sale price.
  b Layla bought 8 T-shirts in the sale.
    Write an expression for the total price.

11 Write an expression for the area of each shape.

  a

  b

  c

  d

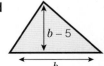

> **Key point** A **formula** uses variables and an equals sign (=) to show the relationship between variables.

12 The diagram shows two kinds of antenna made from metal tubing. Lengths are in metres.

Write a formula for the total length T of tubing in

  a a type A antenna   **b** a type B antenna

  c two type A antennas   **d** three type B antennas

  e two type A and three type B antennas.

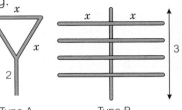

Type A   Type B

13 Expand these expressions.

  a $3(c + 5)$ **b** $-3(c + 5)$ **c** $-3(c - 5)$ **d** $3(2c + 5)$

  e $-3(2c + 5)$ **f** $-3(2c - 5)$ **g** $-2(4t + 3)$ **h** $-2(4t - 3)$

  i $-5(2 + s)$ **j** $-5(2 - s)$ **k** $-10(1 - x)$ **l** $-10(-1 - x)$

  m $1(y + 2)$ **n** $-1(y + 2)$ **o** $-(y + 2)$ **p** $-(3m - 5)$

14 Expand the brackets, then simplify the expressions.

  a $10 - 2(c + 3)$ **b** $8 - 2(b + 2)$ **c** $12 - 3(n - 1)$ **d** $8f - 3(f - 2)$

  e $9u + 10 - 2(u + 4)$ **f** $3p - 4 - 2(p - 5)$ **g** $6(b + 3) - 2(b + 2)$ **h** $6(i - 4) - 3(i - 3)$

15 Expand these expressions.

  a $p(p + 4)$ **b** $p(p - 4)$ **c** $p(p - 2)$ **d** $3d(d - 2)$

  e $4d(d - 2)$ **f** $4d(2d - 2)$ **g** $4a(2a + 3)$ **h** $4a(2a - 3)$

  i $-g(3 - 5g)$ **j** $-g(5g + 3)$ **k** $-g(5g - 3)$ **l** $-2g(5g - 3)$

> **Challenge**
>
> **a** Here is a rectangle.
>
>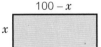
>
> Write a formula for
>
>   **i** its perimeter P **ii** its area A.
>
> **b** How does changing the value of x affect the perimeter?
>
> **c** Draw diagrams to show that the values $x = 20$ and $x = 80$ give the same rectangle.
>
> **d** Write another pair of x values that give the same rectangle.
>
> **e** Work out the area for the values of x given in the table.
>
> | x (cm) | 10 | 20 | 30 | 40 | 50 | 60 | 70 | 80 | 90 |
> |---|---|---|---|---|---|---|---|---|---|
> | Area (cm²) | | | | | | | | | |
>
> **f** Did you need to calculate each area in the table? Explain.
>
> **g** Which value of x gives the rectangle with the largest area?
>
> **h** What shape is the rectangle with the largest area?

> **Reflect** Write a definition, in your own words, for
>
>   • expand
>   • simplify
>
> Compare your definitions with those written by others in your class. Can you improve your definitions?
>
> **Hint** Look back at questions where you were asked to expand and simplify. What did you do?

4.3 Factorising expressions

• Factorise expressions

Active Learn
Homework

Warm up

1 Fluency List the factors of these numbers.
  a 10   **b** 14   **c** 40

2 Expand these expressions.
  a $6(a + 1)$ **b** $4(b - 3)$ **c** $5(2y + 1)$ **d** $d(d + 4)$

3 Copy and complete.
  a $6a = \square \times 2a$ **b** $12p = \square \times 3p$ **c** $18u = 6 \times \square u$
  d $100i = 4 \times \square i$ **e** $-8m = \square \times 4m$ **f** $-14w = 7 \times \square w$

4 What is the highest common factor (HCF) of each pair of numbers?
  a 6 and 3   **b** 8 and 12   **c** 30 and 20   **d** 12 and 18

Worked example

Find the common factor of the terms 6 and $3a$.

$6 = \mathbf{3} \times 2$, so **3** and 2 are factors of 6.
$3a = \mathbf{3} \times a$, so **3** and a are factors of $3a$.
The common factor is **3**.

5 Find the common factor of each pair of terms.
  a $7y$ and 7   **b** $5a$ and 10   **c** $6d$ and 3
  d 6 and $8m$ **e** $6n$ and 9   **f** 10 and $4e$

Key point

Expanding removes brackets from an expression.
Factorising inserts brackets into an expression.
To factorise $5a + 10$, write the common factor of its terms, 5,
outside the brackets. This is called 'taking out the common factor'.

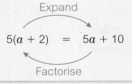

Expand
$5(a + 2) \;=\; 5a + 10$
Factorise

6 Copy and complete these factorisations.
Check your answers by expanding the brackets.
  a $7y + 7 = 7(\square + 1)$ **b** $5a + 10 = \square(a + \square)$
  c $6d - 3 = 3(\square d - \square)$ **d** $12 + 15m = 3(\square + 5m)$
  e $8 + 10c = 2(\square + 5c)$ **f** $14 - 21a = 7(\square - \square a)$
  g $6 + 9w = \square(2 + 3w)$ **h** $20h - 10 = 10(\square h - \square)$
  i $12n + 6 = 6(\square + \square)$ **j** $5a - 10 = \square(\square - \square)$
  k $14u + 7v = \square(\square + \square)$ **l** $16m + 24n = \square(\square + \square)$

7 Factorise each expression. Check your answers by expanding the brackets.

   a $15 + 10h$ **b** $3i + 6$

   c $4c - 10$ **d** $6m - 8$

   e $3d + 3$ **f** $2m - 2$

   g $3s - 9t$ **h** $5 + 5k$

8 **Reasoning** Last year, Gareth paid £e each month for electricity.
This year his monthly payment went down.
His total bill for the first 5 months is given by the expression £$5e - 35$.

   a Factorise $5e - 35$.

   b What does the expression in the brackets represent?

9 Find the HCF of each pair of terms.
The first one is done for you.

   a 6 and $12a$ The common factors of 6 and $12a$ are 3 and 6.
                       The HCF is 6.

   b 10 and $20b$ **c** $8a$ and 12   **d** $9p$ and 18

   e $4a$ and $12b$ **f** $16i$ and $24j$ **g** $15h$ and 30

> **Key point**   To factorise an expression completely, write the HCF of its terms outside the bracket.

10 Factorise each expression completely. Check your answers.

   a $6 + 12a$ **b** $10 - 20b$

   c $9p + 18$ **d** $12 + 16h$

   e $30m - 15$ **f** $6s + 18$

   g $20m - 100$ **h** $27p + 36$

   i $8c + 12$ **j** $15k - 45t$

   k $24r + 36s$ **l** $40n - 120p$

11 **Problem-solving** Copy and complete.

   a $\square + 35 = 5(x + \square)$ **b** $2m - \square = \square(\square - 6)$

   c $\square + 30 = \square(n + 3)$ **d** $15 - \square = \square(5 - 3t)$

12 Find the common factor(s) of each pair of terms.

   a x and x^2 **b** y^2 and y

   c $2n$ and n^2 **d** n^2 and $3n$

   e $6n^2$ and $3n$ **f** $2b^2$ and $6b$

13 Find the HCF of each pair of terms.
The first one is done for you.

   a $3n^2$ and $6n$ The common factors of $3n^2$ and $6n$ are 3 and n.
                       The HCF is $3n$.

   b $2a^2$ and $6a$ **c** $5b$ and $10b^2$

   d $4c^2$ and $10c$ **e** $9d$ and $12d^2$

   f $4e$ and $6e^2$ **g** $12v^2$ and $9v$

14 Fully factorise each expression.
Check your answers by expanding the brackets.

a $p^2 + p$

b $g^2 - g$

c $h + h^2$

d $f - f^2$

e $m - 3m^2$

f $3m^2 - m$

g $4d + 6d^2$

h $4d^2 - 6d$

15 Problem-solving   Give possible side lengths for each rectangle.

a

Area = $2x + 8$

b

Area = $2r^2 + r$

16 Reasoning   Sarah is trying to factorise $3x^2 + 9x$.
She writes

$$3x^2 + 9x = x(3x + 9)$$

a How can you tell from the terms inside the brackets that the expression is
not factorised completely?

b Factorise $3x^2 + 9x$ completely.

Challenge

a   Start with the number n. Multiply it by 4 and add 12. Write this as an expression.
Fully factorise your expression.

b   Divide your factorised expression by 4.

c   Ask a classmate to think of a number, multiply it by 4, add 12, divide the result by 4 and
then tell you the answer.
How does your expression in part **b** show how to quickly find the number your classmate
first thought of?

d   **i**   Starting with n, make your own set of instructions that result in a factorised expression.
ii   Write down the instructions for a classmate to follow. Write down the secret solution.
Check that your trick works before trying it out on a classmate.

Reflect   At the end of Lesson 1.6, you defined 'factor'. (If you didn't do it, or if you
cannot find it, then write a definition of 'factor' now.)
Use your definition of factor to help you write a definition, in your own words, of 'highest
common factor (HCF)'.
Use your definition of HCF to help you write a definition, in your own words, of 'factorising'.
Be as accurate as possible.
How did your factor and HCF definitions help you to define factorising?

4.4 One-step equations

- Find the inverse of a simple function
- Write and solve one-step equations using function machines

Active Learn
Homework

Warm up

1 **Fluency** Write the correct operation for each statement.

a $97 - 48 = 49$

    i $49 \ \square \ 48 = 97$

    ii $97 \ \square \ 49 = 48$

b $29 + 63 = 92$

    i $92 \ \square \ 63 = 29$

    ii $92 \ \square \ 29 = 63$

c $4 \times 17 = 68$

    i $68 \ \square \ 17 = 4$

    ii $68 \ \square \ 4 = 17$

d $128 \div 16 = 8$

    i $16 \ \square \ 8 = 128$

    ii $128 \ \square \ 8 = 16$

2 For each function machine, write down

    i the function   **ii** the missing output.

a

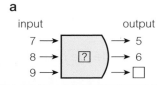

b

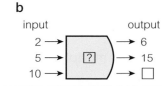

c

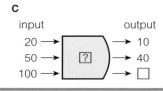

Key point

A **function** is a rule that changes one number into another.

The function +3 adds 3 to a number.

The **inverse function** is −3 because it reverses the effect of the function +3.

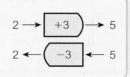

3 Write down the missing function for each inverse function machine.

a

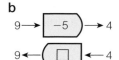

b

c

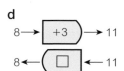

d

4 Use the inverse function to find each missing input.

a

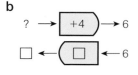

b

c

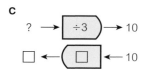

Worked example

Solve the equation $x + 3 = 7$. Check your **solution**.

$x \rightarrow \boxed{+3} \rightarrow 7$ — Draw a function machine for the equation.

$4 \leftarrow \boxed{-3} \leftarrow 7$ — Work out x using the inverse function.

$x = 4$ Check: $x + 3 = 4 + 3 = 7$ ✓ — Check by substituting $x = 4$ back into $x + 3$.

5 Solve these equations. Check your solutions.
    a $x + 4 = 10$ **b** $y + 3 = 15$
    c $z + 9 = 11$ **d** $n - 1 = 5$
    e $m - 3 = 7$ **f** $p - 10 = 6$

6 Solve these equations. Check your solutions.
    a $2x = 8$ $x \rightarrow \boxed{\times 2} \rightarrow 8$ **b** $10v = 80$ **c** $3y = 21$ **d** $12k = 36$
    e $\dfrac{p}{4} = 6$ $p \rightarrow \boxed{\div 4} \rightarrow 6$ **f** $\dfrac{u}{4} = 11$ **g** $\dfrac{x}{5} = 10$ **h** $\dfrac{m}{3} = 12$

7 Priya works out her gross income each month using this rule:

    gross income − tax = take-home pay

At the end of one month Priya pays £130 tax and her take-home pay is £1220.

She writes this equation: $G - 130 = 1220$
Solve the equation to work out Priya's gross income this month.

> **Q7 hint** Gross income is the amount you earn before tax is paid.

8 **Problem-solving**
    a $m + 2 = h$ Find m when $h = 6$.

    b $p = \dfrac{v}{6}$ Find v when $p = 2$.

    c $H = j - 4$ Find j when $H = 7$.

    d $V = IR$ Find R when $I = 2$ and $V = 12$.

    e $S = \dfrac{d}{t}$ Find d when $S = 22$ and $t = 10$.

9 Solve these equations using function machines.

    a $-3 = a - 7$ $a \rightarrow \boxed{-7} \rightarrow \square$ **b** $5d = 0$

    c $7e = -14$ **d** $-2n = 10$ $n \rightarrow \boxed{\times -2} \rightarrow \square$

    e $-4r = -24$ **f** $2n = -3$

Worked example

Bianca cuts 10 cm off a belt of length d cm.

a Write an expression for the new length of the belt.

$d - 10$

b The new length of the belt is 75 cm.
Write an equation involving d.

$d - 10 = 75$

$d \rightarrow \boxed{-10} \rightarrow 75$

[diagram: belt with 10 cm and d cm labelled, $d - 10 = 75$]

c Solve your equation to find the original length of the belt.

$85 \leftarrow \boxed{+10} \leftarrow 75$

$d = 85$ Check: $85 - 10 = 75$ ✓
The original length of the belt was 85 cm.

---

10 Jafar adds 12 more characters to a tweet of t characters.
   a Write an expression for the new length of the tweet.
   b The new length of the tweet is 122 characters.
      Write an equation involving t.
   c Solve your equation to find the original length of the tweet.

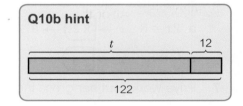

Q10b hint

11 A pair of hiking socks costs £h.
   The cost of 3 pairs is £12.
   a Write an equation involving h.
   b Solve your equation to find the cost of a pair of hiking socks.

12 A carton of juice contains j ml.
   It is shared equally between 8 people.
   Each person receives 150 ml.
   a Write an equation involving j.
   b Solve your equation to find the total volume of juice.

13 Sharon sold 12 CDs from her collection of m CDs.
   She now has 35 CDs.
   a Write an equation involving m.
   b Solve your equation to find the size of her original collection.

14 Simplify the left-hand side of each equation.
   Then solve the equation.
   a $2d + 3d = 20$
   b $2 \times 5a = 60$
   c $2c + 2c + 4c = 16$
   d $6g - 2g = 12 + 6$

> **Q14a hint** Combine the like terms $2d$ and $3d$ first.

15 Problem-solving For each diagram, write an equation and solve it to find the unknown quantity.

a

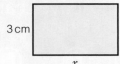

3 cm

x

Area = 15 cm²

b

$3y$

y

Perimeter = 40 cm

16 Problem-solving For each diagram, write an equation and solve it to find the unknown quantity.

a

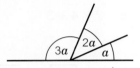

$3a$ $2a$ a

b

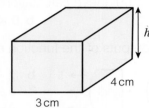

h

4 cm

3 cm

Volume = 24 cm³

Challenge

All of these regular polygons have perimeter 360 cm.

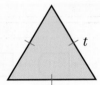

t

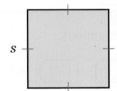

s

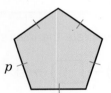

p

1 Write and solve an equation to find the side length of the triangle, square and pentagon. Use the same method to find the side length of a regular hexagon, octagon and decagon with perimeter 360 cm.

2 Two congruent regular hexagons are joined along a side to make a shape with perimeter 360 cm.
Write and solve an equation to find the length of one side.

3 Three congruent regular hexagons are joined at one of their vertices (corners) to make a shape with perimeter 360 cm.
Write and solve an equation to find the length of one side.

4 Join together other regular polygons with the same length sides.
Work out the length of a side when the perimeter of your shape is 360 cm.

Reflect Write the steps you take to solve equations like the ones in this lesson.
You could begin, 'Step 1: Simplify the left-hand side, if needed.'
Beside each step, show whether you found that step OK (☺) or difficult (☹).
Ask a friend or your teacher to help you with any difficult steps.

4.5 Two-step equations

- Solve and write two-step equations using function machines
- Solve problems using equations

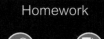 *Active* Learn
Homework

Warm up

1 **Fluency** Work out these calculations.

a $2 \times 4 + 1$ b $6 \times 3 - 5$ c $-2 \times 4 + 3$

2 Work out the outputs of the function machines.

a $1 \rightarrow$ $3 \rightarrow$ $\boxed{\times 2} \rightarrow \boxed{+3} \rightarrow 5$ $10 \rightarrow$

b $12 \rightarrow$ $9 \rightarrow$ $\boxed{\div 3} \rightarrow \boxed{-1} \rightarrow 3$ $30 \rightarrow$

c $2 \rightarrow$ $5 \rightarrow$ $\boxed{\times 5} \rightarrow \boxed{-10} \rightarrow$ $8 \rightarrow$

3 Work out the value of x.

a $x \rightarrow \boxed{\div 2} \rightarrow 13$

b $x \rightarrow \boxed{+1} \rightarrow 5$

c $x \rightarrow \boxed{-5} \rightarrow 23$

4 Copy and complete the inverse function machines.

a $3 \rightarrow \boxed{\times 2} \rightarrow \boxed{+5} \rightarrow 11$
$3 \leftarrow \boxed{} \leftarrow \boxed{} \leftarrow 11$

b $8 \rightarrow \boxed{\div 4} \rightarrow \boxed{-1} \rightarrow 1$
$8 \leftarrow \boxed{} \leftarrow \boxed{} \leftarrow 1$

c $5 \rightarrow \boxed{\times 10} \rightarrow \boxed{+5} \rightarrow 55$
$5 \leftarrow \boxed{} \leftarrow \boxed{} \leftarrow 55$

Worked example

Solve the equation $2a + 1 = 9$ using a function machine.
Check your solution.

$a \rightarrow \boxed{\times 2} \rightarrow \boxed{+1} \rightarrow 9$ ——— Using the priority of operations, multiply a by 2 then add 1.

$a \leftarrow \boxed{\div 2} \leftarrow \boxed{-1} \leftarrow 9$ ——— Reverse the function machine to find the input a.

$9 - 1 = 8$ $8 \div 2 = 4$ $a = 4$

Check by substituting $a = 4$ back into $2a + 1$.
Check: $2a + 1 = 2 \times 4 + 1 = 8 + 1 = 9$ ✓

5 Solve each equation using a function machine.
The first one is started for you.

Q5 hint Check your solutions.

a $3x + 4 = 25$ $x \rightarrow \boxed{\times 3} \rightarrow \boxed{} \rightarrow \square$

b $3x - 4 = 11$

c $4b - 10 = 30$

d $4b + 10 = 30$

e $5n + 2 = 37$

f $2w + 10 = 2$

g $3k + 4 = 28$

h $6h - 7 = 11$

6 Firework rockets cost £f each and Catherine wheels cost £2 each.

   a Write an expression for the total cost of 7 rockets and one Catherine wheel.

   b The cost of 7 rockets and one Catherine wheel is £30 altogether.
     Use your answer to part **a** to write an equation.

   c Solve your equation to find the cost of a rocket.

7 **Problem-solving** Andrew has 12 wooden planks of length c metres,
and an extra 2 metres of wood. He has 38 m of wood altogether.

   a Write an equation involving c.

   b Solve your equation to find the length of a plank.

8 **Problem-solving** Marion thinks of a number n.
She doubles it and adds 12. Her answer is 28.
What was the number, n, she first thought of?

> **Q8 hint** Write an equation and solve it.

9 **Problem-solving** Naeem's bucket holds 5 litres of water.
She used n bucketfuls of water to fill a paddling pool.
After 10 litres of water leaked out, the pool contained 80 litres.
How many bucketfuls did Naeem use to fill the pool?

10 Simplify the left-hand side of each equation by collecting like terms.
Then solve the equation.
Check your solutions.

   a $3d + 2d + 8 = 23$ **b** $4p + 1 + 2p + 3 = 28$

   c $5a - 2 + 3a + 4 = 18$ **d** $10b - 3b + 6 - 12 = 22$

11 Expand the brackets and simplify the left-hand side.
Then solve the equation.

   a $2(5n - 1) = 8$ **b** $3(n + 3) - 2 = 16$

   c $4(g - 2) + 3g = 34$ **d** $5(3u + 5) - 7u = 65$

Challenge   The diagram shows two lawns, A and B.
Lengths are in metres.

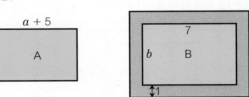

a The area of lawn A is 48 m².

   i Write an expression for the area in
terms of a using brackets.

   ii Write an equation and solve it to find a.

   iii Write down the length of lawn A.

b Lawn B is surrounded by a path of width 1 m.

   i Write an expression for the area of the lawn.

   ii Write an expression for the area of the path.

   iii The area of the path is 26 m².
Write an equation and solve it to find b.

Reflect   Choose an equation from this lesson.
Do the steps for solving equations that you wrote at the end of Lesson 4.4 work for this
equation too? If not, rewrite your steps.
Check that they work for another equation from this lesson.

4.6 The balancing method

- Solve equations using the balancing method

Active Learn
Homework

Warm up

1 **Fluency** Find the inverse of these operations.
   a $- 3$ b $\times 4$ c $\div 7$ d $+ 2$

2 Simplify these expressions.
   a $5c + 10 + 3c - 7$ b $5(z + 3)$ c $7k - 3(k + 4)$

3 Work out these calculations.
   a $8 \div -2$ b $12 \div -3$ c $-6 \div -2$ d $-15 \div 5$

Key point

In an equation, the expressions on both sides of the equals sign have the same value. You can visualise them on balanced scales.

$$x + 3 \quad = \quad 5$$

The scales stay balanced if you do the same operation to both sides.
You can use this **balancing method** to solve equations.

Worked example

Solve the equation $x + 3 = 8$.

$$x + 3 \quad = \quad 8$$
— Visualise the equation as balanced scales.

$$x + 3 - 3 \quad = \quad 8 - 3$$
— The inverse of + 3 is − 3.
Do this to both sides.

$$x + 3 - 3 = 8 - 3$$
$$x = 5$$
— Simplify both sides to find x.

Check: $x + 3 = 5 + 3 = 8$ ✓

4 Use the balancing method to solve each equation.
   Check your answers.

   a $m + 8 = 10$ b $d - 8 = 6$ c $3a = 21$ d $5k = 20$ e $-4g = 12$

   f $\dfrac{n}{4} = 6$ g $\dfrac{t}{10} = 3$ h $\dfrac{s}{10} = -3$ i $\dfrac{x}{-10} = 3$ j $\dfrac{-x}{10} = 20$

5 The formula used to work out the force (F) on an object is

$$F = ma$$

where m is the mass and a is the acceleration of the object.

Work out the value of

a F when $m = 5$ and $a = 3$

b a when $F = 30$ and $m = 6$

c m when $F = 54$ and $a = 9$.

Q5 hint Substitute in the numbers you know and then work out the one you don't know.

Worked example

Solve the equation $2x + 7 = 13$.

$$2x + 7 = 13$$

-7 ⟋⟍ -7

The inverse of $+ 7$ is $- 7$.
Do this to both sides.

$$2x = 6$$

$\div 2$ ⟋⟍ $\div 2$

The inverse of $\times 2$ is $\div 2$.

$$x = 3$$

$$2x + 7 = 13$$
-7 ⟍ -7
$$2x = 6$$
$\div 2$ ⟍ $\div 2$
$$x = 3$$

---

6 Copy and complete to solve $5x - 4 = 6$.

$$5x - 4 = 6$$

$+4$ ⟋⟍ $+\square$

$$5x = \square$$

$\div 5$ ⟋⟍ $\div\square$

$$x = \square$$

7 Solve each equation using the balancing method.

a $2m + 5 = 7$

b $2n - 5 = 11$

c $4t - 3 = 21$

d $3k + 10 = 70$

e $5h + 15 = 50$

f $4w + 10 = 46$

8 **Reasoning** Here is a table of values for the graph of $y = 2x + 3$.

x	1	3	n
y	5	9	15

a Write an equation involving n.

b Solve your equation to find n.

9 Solve these equations.

a $14 = 3m - 1$

b $21 = 5t + 6$

c $47 = 8x + 7$

Q9a hint

$\boxed{14} = \boxed{3m - 1}$

10 Copy and complete to solve these equations.

a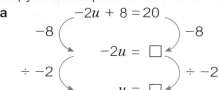
$$-2u + 8 = 20$$
-8 ⟶ ⟵ -8
$$-2u = \square$$
$\div -2$ ⟶ ⟵ $\div -2$
$$u = \square$$

b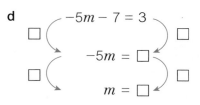
$$10 - 2d = 16$$
-10 ⟶ ⟵ -10
$$\square = \square$$
$\div -2$ ⟶ ⟵ $\div -2$
$$d = \square$$

c
$$11 - 3d = 2$$
$\square$ ⟶ ⟵ $\square$
$$-3d = \square$$
$\div -3$ ⟶ ⟵ $\div -3$
$$d = \square$$

d
$$-5m - 7 = 3$$
$\square$ ⟶ ⟵ $\square$
$$-5m = \square$$
$\square$ ⟶ ⟵ $\square$
$$m = \square$$

11 Copy and complete to solve $2(m + 3) = 8$ in two ways.

a
$$2(m + 3) = 8$$
$$2m + 6 = 8$$
-6 ⟶ ⟵ -6

b
$\div 2$
$$2(m + 3) = 8$$
$$m + 3 = \square$$
$\div 2$

12 Solve these equations using the method you prefer.

a $5(2s - 1) = 25$ **b** $2(3w + 2) = 16$

c $4(5h - 3) = 48$ **d** $2(1 + 3t) = 32$

Challenge   The length y metres of a train is given by $y = 6x + 8$, where x is the number of carriages.

a A train has a length of 50 m.
  i Write down an equation involving x.
  ii Solve the equation to find the number of carriages.

b $y = 6x + 8$ has been plotted on the graph.
  i Find the point on the red line where $y = 50$.
  Read off the number of carriages.
  Is this the same as your solution in part **a**?
  ii Solve an equation to find the number of carriages in a train of length 20 m.
  Check your answer on the graph.

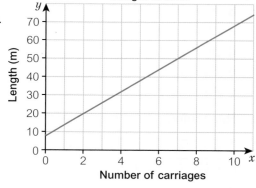
Length of train

c Use the graph to find the length of a train with no carriages.
What part of the train might this be?
Which part of the equation represents this information?

d What does $6x$ in the equation represent?

Reflect   Do the steps for solving equations that you wrote at the end of Lesson 4.5 work for equations with an unknown (a letter) on both sides of the '=' sign? If not, rewrite them.
Check that your steps work for solving equations from Lessons 4.4, 4.5 and 4.6.

Hint You may have to write some extra steps.

4 Check up

Powers, expressions and formulae

1 **a** Write $m \times m \times m \times m$ as a power.
   b Write b^6 as a product.
   c Write each product using index notation.
      i $a \times a \times a \times c \times c$ **ii** $2n \times 3n \times 4n$

2 **a** Write an expression for the area of this rectangle.

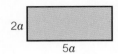

   b Use your expression to find the area when $a = 4$ cm.

3 **a** Write an expression for the volume of each cuboid.

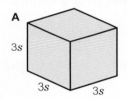 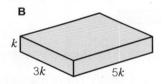

   b Work out the volume of cuboid B when $k = 3$ cm.

4 An ice cube tray is filled with w ml of water. It makes 15 ice cubes.
   a Write a formula for the volume V ml of water in one ice cube.
   b Use your formula to find V when $w = 450$ ml.
   c Write a formula for the total volume T of n ice cubes.

5 A £120 bill for a meal is divided equally between n people.
   Write an expression for the amount each person pays.

Brackets

6 Expand these expressions and simplify where possible.
   a $m(2 + n)$ **b** $2b(b - 3)$ **c** $-4(2t + 5)$
   d $5u - 2(u - 3)$ **e** $4(r - 1) - 2(r + 2)$

7 **a** Write down the highest common factor of $8n$ and 12.
   b Factorise $8n + 12$ completely.

8 Factorise these expressions.
   a $8s - 8$ **b** $12 + 4m$ **c** $3h + 9$
   d $100 - 50t$ **e** $54p + 18r$ **f** $30j - 42q$
   g $k - k^2$ **h** $16v^2 - 4v$ **i** $15a^2 + 25a$

Equations

9 Solve these equations.

   a $h - 7 = 12$ **b** $\frac{w}{2} = 10$ **c** $-4m = 24$

   d $3a + 2 = 20$ **e** $2(d + 5) = 12$ **f** $5(3h - 1) = 40$

10 Jade uses this formula to work out her total pay:

    total pay (P) = wages (W) + tips (T)

   a Work out P when $W = £35$ and $T = £9$.

   b Work out W when $P = £58$ and $T = £12$.

11 The formula $v = at$ gives the velocity v metres per second (m/s) of a sports car after t seconds.
Use the formula to find t when $a = 11$ and $v = 110$ m/s.

12 I think of a number, double it and add 20. My answer is 48.
Write and solve an equation to find the number I thought of.

Challenge

A rectangular paving slab has a width of 1 metre and a length of x metres.

   1m

   x

a Write an expression for the perimeter of a slab.

b A straight path of width 1 m is made by joining four slabs.

Write an expression for the perimeter of the path.

c A 1 m wide path made of six slabs encloses a rectangular growing area. Write an expression for
   i the outer perimeter of the path
   ii the inner perimeter of the path
   iii the total perimeter of the path.

> **Part c hint**
> Here is one of two possible arrangements.
>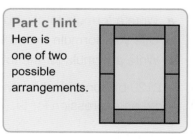

d Repeat part **c** for a path made using eight slabs.

e Write a formula for the total perimeter of a 1 m wide rectangular path made from an even number of slabs.

> **Part e hint** Use your expression from part **d ii**.

f A rectangular growing area has a perimeter of 8 m and is enclosed by a 1 m wide path of eight slabs.
Solve an equation to find the length of a slab.

Reflect

How sure are you of your answers? Were you mostly

   ☹ Just guessing   😐 Feeling doubtful   🙂 Confident

What next? Use your results to decide whether to strengthen or extend your learning.

4 Strengthen

Powers, expressions and formulae

1　Write each power as a product.
   a $u^5 = \square \times \square \times \square \times \square \times \square$
   b a^2
   c d^3

2　Simplify these expressions.

$$\overbrace{c + c + c + c}^{\text{4 lots of } c}$$

   a $c + c + c + c = c + c + c + c = \square\, c$

   b $c \times c \times c \times c = \underbrace{c \times c \times c \times c}_{\text{product}} = c^{\overset{4}{\underset{\text{power}}{}}}$ ←index

   c $h + h + h$
   d $h \times h \times h$
   e $m \times m \times m \times m \times m$
   f $m + m + m + m + m$

3　Write each product using a power or index.
   a $4 \times t \times t = 4 \times t^{\square} = 4t^{\square}$
   b $5 \times a \times a \times a$
   c $g \times g \times g \times g \times g \times 2$
   d $3 \times e \times 2 \times e$
   e $5 \times m \times 2 \times m \times m$
   f $2n \times 4n$
   g $3d \times 2d \times 2d$
   h $-3t \times 5t$

> **Q3h hint** Multiply the numbers −3 × 5.

4　Write each product using a power or index.
   a $e \times e \times e \times d \times d = e^{\square} \times d^{\square} = e^{\square}d^{\square}$
   b $s \times s \times t \times t \times t$
   c $e \times f \times e$
   d $p \times p \times q \times p \times p$

5　Write an expression for the area of each rectangle.
   The first one is started for you.

a　(rectangle with sides $2x$ and 3)
b　(rectangle with sides $2x$ and x)
c　(rectangle with sides 5 and $2y$)
d　(rectangle with sides $4y$ and $2y$)

$l \times w = 2x \times 3$
$\quad\quad = \square\, x$

6 Each rectangle has area A.
Write an expression for the area of the shaded part.
The first one is done for you.

a   **b** 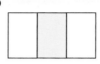 **c** 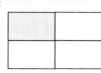 **d**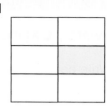

Area $= \dfrac{A}{2}$

7 A meal costs £80.
Work out the cost per person when the meal is shared by
a 2 people **b** 4 people **c** 10 people.
d Write an expression for the cost per person when n people share the meal.

8 Write an expression for the volume of each cuboid.

a 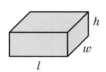 **b**   **c**   **d**

Brackets

1 Expand these brackets. The first one is done for you.
   a $3(3g - 5) = 3 \times 3g + 3 \times -5$
   $= 9g - 15$

   b $2(3g - 5)$
   c $-2(n + 3)$
   d $-2(n - 3)$
   e $-4(3c + 2)$
   f $-4(3c - 2)$
   g $-5(2p + 3)$
   h $-5(2p - 3)$

> **Q1 hint** Use the rule:
> multiplying same signs gives +,
> different signs gives −.

2 Expand the brackets then simplify each expression. Some are started for you.
   a $6t + 2(t + 3) = \Box t + \Box$
   b $6t - 2(t + 3)$
   c $6t + 2(t - 3) = \Box t - \Box$
   d $6t - 2(t - 3)$
   e $8m + 3(m + 2)$
   f $8m + 3(m - 2)$
   g $8m - 3(m + 2)$
   h $8m - 3(m - 2)$

3 Expand the brackets then simplify each expression. Some are started for you.

  a $5(a + 2) + 3(a + 1) = \square a + \square$

  b $5(a + 2) - 3(a + 1) = \square a + \square$

  c $4(a + 1) - 2(a + 3) = \square a - \square$

  d $4(a + 1) - 2(a - 3) = \square a + \square$

  e $3(2m + 3) + 4(2m - 3)$

  f $3(2m + 3) - 4(2m - 3)$

Q3b hint Expand each set of brackets.

$$\underbrace{5(a + 2)}_{5a + 10} \; - \; \underbrace{3(a + 1)}_{3a - 3}$$

Then collect like terms.

4 Expand these expressions.

  a $a(a + 5)$ **b** $a(a - 5)$ **c** $2a(a + 5)$ **d** $2a(a - 5)$

  e $3p(p - 4)$ **f** $3p(p + 4)$ **g** $3p(2p + 1)$ **h** $3p(2p - 1)$

5 Copy and complete to factorise $3c + 6$.

$$3 \times \square = 3c$$
$$3c + 6 = 3(\square + \square)$$
$$3 \times \square = 6$$

HCF of
$3c$ and 6

6 Complete these factorisations. Some are started for you.
Check your answers by expanding the brackets.

  a $4b + 8 = 4(\square + \square)$ **b** $7c - 14 = 7(\square - \square)$

  c $2a + 6$ **d** $5m + 10$

  e $7p - 7$ **f** $3w - 12$

  g $10t - 20$ **h** $8a - 12 = 4(\square - \square)$

  i $10 + 4k$ **j** $12 + 16s$

  k $4a + 6b$ **l** $6c + 10d$

7 Factorise these expressions completely. Some are started for you.
Check your answers by expanding the brackets.

  a $6m^2 + 15m = 3m(\square + \square)$

  b $4a^2 - 6a = \square(\square - 3)$

  c $7u^2 + 14u$

  d $6d^2 - 9d$

Q7a hint The HCF of 6 and 15 is 3.
The HCF of m^2 and m is m.
So $3m$ is the HCF of $6m^2$ and $15m$.
$3m \times \square = 6m^2$
$3m \times \square = 15m$

Equations

1 Solve these equations using function machines. Check your solutions.

  a $x + 2 = 7$

  $x \rightarrow \boxed{+2} \rightarrow 7$

  $\square \leftarrow \boxed{} \leftarrow 7$

  b $x - 5 = 3$

  $x \rightarrow \boxed{-5} \rightarrow 3$

  $\square \leftarrow \boxed{} \leftarrow 3$

Q1a hint The inverse of + 2 is $\square$ 2

  c $2a = 8$

  $a \rightarrow \boxed{\times 2} \rightarrow 8$

  $\square \leftarrow \boxed{} \leftarrow 8$

  d $a \div 3 = 5$

  $a \rightarrow \boxed{\div 3} \rightarrow 5$

  $\square \leftarrow \boxed{} \leftarrow 5$

2 Solve these equations using the balancing method. Check your solutions.

   a $x + 4 = 12$

   b $x - 2 = 7$

   c $a + 10 = 15$

   d $c - 1 = 5$

   e $4p = 12$

   f $5t = 30$

   g $m \div 2 = 7$

   h $\frac{e}{4} = 3$

Q2a hint You can use a function machine or the balancing method to help you find the inverse function.

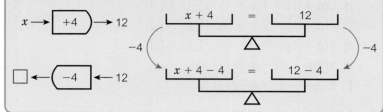

3 Solve these equations. The first one is started for you.

   a

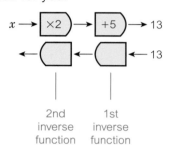

$$-5 \left(\begin{array}{c} 2x + 5 = 13 \\ \Box = \Box \end{array} \right) -5$$
$$\div 2 \left(\begin{array}{c} \\ x = \Box \end{array} \right) \div 2$$

2nd inverse function   1st inverse function

   b $3y - 2 = 10$ **c** $4a + 10 = 30$ **d** $2c - 1 = 5$

4 Expand the brackets. Then solve the equations.

   a $2(t + 1) = 8$ **b** $4(x + 1) = 8$ **c** $3(2d - 1) = 15$ **d** $5(2m - 1) = 15$

Challenge   Esther and Vic live on the same floor in a block of flats.

a Esther takes 10 seconds to go up a floor using the stairs.
Write an expression for the time she takes to walk up n floors.

b Vic uses the lift, which takes 5 seconds to go up a floor.
He has to wait 30 seconds for the lift to arrive.
Write an expression for the time he takes to go up n floors.

c Esther and Vic arrive at their floor at the same time.
   i Write an equation to show this.
   ii Solve the equation to find the floor they live on.

> **Part c i hint** Make your answers to parts **a** and **b** equal.

Reflect   Anna says, 'Algebra is just like arithmetic really, but when you don't know a number, you use a letter.'
Is Anna's explanation a good one? Explain your answer.

4 Extend

1 **Problem-solving** Here are four formula cards.

$$A = B + 3 \qquad B = 3C \qquad B + D = A \qquad A + B + E = 20$$

Copy and complete this table to show the values of A, B, C, D and E.

A	B	C	D	E
9				

2 The area of each shape is given. Solve an equation to find the unknown length of each shape.

a

h | Area = 60 cm² |
12 cm

b

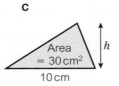

Area = 24 cm² | 8 cm
x

c

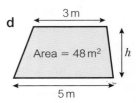

Area = 30 cm² | h
10 cm

d

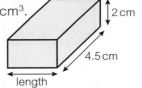

3 m
Area = 48 m² | h
5 m

3 **Problem-solving** The diagram shows a cuboid with volume 31.5 cm³. Work out the length of the cuboid.

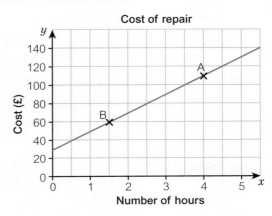

2 cm
4.5 cm
length

4 **Problem-solving** The formula $C = 20n$ gives the total cost C of n pencils, in pence. Solve an equation to find the number of pencils bought for £1.80.

5 **Reasoning** The cost £y for repairing a washing machine is given by the equation $y = 20x + 30$, where x is the number of hours the repair takes.

  a A repair costs £110.

    i Write an equation involving x.

    ii Solve the equation to find the number of hours the repair takes.

  b $y = 20x + 30$ has been plotted on the graph.

    i Explain why point A gives the solution to the equation in part **a**.

    ii Point B gives the solution to the equation $20x + 30 = \square$.
    Complete the equation.

  c Solve an equation to find how long a repair costing £115 takes.
    Check your answer on the graph.
    Which method gives the more accurate answer?

  d What does the number 30 mean in the equation $y = 20x + 30$?

  e What does the number 20 mean in the equation $y = 20x + 30$?

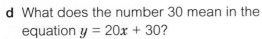

Cost of repair

6 **Reasoning** The formula $C = 10n + 5$ can be used to find the cost, in £, of ordering n umbrellas online, including postage and packing.
   a i Explain what the number 10 means in the formula.
   ii Explain what the number 5 means in the formula.
   b Gavin ordered some umbrellas for £35.
   i Write an equation involving n.
   ii Solve the equation to find how many umbrellas Gavin ordered.
   c i Copy and complete the table of values for $C = 10n + 5$.

Q6c hint Put n on the horizontal axis and C on the vertical axis.

n	0	2	4	6	8
C					

   ii Plot a graph using the data.
   d i Mark the point on your graph where $C = 35$.
   ii How does this point show the answer to part **b ii**?
   e Use your graph to solve the equation $75 = 10n + 5$.
   Check your answer by solving the equation.

7 Solve each equation by working out the unknown length.
   a $5(x + 3) = 20$ **b** $9(x + 2) = 63$ **c** $6(x + 2) + 4 = 28$

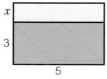
total area = 20

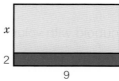
total area = 63

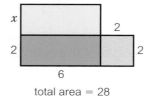
total area = 28

8 **Problem-solving** A bolt has a mass of 20 g and a nut has a mass of n g.
   a Write an expression with brackets for the total mass of 5 nuts and 5 bolts.
   b The total mass of 5 nuts and 5 bolts is 125 g.
   Solve an equation to find the mass of a nut.

9 **Problem-solving** The diagram shows a partly covered swimming pool.
   The dimensions are in metres.
   a Write an expression using brackets for the volume of water the pool holds.
   b The pool holds 180 m³. Write and solve an equation to find the value of a.

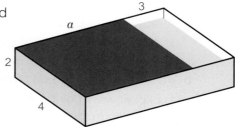

10 **Problem-solving** A rectangle has a length of $4a + 2$ and a width of 3.
   a Write an expression for the area of the rectangle.
   b Work out the length of a rectangle with the same area but a width of 2.

Q10b hint Factorise the expression in part **a**.

Challenge   Two numbers are $3x$ and 11.
The mean of the two numbers is 16.
Write and solve an equation to find x.

Reflect   Which do you find easier, working with expressions or equations? Explain why.

4 Unit test

1 Solve these equations.
   a $t + 3 = 11$ **b** $\frac{y}{3} = 7$ **c** $-5a = 20$

2 On a car journey, four people shared the cost £P of the petrol.
   Write an expression for the amount each person paid.

3 Solve these equations.
   a $2d - 3 = 17$ **b** $7x + 11 = 60$ **c** $15 - 2y = 7$

4 The price of a sweat band in SportsPlus is £t.
   The price of the same sweat band in Jenco's is £1 more.
   a Write an expression for the total cost of four sweat bands from SportsPlus.
   b Write an expression with brackets for the total cost of three sweat bands from Jenco's.

5 **a** $P = \frac{A}{V}$. Find A when $P = 6$ and $V = 11$.

   b $V = IR$. Find I when $R = 8$ and $V = 20$.

6 Expand these expressions. Simplify where possible.
   a $c(2b + 5)$ **b** $3u(u + 1)$
   c $-2(t - 3)$ **d** $5(m + 2) - 3(m - 2)$
   e $u(3u - 2) + 6u$ **f** $2(3a + b) - 2(a - b)$

7 Solve
   a $3(m - 2) = 9$
   b $4(3n + 1) = 88$

8 A company logo is made using three squares of side a cm.
   a Write an expression for
      i the area of one square
      ii the total area of the logo.
   b Use your answer to part **a** to find the total area of the logo when $a = 4$ cm.
   c Write a formula for the total area A of a new logo made using
      i 4 squares   **ii** 5 squares   **iii** n squares.

9 **a** Write $c \times c \times c \times c \times c$ as a power.
   b Write m^4 as a product.
   c Write each product using index notation.
      i $p \times p \times t \times t \times t$ 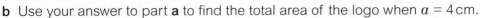 **ii** $5a \times 2a \times a$ **iii** $2x \times 3y^3 \times 4x$

10 **a** **i** Write the highest common factor of $8a$ and 16.
      ii Factorise completely $8a + 16$.
   b Factorise these expressions completely.
      i $12s + 8$ **ii** $w^2 - w$
      iii $2x^2 + 8x$ 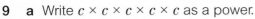 **iv** $15y^2 - 10y$

11 36 sparklers are divided equally between n people.

   a Write an expression for the number of sparklers each person receives.

   b Each person receives two sparklers.

      Write an equation and solve it to find the number of people.

12 A carton of juice holds x ml.

   The juice in the carton fills 5 glasses.

   a Write an expression for the volume of juice in one glass.

   b Each glass contains 300 ml.

      Write and solve an equation to find the volume of juice in the carton.

13 Emma has £37 in her bank account.

   She starts putting £7 into the account each week.

   Write and solve an equation to find how many weeks it will take for Emma to have £100 in her bank account.

14 Write an equation and solve it to find

   a the value of x

   b the size of each angle.

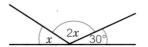

 15 The diagram shows a cuboid with volume 5760 mm³.

   Work out the width of the cuboid.

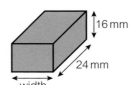

Challenge   The diagram shows two cubes, A and B.

a Write a simplified expression for

   i the volume of cube A

   ii the volume of cube B.

b Copy and complete this statement:

   Volume of cube B = $2^{\square}$ × volume of cube A.

c Cube C has a side of length $3a$.

   i Write a simplified expression for the volume of cube C.

   ii Write a statement comparing the volume of cube C to the volume of cube A.

   iii Calculate the volume of cube C when $a = 4.5$ cm.

d Cube D has a side of length na, where n is a positive integer.

   i Write a simplified expression for the volume of cube D.

   ii Write a statement comparing the volume of cube D with the volume of cube A.

   iii Calculate the volume of cube D when $a = 25$ cm and $n = 7$.

Reflect   This may be the first time you have done any algebra since Year 7.

Choose A, B or C to complete each statement.

In this unit, I did …	**A** well	**B** OK	**C** not very well.
I think algebra is …	**A** easy	**B** OK	**C** difficult.
When I think about doing algebra, I feel …	**A** confident	**B** OK	**C** unsure.

If you answered mostly As and Bs, are you surprised that you feel OK about algebra? Why?

If you answered mostly Cs, look back at the questions in the lessons that you found most tricky.

Ask a friend or your teacher to explain them to you. Then complete the statements above again.

5 Real-life graphs

Master   Check up p137   Strengthen p139   Extend p144   Unit test p146

5.1 Conversion graphs

• Draw, use and interpret conversion graphs

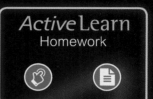

Active Learn
Homework

Warm up

1 Fluency Copy and complete

a 1 cm = ☐ mm   **b** 1 kg = ☐ g   **c** 1 litre = ☐ ml   **d** 1 km = ☐ m

2 Work out the value of one small square in each of these scales.

a

```
0        2 kg
```

b

```
0                    5 litres
```

c

```
0     1 m
```

3 Work out the missing numbers.

a 5 miles ≈ 8 km so 15 miles ≈ ☐ km   **b** 1 gallon ≈ 4.5 litres so 2 gallons ≈ ☐ litres

Key point

A **conversion graph** converts values from one **unit** to another.

4 This **conversion graph** converts between inches
and centimetres, giving approximate values.
The green arrows show that 20 cm ≈ 8 inches.
Use the graph to convert

a 30 cm to inches

b 40 cm to inches

c 6 inches to centimetres

d 11 inches to centimetres

e Problem-solving Use your answers to parts **a** and
b to convert 70 cm into inches.

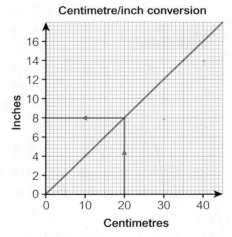

Centimetre/inch conversion

5 The graph converts between British pounds (£) and
US dollars ($).

a Use the graph to convert

    i £5 to dollars   **ii** $4 to pounds   **iii** $12 to pounds.

b Problem-solving Use your answers to part **a** to convert

    i $40 to pounds   **ii** £15 to dollars.

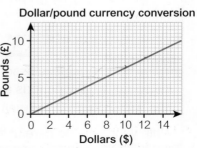

Dollar/pound currency conversion

6 The table shows three temperatures in degrees Celsius (°C) and degrees Fahrenheit (°F).

a Copy these axes onto graph paper.

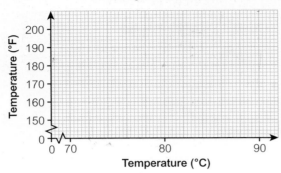

Conversion of degrees Celsius
to degrees Fahrenheit

°C	70	80	90
°F	158	176	194

Q6 hint A zigzag line ─/\/─ shows the axis has 'missing' values.

b Plot the points from the table on the grid and join them with a straight line.

c Nitrogen chloride has a boiling point of 160°F. What is its boiling point in °C?

d Nitric acid has a boiling point of 83°C. What is its boiling point in °F?

e Which has the higher boiling point, nitrogen chloride or nitric acid?

7 a Use the fact the 1 gallon ≈ 4.5 litres to complete this table of values.

Gallons	0	1	5
Litres			

b Draw a conversion graph for litres and gallons.

c Use your graph to complete these conversions.

   i 3.5 gallons ≈ ☐ litres

   ii 0.2 gallons ≈ ☐ litres

   iii 1 litre ≈ ☐ gallons

   iv 12.5 litres ≈ ☐ gallons

Q7b hint Draw your axis scales so that all the values in your table of values will fit.

Challenge The graphs show the currency conversion between British pounds (£) and New Zealand dollars (NZD), and New Zealand dollars (NZD) and Danish krone (DKK).

a Use the graphs to work out the value of

   i £5 in DKK   **ii** 72 DKK in £.

b Draw a conversion graph between British pounds (£) and Danish krone (DKK).

c Check that your graph is correct by converting values in £ to DKK using your graph, and then checking with these two graphs.

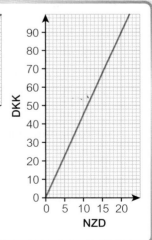

Reflect After this lesson, Caroline says, 'In Q5a i, I almost read 5 on the dollars axis, instead of on the pounds axis.'

She wrote down: *Conversion graphs: be careful to read the correct axis.*

Write your own 'be careful to' list for conversion graphs.

5.2 Distance–time graphs

*Active*Learn
Homework

- Interpret a distance–time graph
- Draw a simple distance–time graph
- Draw and use graphs to solve distance–time problems

Warm up

1 Work out the value in minutes of one small square in each of these scales.

a ⬜⬜ 0 1 hour

b ⬜⬜⬜ 0 1 hour

c ⬜⬜⬜⬜ 0 1 hour

d ⬜⬜⬜⬜⬜ 0 1 hour

2 **Fluency** How many minutes is it
   a from 10 am to 10:45 am
   b from 4:45 pm to 5:15 pm
   c from 15:30 to 16:45
   d from half past 7 to quarter past 8?

Key point In a **distance–time graph**:
- the vertical axis represents the **distance** from the starting point
- the horizontal axis represents the **time** taken.

3 Liam drives from his house to the shops.
  He stays there for a while, then drives home.
  The distance–time graph shows his journey.
  a How far is Liam's house from the shops?
  b At what time does Liam arrive at the shops?
  c How long does he take to drive to the shops?
  d How long does he stay at the shops?
  e How long does he take to drive home?
  f **Reasoning** Did he drive faster to the shops
  or back from the shops?
  Explain how you know.

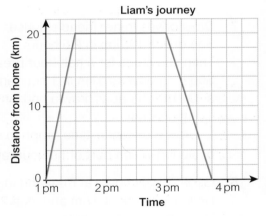

4 Peter walks to the post office.
  He stops to chat to a friend on the way home.
  The graph shows his journey.
  a How far away is the post office from Peter's
  house?
  b How long does Peter spend at the post office?
  c How long does Peter spend chatting to his
  friend?
  d How long does it take for Peter to get from his
  house to the post office?
  e How long does it take for Peter to get from the post office back to his house?
  f **Reasoning** When is Peter walking fastest?

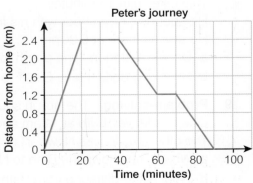

5 One evening Clare walks to the cinema.
The graph shows her journey.
  a How far is the cinema from Clare's home?
  b How far does Clare walk in total?
  c How long is she at the cinema?

Clare's journey

> **Key point** On a distance–time graph the **gradient** (steepness) of the line represents the **speed** of the journey.
> The steeper the line, the faster the speed.

6 The graph shows Lucy's journey from home to the airport.
  a How far is the airport from Lucy's home?
  b Lucy had to reduce her speed for part of the journey, because of roadworks.
    Between what times was she driving through the roadworks?

Lucy's journey to the airport

7 Daya drives to her friend's house.
She drives 125 km in 2.5 hours.
Then she stops for a half-hour break.
She then drives 75 km in 1 hour and arrives at her friend's house.
  a On graph paper draw a horizontal axis from 0 to 4 hours and a vertical axis from 0 to 200 km.
    Draw a distance–time graph to show Daya's journey.
  b During which part of her journey was she travelling fastest?

8 Geoff leaves home at 8 am and jogs 5 km to work. It takes him $\frac{3}{4}$ of an hour.
He leaves work at 4 pm and jogs 2 km further away from home to see his friend.
This takes him 15 minutes.
He spends $\frac{1}{4}$ of an hour with his friend, then jogs directly home.
He arrives there at 5:30 pm.
  a Draw a distance–time graph to show Geoff's journey.
  b How long does it take Geoff to jog home?

9 **Problem-solving** The graph shows two bus journeys.
One bus leaves Bath at 11 am and travels to Newport.
The other bus leaves Newport at 11 am and travels to Bath.
  a Which line shows the Bath to Newport bus?
  b What is the distance from Bath to Newport?
  c What time does each bus arrive?
  d Which is the quicker bus journey?

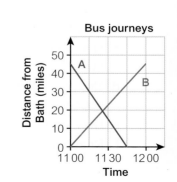

Bus journeys

10 Katy and Aaron take part in a sponsored cycle ride.
The graph shows their journeys.

   a How far is the cycle ride?

   b How long does it take Katy to complete the cycle ride?

   c At what time does Aaron set off?

   d How long does it take Aaron to complete the cycle ride?

   e **Problem-solving** At what time does Aaron overtake Katy?

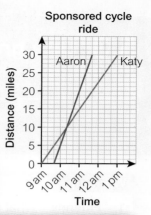

Q10e hint When Aaron overtakes Katy, they are both at the same place at the same time.

Challenge The graph shows a journey taken by Ewan in his car.

On his journey Ewan passed these road signs.

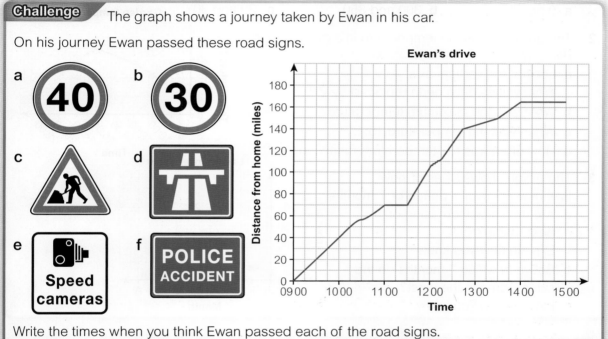

Write the times when you think Ewan passed each of the road signs.

Reflect You have seen lines like lines A, B and C on distance–time graphs:

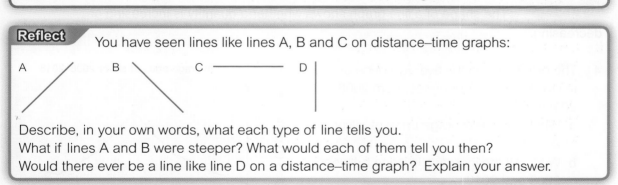

Describe, in your own words, what each type of line tells you.
What if lines A and B were steeper? What would each of them tell you then?
Would there ever be a line like line D on a distance–time graph? Explain your answer.

5.3 Line graphs

- Draw and interpret line graphs

*Active*Learn
Homework

Warm up

1 Fluency What is the number halfway between
a 0 and 1   b 300 and 350   c 20 and 30?

2 The graph shows the temperature in a garden over one day.
  a Look at the vertical axis.
    What values have been replaced by $\lessgtr$?
  b What was the maximum temperature?
  c When was the temperature 15°C?
  d How often was the temperature measured?

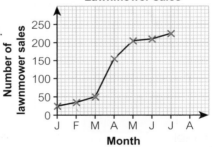
Garden temperature

3 The graph shows sales of new lawnmowers over a period of 7 months.
  a Are the sales increasing or decreasing?
    Explain how you know.
  b Between which 2 months do the sales increase the most?
    Explain how you know.

Lawnmower sales

> **Key point**   The shape of a line graph shows whether a quantity is increasing or decreasing.

4 The graph shows the average price of silver, in US dollars ($) per ounce, from 2006 to 2018.
  a What was the average price of silver in 2010?
  b Work out the increase in price between 2008 and 2010.
  c Between which years was there the biggest increase?
    How can you tell this from the graph?
  d Over which four years did the price decrease?
  e Estimate the price of silver in 2017.
  f **Problem-solving** Describe the change in the price of silver from 2006 to 2018.
    Include when the price increased and decreased, and the smallest and largest increase.

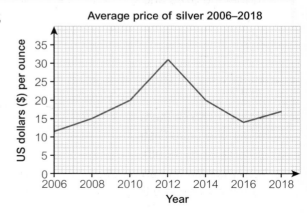
Average price of silver 2006–2018

5   The table shows how much Becky earned every two years from 2010 to 2018.

Year	2010	2012	2014	2016	2018
Amount earned (£)	18 600	19 000	19 200	20 800	20 000

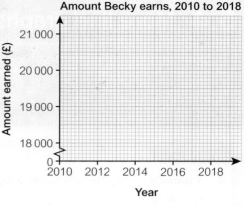

Amount Becky earns, 2010 to 2018

a   Copy these axes onto graph paper.
b   Plot the points from the table on the graph.
    Join them with straight lines to draw a line graph
    for this data.
c   Estimate the amount Becky earned in 2017.
    Explain why this is only an estimate.
d   **Reasoning**   Could you use the graph to predict
    what Becky will earn in the future? Explain your answer.

6   The table shows the number of visitors to a theme park from May to October.
    All the numbers are given to the nearest thousand.

Month	May	Jun	Jul	Aug	Sep	Oct
Number of visitors (thousands)	12	15	22	28	14	11

a   Draw a line graph of this data.
b   i   Between which two months was the difference in visitor
        numbers greatest?
    ii Work out this difference.
c   **Problem-solving**   Write a report about the visitor numbers from
    May to October.

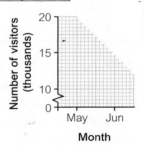

Challenge   The table shows the average temperature each month in the Lake District.

Month	Jan	Feb	Mar	Apr	May	Jun	Jul	Aug	Sep	Oct	Nov	Dec
Temperature (°C)	4.4	4.4	6.1	8.1	11.0	13.6	15.6	15.1	12.9	10.0	6.8	4.5

a   Draw a line graph of this data.
    Label the axes and give the graph a title.

Average monthly rainfall in Lake District

b   Which three months are the hottest?

This graph shows the average monthly
rainfall in the Lake District.

c   Which three months are the driest?
d   Gary is planning an outdoor activity holiday in the Lake District. Use both graphs to
    decide when you think Gary should take his holiday. Explain your answer.

Reflect   In this lesson, Q3 asked you to 'explain how you know'. Think about how you
explained. Did explaining help you to understand more about graphs? Describe how.

5.4 More line graphs

- Draw and interpret line graphs and identify trends

*Active*Learn
Homework

Warm up

1 Fluency The graphs show students' average scores in tests over one year in different subjects.

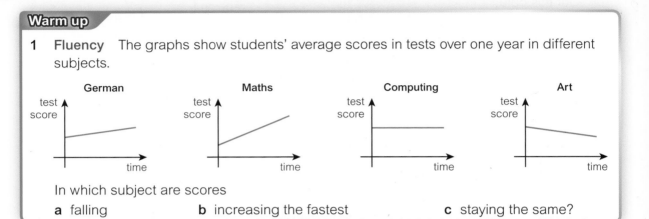

German

Maths

Computing

Art

In which subject are scores

a falling   **b** increasing the fastest   **c** staying the same?

2 A company sells music singles. The graph shows the sales of CD singles and digital singles over time.

a When did the company sell the most CD singles?

b When did the company sell the most digital singles?

c When did digital singles first sell more than CD singles?

d How do you think the graphs for CD singles and digital singles might continue?

Single sales over time

Key:
— digital
— CD

Sales: 6000, 5000, 4000, 3000, 2000, 1000, 0

Year: 1998, 2000, 2002, 2004, 2006, 2008, 2010, 2012

Key point

Line graphs can help you identify **trends** in the data. The trend is the general direction of change, ignoring individual ups and downs.

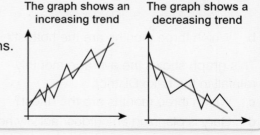

The graph shows an increasing trend

The graph shows a decreasing trend

3 Which kind of trend do you think each graph would show?

a Number of people who have mobile phones, from 2000 to this year.

b Number of people who have a DVD player from 2000 to this year.

4 Reasoning The graph shows the depth of water in a reservoir.

a Why is the blue line horizontal?

b When was the reservoir nearly full?

c Describe the trend in the volume of water

  i from October to May

  ii from May to September.

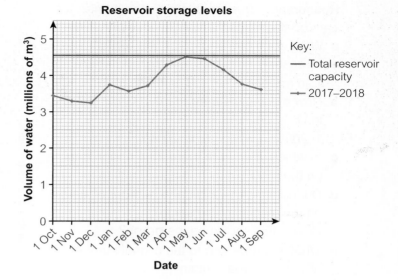

Reservoir storage levels

Key:
— Total reservoir capacity
—•— 2017–2018

5 The table shows the number of holidays taken abroad and in the UK.

Year	1965	1975	1985	1995	2005	2015
Abroad (millions)	4	6	14	21	27	22
UK (millions)	32	34	36	28	34	32

a Draw a line graph of this data, on axes like this:

b Make a key, to show what each graph line represents.

c Describe the trends shown by the graph.

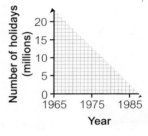

6 Problem-solving / Reasoning The graph shows the total distance travelled using different types of transport in the UK. Information was taken every 10 years from 1970 to 2010.

a Describe the trends in the total distance travelled by each type of transport.

b In 1970, what distance was travelled by

  i bicycle   ii bus/coach?

The 'Cars, vans and taxis' category is missing from the graph. In 1970, 297 billion kilometres were travelled by cars, vans and taxis.

c What percentage of the total distance travelled in 1970 was by cars, vans and taxis?
Give your answer correct to 1 decimal place.

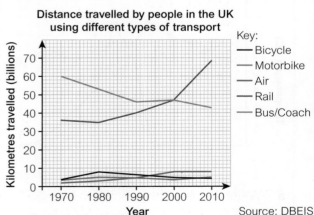

Distance travelled by people in the UK using different types of transport

Key:
— Bicycle
— Motorbike
— Air
— Rail
— Bus/Coach

Source: DBEIS

In 2010, 656 billion kilometres were travelled by cars, vans and taxis.

d What percentage of the total distance travelled in 2010 was by cars, vans and taxis?
Give your answer correct to 1 decimal place.

e Describe how the use of cars, vans and taxis changed between 1970 and 2010.

Q6c hint Use the graph to work out the distance travelled by each type of transport and then find the total.

7   **Reasoning**   The graph shows the number of
     cars on the road in Great Britain since 2004.
     a What does one square on the vertical axis
        represent
        i in millions   **ii** in thousands?
     b How many cars were there in Great Britain
        in
        i 2005   **ii** 2011?
     c In which year were there 28.4 million cars
        on the road?
     d During which year did the number of cars
        on the road stay the same?
        How is this shown on the graph?
     e What is happening to the overall number
        of cars in Great Britain?

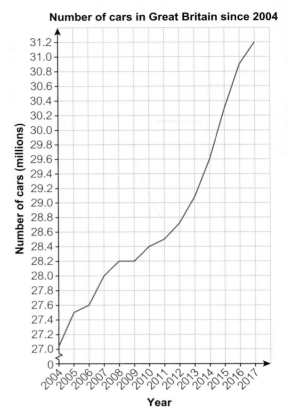

Number of cars in Great Britain since 2004

Challenge   The graph shows the average rainfall and temperature each month in
Mumbai.

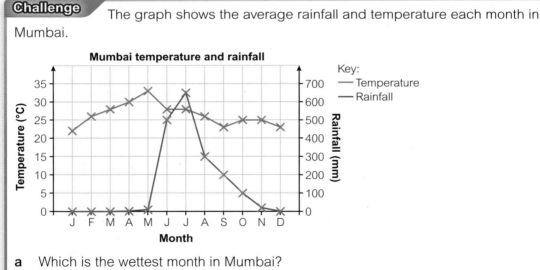

a   Which is the wettest month in Mumbai?
b   Which is the hottest month in Mumbai?
c   Work out the range of the temperatures in Mumbai.
d   Dinesh is travelling to Mumbai for business in October.
     Write a sentence to tell him what the weather should be like.

Reflect   This lesson asked you to interpret information from some real-life graphs.
Which questions were easiest for you to answer? What made them easier?
Which questions were hardest for you to answer? What made them harder?

5.5 Real-life graphs

- Draw and interpret linear and non-linear graphs from a range of sources

Active Learn
Homework

Warm up

1 Fluency In which of these two distance–time graphs was the person travelling faster?

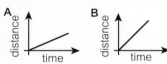

A   B

2 The graph shows Naomi's times for a 5 km run, each week for 6 weeks.
   a Describe the trend shown by the graph.
   b What does the point on the vertical axis represent?

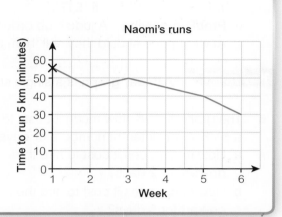

Naomi's runs

3 The graph shows information about internet access in the UK.
   a Is it possible to say how many households had internet access in 2000?
   b Describe the trend shown by the graph.
   c Reasoning Do you expect this trend to continue for ever?

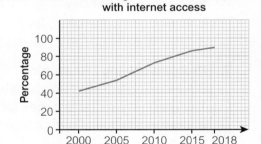

Percentage of UK households with internet access

Source: ONS

4 The graph shows the percentage of adults in the UK who use the internet every day, and the percentage of adults who never use the internet.
   a What percentage of adults used the internet every day in
      i 2006   **ii** 2012   **iii** 2018?
   b Describe the trends shown by the graph.
   c Reasoning Eloise says, 'The percentage of adults who use the internet every day has more than doubled from 2006 to 2018.' Is she correct? Explain your answer.

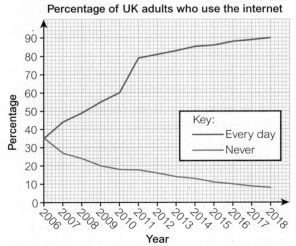

Percentage of UK adults who use the internet

Key:
—— Every day
—— Never

Source: ONS

5 A company prints hoodies. The company charges

- £50 to design the print
- £10 per hoodie for printing.

a Copy and complete this table to show the cost for different numbers of hoodies.

Number of hoodies	1	5	10	15	20
Cost (£)	60				

b Draw a graph for this data.

c Extend your line back to the vertical axis. What does this point on the axis represent?

d How many hoodies can you get for
  i £110   **ii** £175?

> **Q5b hint** Plot the values from the top line of the table on the horizontal axis.

e Problem-solving A judo club orders 17 hoodies. At what price should they sell them to their members, to cover the cost?

Key point A **linear graph** is a single straight line.

---

6 The graph shows how much it costs to hire a go-kart for different numbers of days.

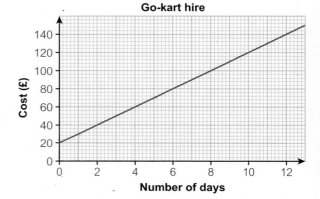

a How much does it cost to hire the go-kart for 2 days?

b How much does it cost to hire the go-kart for 5 days?

Reasoning The hire cost includes a basic fee and a cost per day.

c How much is the basic fee?

d How much is the cost per day?

7 Problem-solving / Reasoning
Dave does gardening and house maintenance. The graph shows his charges for jobs.

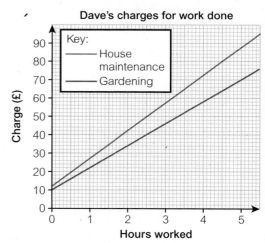

a How much does Dave charge for
  i 3 hours of gardening
  ii $4\frac{1}{2}$ hours of house maintenance?

b What do the values at 0 hours on the graph represent?

c How much does Dave charge per hour for gardening?

d How much does Dave charge per hour for house maintenance?

e How much does Dave charge for $7\frac{1}{4}$ hours of gardening?

f How much should Dave charge for $3\frac{1}{2}$ hours of house maintenance and 3 hours of gardening? Explain your answer.

8   **Reasoning**   The graph shows the
amount a plumber charges his customers.
   a How much does the plumber charge for
      i 1 hour's work
      ii $5\frac{3}{4}$ hours' work?
   b The plumber charges a call-out fee.
      i How much is the call-out fee?
      ii How many minutes of work are
         included in the call-out fee?
      iii How much does the plumber charge
         per hour after the initial call-out fee?

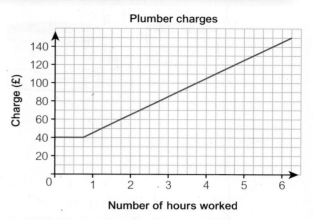

Plumber charges

9   **Reasoning**   The line graph shows the depth of water in Bethan's bath over time.
   Match each point on the graph, labelled 1–6, to one of the statements, labelled A–F.

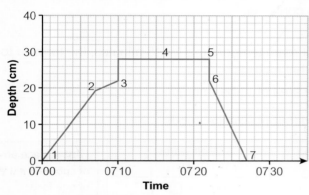

A	Bethan gets in the bath.
B	Bethan gets out of the bath.
C	Bethan turns both taps on.
D	Bethan takes out the plug.
E	Bethan turns off one of the taps.
F	Bethan is in the bath.

10   **Problem-solving / Reasoning**   In an experiment,
a 25 cm length of fishing line was tested to see
when it would break.
The graph shows the tension in the line as the
line was stretched.
   a How much tension was needed to stretch the
      line by 1 cm?
   b By how many centimetres was the fishing line
      stretched when the tension was 20 newtons?
   c How far was the fishing line stretched when it
      broke? Explain how you can tell this from the
      graph.

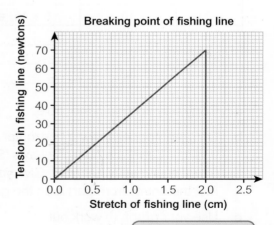

Breaking point of fishing line

> **Q10 hint** A newton
> is a unit of force.

11   **Problem-solving / Reasoning**   The graph shows how the depth of
water in this container changes over time, when water is poured in
at a steady rate.
   a Which bit of the container fills fastest,
      the wide part or the narrow part?
   b How can you tell when it is filling fastest
      from the graph?

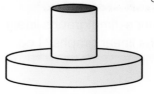

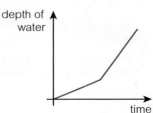

12 Problem-solving / Reasoning

   a Match each of the graphs to the correct container.

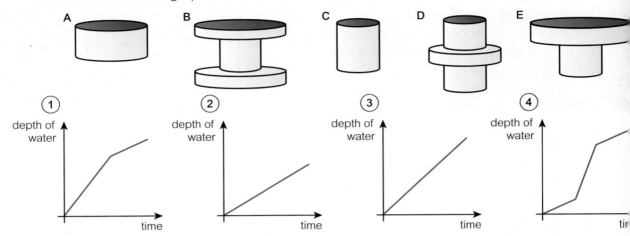

   b Which container has not been matched to a graph?
      Sketch a depth–time graph for this container.

Challenge   When an ice cube is left at room temperature for 15 minutes, the formula to work out the approximate amount of ice that melts is

      melt water (ml) = 0.0002 × surface area of cube (mm²)

The table shows the side lengths of five different size ice cubes.

Ice cube	Side length (mm)	Surface area (mm²)	Melt water (ml)
1	10	6 × 10² = ☐	0.0002 × ☐ = ☐
2	15	6 × 15² = ☐	
3	20		
4	25		
5	30		

Hint surface area of cube = 6 × area of one face

a Copy and complete the table.

b On graph paper, draw a horizontal axis from 0 to 5500 and a vertical axis from 0 to 1.1. Label the horizontal axis 'Surface area (mm²)' and the horizontal axis 'Volume of melt water (ml)'. Give your graph a title.
   Plot the points from part **a** on the graph.

c Use your graph to work out
     i the amount of melt water from a cube of side length 18 mm
    ii the side length of a cube that produced 0.87 ml of melt water.
       Give your answer correct to the nearest millimetre.

Reflect   Are distance–time graphs linear graphs? Look book at lesson 5.2 to check.
Are conversion graphs linear graphs? Look back at lesson 5.1 to check.

5.6 Curved graphs

- Draw and interpret curved graphs from a range of sources

Active Learn
Homework

1 Fluency What does a horizontal line represent on a distance–time graph?

2 A cat is tracked to show its movements during 24 hours.
   a What time did the cat leave in the morning?
   b Write a short description of the cat's movements during the day.

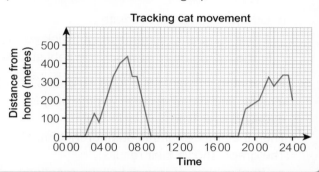

Tracking cat movement

Key point   You can **interpret** graphs from real-life situations by reading values and suggesting what they mean.

---

3 Water is poured into a kettle and heated. The graph shows the temperature of the water.
   a What is the starting temperature of the water?

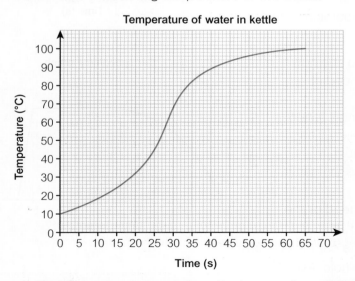

Temperature of water in kettle

   b By how many degrees does the temperature of the water increase
   i in the first 40 seconds
   ii in the last 20 seconds?
   c Suggest why the water stopped getting hotter after it reached 100 °C.

4 To activate a chemical light stick, you bend the tube and shake it.

At 15 °C the light stick gives off 2 lumens of light.

For each 10 °C increase in temperature the number of lumens doubles.

  a Copy and complete this table showing the temperature and the number of lumens.
(A lumen is a measure of the brightness of a light.)

Temperature (°C)	15	25	35	45
Number of lumens	2	4		

> **Q4b hint** It is easier to draw a curve with your hand 'inside' it and moving outwards. Turn your paper round so you can draw the curve comfortably.

  b Draw a graph to show the number of lumens at different temperatures.
Plot the points from your table, then join them with a smooth curve.

  c Use your graph to estimate

    i the number of lumens a light stick will give off at 30 °C

    ii the temperature at which the light stick will give off 10 lumens.

5 **Reasoning** Scientists added sulphuric acid to a metal and measured the volume of gas released over time.
Then they repeated this at different temperatures. The graph shows their results.

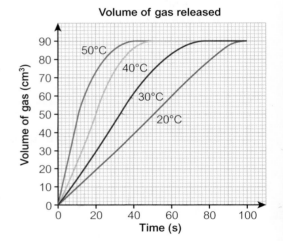

Volume of gas released

  a What volume of gas did all the reactions release?

  b At 20 °C, what volume of gas was released up to 60 seconds?

  c How long did it take to release this volume of gas at

    i 30 °C   **ii** 40 °C   **iii** 50 °C?

  d How does increasing the temperature affect the speed of the reaction?

6 **Reasoning** A car was tested to see how long it took to accelerate to a speed of 50 metres per second (m/s).
It was also tested to see how long it took to stop when the brakes were applied. The graph shows the results of the test.

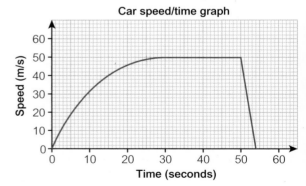

Car speed/time graph

  a How many seconds did it take the car to reach a speed of 50 m/s?

  b What was the approximate speed of the car at 10 seconds?

  c For how many seconds did the car travel at 50 m/s?

  d How many seconds did the whole test take?

  e How many seconds did it take for the car to stop once the brakes were applied?

7 **Reasoning** A fielder throws a cricket ball to a wicket keeper.
The graph shows the height of the cricket ball above the ground.

a How high is the ball above the ground after

   i 1 second

   ii 2.3 seconds?

b What was the highest point above the ground that the ball reached?

c Explain why the ball does not go below 1.6 m.

d After how many seconds is the ball 12 m above the ground?
   Explain why there are two answers to this question.

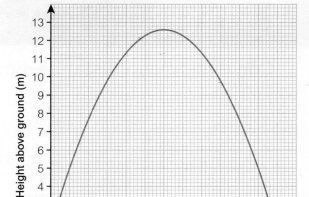

Height of cricket ball above the ground

Challenge The graph shows the growth rate of yeast at different temperatures.

a At what temperature does yeast start growing?

b At what temperatures does yeast reach 40% growth rate?

c Describe what happens to the growth rate of the yeast at

   i 28°C   ii 35°C

d Is the amount of yeast increasing or decreasing when the graph shows a decrease in the percentage growth rate?

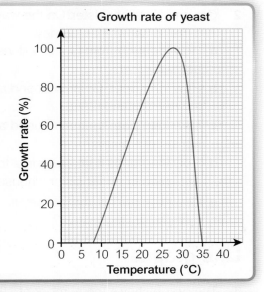

Growth rate of yeast

Reflect Look at the curved graphs from this lesson and the graphs from previous lessons.
Write down two things that are the **same** for linear and curved graphs.
Write down two things that are **different** for linear and curved graphs.

5 Check up

Conversion and distance–time graphs

1 One teaspoon has a capacity of 5 ml.

a Copy and complete this table.

Teaspoons	0	1	2	5
ml	0			

b Copy these axes onto graph paper.

c Plot the points from the table on the graph and join them with a straight line.

d Use your conversion graph to complete these conversions.

    i 3.5 teaspoons = ☐ ml

    ii 21 ml = ☐ teaspoons

Conversion of teaspoons to millilitres

2 Gemma visits her sister. On the way, she stops at a petrol station. The graph shows her journey.

a How far away from Gemma does her sister live?

b How long does Gemma spend at the petrol station?

c How long does Gemma spend at her sister's house?

d How long does it take Gemma to get home from her sister's house?

e On which part of the journey is Gemma driving fastest?

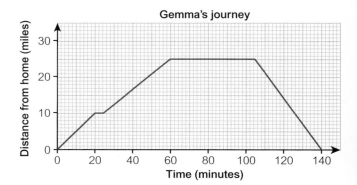

Gemma's journey

Line graphs

3 The graph shows the number of UK airline passengers, in millions, every 2 years between 2007 and 2017.

a How many airline passengers were there in 2011?

b In which years were there approximately 230 million passengers?

c Estimate the number of airline passengers in 2010.

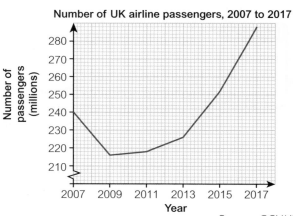

Number of UK airline passengers, 2007 to 2017

Source: GOV.UK

4 The graph shows the percentage of seats occupied on UK airline flights.

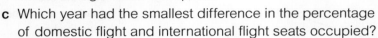

UK airline seat occupancy

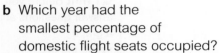

a Amanda says, 'In 2009, 69% of domestic flight seats were occupied.'
Is she correct? Explain your answer.

b Which year had the smallest percentage of domestic flight seats occupied?

c Which year had the smallest difference in the percentage of domestic flight and international flight seats occupied?

d Describe the trend in the percentage of international flight seats occupied.

Key
— International flights
— Domestic flights

5 A vet charges a £40 call-out fee plus £20 per quarter hour.

Length of call out (hours)	0	$\frac{1}{2}$	1	2	3
Total cost (£)	40				

a Copy and complete this table showing the total cost for different call-out times.

b Draw a graph to show the total cost of a call out for up to 3 hours.
Plot 'Length of call out (hours)' on the horizontal axis and 'Total cost (£)' on the vertical axis.

c Use your graph to work out the total cost of a call out that lasts $2\frac{3}{4}$ hours.

Curved graphs

6 The graph shows the average length of baby boys from 0 to 24 months.

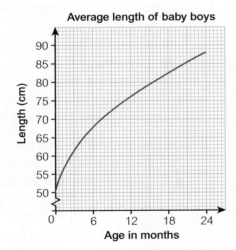

Average length of baby boys

a What is the average length of a baby boy aged 3 months?

b At what age does an average baby boy reach 76 cm?

c Daniel is 15 months and has a length of 78 cm.
Is he longer or shorter than average?

d During which 6-month period does a baby boy grow fastest:
0–6, 6–12, 12–18 or 18–24 months?
Explain how you can tell this from the graph.

Challenge Sketch a distance–time graph from the time you left home this morning to arriving at your first lesson. Plot 'Time' on the horizontal axis and 'Distance travelled (km)' on the vertical axis.

Reflect How sure are you of your answers? Were you mostly

:(**Just guessing** :| **Feeling doubtful** :) **Confident**

What next? Use your results to decide whether to strengthen or extend your learning.

5 Strengthen

Conversion and distance–time graphs

1 The conversion graph shows the approximate conversion of feet to metres.

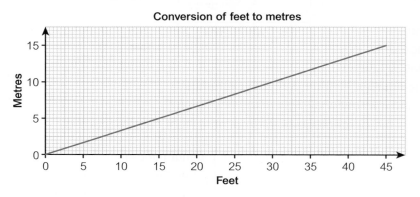

Conversion of feet to metres

Q1 hint Before you answer questions about a graph
• read the title
• read the axes labels
• read the key
• look at the axes scales.

a Look at the scale on each axis.

   i How many feet does one small square represent?

   ii How many metres does one small square represent?

Q1 hint The plural of foot is feet.

Q1a i hint

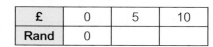

÷10 (10 small squares = 5 feet → 1 small square = ☐ foot) ÷10

b Copy and complete these conversions.
The symbol '≈' means 'is approximately equal to'.

   i 3 feet ≈ ☐ metre

   ii 25 feet ≈ ☐ metres

   iii 12 metres ≈ ☐ feet

   iv 4.5 metres ≈ ☐ feet

c The highest value on the graph is 45 feet.
Use the graph to convert 75 feet into metres.

Q1c hint
45 feet + ☐ feet = 75 feet
☐ m + ☐ m = ☐ m

2 On one day the conversion rate from GB pounds to South African rand was £1 = 15 rand.

a Copy and complete this table of values.

£	0	5	10
Rand	0		

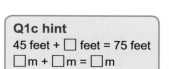

×5 (£1 = 15 rand) ×5
×☐ (£5 = ☐ rand
☐ £10 = ☐ rand) ×☐

b On graph paper draw a horizontal axis from £0 to £10 and a vertical axis from 0 rand to 150 rand.
Plot the points from the table on the graph.
Join them with a straight line.

c Use your conversion graph to complete these conversions.

   i £4 = ☐ rand   **ii** 120 rand = £ ☐

Q2b hint

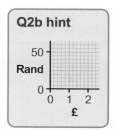

50 Rand 0 | 0 1 2 £

3 Peter goes to the shop by car.
The graph shows his journey.

  a How can you tell from the graph when Peter is at the shop?

  b How long does it take Peter to get from home to the shop?

  c When Peter is at the shop, his distance from home stays the same.
  How many minutes is Peter at the shop?

  d How long does it take Peter to get home from the shop?

  e Which part of the journey was quicker, home to shop or shop to home?

  f **Reasoning** Peter leaves home at 10 am. At what time does he get home?

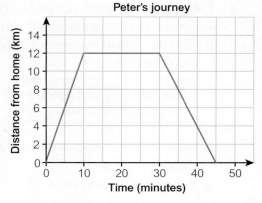

Peter's journey

4 This is a description of Nasim's journey on Saturday.
He sets off from home at 10 am.
He drives 40 miles in one hour. He stops for half an hour at a café.
He then drives 20 more miles.
He arrives at his destination at 12.45 pm. He stays for 90 minutes.
Then he drives straight home in $1\frac{1}{2}$ hours.

  a Copy these axes. Draw a distance–time graph to show Nasim's journey.

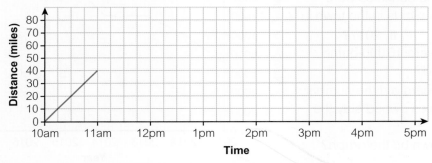

  b How many miles did Nasim drive altogether?

  c At what time did he arrive home?

Line graphs

1 The graph shows the number of views a video got each day.

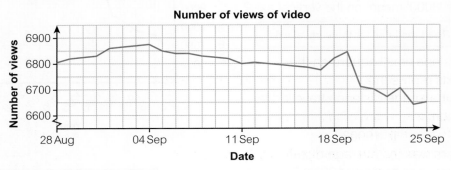

Q1 hint Before you answer questions about a graph
  • read the title
  • read the axes labels
  • read the key
  • look at the axes scales.

  a When did the video have the most views?

  b When did the video have the least views?

  c How many views did the video get on its first day?

2 The graph shows the number of cars sold by a car dealer each week for 10 weeks.

a Between which two weeks is the biggest increase in sales?

Car sales

> **Q2a hint** Look for the steepest line between two points.

b Between which two weeks is the biggest decrease in sales?

c What happened in week 5?

3 The line graph shows the total number of game consoles owned by households in a UK town.

a Look at the scale on each axis. Copy and complete these statements.

   i Ten small squares on the horizontal axis represent ☐ year.

   ii One small square on the vertical axis represents ☐ game consoles.

b How many game consoles were owned by households in the town in

   i 2012   **ii** 2017?

c In which year were 16 000 game consoles owned?

d During which years did the number of game consoles owned stay the same? How is this shown on the graph?

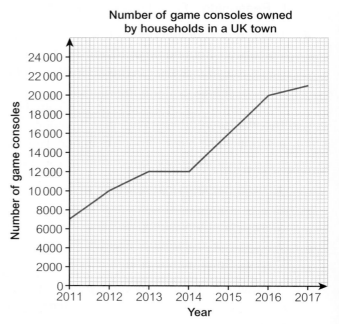

Number of game consoles owned by households in a UK town

4 The line graph shows the average number of kilometres travelled by car per person in the UK.

a Look at the scale on each axis.

   i How many squares on the horizontal axis represent one year?

   ii What does '8000' mean, on the vertical axis?

> **Q4a ii hint** Read the label for the vertical axis.

   iii What does one small square on the vertical axis represent?

b What was the average distance travelled by car per person in

   i 1980   **ii** 1990?

c In which years was the average distance travelled by car per person 7100 km?

d Which year had the highest average distance travelled by car per person?

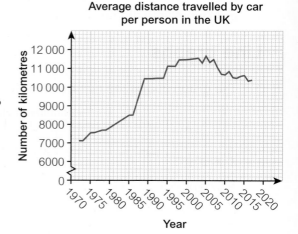

Average distance travelled by car per person in the UK

> **Q4d hint** In which year did the graph reach its highest point?

5 The graph shows the average maximum daytime and minimum night-time temperatures in Keswick, Cumbria.

a What does S stand for on the horizontal axis?

b Which line, A or B, represents the maximum temperatures?

c Which month had the highest maximum temperature?

d Which months had the lowest minimum temperature?

e In October, what was the average
  i maximum temperature
  ii minimum temperature?

f In which month was the smallest difference between the maximum and minimum temperatures?

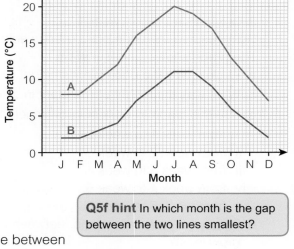
Maximum and minimum temperatures in Keswick

Q5f hint In which month is the gap between the two lines smallest?

6 The graph shows the percentage of adults in the UK who use internet shopping.

a What percentage of adults used internet shopping in 2010?

b By how many percentage points did the number of adults using internet shopping increase between 2010 and 2012?

c Between which two years was the biggest increase in internet shopping?

d Describe the trend in the percentage of adults in the UK who use internet shopping. Use the words 'increasing' or 'decreasing'.

e Use the graph to predict the percentage of adults in the UK who used internet shopping in 2015.

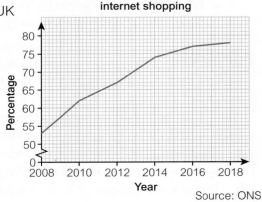
Percentage of UK adults who use internet shopping

Source: ONS

Q6b hint increase = 2012 percentage − 2010 percentage

7 A beach shop hires out kayaks. They charge £6 per half hour.

a Copy and complete this table showing the cost of hiring a kayak.

Rental time (hours)	0	$\frac{1}{2}$	1	4
Cost (£)	0			

Q7a hint
×2 ($\frac{1}{2}$ hour = £6 / 1 hour = £☐) ×2

b Draw a graph to show the cost of renting a kayak for up to 4 hours. Plot 'Rental time (hours)' on the horizontal axis, from 0 to 4 hours. Plot 'Cost (£)' on the vertical axis, from 0 to £50. Add a title.

c Use your graph to work out the cost of renting a kayak for
  i 3 hours
  ii $1\frac{1}{2}$ hours.

Curved graphs

1 Jack plants a bean in week 1.
He measures the bean plant every week.
The graph shows his results.

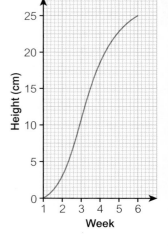

Height of bean plant

a Explain why the bean plant's height was 0 at the start.

b What was the height of the plant in week 4?

c Use the graph to work out how much the plant grew

  i from week 1 to week 2

  ii from week 2 to week 3

  iii from week 3 to week 4

  iv from week 4 to week 5

  v from week 5 to week 6.

d From your answer to part **c**, between which two weeks did it grow least?
How can you tell this from the graph?

e From your answer to part **c**, between which two weeks did it grow most?
How can you tell this from the graph?

Challenge The graph shows the number of T-shirts sold by a shop during the first 6 months of the year.
Write 'True' or 'False' for each statement.
Use readings from the graph to explain.

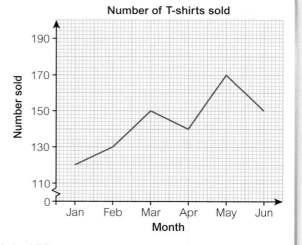

Number of T-shirts sold

a The number of T-shirts sold in February was double the number sold in January.

b The highest number of T-shirts sold was in May.

c The greatest increase in sales was between February and March.

d The greatest decrease in sales was between May and June.

e The mean number of T-shirts sold per month is 150.

Reflect Which do you find harder, reading from graphs or drawing graphs?
What makes it harder?
Write one thing about reading graphs and one thing about drawing graphs you think you need more practice on.

5 Extend

1   **Problem-solving**   The graphs show the conversion of ounces to grams and the cost of gold on a particular day.

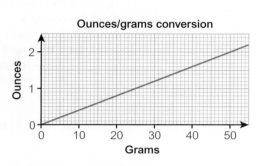

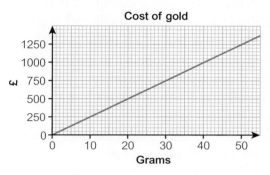

   a   How much does 1.2 ounces of gold cost?

   b   A piece of gold costs £1050. What does it weigh in ounces?

2   Sayeed and Chan take part in a triathlon competition.
    They have to swim, then cycle, then run. The graph shows their results.

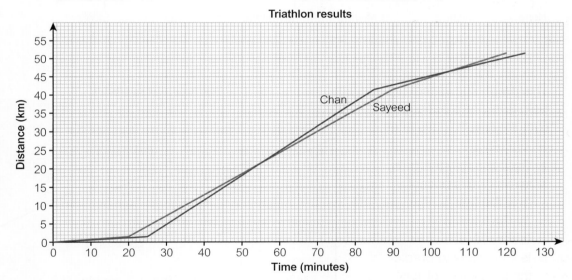

   a   i   Who is in the lead after the swim?   ii   Who is in the lead after the cycle?
      iii   Who wins the triathlon?
   b   Copy the table. Fill in the distances for swim, cycle and run.
   c   Fill in the times for Sayeed and Chan.

	Distance (km)	Sayeed's time (minutes)	Chan's time (minutes)
Swim			
Cycle			
Run			
Total			

3 Problem-solving A taxi firm charges according to the number of minutes a journey takes. The table shows their charges for their three different tariffs.

Tariff 1	Daytime (6 am–8 pm)	£2.40 plus 85p per minute
Tariff 2	Evening (8 pm–10 pm)	£2.40 plus £1 per minute
Tariff 3	Night-time (10 pm–6 am)	£2.40 plus £1.15 per minute

a Draw a line graph showing the cost of taxi journeys up to 20 minutes long. Use a different line for each tariff.

b What is the cost of a 5-minute journey at 2.30 pm?

c How much cheaper is it to make a 12-minute journey at 9.45 pm than at 10.15 pm?

A different taxi firm charges £15 for any daytime journey up to 20 minutes long.

d Use your graph to work out after how many minutes it is cheaper to use the second taxi firm than the first taxi firm.

> **Q3a hint** Use the table to work out the cost of a 20-minute journey on each tariff. The line for each tariff will start at (0 minutes, £2.40).

4 Reasoning In hospital, patients are asked to describe their pain on a scale of 0 to 10. Their answers are recorded, and staff can then decide what pain relief is needed. This is the pain scale used.

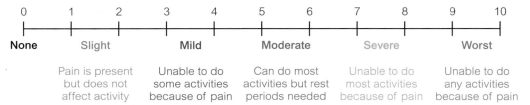

This graph shows the pain levels of a patient over the first 10 days after an operation.

a Describe fully the pain levels of this patient over the first 10 days after the operation.

b Is it possible to predict the pain levels of this patient for days 11 and 12? Explain your answer.

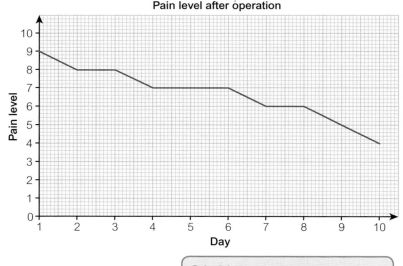

> **Q4a hint** Include words and numbers from the pain scale above.

Reflect Look again at Q4. Why might doctors want to graph a patient's pain?
Look again at Q2. Why might athletes want to graph their performance?

5 Unit test

1 The graph shows the number of CD players owned by households in the UK, every 2 years from 2000 to 2012.

   a How many CD players were owned by households in the UK in
     i 2002   **ii** 2008?

   b In which year did CD player ownership peak?

   c Estimate the number of CD players owned by households in the UK in 2011.

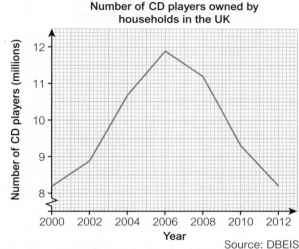

Number of CD players owned by households in the UK

Source: DBEIS

2 **Reasoning** The table shows the average temperature inside a centrally heated home, every 10 years from 1970 to 2010.

Year	1970	1980	1990	2000	2010
Inside temperature (°C)	13.7	14.4	16.7	18.0	16.9

Source: DBEIS

   a Copy the axes and draw a line graph of this data.

   b Describe the trend in the average temperature inside a centrally heated home.

3 On one day the conversion rate from GB £ to Thai baht was £1 = 50 baht.

   a Copy and complete this table of values.

£	0	5	10
Baht	0		

   b On graph paper draw a horizontal axis from £0 to £10 and a vertical axis from 0 baht to 500 baht.
     Plot the points from the table. Join them with a straight line.

   c Use your conversion graph to complete these conversions.
     i £3.50 = ☐ baht   **ii** 460 baht = £☐

4 On Saturday, Raj walks from home to visit a friend.
Then he walks from his friend's house to collect his bike from the repair shop.
He then cycles directly home.
The graph shows Raj's journey.

   a At what time does Raj arrive at his friend's house?

   b How long does he stay at his friend's house?

   c How far does he walk from his friend's house to the repair shop?

   d On which part of the journey is Raj travelling fastest?

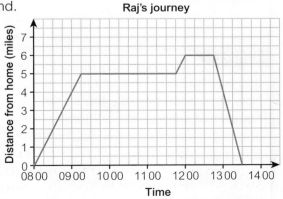

Raj's journey

5 The graph shows the average mass of a kitten up to 15 weeks old.

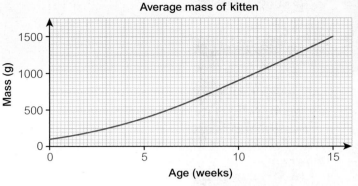

Average mass of kitten

  a What is the average mass of a kitten aged 7 weeks?

  b At what age does an average kitten reach a mass of 1 kg?

  c Sham has a kitten that is 9 weeks old. It has a mass of 750 g.
  Is its mass more or less than average?

  d During which 5-week period does a kitten's mass increase fastest?
  Explain how you can tell this from the graph.

6 A shop owner buys 250 pens.
He sells 40 on Monday, 30 on Tuesday, 35 on Wednesday, 45 on Thursday, 25 on Friday, and 40 on Saturday.

  a Draw a line graph of the number of pens in stock during the week.

  b The shop is closed on Sunday. The shop owner buys 100 more pens.
  How many pens are now in stock?

  c Has the shop owner bought enough pens?
  Explain your answer.

7 Annie goes to a meeting by car. The meeting is 20 km from her home.
She drives there in $\frac{1}{2}$ hour. Her drive home takes $\frac{1}{4}$ hour.
She gets home at 1045.

  a Draw a distance–time graph for Annie's journey.

  b At what time does the meeting start, and at what time does it end?

Challenge The graph shows the height above the ground of a rollercoaster over time.

Write a description of the ride for a marketing brochure. You can include in your description the different sections of the ride, e.g. fastest section, highest section, scariest section, steepest section …

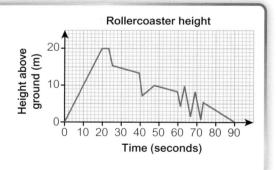

Rollercoaster height

Reflect Look carefully at the numbers and words used in this unit test.
Now copy and complete this spider diagram to show all the different areas of mathematics that you had to use in each question.

Write a sentence about how much mathematics you know and can do.

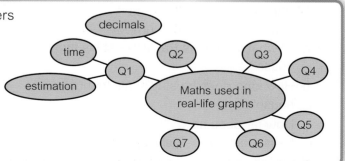

6 Decimals and ratio

6.1 Ordering decimals and rounding

- Round decimals to 2 or 3 decimal places
- Round numbers to a given number of significant figures
- Round numbers to an appropriate degree of accuracy
- Order decimals of any size, including positive and negative decimals

Active Learn
Homework

Warm up

1 **Fluency** Read these numbers aloud.
   a 7 602 385   b 17 400 039

2 a What is the value of the 7 in these numbers?
      i 5.731   ii 5.97   iii 5.827
   b Are the numbers in part **a** written in ascending order, descending order, or neither?
   c Round the numbers in part **a** to 1 decimal place (1 d.p.).

3 What is the place value of the first non-zero digit in these numbers?
   a 0.321   b 0.002   c 0.013

Key point

A number rounded to **2 decimal places** (2 d.p.) has two digits after the decimal point.
A number rounded to **3 decimal places** (3 d.p.) has three digits after the decimal point.

4 Which of these numbers are rounded to
   a 1 decimal place   b 2 decimal places   c 3 decimal places?
      Write the number and then '(1 d.p.)', '(2 d.p.)' or '(3 d.p.)'.
      7.63   12.041   37.3   4.011   14.72   9.00

Key point

For rounding to **2 decimal places**, look at the
thousandths (the third decimal place).
   • 5 thousandths and above, round up.
   • 4 thousandths and below, round down.

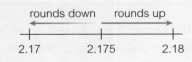

rounds down   rounds up

2.17   2.175   2.18

5 Round each number to 2 decimal places.
   a 2.176   b 7.489
   c 5.083   d 6.199
   e 45.157   f 23.007
   g 0.8631   h 9.002

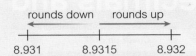
6   Round each number to
     i 2 decimal places   **ii** 3 decimal places.
     a 8.9324   **b** 69.0852   **c** 72.7576   **d** 3.2567
     e 85.8008   **f** 29.7965   **g** 5.0871   **h** 34.0609

7   **Problem-solving / Reasoning**   In a restaurant the tips are divided equally between the workers. One evening the tips total £55 and there are 6 workers.
     The manager uses a calculator to work out how much each worker receives:

     9.16666667

     a How much should each worker receive?
     b Did you round up or down? Explain.

8   **Problem-solving / Reasoning**   Work out the length of one side of a square with perimeter
     a 10 cm   **b** 24.3 cm   **c** 13.65 m
     Round your answers to an appropriate degree of accuracy.

9   The table shows the populations of ten capital cities in Europe.
     Write each population as a decimal number of millions to 1 decimal place.

City	Population		City	Population
Moscow	11 541 000		Paris	2 268 265
London	8 174 100		Budapest	1 728 718
Berlin	3 520 000		Vienna	1 552 789
Madrid	3 233 527		Prague	1 227 332
Rome	2 792 508		Dublin	1 045 769

You can round numbers to a certain number of **significant figures (s.f.)**.
The first significant figure is the one with the highest place value.
It is the first non-zero digit in the number, counting from the left.

Round these numbers to the number of significant figures shown.

a 34.069 (4 s.f.)

34.07 ————————————— The 4th significant digit is 6. The 5th significant digit is 9, so round up.

b 0.046 12 (3 s.f.)

0.0461 ————————————— The 3rd significant digit is 1. The 4th significant digit is 2, so round down.

c 12 575 (2 s.f.)

13 000 ————————————— The 2nd significant digit is 2. The 3rd significant digit is 5, so round up. Write zeros in the ones, tens and hundreds columns to keep the place values of the 1 and 3.

10 Round each number to 1 significant figure.

a 328   **b** 5973

c 21 436   **d** 0.6372

Q10a hint ③28
3 is the 1st significant figure.
2 is the 2nd significant figure, so round down.

11 Round each number to the number of significant figures shown.

a 60.247 (4 s.f.)   **b** 0.005 72 (1 s.f.)   **c** 364 295 (2 s.f.)   **d** 3.1415 (3 s.f.)

12 a Round each number to 2 significant figures.

  i 2.176   **ii** 7.489   **iii** 5.083   **iv** 6.199

  v 45.157   **vi** 23.007   **vii** 0.8631   **viii** 9.002

b Reasoning Do you always, never or sometimes get the same answer when rounding to 2 significant figures and 2 decimal places?

When comparing the size of decimals

- first compare the whole number parts
- then, if they are equal, compare tenths
- then, if they are equal, compare hundredths
- continue like this for thousandths, ten thousandths, hundred thousandths ...

T	O	.	$\frac{1}{10}$	$\frac{1}{100}$	$\frac{1}{1000}$	$\frac{1}{10\,000}$	$\frac{1}{100\,000}$	$\frac{1}{1\,000\,000}$
			tenths	hundredths	thousandths	ten thousandths	hundred thousandths	millionths

13 Copy and complete. Write < or > between each pair of numbers.

a 4.3507 ☐ 4.5307   **b** 0.2453 ☐ 0.2435   **c** 9.6271 ☐ 9.671

d 21.029 ☐ 21.021 11   **e** 6.321 08 ☐ 6.321 072

14 Write each set of decimal numbers in descending order.

   a 1.093, 0.086 66, 1.232, 0.200 71, 0.1258

   b 4.227, 4.051, 4.23, 4.735, 3.2924

   c 0.7113, 0.0732, 7.001, 0.749, 7.0932

   d 24.4570, 25.645, 22.961, 24.833, 25.62

15 Write < or > between each pair of numbers.

   a −0.2 ☐ −0.3

   b −0.3 ☐ −0.29

   c −2.39 ☐ −2.9

   d −9.3 ☐ −9.23

Q15 hint

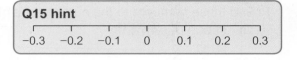

16 Write each list of numbers in ascending order.

   a −4.2, 2.6, −4.6, 2.46

   b 10.5, −10.3, 10.35, −10.53, −10.5

   c −0.07, 0.07, 0.7, −0.77, −0.7

   d −0.125, −0.845, −0.149, −0.135, −0.0122

   e 0.033, −0.0309, −0.0342, −0.0325, 0.0324

   f −5.055, 5.0505, −5.05, 5.0005, −5.5005

Q16 hint Order the negative decimals in ascending order first. Then order the positive decimals in ascending order.

Challenge

Write two sets of numbers in descending order, so that

a 0.112, ☐ , ☐ , ☐ , −0.112

   ↑ number with 2 decimal places

   ↑ number with 3 decimal places

   ↑ number with 3 significant figures

b −6.007, ☐ , ☐ , ☐ , −6.7

   ↑ number with 2 decimal places

   ↑ number with 2 significant figures

   ↑ number with 3 decimal places

Reflect   In this lesson you have been doing lots of work with decimals.

Imagine someone had never seen a decimal point before.

How would you define it?

How would you describe what it does?

Write a description in your own words.

Compare your description with others in your class.

6.2 Place value calculations

*Active*Learn
Homework

- Multiply any number by 0.1 and 0.01
- Multiply larger numbers
- Multiply decimals with up to and including 2 decimal places

Warm up

1 Fluency Name each shape. Work out its area.

a

6 cm
9 cm

b

9 cm
6 cm

c

6 cm   9 cm

2 Copy and complete the place value table and the calculations.

	Th	H	T	O	.	$\frac{1}{10}$	$\frac{1}{100}$	$\frac{1}{1000}$
a 1 ÷ 10 =								
b 1 ÷ ☐ =				0	.	0	1	
c 1 ÷ 10 ÷ 10 =								
d 1 ÷ 10 ÷ 100 =								
e 34 ÷ ☐ =				3	.	4		
f 623 ÷ ☐ =				6	.	2	3	
g 3461 ÷ 1000 =								

3 Work out these multiplications.
  a 0.1 × 6   **b** 0.4 × 6   **c** 0.4 × 0.6   **d** 0.4 × 1.2

4 Work out these multiplications.

  a   445   **b**   53   **c**   32   **d**   267
       × 3   × 28   × 87   × 15
      ─────   ─────   ─────   ─────

                         ─────   ─────   ─────

5 a Copy and complete the patterns.
   i 29 × 10 = ☐   **ii** 107 × 10 = ☐
      29 × 1 = ☐   107 × 1 = ☐
      29 × 0.1 = ☐   107 × 0.1 = ☐
      29 × 0.01 = ☐   107 × 0.01 = ☐

> **Q5a i hint**
>
> 29 × 1 = ☐   29 × 1 = ☐
>   ÷10 ↓   ↓ ÷10   ÷100 ↓   ↓ ÷100
> 29 × ☐ = ☐   29 × ☐ = ☐

b Reasoning What division calculation is equivalent to
   i × 0.1   **ii** × 0.01?

6 Work out these multiplications.

   a 8.6 × 0.1   **b** 11.6 × 0.1   **c** 0.53 × 0.1

   d 3621 × 0.01   **e** 4568 × 0.01   **f** 88.6 × 0.01

   g 11.6 × 0.01   **h** 534 × 0.01   **i** 683 × 0.01

7 Work out these calculations. The first one is started for you.

   a 0.3 × 0.07 = 3 ÷ 10 × 7 ÷ 100

                    = 3 × 7 ÷ 10 ÷ 100

                    = □ ÷ 1000

                    = □

   b 0.8 × 0.03   **c** 0.06 × 0.2   **d** 0.09 × 0.8

8 Copy and complete this long multiplication.

```
    137
  × 245
          ← 137 × 5
          ← 137 × 40
          ← 137 × 200
  _____
  _____  ← Add these together
```

9 Work out these multiplications.

   a 237 × 151   **b** 329 × 238   **c** 578 × 312   **d** 923 × 455

Q9a hint

```
   237
 × 151
```

10 **Problem-solving** A 747 plane holds 416 passengers.
There are 536 of these planes in service.
All of them are flying on a given day.
How many passengers can they carry in total?

Q10 hint Read the question carefully. Make sure you multiply the correct numbers.

11 Use the multiplication facts given to work out the answers.

   a   12 × 17 = 204   Work out 1.2 × 1.7

   b   34 × 89 = 3026   Work out 3.4 × 8.9

   c   23 × 43 = 989   Work out 2.3 × 4.3

Q11 hint

```
12  ×  17  = 204
 ↓÷10   ↓÷10   ↓÷100
1.2  ×  1.7  = □
```

Worked example

Work out 2.6 × 3.2

Estimate: 3 × 3 = 9

```
    2 6
  ×  3 2
    5 2
+ 7 8 0
  8 3 2
```
            — Use long multiplication to work out 26 × 32

   26 × 32 = 832   — Compare the size of the numbers in the standard method to the numbers in the calculation.

  ÷10 ↓ ÷10 ↓   ÷100 ↓

  2.6 × 3.2 = 8.32

8.32 ≈ 9   — Use your estimate to check your answer.

12 Estimate then work out these multiplications.

    a 3.7 × 2.2   **b** 2.5 × 4.3

    c 9.3 × 8.4   **d** 7.22 × 3.1

    e 3.46 × 8.9   **f** 4.04 × 8.2

    g 4.1 × 2.13   **h** 19.7 × 8.25

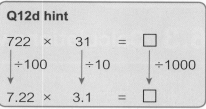

Q12d hint

722 × 31 = ☐
÷100 ÷10 ÷1000
7.22 × 3.1 = ☐

13 a For each part in Q12, count the number of digits
after the decimal point in both numbers in the question.
Do the same for the answer. What do you notice?

    b Reasoning Use your answer to part **a** to help you work out 3.26 × 5.12.

14 Problem-solving A car can travel 13.8 kilometres on 1 litre of petrol.
How far can it travel on 8.8 litres of petrol?

15 Use the multiplication facts given to work out the answers.

    a | 36 × 14 = 504 | Work out 3.6 × 0.14

    b | 108 × 4 = 432 | Work out 10.8 × 0.04

    c | 36 × 72 = 2592 | Work out 0.36 × 7.2

    d | 894 × 32 = 28 608 | Work out 8.94 × 0.32

16 Work out the area of each shape.

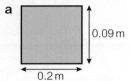
a 0.09 m, 0.2 m

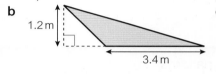
b 1.2 m, 3.4 m

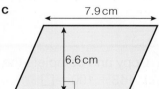
c 7.9 cm, 6.6 cm

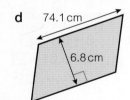
d 74.1 cm, 6.8 cm

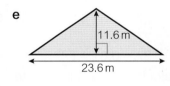
e 11.6 m, 23.6 m

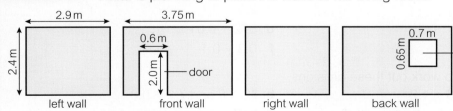
Reflect   Look back at Q13. At the end of this question you discovered a
mathematical 'rule'.
The rule tells you where to put the decimal point in the answer when multiplying decimals.
Write the 'rule' in your own words.
Does the rule still work for 2.5 × 4.2?

6.3 Calculations with decimals

Active Learn
Homework

- Divide by 0.1 and 0.01
- Multiply and divide by decimals
- Solve problems involving decimals and all four operations

Warm up

1 Fluency Work out these calculations.
  a 63 ÷ 7   **b** 56.2 × 10   **c** 9 ÷ 100   **d** 37 ÷ 10   **e** 423 ÷ 100

2 Work out these calculations.
  a 26.3 + 53 082 + 0.617   **b** 73.8 − 46.93 − 12.06
  c 4.83 × 2.5   **d** 2.45 × 3.32

3 Use a written method to calculate these divisions.

  a 3)294   **b** 13)412.1   **c** 23)943

> **Q3b hint**
> $$\begin{array}{r} 3 \\ 13\overline{)412.1} \\ -\underline{39} \\ 3 \end{array}$$

4 **a** Copy and complete the patterns.
      i 143 ÷ 100 = ☐   **ii** 27 ÷ 100 = ☐   **iii** 8 ÷ 100 = ☐
         143 ÷ 10 = ☐   27 ÷ 10 = ☐   8 ÷ 10 = ☐
         143 ÷ 1 = ☐   27 ÷ 1 = ☐   8 ÷ 1 = ☐
         143 ÷ 0.1 = ☐   27 ÷ 0.1 = ☐   8 ÷ 0.1 = ☐
         143 ÷ 0.01 = ☐   27 ÷ 0.01 = ☐   8 ÷ 0.01 = ☐

  b Reasoning What multiplication calculation is equivalent to
      i ÷ 0.1   **ii** ÷ 0.01?

5 Work out these divisions.
  a 15 ÷ 0.1   **b** 2.6 ÷ 0.1
  c 85.3 ÷ 0.01   **d** 572 ÷ 0.01
  e 7.6 ÷ 0.01   **f** 0.3 ÷ 0.1

6 Use a calculator to work out these divisions.
  a 36 ÷ 12 and 3.6 ÷ 1.2   **b** 72 ÷ 8 and 7.2 ÷ 0.8
  c 484 ÷ 4 and 4.84 ÷ 0.04   **d** 625 ÷ 25 and 6.25 ÷ 0.25

7 Reasoning What do you notice about your answers to Q6?
How does this help you work out 8.1 ÷ 0.9 and 0.64 ÷ 0.08 without a calculator?

8 Work out these divisions.
  a 6.3 ÷ 0.7   **b** 4.8 ÷ 0.6
  c 12.1 ÷ 1.1   **d** 0.28 ÷ 0.07
  e 0.9 ÷ 0.3   **f** 14.4 ÷ 1.2

9 **Reasoning**

    a Work out $0.8 \div 0.2$.

    b Would you expect $0.8 \div 0.02$ to be larger or smaller than your answer to part **a**? Explain.

    c Predict the answer to $0.8 \div 0.02$.

    d Check your answer on a calculator.

10 Work out these divisions.

    a $3.5 \div 0.07$ **b** $5.6 \div 0.08$ **c** $8.4 \div 0.12$ **d** $12.1 \div 0.11$

> **Key point**   To divide by a decimal, multiply both numbers by a power of 10 (10, 100, …) until you have a whole number to divide by. Then work out the division.

Worked example

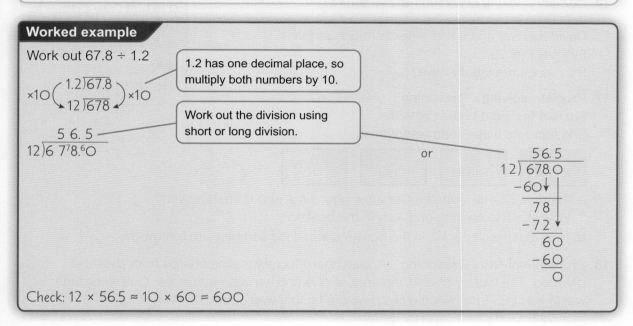

Work out $67.8 \div 1.2$

1.2 has one decimal place, so multiply both numbers by 10.

Work out the division using short or long division.

Check: $12 \times 56.5 \approx 10 \times 60 = 600$

11 Work these out using a written method.

    a $18.9 \div 0.9$ **b** $25.2 \div 0.7$ **c** $39 \div 0.75$ **d** $124.6 \div 0.35$

    e $348 \div 2.4$ **f** $43.32 \div 0.3$ **g** $82.3 \div 6.25$

12 Work these out using a written method.
    Give your answers to 1 decimal place.

    a $367 \div 2.4$ **b** $0.556 \div 3.6$ **c** $72.5 \div 0.7$

> **Q12 hint** You will need to work out the second decimal place and then round.

13 **Problem-solving** A scientist has 27.9 g of substance X.
    He needs to divide it into samples for testing.
    Each testing dish holds 2.4 g.
    How many testing dishes does the scientist need?

14 Estimate then work out these multiplications.

    a 2.724×3.25

    b 4.59×2.764

    c 8.91×5.126

    d 7.261×9.28

    e 6.903×0.425

> **Q14a hint**
> $$\begin{array}{r} 2724 \\ \times\ \ 325 \\ \hline \\ \hline \end{array}$$
> Count the number of digits after the decimal point in both numbers in the decimal calculation.

15 a Work out the volume of this cuboid.

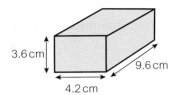

3.6 cm
9.6 cm
4.2 cm

b Problem-solving Another cuboid has a volume of 35.52 m³. Its length is 4 m and its width is 2.4 m. What is its height?

Q15b hint Make a sketch.

16 Problem-solving / Reasoning Sally has £300.05 more than David.
David has two and a half times as much as Eve.
Eve has £98.70.
How much does Sally have?

Q16 hint Draw a picture to help you solve problems.
Sally:
David:
Eve:

17 Problem-solving / Reasoning
Suzie is testing a beaker of water.
She removes these samples for analysis.

A 2.13 ml   B 0.005 ml   C 3.075 ml   D 0.321 ml

a There is 32.4 ml in the beaker after samples A and B are removed.
How much water was originally in the beaker?
b How much water is left in the beaker after all the samples are removed?

18 Problem-solving / Reasoning A skateboard factory makes boards from sheets of plywood. The factory checks the area of plywood wasted each week. One week the total waste was 28.75 m² over the five days the factory was open.

Day	Waste
Monday	4.35 m²
Wednesday	5.4 m²
Thursday	6.14 m²

a How much plywood was wasted on Tuesday and Friday?
On Friday 2.4 m² more plywood was wasted than on Tuesday.
b How much was wasted on Tuesday?

Challenge

a What happens when you divide a positive number by a number between 0 and 1?
b What happens when you multiply a positive number by a number between 0 and 1?
c Write your own 'What happens when …?' question and answer it.

Hint
a Look back at some of the calculations you did in Q8.
b Look back at some of the calculations you did in lesson 6.2.

Reflect What is the same and what is different when dividing an integer by an integer compared with dividing a decimal by a decimal?

157

6.4 Ratio and proportion with decimals

- Divide a quantity into three or more parts in a given ratio
- Use ratios involving decimals
- Solve ratio and proportion problems
- Use unit ratios

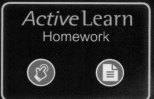

Active Learn
Homework

Warm up

1 Fluency

a Which of these ratios are equivalent to 2 : 3?

$3 : 5$ $6 : 9$ $5 : 16$ $14 : 21$ $12 : 19$ $30 : 45$ $4 : 9$

b Which of these fractions are equivalent to $\frac{2}{3}$?

$\frac{3}{5}$ $\frac{6}{9}$ $\frac{5}{16}$ $\frac{14}{21}$ $\frac{12}{19}$ $\frac{30}{45}$ $\frac{4}{9}$

2 This bar is split into equal parts.

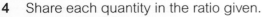

a Write down the ratio of red to blue parts. Give your answer in its simplest form.

b What proportion of the parts are

  i red   ii blue?

Give your answers as fractions in their simplest form.

3 a Share £20 in the ratio 2 : 3.

b Share £36 in the ratio 4 : 5.

c A piece of rope 24 m long is cut in the ratio 5 : 3.
How long is each piece of rope?

Worked example

Share £114 between Alice, Bert and Chen in the ratio 5 : 2 : 1.

5 + 2 + 1 = 8 parts —————————————— First find out how many parts there are in total.

£114 ÷ 8 = £14.25 per part ————

Alice: 5 × £14.25 = £71.25 —————— Find out how much one part is worth.

Bert: 2 × £14.25 = £28.50

Chen: 1 × £14.25 = £14.25 —————— Multiply the amount that one part is

Check: £71.25 + £28.50 + £14.25 = £114   worth by each value in the ratio.

4 Share each quantity in the ratio given.

a £3.50 in the ratio 2 : 3

b 6.3 m in the ratio 4 : 5

c 19.2 kg in the ratio 5 : 3

d $2035.60 in the ratio 3 : 7

5 Share each quantity in the ratio given.
   a £108 in the ratio 2 : 3 : 4   **b** £486 in the ratio 1 : 3 : 5
   c £510 in the ratio 1 : 2 : 3   **d** £242 in the ratio 1 : 2 : 3 : 5
   e 429 m in the ratio 2 : 3 : 6   **f** 591 km in the ratio 1 : 2 : 4 : 5
   g £1032 in the ratio 3 : 5 : 9   **h** 87 cm in the ratio 1 : 3 : 7

Q5 hint When working with measures, round to an appropriate number of decimal places. For example £ __ . ☐☐ or __ . ☐ cm.

6 **Problem-solving** In a company's website team, there are 5 programmers, 3 graphic artists and 2 copy writers.
   a What is the ratio of programmers to graphic artists to copy writers?
   b The team win a £500 prize for one of their websites.
      The prize money is to be shared equally.
      How much should the graphic artists receive?
   c What proportion of the team is currently
      i graphic artists   **ii** copy writers?
   d One more graphic artist and one more copy writer are employed.
      i What is the ratio of programmers to graphic artists to copy writers now?
      ii What proportion of the team is graphic artists now?
      iii What proportion of the team is copy writers now?

Worked example

Simplify 40 : 28.5 into a whole number ratio in its simplest form.

×10 ⟮ 40 : 28.5 ⟯ ×10
 ÷5 ⟮ 400 : 285 ⟯ ÷5
        80 : 57

Simplify using powers of 10.
28.5 has one decimal place, so multiply both sides of the ratio by 10 to give a whole number, then simplify.

---

7 Simplify each ratio into a whole number ratio in its simplest form.
   a 70 : 13.5   **b** 70 : 51.2
   c 25.5 : 17   **d** 33.6 : 4.8 : 24
   e 28.6 : 5.15   **f** 1.05 : 1.68 : 21

Q7d hint Multiply *all* parts of the ratio.

Q7e hint
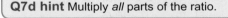
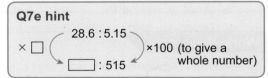
× ☐ ⟮ 28.6 : 5.15 ⟯ ×100 (to give a
        ☐ : 515   whole number)

8 **Problem-solving / Reasoning** The triathlon is a race where competitors swim, cycle and run.
   Four recognised lengths of race are shown in the table below.

Race	Swim	Cycle	Run
Sprint	0.75 km	20 km	5 km
Olympic	1.5 km	40 km	10 km
Half Ironman	1.9 km	90 km	21.1 km
Ironman	3.8 km	180.2 km	42.2 km

   a Write the ratio of swim to cycle to run for each race.
      Simplify each ratio into a whole number ratio in its simplest form.
   b What proportion of the Olympic triathlon is
      i swimming   **ii** cycling   **iii** running?

Q8b hint Write the proportion as a fraction. Simplify by first multiplying by 10.

9 Share each quantity in the ratio given.

   a £252 in the ratio 1.3 : 5

   b 648 m in the ratio 11.9 : 9.7

   c 2040 km in the ratio 6.2 : 4.8 : 1

   d 588 kg in the ratio 4.5 : 2.3 : 1.6

Q9 hint First simplify the ratio into a whole number ratio in its simplest form.

10 Problem-solving Mortar is made by mixing water with cement and sand in the ratio 1 : 2 : 3.

Copy and complete the table to show how much of each component is needed to make the quantities shown.

Q10 hint 1 litre of water has a mass of 1 kg.

Q10 hint Share 1.2 kg in the ratio 1 : 2 : 3.

Amount of mortar	Water (litres)	Cement (kg)	Sand (kg)
1.2 kg			
3 kg			
3.9 kg			

11 Problem-solving Turquoise paint is made by mixing blue, green and yellow in the ratio 2.5 : 1.4 : 0.1.

Copy and complete the table to show how much of each colour is needed to make the quantities shown.

Q11 hint 1 litre = ☐ ml

Quantity	Blue	Green	Yellow
1 litre			
1.5 litres			
2.5 litres			

12 Problem-solving The aspect ratio describes the ratio 'width : height' of an image.

Most modern televisions have an aspect ratio of 16 : 9.

   a What would be the height of screens with these widths? Give your answers to a maximum of 2 decimal places.

     i 24 cm   **ii** 30.4 cm

     iii 41.7 cm   **iv** 44.3 cm

   b What would be the width of screens with these heights?

     i 31.5 cm   **ii** 18.9 cm

     iii 26.4 cm   **iv** 35.2 cm

Q12a i hint
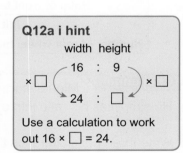
Use a calculation to work out 16 × ☐ = 24.

Key point You can compare ratios by writing them as **unit ratios**.
In a unit ratio, one of the numbers is 1.

Worked example

Express 13 : 9 as a **unit ratio**. Give your answer to 2 decimal places.

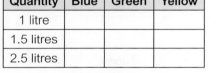

Divide both sides of the ratio by the smaller number.

13 Write each ratio as a unit ratio.

   a 7 : 2   **b** 10 : 21   **c** 149 : 100

Q13a hint

$\div 2 \left(\begin{array}{c} 7 : 2 \\ \square : \square \end{array} \right) \div 2$

write as a decimal

14 Write each ratio as a unit ratio.
   Give each answer to a maximum of 2 decimal places.
   a 9 : 5   **b** 11 : 4
   c 17 : 33   **d** 11 : 23

15 **Problem-solving / Reasoning**
   a Convert each aspect ratio to a unit ratio.
     i 5 : 3 (European widescreen)   **ii** 3 : 2 (35 mm film)
     iii 8 : 5 (computer screen)   **iv** 4 : 3 (cathode ray tube TV)
     v 37 : 20 (US widescreen)   **vi** 12 : 5 (cinema widescreen)
   b Which of these aspect ratios shows the widest picture?

16 **Problem-solving** Most modern bikes
   have a variety of gears, with a number of
   different-sized cogs. A road-racing bike
   has a front cog at the pedals with 53 teeth
   and a choice of five cogs at the rear. One
   turn of the pedals turns the front cog once.

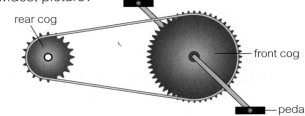

rear cog / front cog / pedal

   Copy and complete the table to work out the number of turns the rear wheel will make when
   the pedals are turned once for different gears.

Front cog teeth	53	53	53	53	53
Gear	1	2	3	4	5
Rear cog teeth	32	25	19	14	11
Ratio of front teeth to rear teeth	53 : 32				
Unit ratio	1.66 : 1				
Number of rear wheel turns per turn of the pedals	1.66				

Challenge   Miguel starts with a ratio that is decimal number : integer
He simplifies his ratio into a whole number ratio in its simplest form and gets the answer
3 : 200.
Write three possible ratios that Miguel could have started with.

Reflect   Look back at Q6d.
a Write all the steps you took to work out the answer to part **i**.
b Write all the steps you took to work out the answers to parts **ii** and **iii**.
c Lou says, 'Part **i** was about ratio. A ratio compares one part to another part. Parts **ii** and
   iii were about proportion. A proportion compares one part to the whole thing.'
   Is Lou correct?

6 Check up

Ordering and rounding

1 Copy and complete. Put the correct sign, < or >, between each pair of numbers.
　a 4.0531 □ 4.0501
　b 0.6091 □ 0.6901
　c 32.49 □ 32.3011

2 Write each number as a decimal number of millions to 1 decimal place.
　a 4 250 000　　　**b** 85 650 000

3 Write these decimal numbers in *ascending* order.
　　5.9281　　　5.90113　　　5.0982　　　5.9408

4 Write these decimal numbers in *descending* order.
　　−0.57　　　−0.5　　　0.5691　　　−0.563　　　0.59

5 Round each number to　**i**　3 decimal places　**ii**　3 significant figures.
　a 7.1335　　　　**b** 108.44958

Decimal calculations

6　$81 \times 56 = 4536$

　Use this multiplication fact to work out these multiplications.
　a 8.1 × 56　　　**b** 8.1 × 0.56

7 Work out these multiplications.
　a 708 × 0.1
　b 3.7 × 0.1
　c 41 × 0.01
　d 62.2 × 0.01
　e 0.08 × 0.4

8 Jane says that she can use an equivalent calculation to find the answer to 4.03 ÷ 0.1
　What calculation could she do?

9 Work out these divisions.
　a 734 ÷ 0.1
　b 174 ÷ 0.01
　c 253 ÷ 0.01

10 Work out these divisions.
　a 64 ÷ 0.8
　b 5.4 ÷ 0.9
　c 0.42 ÷ 0.6
　d 7.2 ÷ 0.12

11 Estimate and then work out 18.2 × 3.15.

12 Serpil has £140.80 in her bank account.
This is 2.2 times the amount that Tarik has in his bank account.
How much does Tarik have in his bank account?

13 Work out 3.46 × 2.181.

Ratio and proportion with decimals

14 Write each ratio in its simplest form.
  a 6 : 4.8
  b 1.2 : 1.44

15 Share each quantity in the ratio given.
  a 6.5 kg in the ratio 2 : 3
  b 451 litres in the ratio 2 : 4 : 5
  c £1000 in the ratio 10 : 2.5

16 A small pot of custard has 1.8 g of protein, 9 g of carbohydrate and 3.6 g of fat.
  a Write the ratio of protein to carbohydrate to fat as a whole number ratio in its simplest form.
  b What proportion of the custard is fat?

17 Write each ratio as a unit ratio.
  a 9 : 2
  b 10 : 19

Challenge

1 A string factory makes 1563.25 m of string each day.
One ball of string uses 6.5 m.
  a How many balls of string does the factory make in one day?
  b How many balls of string does the factory make in a week (Monday to Friday)?

2 Work out 1 ÷ 0.7 using a written method.
Write your answer to 6 decimal places.
Repeat for 2 ÷ 0.7, 3 ÷ 0.7, 4 ÷ 0.7, and so on.
What do you notice?
Use a calculator work out 1 ÷ 1.4, 2 ÷ 1.4, and so on. What do you notice?

Reflect

How sure are you of your answers? Were you mostly

😟 Just guessing   😐 Feeling doubtful   😊 Confident

What next? Use your results to decide whether to strengthen or extend your learning.

6 Strengthen

Ordering and rounding

1 Copy these number lines and mark on the number given.

a
Mark 4.631 on your number line.

b
Mark 15.869 on your number line.

c
Mark 7.9248 on your number line.

d
Mark 23.0314 on your number line.

2
a Is 4.631 closer to 4.63 or 4.64?
b Is 15.869 closer to 15.86 or 15.87?
c Is 7.9248 closer to 7.924 or 7.925?
d Is 23.0314 closer to 23.031 or 23.032?
e Is 2.196 closer to 2.19 or 2.20?
f Is 47.8328 closer to 47.832 or 47.833?

> **Q2a–d hint** Use the number lines in Q1.

3 Round each number to 2 decimal places.
a 4.637   **b** 15.861
c 3.624   **d** 3.629
e 14.561   **f** 2.066
g 3.615   **h** 29.075

> **Q3 and Q4 hint**
> Draw number lines.
> If a number ends in 5, round up.
>
> 3.61   3.615   3.6□

4 Round each number to 3 decimal places.
a 7.9241   **b** 23.0317   **c** 5.1284
d 4.8652   **e** 12.4769   **f** 26.0485

5 Write each number as millions.
Parts **a** and **d** are done for you.
a 2 000 000 = 2 million   **b** 8 000 000 = □ million
c 12 000 000 = □ million   **d** 8 600 000 = 8.6 million
e 7 400 000 = □ million   **f** 15 700 000 = □ million

6 These are some previous Sunday night TV viewing figures.

> **Q6 hint**
> 9 623 145 = 9.623 145 million
>   = 9.□ million (1 d.p.)

Programme	Viewers
Downton Abbey	9 623 145
By Any Means	3 450 238
Countryfile	6 285 016
The Crane Gang	926 818
X Factor	9 528 586

Round each number to a decimal number of millions to 1 decimal place.

7 Copy these numbers. Circle the first significant figure.
Write its value.

a 56.882   **b** 0.00456

c 673500   **d** 0.8834

Q7 hint

④68.23   4 hundreds

0.0⑦95   7 hundredths

8 Round each number to 1 significant figure.

a 486

b 394.55

c 3495

d 187340

e 0.03394

f 0.000479

Q8a hint

④86

Circle the first significant figure.
It's in the 100s column, so you
are rounding to the nearest 100.

9 Copy these numbers. Circle the second significant figure.
Then round to 2 significant figures.

a 568   **b** 63349   **c** 0.6528   **d** 0.004781

10 Copy these numbers. Circle the third significant figure.
Then round to 3 significant figures.

a 7084   **b** 478901   **c** 0.73819   **d** 0.01637

11 In these place value tables, which number is
bigger in each pair?

Q11a hint There are the same number
of ones, tenths and hundredths in 3.64.
But which number has more thousandths?

	O	.	$\frac{1}{10}$	$\frac{1}{100}$	$\frac{1}{1000}$	$\frac{1}{10000}$	$\frac{1}{100000}$	
a	3	.	6	4	2	9		or
b	4	.	5	3	1	8		or
c	0	.	0	6				or
d	0	.	0	0	3			or

O	.	$\frac{1}{10}$	$\frac{1}{100}$	$\frac{1}{1000}$	$\frac{1}{10000}$	$\frac{1}{100000}$
3	.	6	4	7		
4	.	5	9			
0	.	0	6	1	8	
0	.	0	0	2	9	9

12 Write these numbers in *ascending* order (smallest first).

7.605   7.2041   7.3   7.6011   7.2049

13 Write each number to 2 decimal places.

a 5.128   **b** 4.865   **c** 12.476   **d** 26.048

Decimal calculations

1 Here is a spider diagram for 27 showing the links between
multiplying and dividing by powers of 10.
Draw a spider diagram like this for 157.

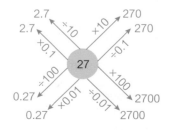

2 Draw a similar spider diagram for each of these numbers.

a 57   **b** 101   **c** 45.2   **d** 2.8

3 Multiply each number by 0.1

a 9.06   **b** 4.73   **c** 6.43   **d** 13.87

4 Multiply each number by 0.01

   a 3.42   **b** 1.14   **c** 7.36

   d 6.214   **e** 57.972   **f** 61.03

5 Use equivalent calculations to work out these multiplications and divisions.

   a 5.28×0.1 **b** 9.75×0.1 **c** $7.51 \div 0.1$

   d $0.98 \div 0.01$ **e** 0.43×0.01 **f** $25.65 \div 0.1$

> **Q5 hint** Look at the spider diagram in Q1.
> '×10' is equivalent to '÷0.1'
> '×0.1' is equivalent to '÷10'

6 Copy and complete these calculations.

   a
```
    312
  ×   3
  _____
```

   b
```
    312
  ×  43
  _____
  +    0
  _____
```

   c
```
    312
  × 143
        0
  +   00
  _____
```

   d
```
    251
  ×   8
  _____
```

   e
```
    251
  ×  38
  _____
  +    0
  _____
```

   f
```
    251
  × 238
        0
  +   00
  _____
```

7 Copy and complete to estimate these multiplications.

   a $3.12 \times 4.3 \approx \square$
          $\downarrow$ $\downarrow$
        ≈ 3 $\times$ ≈ 4

   b $25.1 \times 2.38 \approx \square$
           $\approx \square \times \approx 2$

8 Work out these calculations. The first one is started for you.

   a $5.06 \times 4.1 \approx 5 \times 4 = \square$
```
      506
    ×  41
      506
    20240
    20746
```
      $5.06 \times 4.1 = \square$

   b 3.12×4.3

   c 2.51×2.38

   d 7.01×4.2

   e 4.23×1.3

> **Q8a hint** Use your estimated answer to decide where to put the decimal point in 20746. Is the answer likely to be 2.0746? ... 20.746? ... 207.46? ... or 2074.6?

9 Copy and complete these divisions.

   a ×10 $\left(\dfrac{15 \div 0.3}{150 \div 3 = \square} \right)$ ×10

   b ×10 $\left(\dfrac{2.8 \div 0.7}{\square \div \square = \square} \right)$ ×10

   c ×100 $\left(\dfrac{0.32 \div 0.08}{\square \div \square = \square} \right)$ ×100

   d ×100 $\left(\dfrac{6.6 \div 0.11}{\square \div \square = \square} \right)$ ×100

> **Q10b hint** It is easier to divide by a whole number.
>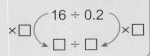
> ×□ $\left(\dfrac{16 \div 0.2}{\square \div \square} \right)$ ×□

10 Work out these divisions.

   a $1.4 \div 0.2$ **b** $16 \div 0.2$

   c $0.24 \div 0.03$ **d** $2.4 \div 0.12$

11 Work out these divisions.
Use a written method.
  a 20.04 ÷ 1.2
  b 70.95 ÷ 1.1
  c 43.68 ÷ 2.1

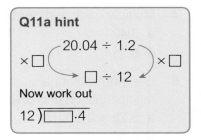

Q11a hint

20.04 ÷ 1.2

×☐ ⟶ ☐ ÷ 12 ⟵ ×☐

Now work out

12)☐·4

12 Problem-solving A car boot sale raises £104.95.
This is 2.5 times as much as was raised by a
sponsored walk.
How much was raised by the sponsored walk?

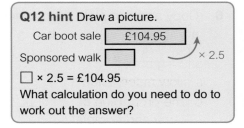

Q12 hint Draw a picture.

Car boot sale | £104.95

Sponsored walk | ☐   × 2.5

☐ × 2.5 = £104.95
What calculation do you need to do to
work out the answer?

Ratio and proportion with decimals

1 A rope is 8.5 m long. Josie cuts it in the ratio 3 : 2.
How long is each piece?

Q1 hint 8.5 ÷ 5 gives
the length of one part.

8.5 m

3   2

2 A plank of wood is 184 cm long.
Alex cuts it in the ratio 4 : 3 : 1.
How long is each piece?

Q2 hint
184 cm

4   3   1

3 Tips at a hotel one weekend amount to £422.40.
The tips are shared between the receptionists, porters and
cleaners in the ratio 2 : 4 : 5.
How much did each group receive?

4 Copy and complete to simplify each ratio into a whole number ratio in its simplest form.

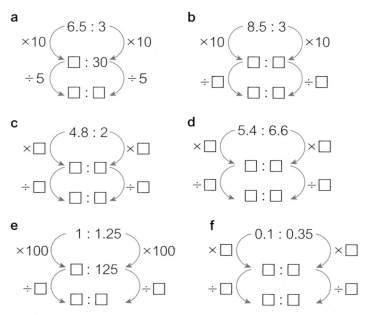

a
×10 (6.5 : 3) ×10
☐ : 30
÷5 ( ) ÷5
☐ : ☐

b
×10 (8.5 : 3) ×10
☐ : ☐
÷☐ ( ) ÷☐
☐ : ☐

c
×☐ (4.8 : 2) ×☐
☐ : ☐
÷☐ ( ) ÷☐
☐ : ☐

d
×☐ (5.4 : 6.6) ×☐
☐ : ☐
÷☐ ( ) ÷☐
☐ : ☐

e
×100 (1 : 1.25) ×100
☐ : 125
÷☐ ( ) ÷☐
☐ : ☐

f
×☐ (0.1 : 0.35) ×☐
☐ : ☐
÷☐ ( ) ÷☐
☐ : ☐

Q4e and f hint The
ratio has a number
with 2 decimal places.
Multiply this by 100 to
give an integer.

5 Copy and complete to write each number as a unit ratio □ : 1.

a
$\div 2$
6 : 2
□ : □
$\div 2$

b
$\div 3$
6 : 3
□ : □
$\div 3$

c
$\div 4$
6 : 4
□ : □
$\div 4$

d
$\div \square$
6 : 5
□ : □
$\div \square$

6 Write each ratio as a unit ratio (□ : 1 or 1 : □).

a 4 : 5

b 2 : 7

c 8 : 5

d 7 : 4

> **Q6 hint** Always divide by the smaller number in the ratio.
>
> $\div 4$
> 4 : 5
> □ ÷ □
> $\div 4$

7 A spice mix uses 5 g of garlic powder, 2.5 g of onion powder and 1 g of salt.

a How much spice mix is there altogether?

b The proportion of garlic powder in the spice mix is $\frac{5}{8.5}$.
Copy and complete to write this proportion as a fraction in its simplest form.

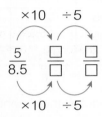

×10   ÷5

$\frac{5}{8.5}$ $\frac{\square}{\square}$ $\frac{\square}{\square}$

×10   ÷5

c Write the proportion of salt in the spice mix.
Give your answer as a fraction in its simplest form.

d Write the proportion of onion powder in the spice mix.
Give your answer as a fraction in its simplest form.

Challenge   All three pictures have their sides in the same ratio.

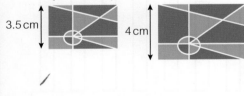
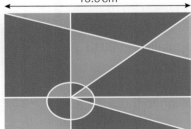

4.5 cm   13.5 cm

3.5 cm

4 cm

a Write the ratio of length : width for the first picture.

b Work out the missing lengths on the second and third pictures.

c Work out the area of each picture.

d How many times as big is the area of the largest picture than the area of the smallest one?

Reflect   This Strengthen lesson used lots of diagrams.
Look back at these diagrams.
Which diagrams did you find most useful? Why?
Which diagrams did you find least useful? Why?

6 Extend

1 **a** Work out the mean of these 10 km race times.

    58 minutes   1 hour 6 minutes   55 minutes

    1 hour 20 minutes   1 hour 17 minutes   1 hour 37 minutes

  Give your answer

    i in minutes rounded to 2 d.p.   **ii** in minutes rounded to 2 s.f.

    iii in hours, minutes and seconds.

  b **Reasoning** Which answer to part **a** is

    i most accurate? Explain.   **ii** least accurate? Explain.

2 **Problem-solving** Donna, Shakira and Myles are going out for a meal.
They decide to put their money together. Donna has £13.50, Shakira has £18.20 and Myles has £22.75.
The prices of their food are given in the table.

Item	Donna	Shakira	Myles
drink	£1.95	£1.95	£1.95
starter	£2.95	£2.95	£2.50
main	£6.95	£7.75	£7.95
dessert	£3.50	£3.50	£3.50

  a How much is the total bill?

  b Could Donna afford to pay for all of her own food if they hadn't pooled their money?

  c They leave a tip of 10% of the bill. How much is this?

  d How much money do they have left?

  e They share the remaining money equally between them.
How much do they get each?

3 The graph shows the population of the UK between 2010 and 2017.

  a Describe what happened to the UK population between 2010 and 2017.

  b What was the population in 2013 to the nearest million?

  c In which years was the population 65 million to the nearest million?

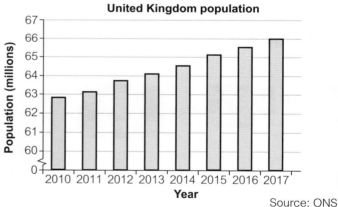

Source: ONS

4 Bank statements show overdrawn balances as negative numbers.
All of these students are overdrawn. Two bank balances are missing.

Student	Bank balance (£)
Lily	−65.94
Mia	
Freya	−72.31
Maya	−12.62
Arjan	−12.84

Student	Bank balance (£)
Josh	−47.15
Luke	−17.03
Ali	−22.67
Junior	−5.82
Lincoln	

  a Mia owes the most. Write a possible balance for Mia's account.

  b Lincoln owes the least. Write a possible balance for Lincoln's account.

5 **Problem-solving**   Prescription medicine doses are measured in grams and milligrams.
A high dose tablet of ibuprofen has 600 mg of active ingredient.
a How much is this in grams?

> **Q5 hint** 1000 mg = 1 g

A tablet with 600 mg of active ingredient weighs 2.4 g in total.

b How much of the tablet is *not* active ingredient?

6 **Reasoning**   Work out these calculations.
   a 105 ÷ 5   **b** 105 × 0.2   **c** 425 ÷ 5   **d** 425 × 0.2
   e Copy and complete.
   ÷10 is equivalent to ×0.1   ÷5 is equivalent to ☐   ÷0.2 is equivalent to ☐
   ÷2 is equivalent to ☐   ÷4 is equivalent to ☐

7 5 g of grass seed covers a 10 m by 10 m square.
   a How many m² will 5 g cover?
   b How many grams do you need to cover a football pitch that is 110 m × 60 m?

8 A cereal box is 19.6 cm wide, 7.2 cm deep and 27.5 cm high.
   a What is the volume of the cereal box?
   b **Problem-solving / Reasoning**   All three dimensions are halved.
      What is the ratio of the volume of the small box to the volume of the original one?

9 8 km is approximately 5 miles.
   a How many miles is each km?   **b** How many km is each mile?

10 Use suitable equivalent calculations to work out
   a 3.5 × 62   **b** 1.6 × 125   **c** 2.25 × 848
   d 1.5 × 4682   **e** 1.8 × 4235   **f** 6.25 × 488

> **Q10a hint** Multiplying by 3.5 is the same as multiplying by 7 and dividing by 2.

11 **Reasoning**   A film projected in widescreen has an aspect ratio of 2.35 : 1.
How tall would the film appear if projected on a screen 16.75 m wide?

12 **Problem-solving / Reasoning**   Although not as visible,
cars use gears in the same way as bikes. Different gear
ratios (number of turns in the engine : number of turns in the
wheels) make the wheels travel different distances for each
revolution in the engine.
In a typical car each revolution of the wheels is about 2 m.

   a Explain why 6th gear is the fastest gear.
   b A revolution is a full rotation of 360°. How many
      revolutions of the engine does it take to travel 1 km
      in 6th gear?

Gear	Turns in the engine : turns in the wheels
1st	2.97 : 1
2nd	2.07 : 1
3rd	1.43 : 1
4th	1 : 1
5th	0.84 : 1
6th	0.56 : 1

> **Challenge**   Estimate the volume and the surface area of a typical adult. Use a cuboid as
> a model. You may wish to use measuring equipment to help you.
> Use a sensible degree of accuracy for all your measurements and calculations.

> **Reflect**   What kinds of jobs might need the maths skills you have used in this
> Extend lesson?
> Look back at the questions to help you. For example, Q12 was about car gears. Someone
> working as a Formula One engineer would need to understand car gears.

y

z

6 Unit test

1 Round each number to the number of decimal places shown.
  a 4.7913 (3 d.p.)
  b 37.0004 (2 d.p.)
  c 21.4897 (3 d.p.)

2 Round each number to the number of significant figures shown.
  a 75650 (2 s.f.)
  b 0.00872 (1 s.f.)
  c 45.669 (3 s.f.)

3 Write these numbers in *ascending* order.
      45.8, 45.275, 45.33, 66.0981, 66.5, 66.39

4 Write these numbers in *ascending* order.
      −9.31, −9.78, −9.57, −9.3, −9.53, −9.511, −9.9

5 Work out these multiplications.
  a 57 × 0.01
  b 9.2 × 0.1

6 Work out these divisions.
  a 36 ÷ 0.1
  b 419 ÷ 0.01
  c 4.8 ÷ 0.6
  d 48 ÷ 0.08
  e 8.4 ÷ 0.2
  f 0.63 ÷ 0.3

7 471 × 34 = 16014

  Use this multiplication fact to work out these calculations.
  a 4.71 × 0.34
  b 0.471 × 34
  c 47.1 × 0.034
  d 0.471 × 0.34

8 Long rolls of cloth need to be cut in the ratio 5 : 1 : 2.
  How long is the longest piece of cloth from a roll 48 m long?

9 Simplify each ratio.
  a 1.5 : 7.5
  b 2 : 1.28

10 Write each ratio as a unit ratio.
  a 13 : 2
  b 10 : 25

11 Sophie mixes acid and water in the ratio 2 : 5.2.
She makes 144 ml of the mixture.
How much acid and how much water does she mix?

12 Ben makes orange paint by mixing red, yellow and white paint in the ratio 20 : 16 : 1.5.
How much of each colour does he need to make 1.5 litres of orange paint?

13 A journey from Canterbury to Dunkirk in France involves travelling 35 km by taxi,
35 km by ferry and then 50 km by train.
   a Write the ratio of travel by taxi to ferry to train.
      Simplify into a whole number ratio in its simplest form.
   b What proportion of the journey is by train?

14 A company buys 152 laptops. Each laptops costs £478.
How much money does the company spend?

15 Work out these calculations.
   a 54.18×6.7 **b** $78.03 \div 1.7$

16 Ben's dad is one and a half times the height of Ben.
Ben is 33.4 cm shorter than his mum.
Ben's dad is 190.2 cm tall.
How tall is Ben's mum?

Challenge

0.12	0.86	12.5
5.04	0.7	9
11.3	6.3	0.1
51.3	2.97	10.7

Each of the numbers in the rectangle can be made by adding, subtracting, multiplying or
dividing some or all of these decimal numbers.

0.3	0.4	1.4	9.9	3.6	6.2	5.7

a   You can use each number a maximum of once in each calculation.
    Make as many of the numbers from the rectangle as you can.
    Keep a note of the calculations you do to avoid duplication.

b   Following the same rules:
    What is the highest number you can make?
    What is the lowest number you can make?
    What is the number closest to zero you can make?

Reflect   Look back at the questions in this unit test.
Which took the shortest time to answer? Why?
Which took the longest time to answer? Why?
For those that took the longest time, could you estimate the answer more quickly?
Why is this a useful skill when using a calculator to work out answers?

7 Lines and angles

7.1 Quadrilaterals

*Active*Learn
Homework

- Classify quadrilaterals by their geometric properties
- Solve geometric problems using side and angle properties of special quadrilaterals

Warm up

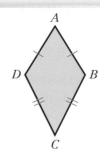

1 **Fluency**
   a What do the angles in a quadrilateral add up to?
   b What do the angles in a triangle add up to?

2 What do the dashes on the sides tell you about this shape?

3 Write the number of lines of symmetry and the order of rotational symmetry of each quadrilateral.

a	b	c	d	e	f	g
Square	Rectangle	Parallelogram	Rhombus	Kite	Trapezium	Isosceles trapezium

Key point

A **diagonal** is a line that joins two opposite vertices of a shape.
When diagonals **bisect** each other, they cut each other in half.
The **properties** of a shape are facts about its sides, angles, diagonals and symmetry.
Here are some of the properties of the special quadrilaterals that you should know.

Square		Rectangle	
	• all sides are equal in length • opposite sides are parallel • all angles are 90° • diagonals bisect each other at 90°		• opposite sides are equal in length • opposite sides are parallel • all angles are 90° • diagonals bisect each other
Rhombus		**Parallelogram**	
	• all sides are equal in length • opposite sides are parallel • opposite angles are equal • diagonals bisect each other at 90°		• opposite sides are equal in length • opposite sides are parallel • opposite angles are equal • diagonals bisect each other
Kite		**Trapezium**	
	• 2 pairs of sides are equal in length • no parallel sides • 1 pair of equal angles • diagonals bisect each other at 90°		• 1 pair of parallel sides
		Isosceles trapezium	• 2 sides are equal in length • 1 pair of parallel sides • 2 pairs of equal angles

4 Write which quadrilaterals
   a have all sides equal
   b have four right angles
   c have two pairs of equal sides
   d have exactly one pair of parallel sides
   e have bisecting diagonals
   f can have four different sized angles.

5 Name each quadrilateral from its description.
   a My opposite sides are parallel and equal in length.
      None of my angles are 90°.
   b I have one pair of parallel sides, and two sides the same length.
   c I have one pair of equal angles, and no parallel sides.
   d All my angles are 90°. My diagonals bisect each other, but not at 90°.

6 **Reasoning** Is this shape a trapezium?
List its properties to explain.

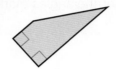

7 **Problem-solving** Find the coordinates of the fourth vertex of
   a a rectangle with vertices (4, 5), (6, 5), (6, 6)
   b a parallelogram with vertices (1, –2), (2, –6), (7, –6)
   c a square with vertices (2, 1), (2, –5), (–4, –5).

8 **Problem-solving / Reasoning** Three vertices of a quadrilateral are plotted.

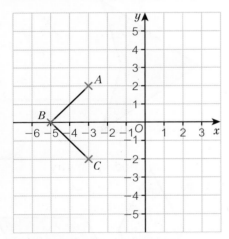

   a What are the coordinates of the missing vertex if the shape is a square?
   b Give two different possible coordinates for the missing vertex if the shape is a kite.
   c Are there more than two different possible solutions to part **b**?

Worked example

In this parallelogram, one of the angles is 55°.
Work out the sizes of the other angles.

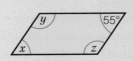

$x = 55°$ (opposite angles of a parallelogram are equal) ──────── Identify equal angles.
Write the reason.

$360 - 55 - 55 = 250°$ (angles in a quadrilateral add up to to 360°)

$250 ÷ 2 = 125°$ (opposite angles of a parallelogram are equal)

$y = 125°$ and $z = 125°$

9 In this parallelogram, one of the angles is 130°. Work out the sizes of the other angles.

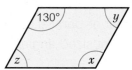

10 Work out the sizes of the angles marked with letters in this isosceles trapezium.

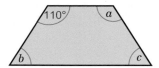

11 Work out the sizes of the angles marked with letters in this kite.

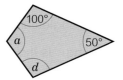

12 Reasoning

   a Quadrilateral *ABCD* is called an arrowhead.

      Copy and complete these statements.

      i Length *AD* is equal to length □.

      ii Length *AB* is equal to length □.

      iii $\angle BAD = \angle$□

      iv *ABCD* has □ line(s) of symmetry and rotational symmetry of order □.

   b In this arrowhead $\angle KJM = 40°$ and $\angle JKM = 35°$.

      Calculate the size of these angles.

      i $\angle KLM$

      ii $\angle KML$

      iii $\angle JML$

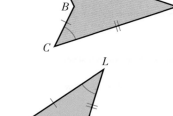

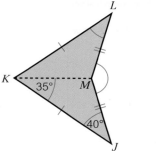

Challenge   Lowri uses this rhombus and parallelogram in her patchwork quilt design.

a Work out the sizes of the angles marked with letters. Give a reason for each answer.

b Shapes tessellate if they make a repeating pattern with no gaps.

Draw a sketch to show how these shapes tessellate. Include at least four of each shape. Label the angles to show how they fit together.

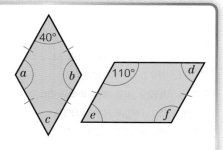

Reflect   Frankie says that to identify a shape, he begins by asking himself these questions.

• Are any sides equal in length?

• Are the equal sides next to each other, or opposite?

Write all the questions you ask yourself to identify a shape.

Test your questions on some quadrilaterals. Can you improve your questions?

Compare your questions with other people's. Can you improve your questions?

7.2 Alternate angles and proof

Active Learn
Homework

- Identify alternate angles on a diagram
- Understand proofs of angle facts

Warm up

1 Fluency Complete these statements.

a The angles on a straight line add up to ☐°.

b The angles in a triangle add up to ☐°.

2 Work out the size of each angle marked with a letter.

a

b

c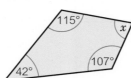

d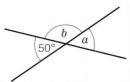

Key point

We show parallel lines using arrows.

3 Reasoning The diagram shows a line crossing two parallel lines.

a Measure angles a, b, c and d.

b Write two pairs of equal angles.

Key point

When a line crosses two parallel lines it creates a 'Z' shape.

Inside the Z shape are **alternate angles**.

Alternate angles are equal.

Alternate angles are on different (alternate) sides of the diagonal line.

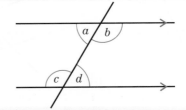

4 The diagram shows a line crossing two parallel lines and angles labelled a, b, c and d.

a and d are alternate angles.
a and d are equal.

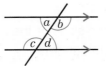

b and c are alternate angles.
b and c are equal.

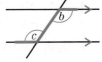

Now look at this diagram.
Write two pairs of alternate angles.

Worked example

Write the sizes of angles x and y.
Give reasons for your answers.

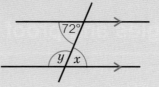

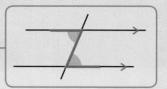

$x = 72°$ (alternate angle with 72°)

$y = 180 - 72 = 108°$ (angles on a straight line add up to 180°)

5 **Reasoning**   Write the sizes of the angles marked with letters.
Give a reason for each answer.

a

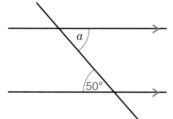

b

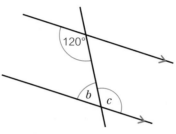

6 **Reasoning**   Write the sizes of the angles marked with letters.
Give a reason for each answer.

a    b 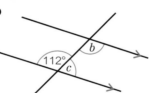   c 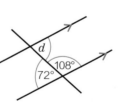   d

7 **Reasoning**   The diagram shows two lines crossing parallel lines.
Copy and complete these statements.
a Angle r and angle ☐ are alternate angles.
b Angle t and angle ☐ are alternate angles.
c Angle ☐ is the same size as angle q because _____ .
d Angle ☐ is the same size as angle p because _____ .

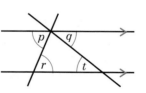

8 **Reasoning**   Write the sizes of the angles marked with letters.
Give a reason for each answer

a 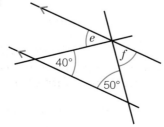   b 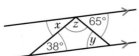   c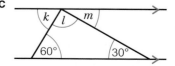

Key point It is not enough to show that a theory works for a few values. You need to **prove** that it works for all values. A **proof** uses logical reasoning to show that a theory is true.

9 **Reasoning** Sketch a copy of this diagram.
Copy and complete these sentences that prove that the angles in a triangle add up to 180°.

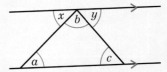

a Angle x is equal to angle ☐ because they are alternate angles.
b Angle y is equal to angle ☐ because they are _____ angles.
c $x + b + y = $ ☐° because they lie on a _____ line.
d Since $x = a$ and $y = $ ☐
$x + b + y = $ ☐ $+ b + $ ☐
so $a + b + c = $ ☐°.
e This proves that the angles in a triangle add up to ☐°.

10 **Reasoning** Sketch a copy of this diagram.
The quadrilateral has been split into two triangles.
Copy and complete this proof to show that the angles in a quadrilateral add up to 360°.

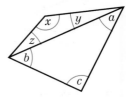

$x + y + z = $ ☐° because the angles in a triangle add up to ☐°.
$a + b + c = $ ☐° because the angles in a triangle add up to ☐°.
$x + y + z + a + b + c = $ ☐°
This proves that the angles in a quadrilateral add up to ☐°.

Challenge

1 For each diagram, answer these questions.

a

b

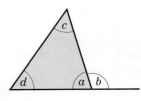

i Work out the sum of the two given angles in the triangle.
ii Work out the size of angle a.
iii Work out the size of angle b.

2 What do you notice about your answers to parts **i** and **iii** in Q1?

3 Will this be true for every triangle? Explain why.

4 Draw two triangles of your own to test your answer.
Choose your own values for angles c and d, then work out a and b.

5 Copy and complete the formula: $b = $ ☐ $+ $ ☐.

Reflect Marco says, 'A mathematical proof is an argument that convinces people something is true.'
Read each line of the proofs you worked on in Q9 and Q10.
How does the way they are written help to convince people?

Hint What type of language are the proofs using? How are they set out? Why is algebra used?

7.3 Angles in parallel lines

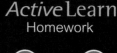

Active Learn
Homework

- Identify corresponding angles
- Solve problems using properties of angles in parallel and intersecting lines

Warm up

1 **Fluency**   Identify the pairs of alternate and vertically opposite angles in these parallel lines.

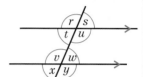

2 Work out the sizes of the angles marked with letters.

a

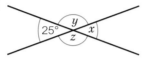

b

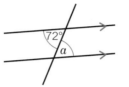

c

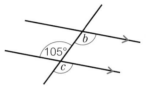

3 Work out the sizes of the angles marked with letters.

a

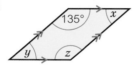

b

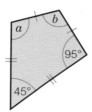

c

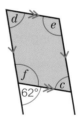

4 **Reasoning**   The diagram shows a line crossing two parallel lines.
   a Measure angles a, b and c.
   b Which angles are equal?
   c Which angles add to 180°?

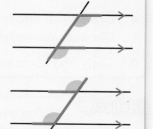

Key point

When a line crosses two parallel lines it creates an 'F' shape.
There are **corresponding angles** on an F shape.
Corresponding angles are equal.
Corresponding angles are on the same (corresponding) side of the diagonal line.

Write the sizes of angles x, y and z.
Give reasons for your answers.

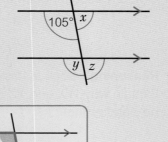

$x = 180 - 105 = 75°$ (angles on a straight line add up to 180°)

$y = 105°$ (corresponding angle with 105°)

$z = 75°$ (corresponding angle with x)

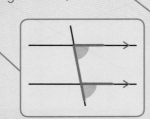

5 **Reasoning** Write the sizes of the angles marked with letters.
Give a reason for each answer.

a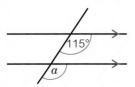

b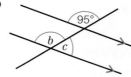

c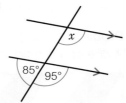

d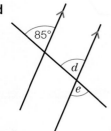

e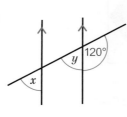

f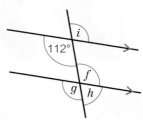

6 **Reasoning** Copy each diagram.
Find and label the angles you need until you can write the size of each angle marked
with a letter.

a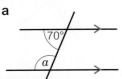

b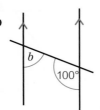

c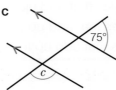

d

7 **Reasoning** Write the sizes of the angles marked with letters.
Give a reason for each answer.

a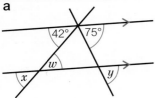

b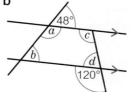

c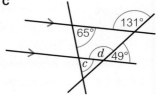

8 Reasoning Write the sizes of the angles marked with letters. Give a reason for each answer.

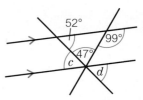

9 Reasoning Look at this diagram. Explain why WX and YZ cannot be parallel lines.

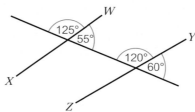

Q9 hint Are there any corresponding angles?

10 Reasoning The diagram shows the road markings on a 'no parking' zone.

  a Work out the size of angle x.

  b Use properties of a parallelogram to work out the size of angle y.

11 Problem-solving The diagram shows a chevron road sign. A chevron is made from two congruent parallelograms.

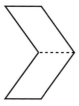

Work out the size of angle z.

Challenge The diagram shows two sets of parallel lines.

Write

a two pairs of alternate angles

b two pairs of corresponding angles

c two pairs of angles that add up to 180°

d two sets of three angles that add up to 180°

e two sets of four angles that add up to 360°

f two sets of six angles that add up to 360°.

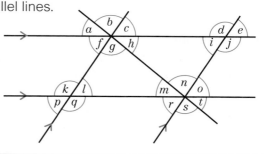

Reflect After the lesson Otmane wrote this list.

Hint You could begin your list with the same points as Otmane.

> To solve shape and angle problems, look out for
> • right angles (marked with a small square)
> • parallel lines (marked with arrows)
> • alternate angles (alternate sides of any line that crosses parallel lines)

Look back at the questions you answered in this lesson. Write your own 'Look out for' list.

7.4 Exterior and interior angles

*Active*Learn
Homework

- Calculate the sum of the interior and exterior angles of a polygon
- Work out the sizes of interior and exterior angles of a polygon

Warm up

1 Fluency What is special about a regular polygon?

2 Fluency How many sides does each shape have?
  a pentagon **b** hexagon **c** heptagon **d** octagon **e** nonagon **f** decagon

3 Work out the sizes of the angles marked with letters.

a

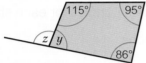

b

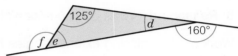

Key point

The **interior** and **exterior angles** of a polygon are shown in the diagram.

In an **irregular polygon** sides are not all equal lengths, and angles are not all equal.

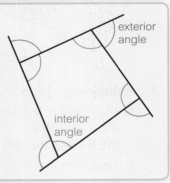

exterior angle

interior angle

4 **a** Measure each exterior angle of this pentagon.
  b Work out the sum of the exterior angles.
  c **Reasoning** What do you notice about the sum of the exterior angles?

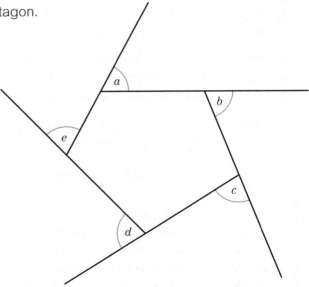

5 a For each polygon, work out the size of each exterior angle, and then the sum of the exterior angles.

i

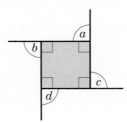

ii

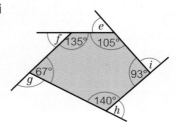

iii

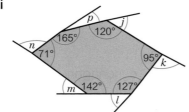

iv

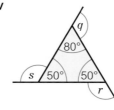

b Reasoning What do you notice about the sum of the exterior angles for each shape?

6 Work out the missing exterior angles for each of these polygons.

a

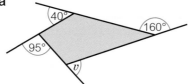

b

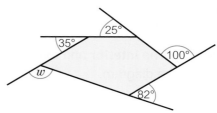

7 Reasoning Here are two regular polygons.
  a In a regular polygon, all the interior angles are the same size.
  What does this tell you about the exterior angles?
  b Describe in words how to work out the exterior angle of a regular polygon.
  c Work out the sizes of the exterior angles x and w.
  d Work out the sizes of the interior angles y and t.

8 For each regular polygon, sketch the shape and work out
    i the exterior angle   **ii** the interior angle.
  a equilateral triangle   **b** decagon (10-sided polygon)   **c** regular 16-sided polygon

9 Reasoning A diagonal divides a quadrilateral into two triangles.
  The sum of the interior angles in a quadrilateral = $2 \times 180° = 360°$.

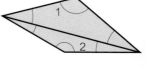

  a Draw a pentagon and divide it into triangles using diagonals.
  The diagonals must all start from the same vertex (corner) of the pentagon.
  b Copy and complete:
  A pentagon divides into ☐ triangles.
  The sum of the interior angles in a pentagon = ☐ $\times$ 180° = ☐°.

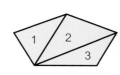

  c Use the same method to work out the sum of the interior angles in a hexagon.

d Copy and complete this table.

Shape	triangle	quadrilateral	pentagon	hexagon
Number of sides	3	4	5	6
Number of triangles	1	2	3	☐
Sum of interior angles	180°	360°	☐°	☐°

e Describe in words how to work out the number of triangles from the number of sides.

f Describe in words how to work out the sum of interior angles from the number of sides.

> **Key point** Sum of interior angles of an n-sided polygon = $180°(n - 2)$

10 For each irregular polygon, work out
  i the sum of the interior angles
  ii the size of the angle marked with a letter.

a

b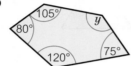

c

11 Reasoning
  a What is the sum of the interior angles of a heptagon?
  b Work out the size of one interior angle in a regular heptagon.

Challenge

a The diagram shows an equilateral triangle inside a square.
Show that $x = 30°$.

b The diagram shows a square inside a regular pentagon.
Work out the size of angle y.

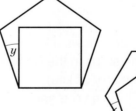

c The diagram shows a regular pentagon inside a regular hexagon.
Work out the size of angle z.

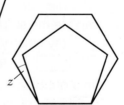

Reflect Write the steps for finding the sum of the interior angles of any polygon. You might begin with, 'Step 1: count the number of sides'. Do your steps work to find the interior angles of one of the regular polygons in Q8?
If not, rewrite your steps for any regular polygon.
Now write the steps to find the exterior angle of any regular polygon.

> **Hint** Use your answers to Q9 to help you.

7.5 Solving geometric problems

*Active*Learn
Homework

- Solve geometric problems, showing reasoning
- Solve problems involving angles by setting up equations

Warm up

1 Fluency Work out the sizes of the angles marked with letters.

a
50°
a
b

b
3 cm 36° 3 cm
p

c
m

2 Solve these equations.
  a $5x + 30 = 180$ **b** $8x - 40 = 360$

3 Work out the sizes of the angles marked with letters.

a
x
27°

b
y
40°

c
z

4 Reasoning Work out the size of angle x in each diagram.

a
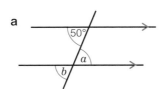

b

c

5 Reasoning The diagram shows a kite.
Copy and complete the steps in the working and reasoning, to find the size of angle y.

$\angle ADC = \boxed{}$ (symmetry of kite)

$112 + \boxed{} + \boxed{} + \angle BAD = 360°$

  (angles in a quadrilateral add up to 360°)

$\angle BAD = \boxed{}$

$\angle ABX = \angle ADX = y$ (*ABD* is an isosceles triangle)

$y + y + \boxed{} = 180°$ (angles in a triangle add up to 180°)

$y = \boxed{}$

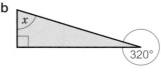

6 Problem-solving In this rectangle, work out the size of $\angle EBD$.
Show your steps for solving the problem.
Give your reasons.

Q6 hint Sketch the diagram. Label the angles as you work them out.

Worked example

a Work out the value of x in this diagram.

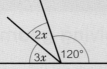

$3x + 2x + 120 = 180°$ (angles on a straight line add up to 180°)

$5x + 120 = 180$ ⟵ Give a reason.

$5x = 60$

$x = \frac{60}{5} = 12°$ ⟵ Simplify by collecting like terms.

b Work out the sizes of the angles.

Angle $2x = 2 \times 12° = 24°$ Angle $3x = 3 \times 12° = 36°$ ⟵ Substitute the value of x into $2x$ and $3x$.

Check: $24° + 36° + 120° = 180°$ ✓

7 **Reasoning** For each diagram, write an equation and then solve it to find the value of x. Work out the sizes of the angles. Check that your answers are correct.

a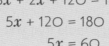

b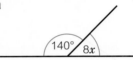

c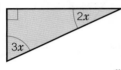

d

e **Reasoning** Is there more than one equation that you can write for part **c**?

8 The diagram shows a quadrilateral.
   a Write an equation in terms of x for the sum of the angles.
   b Simplify your equation by collecting like terms.
   c Solve your equation to find the value of x.
   d Write the sizes of the four angles in the quadrilateral.

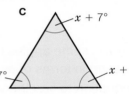

9 **Reasoning** A regular polygon has an exterior angle of 24°.
   Write and solve an equation to work out how many sides the polygon has.

10 **Reasoning** In this isosceles trapezium $ABCD$,
   $\angle DAB$ is three times the size of $\angle ADC$.
   a Sketch the trapezium. Label $\angle ADC$ as x.
   b Label the angles in the trapezium in terms of x.
   c Work out the sizes of the angles in the trapezium.

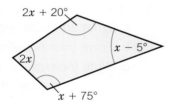

Challenge

Work out the sizes of angles a, b, c and d.

Give reasons at each step of your working.

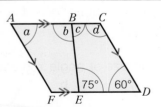

Reflect Q6 had a hint to sketch a diagram. Did you sketch the diagram? Did it help you?

Explain.

7 Check up

Solving geometric problems

1 Work out the sizes of the angles marked with letters, stating any angle facts that you use.

a

b
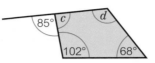

c
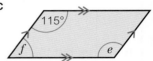

d
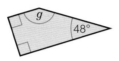

e
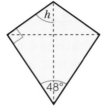

2 The diagram shows some angles on a straight line.
  a Write an equation in terms of x.
  b Solve your equation to find the value of x.
  c Write the sizes of the three angles on the straight line.

3 The diagram shows a triangle.
  a Write an equation in terms of x.
  b Solve your equation to find the value of x.
  c Write the sizes of the three angles in the triangle
     in order of size, starting with the smallest.

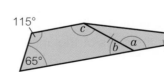

4 In this rectangle, calculate the size of $\angle BCE$.
Show your steps for solving the problem.
Give your reasons.

5 The diagram shows a trapezium and an
isosceles triangle.
Work out the sizes of angles a, b and c.
Give your reasons.

Parallel lines

6 Work out the size of angle x in each diagram. Give your reasons.

a
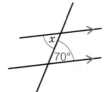

b
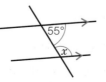

c
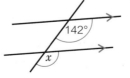

d
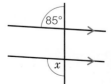

7 Work out the sizes of the angles marked with letters in these diagrams.
Give your reasons.

a

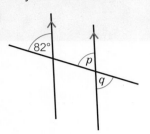

b

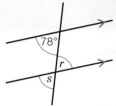

c

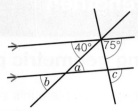

d

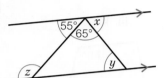

e

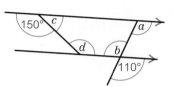

Interior and exterior angles

8 Work out the sum of the interior angles of a pentagon.
You can use this diagram to help.

9 The diagram shows an irregular hexagon.
  a What is the sum of the interior angles of a hexagon?
  b Work out the size of angle z.

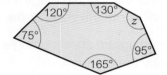

10 The diagram shows a regular hexagon.
Work out the sizes of angles x and y.

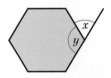

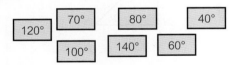
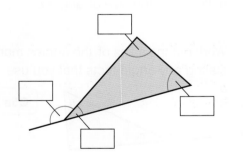

7 Strengthen

Solving geometric problems

1 Copy and complete this statement.
The angles in any quadrilateral add up to ⬚°.

2 **a** Copy each quadrilateral.

    i parallelogram   **ii** rhombus   **iii** kite

      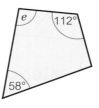

    Draw in any lines of symmetry.
    Mark any equal lengths or angles.
  b Work out the sizes of the angles marked with letters.

3 The diagram shows triangle ABC.
Copy the diagram.
Write on it the sizes of the angles you know.
Work out the size of angle q.

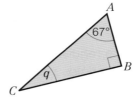

4 The diagram shows triangle LMN.
  a Which two sides are equal?
  b What type of triangle is LMN?
  c What does this tell you about angles p and r?
  d Work out the size of angle p.

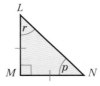

5 Work out the sizes of the angles marked with letters,
stating any angle facts that you use.

  a

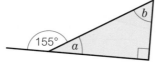

> **Q5a hint** Work out angle a first.

  b   **c**

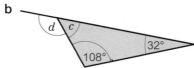   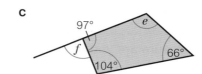

6 **Reasoning** In this rectangle, work out the size of ∠*CED*.
Show your steps for solving this problem and explain your reasoning.

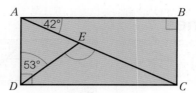

7 a Copy this diagram.

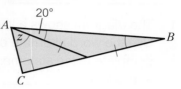

   b Which other angle is 20°? Label it on your diagram.

   c Use the angles of triangle *ABC* to write an equation.

     $z + 20° + \square° + \square° = 180°$

   d Solve your equation to find the value of *z*.

8 For each diagram, write and solve an equation to find the value of the letter.

a

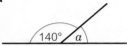

b

c

d

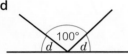

e

f

9 For each diagram, write and solve an equation to find the value of *x*.

> **Q9a hint** $x + 5x + 60 = \square$

a

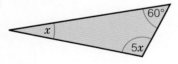

b

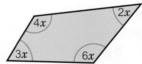

10 The diagram shows a quadrilateral.

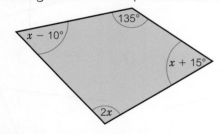

   a Write an equation to find the value of *x*.

> **Q10a hint** $2x + x - 10 + \square + \square + \square = 360$

   b Simplify your equation by collecting like terms.

   c Solve your equation to find the value of *x*.

   d Write the sizes of the four angles in the quadrilateral, starting with the smallest.

Parallel lines

alternate (Z shape)

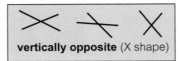
vertically opposite (X shape)

corresponding (F shape)

1   The diagram shows a line crossing two parallel lines.
    Use the word alternate or corresponding to
    complete these statements.
    a *a* and *b* are _____ angles.
    b *c* and *d* are _____ angles.

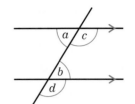

2   The diagram shows a set of parallel lines.
    Copy and complete these statements using words
    from the boxes.
    a *a* and *b* are _____ angles.
    b *a* and *d* are _____ angles.
    c *a* and *c* are _____ angles.
    d *b* and *d* are _____ angles.
    e *c* and *d* are _____ angles.

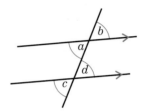

3   Write the sizes of the angles marked with letters in each of these diagrams.
    Give a reason for each answer.
    Choose from
    • alternate angles
    • corresponding angles
    • angles on a straight line
    • vertically opposite angles.

a
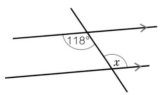

b
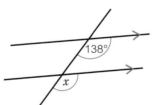

c
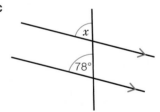

d
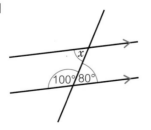

e
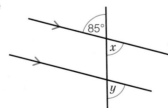

f
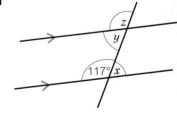

4 Reasoning Write the sizes of the angles marked with letters in each of these diagrams. Give a reason for each answer.

a

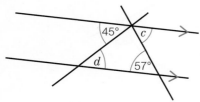

b

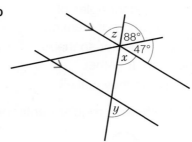

Interior and exterior angles

1 Reasoning

a These two triangles have been joined along one edge to create a quadrilateral. What is the sum of the interior angles of the quadrilateral?

b Copy and complete
The sum of the interior angles of a quadrilateral is ☐ × 180° = ☐°

c Copy this pentagon.
Draw diagonals from the marked corner to split it into three triangles.

d Copy and complete
The sum of the interior angles of a pentagon is ☐ × 180° = ☐°

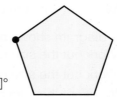

e Copy this hexagon.
Draw diagonals from the marked corner to split the hexagon into triangles.

f Copy and complete
The sum of the interior angles of a hexagon is ☐ × 180° = ☐°

2 **i** Sketch each shape.
ii Divide each shape into triangles using diagonals from the same vertex.
iii Work out what the angles in each shape add up to.
iv Work out the size of angle x.

a

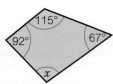

b

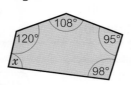

c

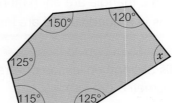

3 The diagram shows an irregular hexagon.
Work out the size of angle x.

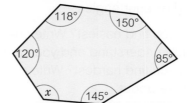

4 Reasoning The diagram shows the exterior angles of a quadrilateral.

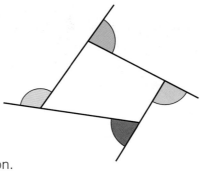

a Trace the exterior angles of this polygon and cut them out.

b Place them together so that the points are together.

c What angle do they make?

5 The diagram shows a regular pentagon.

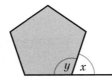

a What do the exterior angles add up to?

b How many equal exterior angles does the regular pentagon have?

c Work out the size of the exterior angle x.

d Use angles on a straight line to work out the size of the interior angle y.

e Work out the sum of all the interior angles.

6 The diagram shows a regular hexagon.

a Work out the size of the exterior angle x.

b Work out the size of the interior angle y.

c Work out the sum of the interior angles.

Challenge Decide whether each of these statements is *always true*, *sometimes true* or *never true*.

If the statement is *always true* or *sometimes true*, draw a diagram to show it.

If the statement is *never true*, explain why.

For example: 'A trapezium has two right-angles'.

Sometimes true

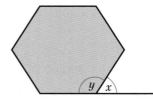

a All the angles in a triangle are less than 90°.

b Two angles in a triangle are each more than 90°.

c All the angles in a quadrilateral are less than 90°.

Reflect This Strengthen lesson covers these topics:
- solving geometric problems
- parallel lines
- interior and exterior angles.

Hint Show what you have written to a friend or your teacher. Ask them to explain to you the thing you did not understand.

Which topic did you find easiest? Write one thing about this topic you fully understand and you are sure about.

Which topic did you find hardest? Write one thing about this topic you still do not understand or you are not sure about.

7 Extend

1 **Reasoning** Anil designs a kite on his computer.
The diagram shows some of the angles.
Work out the sizes of angles a, b and c.
Give a reason for each answer.

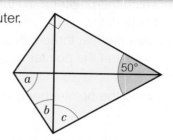

2 **Problem-solving** In triangle ABC,
$\angle ABC$ is 20° more than $\angle BAC$.
$\angle BCA$ is 50° less than $\angle BAC$.
Work out the size of the smallest angle in the triangle.

3 **Problem-solving** In triangle ABC, $\angle ABC$ is twice the size of $\angle BAC$
and $\angle BCA$ is three times the size of $\angle BAC$.
Work out the sizes of the three angles in the triangle.

4 **a** Work out the sum of the interior angles of a pentagon.
   b Work out the value of y in this pentagon.
   c Work out the sizes of all the angles in the pentagon.

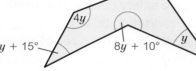

5 **Problem-solving**
   a Plot these points on a coordinate grid:
      $A(1, 2)$, $B(1, 4)$, $C(3, 6)$ and $D(3, 0)$.
   b Join the points in order to make quadrilateral $ABCD$.
   c Write the sizes of $\angle ADC$ and $\angle DAB$.

6 **Problem-solving** In this diagram, angles a and b are in the ratio 5 : 7.
Work out the size of angle c. Give reasons for your answer.

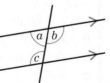

7 **Reasoning** Work out the value of x in each diagram.

  a 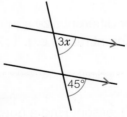   **b** 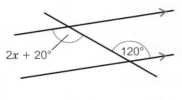   **c**

8 **Problem-solving** The diagram shows a parallelogram and
an isosceles triangle.
Work out the sizes of the angles marked with letters.

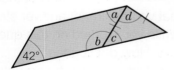

9 **Problem-solving** The diagram shows a right-angled
triangle and a rhombus.
Work out the sizes of the angles marked with letters.

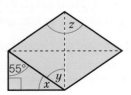

10 **Problem-solving** A computer programmer writes a
program to create a 12-sided regular polygon.
Each side of the polygon is 50 mm.
After each length of 50 mm the programmer gives the
angle through which the pointer must turn anticlockwise
to start the next side.
The diagram shows the first three sides.

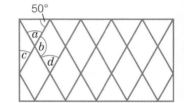

a What is the angle that the pointer needs to
turn through?

b What angle would the pointer need to turn through to create a regular nonagon (9 sides)?

11 **Reasoning**
a A regular polygon has an exterior angle of 18°.
i How many sides does the polygon have?
ii Work out the size of each interior angle.
b A regular polygon has an interior angle of 168°.
How many sides does the polygon have?

12 **Problem-solving** The diagram shows part of the design of
a safety gate. The wooden bars form isosceles triangles
and rhombuses.
Work out the sizes of angles a, b, c and d.

Challenge This diagram shows a triangle drawn inside a square.
The base of the triangle is the base of the square.
The top of the triangle divides the top of the square in the ratio 1 : 1,
i.e. it is the midpoint.

a Make a copy of the diagram on squared paper.
b With a protractor, measure the size of angle x.
c Will angle x always be the same, whatever the size of the square? Explain your answer.
d Draw different squares to test your answer to part **c**.
e Investigate further to see whether angle x is always the same for different size squares
when the top of the triangle divides the top of the square in different ratios, e.g. 1 : 2,
1 : 3 or 1 : 4.

Reflect Look back at the questions you answered in this Extend lesson. Find a question
that you could not answer straight away, or that you really had to think about.
While you worked on this question:
- How did you feel?
- Did you keep trying until you had an answer? Did you give up before reaching an
answer, and move on to the next question?
- Did you think you would get the answer correct or incorrect?

Write any strategies you could use to help you stay calm when answering tricky maths
questions. Compare your strategies with other people's.

7 Unit test

1 Work out the size of angle y in each diagram. State any angle facts that you use.

a

b
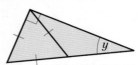

2 Work out the sizes of the angles marked with letters. State any angle facts that you use.

a
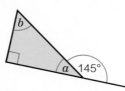

b
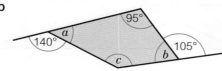

3 Work out the sizes of the angles marked with letters. State any angle facts that you use.

a   **b**   **c**
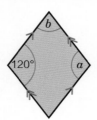
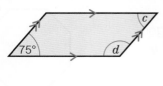
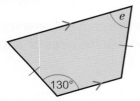

4 The diagram shows some angles on a straight line.
Work out the value of x.

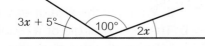

5 The diagram shows a quadrilateral.
a Work out the value of x.
b Write the sizes of the four angles in the quadrilateral, smallest first.

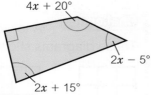

6 The diagram shows a kite and a right-angled triangle.
Work out the size of angle w.

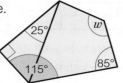

7 a Copy and complete these statements.
  i The angles in a triangle add up to ☐°.
  ii The angles in a quadrilateral add up to ☐°.
  iii The angles in a pentagon add up to ☐°.
  iv The angles in a hexagon add up to ☐°.
b The diagram shows an irregular hexagon.
Work out the size of angle m.

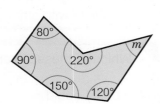

8 Work out the sizes of the angles marked with letters.
Give a reason for each answer.

a 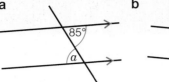 **b** 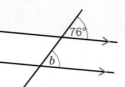 **c** 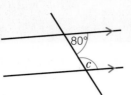 **d**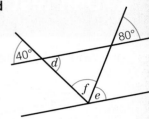

9 The diagram shows a trapezium, *ABCD*.

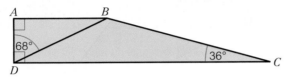

Work out the size of ∠*DBC*.
Show your steps for solving this problem
and explain your reasoning.

10 The diagram shows a regular octagon.
Work out the sizes of angles x and y.

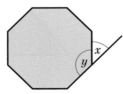

11 a The exterior angle of a regular polygon is 36°.
   i How many sides does the polygon have?
  ii Work out the size of each interior angle.
b The interior angle of a regular polygon is 165°.
   How many sides does this polygon have?

Challenge   A tessellation is a pattern of repeated shapes with no gaps in between.
These diagrams show some different tessellations.

  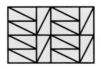

a Do all quadrilaterals tessellate?
b Do all triangles tessellate?
c Which regular polygons will tessellate?
d Some regular polygons will not tessellate.
   Do they tessellate with other shapes?

Hint Draw a diagram to help
you explain each answer.

Reflect   Which of these statements best describes your work on lines and angles in
this unit?
   • I did the best I could.
   • I could have tried harder.

Why did you choose that statement?
Was it true for every lesson?
Write one thing you will do to make sure you do the best you can in the next unit.

8 Calculating with fractions

Master   Check up p212   Strengthen p214   Extend p219   Unit test p221

8.1 Ordering fractions

Active Learn
Homework

- Identify fractions as more than $\frac{1}{2}$ or less than $\frac{1}{2}$
- Order fractions

Warm up

1 **Fluency**   Which fraction is larger in each pair?

   a $\frac{9}{12}$ and $\frac{8}{12}$ **b** $\frac{3}{20}$ and $\frac{13}{20}$ **c** $\frac{1}{2}$ and $\frac{1}{4}$ **d** $\frac{1}{8}$ and $\frac{1}{5}$ **e** $\frac{1}{10}$ and $\frac{1}{9}$

2 Copy and complete these equivalent fractions.

   a
   $$\frac{1}{2} = \frac{\square}{8} \quad {\scriptstyle \times 4}$$

   b ${\scriptstyle \times 5}$
   $$\frac{1}{2} = \frac{\square}{10} \quad {\scriptstyle \times 5}$$

   c ${\scriptstyle \times \square}$
   $$\frac{5}{6} = \frac{\square}{12} \quad {\scriptstyle \times \square}$$

   d ${\scriptstyle \times \square}$
   $$\frac{3}{4} = \frac{\square}{20} \quad {\scriptstyle \times \square}$$

   e $$\frac{1}{2} = \frac{\square}{6}$$

   f $$\frac{2}{5} = \frac{\square}{20}$$

3 Work out the lowest common multiple (LCM) of
   a 3 and 4
   b 4 and 5
   c 5 and 10
   d 4, 8 and 16
   e 3, 6 and 9
   f 3, 5 and 10.

4 Which of these fractions are more than $\frac{1}{2}$?

   $\frac{3}{4}$ $\frac{2}{5}$ $\frac{5}{6}$ $\frac{4}{7}$ $\frac{5}{8}$ $\frac{4}{9}$

> **Q4 hint** Is the numerator more than $\frac{1}{2}$ the denominator?

5 Write each fraction under the heading 'more than $\frac{1}{2}$' or 'less than $\frac{1}{2}$'.

   $\frac{7}{10}$ $\frac{5}{9}$ $\frac{2}{7}$ $\frac{2}{5}$ $\frac{11}{20}$ $\frac{9}{20}$ $\frac{4}{11}$ $\frac{6}{11}$

6 **Reasoning**   Write a fraction larger than $\frac{1}{2}$ with a denominator of 17.

> **Q6 hint** $\frac{\square}{17} > \frac{1}{2}$

7 **Reasoning**   Write a fraction smaller than $\frac{1}{2}$ with a numerator of 5.

8 **Problem-solving / Reasoning**   How many positive fractions are there less than $\frac{1}{2}$, with a numerator of 13?

9 Write each set of fractions in order, smallest first.

a $\frac{1}{2}$ $\frac{5}{8}$ $\frac{1}{4}$ **b** $\frac{1}{2}$ $\frac{2}{5}$ $\frac{7}{9}$ **c** $-\frac{1}{2}$ $-\frac{5}{8}$ $-\frac{1}{4}$ **d** $-\frac{1}{2}$ $-\frac{2}{5}$ $-\frac{7}{9}$

10 **a** Write each fraction with a denominator of 12.

i $\frac{1}{6} = \frac{\Box}{12}$ **ii** $\frac{3}{4} = \frac{\Box}{12}$ **iii** $\frac{2}{3} = \frac{\Box}{12}$

b Order the fractions $\frac{1}{6}$, $\frac{3}{4}$ and $\frac{2}{3}$ from smallest to largest.

> **Q10b hint** In part **a** you wrote these fractions with the same denominator of 12.

11 **a** Write each fraction with a common denominator of 40.

i $\frac{3}{4}$ **ii** $\frac{7}{10}$ **iii** $\frac{5}{8}$ **iv** $\frac{11}{20}$

b Order the fractions in part **a** in descending order.

12 Write each set of fractions in ascending order.

a $\frac{2}{3}$ $\frac{1}{6}$ $\frac{7}{9}$ **b** $\frac{3}{4}$ $\frac{4}{5}$ $\frac{13}{20}$

c $\frac{3}{8}$ $\frac{9}{16}$ $\frac{1}{4}$ **d** $\frac{1}{3}$ $\frac{2}{5}$ $\frac{3}{10}$

e $\frac{11}{15}$ $\frac{7}{10}$ $\frac{2}{3}$ $\frac{4}{5}$ **f** $\frac{5}{8}$ $\frac{2}{3}$ $\frac{7}{12}$ $\frac{5}{6}$

> **Q12a hint** What is the lowest common multiple (LCM) of 3, 6 and 9? Write each fraction with the LCM as the denominator. Then order them.

13 **a** List these fractions in descending order.

$-\frac{3}{4}$ $\frac{9}{14}$ $-\frac{5}{7}$ $\frac{1}{2}$

b **Problem-solving** Add these two fractions to your list in part **a**, so that your six fractions are still in descending order:

i one fraction at the beginning of your list

ii one fraction at the end of your list.

8.2 Adding and subtracting fractions

Active Learn
Homework

- Add and subtract fractions with any size denominator

Warm up

1 Fluency

a Which of these fractions are equal to 1?

$$\frac{1}{3} \quad \frac{4}{4} \quad \frac{2}{5} \quad \frac{4}{5} \quad \frac{6}{7} \quad \frac{7}{7}$$

b Which pairs of fractions in part **a** have a common denominator?

2 Work out these calculations.
Give your answers as fractions in their simplest form.

a $\frac{1}{8} + \frac{3}{8}$ **b** $\frac{2}{12} + \frac{7}{12}$ **c** $\frac{6}{15} + \frac{4}{15}$ **d** $1 - \frac{6}{10}$

3 Write these improper fractions as mixed numbers.

a $\frac{7}{2}$ **b** $\frac{10}{9}$ **c** $\frac{101}{25}$ **d** $\frac{26}{9}$ **e** $\frac{15}{4}$

4 Write each pair of fractions so that they have a common denominator.
The first one is started for you.

a $\frac{1}{4} \quad \frac{1}{8}$ **b** $\frac{4}{5} \quad \frac{7}{10}$ **c** $\frac{1}{12} \quad \frac{5}{6}$ **d** $\frac{1}{4} \quad \frac{1}{3}$

$\frac{1}{4} = \frac{\square}{8}$

Key point

To add or subtract fractions, they must have a common denominator.

Worked example

Work out these calculations.

a $\frac{1}{3} + \frac{1}{6}$

$$\frac{1}{3} + \frac{1}{6} = \frac{2}{6} + \frac{1}{6}$$

$\frac{1}{3} = \frac{2}{6} \quad \frac{1}{6}$

The LCM of 3 and 6 is 6.

$$= \frac{3}{6}$$

$$= \frac{1}{2}$$

Simplify the answer, if possible.

b $\frac{1}{3} - \frac{1}{6}$

$$\frac{1}{3} - \frac{1}{6} = \frac{2}{6} - \frac{1}{6}$$

$$= \frac{1}{6}$$

5 Work out these calculations.
Give your answers as fractions in their simplest form.

a $\frac{1}{4} + \frac{1}{8}$ **b** $\frac{1}{5} + \frac{3}{10}$

c $\frac{1}{12} + \frac{5}{6}$ **d** $\frac{2}{3} + \frac{1}{12}$

e $\frac{2}{15} + \frac{2}{5}$ **f** $\frac{3}{20} + \frac{7}{20}$

g $\frac{20}{24} + \frac{1}{6}$ **h** $\frac{3}{5} + \frac{6}{25}$

6 Work out these calculations.
Write any improper fraction answers as mixed numbers and fractions in their simplest form.

a $\frac{2}{3} + \frac{4}{9}$ **b** $\frac{3}{4} + \frac{7}{12}$

c $\frac{9}{10} + \frac{3}{5}$ **d** $\frac{5}{6} + \frac{21}{18}$

7 Work out these calculations.
Give your answers as fractions in their simplest form.

a $\frac{1}{5} - \frac{1}{10}$ **b** $\frac{3}{5} - \frac{2}{10}$

c $\frac{4}{9} - \frac{1}{3}$ **d** $\frac{11}{12} - \frac{3}{4}$

8 **Problem-solving / Reasoning**
a Ahmed has eaten $\frac{5}{12}$ of his pizza. Dom has eaten $\frac{5}{6}$ of his.
How much more has Dom eaten?
b Which of the boys has eaten more than half of his pizza?

9 **Reasoning** Kieran says, '$\frac{1}{4} + \frac{1}{3} = \frac{2}{7}$'

a What mistake has he made?

b Work out $\frac{1}{4} + \frac{1}{3}$ by writing both fractions with denominator 12.

10 Work out these calculations. The first one is started for you.

a $\frac{1}{2} + \frac{1}{3} = \frac{\square}{6} + \frac{\square}{6}$

$= \frac{\square}{6}$

> **Q10b hint** Use
> 15 as the common
> denominator because it
> is the LCM of 3 and 5.

b $\frac{2}{3} + \frac{1}{5}$ **c** $\frac{1}{2} + \frac{1}{7}$ **d** $\frac{3}{4} - \frac{1}{6}$ **e** $\frac{7}{10} + \frac{4}{15}$

11 **Problem-solving**

a How much more than $\frac{11}{15}$ is $\frac{5}{6}$?

b How much less than $\frac{7}{8}$ is $\frac{3}{5}$?

c What is the sum of $\frac{2}{5}$ and $\frac{3}{8}$?

12 $\frac{3}{4} - \frac{2}{7} = \frac{13}{28}$ $\frac{3}{4} + \frac{2}{7} = 1\frac{1}{28}$

Use these facts to work out these calculations.

a $\frac{13}{28} + \frac{2}{7}$ **b** $1\frac{1}{28} - \frac{3}{4}$

c $\frac{13}{28} - \frac{3}{4}$ **d** $\frac{13}{28} - \left(\frac{3}{4} - \frac{2}{7}\right)$

13 Use your calculator to work out these calculations.
Write your answers as mixed numbers.

a $\frac{1}{2} + \frac{3}{5} + \frac{1}{4}$ b $\frac{2}{5} - \frac{3}{5} - \frac{9}{10}$

c $\frac{13}{28} + \frac{21}{3}$ d $\frac{11}{2} + \frac{21}{6} - \frac{3}{5}$

> **Q13 hint** Use the fraction button on your calculator to enter a fraction.

e Copy the way that your calculator displays fractions.
Compare with others in your class.

14 Answer these questions in fractions of an hour.

a On Monday, Katherine spends $\frac{3}{4}$ of an hour on maths homework and $\frac{1}{2}$ an hour on French homework.
How long does she spend doing homework on Monday?

b On Wednesday, she spends $\frac{2}{3}$ of an hour on art homework and 15 minutes on creative writing.
How long does she spend doing homework on Wednesday?

c This is all of her homework.
How long has she spent in total doing homework this week?

15 Problem-solving At a school, $\frac{1}{3}$ of Year 8 students have school dinners.
$\frac{3}{5}$ bring packed lunches.
The rest go home for lunch.
What fraction of Year 8 students go home for lunch?

Challenge

> **Hint** Consecutive numbers follow on, in order. 2 and 3 are consecutive numbers.

1 a Find the difference between fractions where the numerator and denominator are consecutive numbers.

$\frac{2}{3} - \frac{1}{2} = \frac{\square}{6} - \frac{\square}{6} =$ $\frac{3}{4} - \frac{2}{3} =$ $\frac{4}{5} - \frac{3}{4} =$ $\frac{5}{6} - \frac{4}{5} =$

b Predict the answer to $\frac{9}{10} - \frac{8}{9}$. Work out the answer to check your prediction.

2 a Find these differences.

$\frac{3}{4} - \frac{1}{2} =$ $\frac{5}{6} - \frac{3}{4} =$ $\frac{6}{7} - \frac{4}{5} =$

b Is the answer getting smaller or larger?
Predict the answer to $\frac{9}{10} - \frac{7}{8}$.

Reflect   Look back at Q5, Q6 and Q7.

What steps did you take to work out these calculations?
You might begin with, 'Step 1: I looked at the denominators and noticed ...'
Do your steps work for Q10?
If not, rewrite your steps so that they work for all the questions in this lesson.

8.3 Multiplying fractions

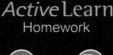

- Multiply integers and fractions by a fraction
- Use appropriate methods for multiplying fractions

Warm up

1 Fluency Which of these calculations give the same answer?

A 15 × 3   **B** 3 × 10   **C** 8 × 3   **D** 3 × 15

E 7 ÷ 7   **F** 4 × 6   **G** 10 × 3   **H** 1 × 1

2 Work out

a $\frac{1}{4}$ of 100 kg   **b** $\frac{3}{4}$ of 100 kg   **c** $\frac{1}{5}$ of 50 cm   **d** $\frac{4}{5}$ of 50 cm.

3 Simplify these fractions.

a $\frac{4}{12}$ **b** $\frac{8}{36}$ **c** $\frac{13}{10}$ **d** $6\frac{3}{9}$

4 Work out

a $\frac{4}{5}$ of 30   **b** $\frac{2}{3}$ of 90   **c** $\frac{2}{7}$ of 42   **d** $\frac{3}{10}$ of 10.

> **Key point** Finding a fraction of an integer is the same as multiplying a fraction and an integer. For example, $\frac{3}{4}$ of 100 is the same as $\frac{3}{4}$ × 100.

5 Work out

a $\frac{3}{4}$ × 100   **b** $\frac{2}{5}$ × 10   **c** 16 × $\frac{7}{8}$ **d** 22 × $\frac{4}{11}$

> **Q5c hint** 16 × $\frac{7}{8}$ = $\frac{7}{8}$ × 16

6 Reasoning

a Jesse and Lucy are working out 45 × $\frac{2}{9}$

Jesse begins his working like this: 45 × 2

Then he divides his answer by 9.

Lucy begins her working like this: 45 ÷ 9

Then she multiplies her answer by 2.

Do they both get the same answer?

b Work out 20 × $\frac{3}{5}$ by multiplying first (like Jesse).

Then work it out by dividing first (like Lucy).

Does it matter whether you divide or multiply first?

7 Work out the areas of these shapes. Simplify your answers.

a

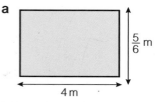

$\frac{5}{6}$ m

4 m

b

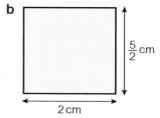

$\frac{5}{2}$ cm

2 cm

c

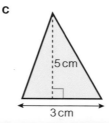

5 cm

3 cm

8 **Problem-solving** A hedge is 6 metres long. A gardener trims $\frac{2}{3}$ of the hedge.
  a What length of hedge has been trimmed?
  b What length of hedge is left to trim?

9 **Problem-solving** A car has 45 litres of fuel in the tank. The driver uses $\frac{3}{5}$ of the fuel.
  How many litres of fuel are left?

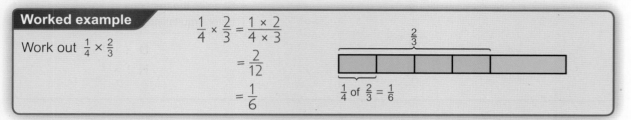

Key point To multiply two fractions, multiply their numerators and multiply their denominators.

Worked example

Work out $\frac{1}{4} \times \frac{2}{3}$

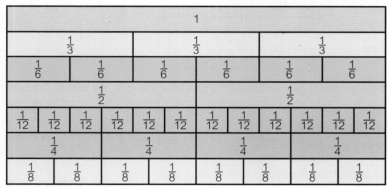

$$\frac{1}{4} \times \frac{2}{3} = \frac{1 \times 2}{4 \times 3}$$
$$= \frac{2}{12}$$
$$= \frac{1}{6}$$

$\frac{1}{4}$ of $\frac{2}{3} = \frac{1}{6}$

10 Work out these multiplications. Use the fraction wall to check your answers.

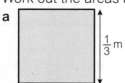

a $\frac{1}{2} \times \frac{1}{2}$ **b** $\frac{1}{3} \times \frac{1}{2}$ **c** $\frac{1}{4} \times \frac{1}{3}$ **d** $\frac{3}{4} \times \frac{1}{2}$

11 Work out each calculation. Simplify your answer where needed.

  a $\frac{2}{3} \times \frac{3}{4}$ **b** $\frac{1}{4} \times \frac{4}{5}$ **c** $\frac{2}{3} \times \frac{2}{5}$ **d** $\frac{3}{4} \times \frac{3}{4}$
  e $\frac{3}{4} \times \frac{6}{11}$ **f** $\frac{4}{9} \times \frac{3}{7}$ **g** $\frac{3}{5} \times \frac{7}{12}$ **h** $\frac{5}{6} \times \frac{3}{8}$

12 Work out the areas and perimeters of these squares.

  a $\frac{1}{3}$ m

  b $\frac{3}{4}$ cm

  c 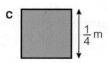 $\frac{1}{4}$ m

13 **Problem-solving** In 2012, $\frac{1}{20}$ of a council's members were from minority ethnic groups.
  Of these, $\frac{1}{3}$ were women.
  What fraction of the council were minority ethnic women?

14 Work out

  a $-\frac{2}{3} \times \frac{1}{4}$ **b** $-\frac{5}{6} \times \frac{1}{2}$ **c** $\frac{1}{5} \times -\frac{3}{4}$ **d** $-\frac{4}{7} \times -\frac{1}{2}$

> **Q14 hint** Use the rules for multiplying negative numbers.

Worked example

Work out $\frac{3}{8} \times \frac{2}{9}$

$$\frac{3}{8} \times \frac{2}{9} = \frac{3 \times 2}{8 \times 9}$$

$$= \frac{2 \times 3}{8 \times 9}$$

$$= \frac{2}{8} \times \frac{3}{9}$$

$$= \frac{1}{4} \times \frac{1}{3}$$

$$= \frac{1}{12}$$

Rewrite the calculation with a fraction that can be simplified. 2 is a factor of 8 and 3 is a factor of 9.

Simplify the fractions before multiplying.

15 Problem-solving / Reasoning

Chris works out $\frac{5}{12} \times \frac{3}{10}$ like this: $\quad \frac{5}{12} \times \frac{3}{10} = \frac{5 \times 3}{12 \times 10} = \frac{15}{120}$

Kamran works it out like this: $\quad \frac{5}{12} \times \frac{3}{10} = \frac{5 \times 3}{12 \times 10} = \frac{3 \times 5}{12 \times 10} = \frac{{}^1 3 \times 5^1}{{}_4 12 \times 10_2} = \frac{1}{8}$

a Copy Chris's working then simplify his answer to show that he got the same answer as Kamran.

b Whose method do you prefer? Why?

c Use your preferred method to work out $\frac{8}{49} \times \frac{7}{24}$.

16 Work these out, using your preferred method from Q15.

a $\frac{5}{6} \times \frac{9}{10}$ b $\frac{5}{12} \times \frac{6}{15}$ c $\frac{7}{8} \times \frac{4}{7}$

Q16f hint $\frac{20}{10} = 20 \div 10 = \square$

d $\frac{5}{14} \times \frac{6}{15}$ e $\frac{17}{33} \times \frac{11}{34}$ f $\frac{20}{21} \times \frac{3}{10}$

17 Problem-solving Holly drank $\frac{2}{3}$ of a $\frac{1}{2}$ litre bottle of juice. How much did she drink?

18 Work out

a $-\frac{2}{3} \times \frac{7}{8}$ b $-\frac{3}{7} \times \frac{7}{12}$ c $\frac{4}{9} \times -\frac{2}{9}$ d $-\frac{5}{6} \times -\frac{2}{9}$

Challenge Work out the missing numbers.

a $\frac{9}{11} \times \frac{2}{3} \times \frac{11}{20} = \frac{\square}{\square}$ b $\frac{9}{14} \times \frac{3}{18} \times \frac{7}{8} = \frac{\square}{\square}$ c $\frac{1}{3} \times \frac{5}{7} \times \frac{\square}{\square} = \frac{5}{42}$ d $\frac{1}{5} \times \frac{\square}{\square} \times \frac{1}{2} = \frac{1}{45}$

Reflect Look back at Q10.

How did you learn how to multiply fractions?

What is good about learning a new mathematics skill this way?

Explain your answer.

Is anything not so good?

What other ways do you like to learn new mathematics skills?

Hint Did you read the worked example? Did your teacher explain it to you?

8.4 Dividing fractions

- Find the reciprocal of a number
- Divide integers and fractions by a fraction
- Use strategies for dividing fractions

Active Learn
Homework

Warm up

1 Fluency How many
  a 2s are there in 10
  b 5s are there in 10
  c 1s are there in 3
  d 4s are there in 16?

2 Write these improper fractions as mixed numbers.
  a $\frac{3}{2}$ **b** $\frac{5}{2}$ **c** $\frac{13}{3}$ **d** $\frac{23}{4}$ **e** $\frac{45}{2}$

3 Work out
  a $\frac{1}{4} \times 2$ **b** $\frac{1}{3} \times \frac{1}{2}$ **c** $\frac{3}{5} \times \frac{2}{7}$ **d** $\frac{2}{3} \times \frac{3}{4}$
  e $\frac{5}{9} \times \frac{3}{10}$ **f** $\frac{1}{2} \times -4$ **g** $-\frac{1}{3} \times -\frac{2}{5}$ **h** $-\frac{4}{5} \times -\frac{1}{6}$

4 Work out
  a $\frac{4}{5} \times \frac{5}{4}$ **b** $\frac{2}{3} \times \frac{3}{2}$ **c** $\frac{1}{3} \times 3$ **d** $\frac{1}{8} \times 8$
  e What do you notice about the fractions in parts **a** to **d** and your answers?

5 Write your own calculation with two fractions. $\frac{\square}{\square} \times \frac{\square}{\square} = 1$

> **Key point**   The **reciprocal** of a fraction is the 'upside down' fraction.
> A number multiplied by its reciprocal is always 1. The reciprocal of $\frac{3}{5}$ is $\frac{5}{3}$.

6 Write the reciprocal of each of these numbers.
  a $\frac{2}{7}$ **b** $\frac{3}{5}$ **c** $\frac{8}{9}$ **d** $\frac{11}{3}$ **e** $\frac{20}{7}$

> **Key point**   You can write integers (whole numbers) as fractions with a denominator of 1.
> Dividing by 1 doesn't change the number. For example, $\frac{3}{1} = 3$.

7 Write the reciprocal of each of these numbers.
  The first one is started for you.
  a $4 = \frac{4}{1}$ reciprocal $= \frac{\square}{\square}$
  b 5   **c** 7   **d** $\frac{1}{10}$ **e** $\frac{1}{23}$ **f** $\frac{1}{100}$

8 Write a calculation to match each question. The first one has been done for you.

a How many fifths are there in 1?

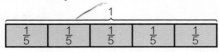

$1 \div \frac{1}{5} = 5$

b How many quarters are there in 1?

c How many thirds are there in 1?

d How many halves are there in 3?

e How many quarters are there in 2?

> **Q8b hint**
>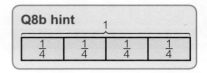

9 Copy and complete.

a $3 \div \frac{1}{2} = \square = 3 \times \square$

b $2 \div \frac{1}{4} = \square = 2 \times \square$

c $3 \div \frac{1}{5} = \square = 3 \times \square$

d $4 \div \frac{1}{3} = \square = 4 \times \square$

e Reasoning Look at your answers to parts **a** to **d**.
Explain how you use the reciprocal of a fraction to divide.

10 Match each calculation to a diagram and work out the answer.

a $\frac{3}{5} \div \frac{3}{10}$

A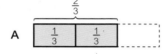

b $\frac{2}{3} \div \frac{1}{3}$

B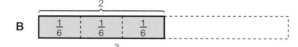

c $\frac{3}{4} \div \frac{1}{8}$

C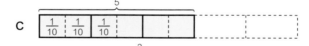

d $\frac{1}{2} \div \frac{1}{6}$

D

e Work out the calculations in parts **a** to **d** using your rule from Q9 part **e**. Does it work?

11 Use your rule from Q9 part **e** to work out

a $\frac{2}{5} \div \frac{1}{5}$

b $\frac{3}{4} \div \frac{3}{8}$

c $\frac{5}{6} \div \frac{1}{12}$

d $\frac{1}{7} \div \frac{1}{21}$

> **Key point** Dividing by a fraction is the same as multiplying by its reciprocal.

12 Work out these calculations. Give your answers as fractions in their simplest form.

a $\frac{1}{5} \div \frac{1}{3}$

b $\frac{2}{9} \div \frac{1}{4}$

c $\frac{3}{10} \div \frac{1}{2}$

d $\frac{2}{15} \div \frac{1}{7}$

e $\frac{4}{9} \div \frac{2}{3}$

f $\frac{2}{5} \div \frac{8}{15}$

g $\frac{5}{12} \div \frac{15}{16}$

h $\frac{9}{20} \div \frac{21}{40}$

> **Q12e hint** $\frac{4}{9} \times \frac{3}{2}$
> Simplify the fractions before multiplying.

Worked example

Work out $5 \div \frac{2}{3}$

$$5 \div \frac{2}{3} = \frac{5}{1} \times \frac{3}{2}$$

$$= \frac{15}{2}$$

$$= 7\frac{1}{2}$$

$5 = \frac{5}{1}$.
Multiply by the reciprocal of $\frac{2}{3}$.

Write as a mixed number in its simplest form.

13 Work out these calculations.
Write any improper fraction answers as mixed numbers.

Q13d hint
$10 \times \frac{9}{5} = \frac{10 \times 9}{1 \times 5} = \frac{9 \times 10}{1 \times 5}$

a $6 \div \frac{2}{3}$

b $3 \div \frac{4}{5}$

c $4 \div \frac{3}{4}$

d $10 \div \frac{5}{9}$

e $12 \div \frac{3}{10}$

f $18 \div \frac{2}{9}$

g $21 \div \frac{7}{10}$

h $15 \div \frac{2}{3}$

i $7 \div \frac{2}{5}$

14 **Problem-solving** An electrician cuts a 10 m roll of cable into lengths.
Each length is $\frac{5}{6}$ of a metre. How many lengths can she cut from the roll?

15 **Problem-solving** A sewing pattern uses $\frac{5}{8}$ of a yard of fabric for a pair of shorts.
How many pairs can you make from 4 yards?

16 Work out

a $-20 \div \frac{2}{5}$

b $24 \div -\frac{8}{15}$

c $-16 \div \frac{4}{9}$

d $40 \div -\frac{4}{5}$

e $-\frac{3}{20} \div -\frac{2}{5}$

f $\frac{3}{7} \div -\frac{9}{14}$

g $\frac{9}{16} \div -\frac{3}{4}$

h $-\frac{3}{4} \div \frac{5}{6}$

17 **Problem-solving** Continue these patterns.

a $\frac{1}{2} \times 8 = 4$

$\frac{1}{2} \times 4 =$

$\frac{1}{2} \times 2 =$

$\frac{1}{2} \times 1 =$

$\frac{1}{2} \times \frac{1}{2} =$

$\frac{1}{2} \times \frac{1}{4} =$

$\frac{1}{2} \times \frac{1}{8} =$

b $\frac{1}{2} \div 8 = \frac{1}{16}$

$\frac{1}{2} \div 4 =$

$\frac{1}{2} \div 2 =$

$\frac{1}{2} \div 1 =$

$\frac{1}{2} \div \frac{1}{2} =$

$\frac{1}{2} \div \frac{1}{4} =$

$\frac{1}{2} \div \frac{1}{8} =$

c Describe and explain the different sequences and patterns you can see.

Challenge Use your calculator to work out these divisions.

a $\frac{1}{2} \div \frac{6}{5}$

b $\frac{8}{3} \div \frac{2}{3}$

c $\frac{10}{11} \div \frac{5}{2}$

d $\frac{6}{7} \div \frac{1}{2}$

e $\frac{2}{3} \div \frac{8}{3}$

f How can you tell by comparing the two fractions whether the answer is going to be bigger or smaller than the first fraction?

Reflect Q10 used bar models to show dividing by fractions.
Did the bar models help you to understand? Explain your answer.

8.5 Calculating with mixed numbers

Active Learn
Homework

- Write a mixed number as an improper fraction
- Use the four operations with mixed numbers

Warm up

1 Fluency What are the missing lengths?

a
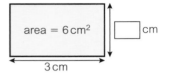
area = 6 cm²   □ cm
3 cm

b
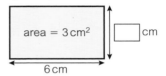
area = 3 cm²   □ cm
6 cm

2 Write these improper fractions as integers or mixed numbers

a $\frac{8}{4}$ **b** $\frac{7}{4}$ **c** $\frac{15}{3}$ **d** $\frac{15}{2}$

e $\frac{21}{7}$ **f** $\frac{10}{7}$ **g** $\frac{54}{9}$ **h** $\frac{15}{9}$

3 Work out

a $\frac{3}{4} + \frac{1}{8}$ **b** $\frac{1}{2} + \frac{2}{3}$ **c** $\frac{2}{5} - \frac{1}{4}$ **d** $\frac{5}{2} \times 3$

e $\frac{7}{9} \times \frac{2}{3}$ **f** $\frac{1}{2} \div \frac{3}{4}$ **g** $\frac{8}{9} \div \frac{1}{3}$ **h** $\frac{4}{11} \div 6$

Key point   You can add or subtract mixed numbers by adding or subtracting the whole numbers first, then writing the fraction parts with a common denominator to add or subtract them.

4 Work out these mixed number calculations. Write the answers in their simplest form. The first one is started for you.

a $3\frac{1}{4} + 2\frac{1}{2} = 5 + \frac{1}{4} + \frac{2}{4} =$

b $1\frac{1}{2} + 5\frac{1}{3}$ **c** $5\frac{3}{10} + 2\frac{1}{5}$ **d** $3\frac{2}{3} + 4\frac{4}{5}$

e $5\frac{3}{8} - 2\frac{7}{9}$ **f** $2\frac{3}{4} - 1\frac{1}{2}$ **g** $10\frac{1}{8} - 4\frac{1}{10}$

> **Q4d hint** $7 + \frac{\square}{15} = 7 + 1\frac{\square}{15}$
> $= 8\frac{\square}{15}$

5 Problem-solving Paul is travelling from Turkey to Iran.
He spends $2\frac{1}{2}$ hours on the bus. He then travels for $3\frac{3}{4}$ hours by train.
How long does he spend travelling?

6 Problem-solving Work out the missing mixed numbers in these calculations. Write the mixed numbers in their simplest form.

a $3\frac{1}{2} + \square = 4\frac{7}{10}$ **b** $\square + 2\frac{1}{4} = 4\frac{5}{12}$

c $2\frac{6}{7} - \square = 1\frac{11}{21}$ **d** $\square - 3\frac{1}{3} = 1\frac{5}{6}$

Write $5\frac{2}{3}$ as an improper fraction.

Write the whole number as a fraction with the same denominator as the fraction part.

$5\frac{2}{3} = \frac{15}{3} + \frac{2}{3}$

$= \frac{17}{3}$

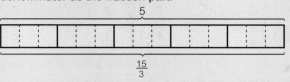

7 Write these mixed numbers as improper fractions.

a $5\frac{1}{2}$ **b** $9\frac{1}{6}$ **c** $2\frac{3}{8}$ **d** $10\frac{3}{4}$

Key point   It can be easier to write mixed numbers as improper fractions before subtracting.

Work out $5\frac{2}{3} - 1\frac{5}{6}$.

$5\frac{2}{3} - 1\frac{5}{6} = \frac{17}{3} - \frac{11}{6}$ Write both numbers as improper fractions.

$= \frac{34}{6} - \frac{11}{6}$ Write the fractions with a common denominator.

$= \frac{23}{6}$ Write the answer as a mixed number.

$= 3\frac{5}{6}$

8 Work out these subtractions.

a $5\frac{1}{2} - 2\frac{3}{4}$ **b** $2\frac{1}{5} - 2\frac{3}{10}$ **c** $2\frac{5}{6} - 5\frac{1}{3}$ **d** $3\frac{2}{3} - 5\frac{8}{9}$

e $8\frac{1}{2} - 4\frac{3}{5}$ **f** $3\frac{2}{3} - 2\frac{3}{4}$ **g** $4\frac{3}{4} - \frac{11}{16}$ **h** $4\frac{3}{7} - 3\frac{1}{3}$

9 **Problem-solving** Sanjay has completed $15\frac{2}{3}$ miles of a $24\frac{5}{7}$ mile race. How far does he have left to run?

10 **Problem-solving / Reasoning** Write two mixed numbers that

a add to give $13\frac{5}{9}$ **b** subtract to give $13\frac{5}{9}$.

Key point   Write mixed numbers as improper fractions before multiplying or dividing.

11 Work out these calculations.
Give your answers as mixed numbers.

a $2\frac{1}{2} \times 3$ **b** $4\frac{1}{10} \times 2$ **c** $1\frac{3}{5} \times 10$ **d** $3\frac{1}{10} \times \frac{2}{3}$

e $\frac{4}{7} \times 1\frac{4}{5}$ **f** $2\frac{1}{2} \times 2\frac{1}{2}$ **g** $3\frac{1}{4} \times 1\frac{2}{3}$ **h** $1\frac{3}{7} \times 5\frac{1}{5}$

12 **Problem-solving** The length of a wall is twice its height. The height is $1\frac{7}{10}$ m. How long is the wall?

13 Work out these calculations.
Give your answers as mixed numbers.

a $6\frac{1}{4} \div 2$ **b** $9\frac{2}{5} \div 3$ **c** $10\frac{2}{3} \div \frac{1}{2}$ **d** $2\frac{1}{4} \div \frac{2}{5}$

e $2\frac{5}{8} \div \frac{3}{5}$ **f** $4\frac{4}{5} \div \frac{5}{6}$ **g** $3\frac{3}{10} \div 1\frac{1}{2}$ **h** $3\frac{1}{3} \div 2\frac{1}{6}$

14 Sally uses $5\frac{1}{5}$ kg of clay to make a set of four pots that are exactly the same.
How much clay does Sally use for each pot?

15 Problem-solving Work out the area
of this trapezium.

$3\frac{1}{4}$ cm

$3\frac{1}{2}$ cm

$5\frac{1}{2}$ cm

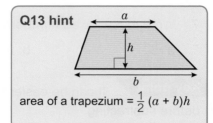

Q13 hint

a

h

b

area of a trapezium = $\frac{1}{2}(a + b)h$

16 Problem-solving A relay race is $1\frac{1}{4}$ miles.
There are three relay runners on the team.
Each person runs the same distance.
How far does each person run?

17 Problem-solving Antony says he is $1\frac{1}{2}$ times as tall as Ross.
Antony is 156 cm tall.
How tall is Ross?

18 Problem-solving A pancake recipe uses $1\frac{3}{4}$ pints of milk to make 20 pancakes.
How much is needed to make 10 pancakes?

19 Problem-solving Mumtaz can swim $1\frac{1}{5}$ times as fast as Ethan.
Ethan can swim one length in 30 seconds.
How long will it take Mumtaz to swim one length?

20 Problem-solving Find the lengths of these rectangles.

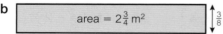

a area = $6\frac{1}{3}$ m² $\frac{3}{4}$ m   **b** area = $2\frac{3}{4}$ m² $\frac{3}{8}$ m

21 An equilateral triangle has side length $8\frac{1}{5}$ cm.
Sara uses this calculation to work out its perimeter $8\frac{1}{5} + 8\frac{1}{5} + 8\frac{1}{5}$.
a Work out the answer to Sara's calculation.
b What other calculation can you use to work out the perimeter?
Show your working and an answer.

Challenge Sort these calculations into the two groups.

$4\frac{2}{3} \times 1\frac{1}{5}$ $15\frac{1}{8} - 5\frac{1}{4}$ $1\frac{1}{2} \times 8$ $6\frac{2}{5} + 20\frac{1}{2}$ $1\frac{3}{7} \times 1\frac{1}{7}$ $18\frac{3}{10} - 1\frac{4}{5}$

• Group 1: Write as improper fractions first.
• Group 2: Calculate the whole number parts first.

Reflect What is the same when you calculate with fractions and with mixed numbers?
What is different?

8 Check up

Ordering fractions

1 Order these fractions, from smallest to largest.

$\frac{1}{2}$ $\frac{7}{12}$ $\frac{2}{17}$

2 Write these fractions in ascending order. Show your working.

$\frac{18}{25}$ $\frac{7}{10}$ $\frac{4}{5}$

Calculating with fractions

3 Work these out. Simplify your answers where needed.

a $\frac{3}{16} + \frac{5}{8}$ **b** $\frac{7}{12} - \frac{1}{4}$ **c** $\frac{9}{20} + \frac{4}{5}$ **d** $\frac{7}{10} + \frac{3}{15}$ **e** $\frac{5}{12} - \frac{1}{8}$

4 $\frac{4}{9}$ of the memory on Harry's computer stores MP3 files.
Video files take up another $\frac{1}{7}$.
How much memory is left on Harry's computer?

5 Work out

a $\frac{1}{4} \times 20$ **b** $30 \times \frac{7}{10}$

6 Work out

a $4 \div \frac{1}{3}$ **b** $10 \div \frac{2}{5}$ **c** $7 \div \frac{5}{6}$

7 Work out

a $\frac{1}{2} \times \frac{1}{4}$ **b** $\frac{9}{15} \times \frac{5}{6}$ **c** $-\frac{6}{11} \times \frac{1}{3}$

8 Write the reciprocal of these numbers.

a 3 **b** $\frac{1}{5}$ **c** $\frac{2}{11}$

9 Work out these calculations. Give your answers as mixed numbers where needed.

a $\frac{1}{4} \div 6$ **b** $\frac{4}{9} \div 3$

c $\frac{2}{3} \div \frac{1}{15}$ **d** $\frac{5}{13} \div \frac{4}{25}$

e $-\frac{1}{25} \div \frac{2}{25}$ **f** $\frac{16}{21} \div \frac{8}{3}$

10 A rectangle is $\frac{4}{5}$ m long and $\frac{3}{10}$ m wide.

a Calculate the perimeter of the rectangle.
b Calculate the area of the rectangle.

Calculating with mixed numbers

11 Write $3\frac{2}{5}$ as an improper fraction.

12 Work out these calculations.
Give your answers as mixed numbers and fractions in their simplest form.

   a $1\frac{3}{5} + 2\frac{1}{10}$

   b $5\frac{5}{6} + 2\frac{3}{4}$

   c $12\frac{1}{2} - 6\frac{1}{4}$

   d $2\frac{2}{3} - 1\frac{4}{5}$

13 Work out these calculations.
Give your answers as integers or mixed numbers and fractions in their simplest form.

   a $\frac{2}{3} \times 2\frac{1}{2}$

   b $1\frac{1}{3} \times \frac{5}{6}$

   c $3\frac{3}{4} \times 2\frac{2}{5}$

   d $2\frac{5}{8} \div \frac{7}{8}$

   e $5\frac{1}{2} \div \frac{1}{3}$

   f $2\frac{1}{3} \div 1\frac{2}{3}$

14 Ali is $1\frac{2}{5}$ times the age of Sally. Sally is $12\frac{1}{2}$.
How old is Ali?

Challenge

1 Susannah multiplies an integer by a fraction and gets the answer 10.
Suggest two numbers she could have multiplied.

2 A rectangle has area $4\frac{5}{8}$ m².
Sketch two possible rectangles. Write their lengths and widths.

Reflect   **How sure are you of your answers? Were you mostly**

🙁 **Just guessing**   😐 **Feeling doubtful**   🙂 **Confident**

What next? Use your results to decide whether to strengthen or extend your learning.

8 Strengthen

Ordering fractions

1 Copy these number lines. Put an arrow at $\frac{1}{2}$ on each line.

a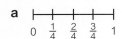
0 $\frac{1}{4}$ $\frac{2}{4}$ $\frac{3}{4}$ 1

b
0 $\frac{1}{5}$ $\frac{2}{5}$ $\frac{3}{5}$ $\frac{4}{5}$ 1

c
0 $\frac{1}{6}$ $\frac{2}{6}$ $\frac{3}{6}$ $\frac{4}{6}$ $\frac{5}{6}$ 1

d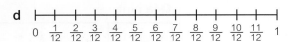
0 $\frac{1}{12}$ $\frac{2}{12}$ $\frac{3}{12}$ $\frac{4}{12}$ $\frac{5}{12}$ $\frac{6}{12}$ $\frac{7}{12}$ $\frac{8}{12}$ $\frac{9}{12}$ $\frac{10}{12}$ $\frac{11}{12}$ 1

e
0 $\frac{1}{17}$ $\frac{2}{17}$ $\frac{3}{17}$ $\frac{4}{17}$ $\frac{5}{17}$ $\frac{6}{17}$ $\frac{7}{17}$ $\frac{8}{17}$ $\frac{9}{17}$ $\frac{10}{17}$ $\frac{11}{17}$ $\frac{12}{17}$ $\frac{13}{17}$ $\frac{14}{17}$ $\frac{15}{17}$ $\frac{16}{17}$ 1

2 Which of these fractions are larger than $\frac{1}{2}$?

a $\frac{3}{4}$ **b** $\frac{2}{5}$ **c** $\frac{5}{6}$

d $\frac{7}{12}$ **e** $\frac{2}{17}$ **f** $\frac{11}{17}$

> **Q2 hint** Use the number lines in Q1 to help you.

3 Which of these fractions are smaller than $\frac{1}{2}$?

a $\frac{5}{12}$ **b** $\frac{7}{17}$ **c** $\frac{3}{8}$

d $\frac{4}{7}$ **e** $\frac{6}{11}$

> **Q3c hint** Imagine a number line with $\frac{1}{8}$s marked. Where is $\frac{1}{2}$ on the number line?

4 Order each set of fractions in ascending order (from smallest to largest).

a $\frac{7}{12}$ $\frac{1}{2}$ $\frac{2}{5}$ **b** $\frac{4}{7}$ $\frac{5}{12}$ $\frac{1}{2}$ **c** $\frac{6}{11}$ $\frac{1}{2}$ $\frac{6}{17}$

d $\frac{1}{2}$ $\frac{5}{8}$ $\frac{3}{8}$ **e** $\frac{5}{6}$ $\frac{1}{2}$ $\frac{3}{8}$ $\frac{1}{8}$ **f** $\frac{4}{9}$ $\frac{5}{7}$ $\frac{1}{9}$ $\frac{1}{2}$

5 a What is the lowest common multiple (LCM) of 2, 3 and 4?

b Write equivalent fractions to $\frac{1}{2}$, $\frac{2}{3}$ and $\frac{3}{4}$ with a common denominator.

c Order the fractions $\frac{1}{2}$, $\frac{2}{3}$ and $\frac{3}{4}$ in descending order (from largest to smallest).

> **Q5b hint** Use the LCM found in part **a** as the common denominator.

6 a What is the lowest common multiple (LCM) of 5, 10 and 20?

b Write equivalent fractions to $\frac{3}{5}$, $\frac{7}{10}$ and $\frac{9}{20}$ with a common denominator.

c Order the fractions $\frac{3}{5}$, $\frac{7}{10}$ and $\frac{9}{20}$ in descending order.

Calculating with fractions

1 Add together these fractions by writing them with the same denominator.

a $\frac{1}{5} + \frac{1}{10}$ **b** $\frac{2}{5} + \frac{3}{10}$ **c** $\frac{3}{5} + \frac{3}{10}$

> **Q1 hint**
>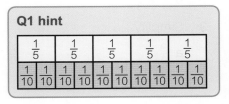

2 Add together these fractions by writing them with the same denominator.

a $\frac{1}{3} + \frac{2}{9}$ **b** $\frac{1}{3} + \frac{4}{9}$

c $\frac{2}{3} + \frac{1}{9}$ **d** $\frac{2}{3} + \frac{2}{9}$

Q2 hint

$\frac{1}{3}$			$\frac{1}{3}$			$\frac{1}{3}$		
$\frac{1}{9}$	$\frac{1}{9}$	$\frac{1}{9}$	$\frac{1}{9}$	$\frac{1}{9}$	$\frac{1}{9}$	$\frac{1}{9}$	$\frac{1}{9}$	$\frac{1}{9}$

3 Work out these fraction subtractions by writing them with the same denominator.

a $\frac{2}{3} - \frac{1}{9}$ **b** $\frac{2}{3} - \frac{4}{9}$

c $\frac{3}{5} - \frac{3}{10}$ **d** $\frac{4}{5} - \frac{7}{10}$

4 Copy and complete. The first two are started for you.
  a The lowest common multiple of 3 and 5 is 15.

$$\frac{1}{3} + \frac{1}{5} = \frac{5}{15} + \frac{\square}{15} = \frac{\square}{15}$$

  b The lowest common multiple of 3 and 4 is 12.

$$\frac{1}{3} + \frac{1}{4} = \frac{\square}{12} + \frac{\square}{12} = \frac{\square}{12}$$

Q4a hint

$\frac{1}{5}$			$\frac{1}{3}$				
$\frac{1}{15}$	$\frac{1}{15}$	$\frac{1}{15}$	$\frac{1}{15}$	$\frac{1}{15}$	$\frac{1}{15}$	$\frac{1}{15}$	$\frac{1}{15}$

  c The lowest common multiple of 10 and 3 is $\square$.

$$\frac{3}{10} + \frac{2}{3} =$$

5 Work out

a $\frac{5}{8} + \frac{1}{6}$ **b** $\frac{2}{5} - \frac{1}{12}$ **c** $\frac{6}{11} - \frac{2}{3}$

Q5 hint When you add or subtract fractions, the denominator must be the same. Use the LCM of the denominators.

6 **Reasoning** Marie says, '$\frac{1}{10} + \frac{1}{20} = \frac{2}{30} = \frac{1}{15}$'

  a Explain what mistake she has made.

  b What is the correct answer to $\frac{1}{10} + \frac{1}{20}$?

7 Work out these multiplications. The first three are started for you.

a $5 \times \frac{1}{3} = 5$ lots of $\frac{1}{3} = \frac{1}{3} + \frac{1}{3} + \frac{1}{3} + \frac{1}{3} + \frac{1}{3} = \frac{\square}{3} = \square\frac{\square}{3}$

b $2 \times \frac{1}{7} = \frac{1}{7} + \frac{1}{7} = \frac{\square}{\square}$

c $\frac{3}{5} \times 4 = 4 \times \frac{3}{5} = \frac{3}{5} + \frac{3}{5} + \frac{3}{5} + \frac{3}{5} = \frac{\square}{5} = \square\frac{\square}{5}$

d $\frac{6}{11} \times 3$ **e** $5 \times \frac{2}{7}$ **f** $\frac{1}{4}$ of 18 **g** $\frac{9}{10}$ of 40

8 Work out these multiplications. The first two are started for you.

a $\frac{1}{2} \times \frac{1}{2} = \frac{1 \times 1}{2 \times 2} = \frac{\square}{\square}$

b $\frac{2}{3} \times \frac{1}{5} = \frac{2 \times 1}{3 \times 5} = \frac{\square}{\square}$

c $\frac{3}{4} \times \frac{3}{5}$

d $\frac{4}{7} \times \frac{2}{3}$

9 Simplify

a $\frac{3}{6}$ **b** $\frac{5}{10}$ **c** $\frac{11}{33}$ **d** $\frac{12}{4}$

10 Work out these multiplications. The first two are started for you.

a $\frac{5}{6} \times \frac{3}{10} = \frac{5 \times 3}{6 \times \square}$

$= \frac{3 \times 5}{6 \times \square}$

$= \frac{3}{6} \times \frac{5}{\square}$

$= \frac{1}{2} \times \frac{\square}{\square}$

$= \frac{\square}{\square}$

b $\frac{12}{33} \times \frac{11}{4} = \frac{12 \times 11}{33 \times 4}$

$= \frac{11 \times 12}{33 \times 4}$

$=$

c $\frac{8}{15} \times \frac{5}{24}$

d $\frac{14}{25} \times \frac{10}{7}$

e $\frac{20}{63} \times \frac{9}{10}$

11 Copy and complete.

a The reciprocal of $\frac{2}{5}$ is $\frac{5}{\square}$

b The reciprocal of $\frac{3}{5}$ is $\frac{5}{\square}$

c The reciprocal of $\frac{4}{5}$ is $\frac{5}{\square}$

d The reciprocal of $\frac{3}{4}$ is $\frac{4}{\square}$

e The reciprocal of $\frac{6}{7}$ is $\frac{\square}{\square}$

f The reciprocal of $\frac{8}{7}$ is $\frac{\square}{\square}$

12 Write the reciprocals of these numbers. The first two are started for you.

a $2 = \frac{2}{1}$ reciprocal $= \frac{1}{\square}$

b $\frac{1}{4}$ reciprocal $= \frac{\square}{1} = \square$

c 3

d 6

e 11

f $\frac{1}{5}$

g $\frac{1}{7}$

h $\frac{1}{12}$

> **Q12b hint**
> $\frac{4}{1} = 4 \div 1 = \square$

13 Copy and complete to work out these divisions.

a $\frac{2}{7} \div \frac{3}{5} = \frac{2}{7} \times \frac{5}{\square} = \frac{10}{\square}$

b $\frac{1}{4} \div \frac{6}{7} = \frac{1}{4} \times \frac{\square}{6} = \frac{\square}{24}$

c $\frac{1}{6} \div \frac{2}{5} = \frac{1}{6} \times \frac{\square}{\square} = \frac{\square}{\square}$

d $\frac{1}{3} \div \frac{8}{7} = \frac{\square}{\square} \times \frac{\square}{\square} = \frac{\square}{\square}$

e $\frac{1}{6} \div \frac{3}{5} = \frac{\square}{\square} \times \frac{\square}{\square} = \frac{\square}{\square}$

f $\frac{2}{3} \div \frac{7}{10} = \frac{\square}{\square} \times \frac{\square}{\square} = \frac{\square}{\square}$

> **Q13 hint**
> Multiply the first number by the reciprocal of the second.

14 Copy and complete to work out these divisions.

a $\frac{2}{7} \div 4 = \frac{\square}{\square} \times \frac{1}{\square} = \frac{\square}{\square}$

b $\frac{1}{4} \div \frac{1}{3} = \frac{\square}{\square} \times \frac{\square}{1} = \frac{\square}{\square}$

c $6 \div \frac{1}{2} = 6 \times \frac{\square}{1} = \square$

d $6 \div \frac{2}{3} = \square \times \frac{\square}{\square} = \frac{\square}{\square} = \square$

> **Q14c hint** $\frac{12}{1} = 12 \div 1 = \square$

Calculating with mixed numbers

1 How many

  a $\frac{1}{3}$s in 1

  c $\frac{1}{3}$s in 2

  e $\frac{1}{5}$s in 1

  g $\frac{1}{8}$s in 1

Q1a hint

1

$\frac{1}{3}$	$\frac{1}{3}$	$\frac{1}{3}$

$\frac{3}{3} = 1$

  b $\frac{1}{4}$s in 1

  d $\frac{1}{4}$s in 2

  f $\frac{1}{5}$s

  h

Q1b hint

1

$\frac{1}{4}$	$\frac{1}{4}$	$\frac{1}{4}$	$\frac{1}{4}$

$\frac{4}{4} = 1$

2 Write these numbers as improper fractions.
The first two are started for you.

  a $1\frac{2}{3} = \frac{3}{3} + \frac{2}{3} = \frac{\square}{3}$

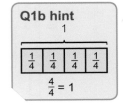

$\frac{2}{3}$

$\frac{}{3}$

  b $2\frac{3}{4} = \frac{8}{4} + \frac{3}{4} = \frac{\square}{4}$

Q2b hint

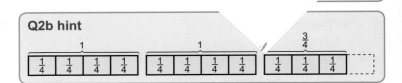

1   1 $\frac{3}{4}$

$\frac{1}{4}$	$\frac{1}{4}$	$\frac{1}{4}$	$\frac{1}{4}$	$\frac{1}{4}$	$\frac{1}{4}$	$\frac{1}{4}$	$\frac{1}{4}$	$\frac{1}{4}$	$\frac{1}{4}$	$\frac{1}{4}$

  c $1\frac{1}{5}$ **d** $2\frac{3}{5}$ **e** $2\frac{3}{8}$ **f** $1\frac{1}{10}$ **g** $2\frac{7}{10}$ **h** $9\frac{3}{10}$

3 Work out these mixed number calculations.

  a $2\frac{2}{3} + 1\frac{1}{3}$

  b $1\frac{2}{5} + 3\frac{1}{5}$

  c $5\frac{1}{6} + 2\frac{5}{6}$

Q3a hint

2   1

1	1		1		$\frac{2}{3}$	$\frac{1}{3}$

4 Copy and complete to work out these additions.

  a $1\frac{2}{3} + 2\frac{1}{6} = \underline{1 + 2} + \frac{2}{3} + \frac{1}{6}$

           $= \quad 3 \quad + \frac{\square}{6} + \frac{1}{6}$

           $= 3\frac{\square}{6}$

  b $4\frac{7}{10} + 2\frac{1}{5} = \underline{4 + 2} + \frac{7}{10} + \frac{1}{5}$

           $= \quad 6 \quad + \frac{7}{10} + \frac{\square}{10}$

           $= 6\frac{\square}{10}$

  c $3\frac{1}{3} + 2\frac{1}{4} = \underline{\square + \square} + \frac{1}{3} + \frac{1}{4}$

           $= \quad \square \quad + \frac{\square}{12} + \frac{\square}{12}$

           $= \quad \square$

  d $5\frac{1}{5} + 7\frac{3}{4} = \underline{\square + \square} + \frac{1}{5} + \frac{3}{4}$

           $= \quad \square \quad + \frac{\square}{20} + \frac{\square}{\square}$

           $= \quad \square$

5 Work out these subtractions. Give your answers as mixed numbers.
Some are started for you.

  a $5 - 3\frac{1}{2} = \frac{10}{2} - \frac{\square}{2}$

  b $4\frac{2}{3} - 1\frac{1}{3} = \frac{\square}{3} - \frac{\square}{3}$

Q5a hint Write as halves.
10 halves − ☐ halves = ☐ halves

  c $10\frac{3}{4} - 2\frac{1}{4} = \frac{\square}{4} - \frac{\square}{4}$

  d $5\frac{4}{5} - 2\frac{1}{10} = \frac{\square}{5} - \frac{\square}{10} = \frac{\square}{10} - \frac{\square}{10}$

  e $1\frac{1}{2} - \frac{3}{4} = \frac{\square}{2} - \frac{\square}{4} = \frac{\square}{4} - \frac{\square}{4}$

  f $2\frac{3}{4} - 1\frac{1}{6} = \frac{\square}{4} - \frac{\square}{6} = \frac{\square}{12} - \frac{\square}{12}$

6 Work out these multiplications. The first and last are started for you.

Q6 hint Write mixed numbers as improper fractions. Give your answers as mixed numbers.

a $\frac{4}{5} \times 2\frac{1}{3} = \frac{4}{5} \times \frac{\square}{3}$

b $\frac{7}{10} \times 1\frac{2}{3}$

c $\frac{1}{15} \times 2\frac{1}{2}$

d $3\frac{8}{9} \times \frac{1}{6}$

e $1\frac{2}{11} \times 6\frac{1}{3} = \frac{\square}{11} \times \frac{\square}{3} = \frac{\square \times \square}{11 \times 3}$

7 Work out these divisions. The first two are started for you.

a $5\frac{1}{2} \div \frac{1}{2} = \frac{\square \times 2}{2 \times 1}$ **b** $3\frac{2}{11} \div \frac{4}{5} = \frac{\square \times 5}{11 \times 4}$ **c** $4\frac{1}{9} \div \frac{2}{3}$

d $12\frac{1}{2} \div \frac{1}{4}$ **e** $10\frac{1}{3} \div 2\frac{3}{4}$

8 **Problem-solving** A blue pencil is $1\frac{1}{3}$ times the length of a red pencil. The red pencil is $5\frac{1}{2}$ cm.

a Choose the correct calculation to work out the length of the blue pencil.

   A $1\frac{1}{3} + 5\frac{1}{2}$ **B** $1\frac{1}{3} - 5\frac{1}{2}$ **C** $1\frac{1}{3} \times 5\frac{1}{2}$ **D** $1\frac{1}{3} \div 5\frac{1}{2}$

b How long is the blue pencil?

Challenge

1 Jatin pays $\frac{1}{5}$ of his salary as tax.
He uses $\frac{1}{10}$ of his salary to pay back his student loan.
He pays $\frac{1}{4}$ of his salary into a pension scheme.
What fraction of his salary is he left with?

2 Ann is $1\frac{3}{5}$ m tall.
Her father is $1\frac{1}{4}$ times her height. Her brother is $\frac{3}{4}$ of her height.
How tall are her father and her brother?
Write her brother's height in metres and centimetres.

Reflect   List these tasks (A–F) in order from easiest to hardest.

A   Adding and subtracting fractions
B   Multiplying fractions
C   Dividing fractions
D   Adding and subtracting mixed numbers
E   Multiplying mixed numbers
F   Dividing mixed numbers

Hint List the letters of the tasks in order. You don't need to write out the descriptions.

Look at the first task in your list (the easiest).
What made it easiest?
Look at the two tasks at the bottom of your list (the hardest).
What made them hardest?

Write hints to help you with the two tasks you found hardest.

8 Extend

1 **Reasoning** Copy and complete this list so that the fractions are in descending order.

$$\frac{2}{3} \quad \square \quad \frac{5}{12} \quad \square \quad \frac{3}{8}$$

2 The musicians in a band share $\frac{1}{3}$ of a royalty fee for their song.
There are six musicians. What fraction of the fee does each musician get?

3 **Reasoning** Petra has 10 cakes at her party.
She wants to give all 75 guests an equal piece.
  a Explain why she won't have enough if she cuts the cakes into sevenths.
  b How many pieces should she cut the cakes into?
  c How many pieces will she have left over?

4 Work out

  a $\left(\frac{1}{2}\right)^2 = \frac{1^2}{2^2} = \frac{\square}{\square}$
  b $\left(\frac{1}{4}\right)^2$
  c $\left(\frac{2}{3}\right)^2$
  d $\sqrt{\frac{16}{25}} = \frac{\sqrt{16}}{\sqrt{25}} = \frac{\square}{\square}$
  e $\sqrt{\frac{1}{64}}$
  f $\sqrt{\frac{9}{16}}$

5 Use your calculator to work out

  a $2\frac{3}{8} + 1\frac{1}{3}$

  b $2\frac{3}{4} \times 3\frac{1}{8}$

  c $1\frac{1}{3} \div -3\frac{1}{2}$

  d $\left(2\frac{1}{4} + 9\frac{1}{5}\right) - \left(\frac{3}{5}\right)^2$

  e $\left(5\frac{1}{2} \times 2\right) + \left(1\frac{3}{4} - 1\frac{3}{8}\right)$

  f $\left(\frac{9}{10} \div 1\frac{2}{3}\right) \times \left(2\frac{1}{2} + 9\frac{1}{3}\right)$

6 **Problem-solving**
  a Complete this magic square so that each row, column and diagonal sums to the same number.

$1\frac{1}{3}$		
	$1\frac{2}{3}$	
$2\frac{2}{3}$		2

  b Make your own magic square using fractions.

7 Simplify these fractional ratios.

  a $3\frac{1}{2} : \frac{1}{4}$

  b $2\frac{1}{5} : \frac{3}{10}$

  c $1\frac{3}{4} : 2\frac{1}{6}$

> **Q7a hint** Multiply both numbers to give integers.

8 Problem-solving Meteorologists use these ratings to describe the level of cloud cover.

   1 Clear: 0 to $\frac{1}{10}$ cloud cover

   2 Scattered: $\frac{1}{10}$ to $\frac{5}{10}$ cloud cover

   3 Broken: $\frac{5}{10}$ to $\frac{9}{10}$ cloud cover

   4 Overcast: fully covered

A forecast for five days was:

   Monday: $\frac{1}{4}$ covered

   Tuesday: $\frac{3}{5}$ covered

   Wednesday: $\frac{3}{4}$ covered

   Thursday: $\frac{1}{3}$ covered

   Friday: clear sky

   a What was the mean amount of cloud cover for the five days?

   b Work out the mean of the cloud cover ratings (the numbers 1 to 4) for the five days.

9 Problem-solving / Reasoning The owner of a café calculates that $\frac{2}{3}$ of her customers order cake.
Half of the people who order cake have cheesecake.
How many pieces of cheesecake should she have for 60 customers?

10 Problem-solving A rectangle has length $2\frac{1}{4}$ m and area $7\frac{1}{2}$ m². What is the perimeter of the rectangle?

11 Problem-solving A pair of mixed numbers have a mean of $6\frac{1}{5}$.
   a Write a possible pair of mixed numbers.
   b Write another two possible pairs of mixed numbers.

12 Problem-solving
   a Find the volume of this cube.

$2\frac{1}{2}$ cm

   b This solid is made using the cube.

   Find the volume of the solid.

Reflect The word fraction is used in lots of ways. Here are two examples:

- In everyday English, a fraction means 'a small amount'. When hanging a picture you might 'move it up a fraction' or you might ask someone to 'budge up a fraction' so you can sit beside them.
- In chemistry, the fractionating process separates a mixture into its components.

Write a definition, in your own words, of 'fraction' in mathematics.
What do you think 'fractional ownership' means? When might it be a good idea?

8 Unit test

1 Write these fractions in ascending order.

$\frac{4}{9}$ $\frac{5}{6}$ $\frac{3}{4}$ $\frac{11}{18}$ $\frac{1}{2}$

2 Work out

a $\frac{1}{3} + \frac{1}{6}$ b $\frac{3}{4} + \frac{1}{8}$

c $\frac{7}{10} - \frac{2}{5}$ d $\frac{5}{8} - \frac{1}{10}$

3 Work out

a $2\frac{1}{2} + 6\frac{1}{4}$ b $3\frac{2}{5} + 4\frac{1}{3}$

c $15\frac{5}{6} - 2\frac{1}{3}$ d $3\frac{1}{4} - 2\frac{3}{8}$

4 Work out these multiplications.
   Simplify your answers where needed.

a $\frac{1}{5} \times 35$ b $\frac{2}{3} \times 18$

c $\frac{3}{4} \times \frac{1}{5}$ d $-\frac{1}{3} \times \frac{3}{5}$

e $\frac{7}{10} \times \frac{2}{3}$ f $-\frac{9}{15} \times -\frac{5}{6}$

5 Work out these multiplications.
   Give your answers in their simplest form.

a $1\frac{1}{3} \times \frac{9}{20}$ b $1\frac{2}{3} \times 1\frac{4}{5}$

c $2\frac{1}{2} \times \frac{4}{25}$ d $3\frac{2}{3} \times \frac{9}{22}$

6 Write the reciprocal of these numbers.
   a 5   b $\frac{1}{2}$ c $\frac{6}{11}$

7 Work out

a $5 \div \frac{1}{4}$ b $10 \div \frac{2}{3}$

c $\frac{2}{5} \div 8$ d $5 \div \frac{8}{9}$

8 Work out

a $\frac{1}{3} \div \frac{1}{2}$ b $\frac{2}{5} \div \frac{1}{4}$

c $\frac{3}{8} \div \frac{1}{2}$ d $\frac{2}{5} \div \frac{8}{15}$

e $-\frac{3}{4} \div \frac{7}{9}$ f $-\frac{5}{12} \div -\frac{2}{5}$

9 Work out

a $4\frac{3}{10} \div \frac{18}{21}$ b $2\frac{2}{5} \div 1\frac{1}{10}$

10 On Saturday, Tim walks his dog in the park for $\frac{3}{4}$ hour.
Then he jogs in the park for 20 minutes.
How long was Tim in the park?

11 An electrician buys a 3 metre lead.
He uses $\frac{2}{5}$ of the lead.
What length of lead is left?

12 Alex ran $2\frac{1}{2}$ miles, then cycled $5\frac{2}{7}$ miles.
How many miles did he travel in total?

13 Miguel walks $2\frac{1}{8}$ km to work.
Jean walks $1\frac{1}{3}$ km to work.
How much further does Miguel walk than Jean?

14 A rectangle has length $7\frac{7}{9}$ cm and area $8\frac{3}{4}$ cm².
What is the width of the rectangle?

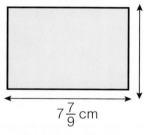

$7\frac{7}{9}$ cm

Area = $8\frac{3}{4}$ cm²

9 Straight-line graphs

9.1 Direct proportion on graphs

Active Learn
Homework

- Recognise when values are in direct proportion with or without a graph
- Plot graphs and read values to solve problems

Warm up

1 Fluency What value is each arrow pointing to?

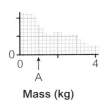

Mass (kg)

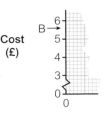

2 Which of these quantities are in direct proportion?

  A 30 litres of petrol cost £40; 60 litres of petrol cost £80.

  B 1 pair of bicycle brake pads cost £1.99; 2 pairs of bicycle brake pads cost £3.75.

  C Sarah is paid £54 for 6 hours' work one week; she is paid £27 for 3 hours' work the next week.

  D A plumber charges £80 for 1 hour's work; she charges £110 for 2 hours' work.

> **Q2 hint** Two quantities in direct proportion increase or decrease at the same rate. For example, if one doubles, the other doubles; and if one halves, the other halves.

3 This graph can be used for converting between a length in metres (m) and a length in feet (ft).

  a Convert 6 m to feet.

  b Convert 30 feet to metres.

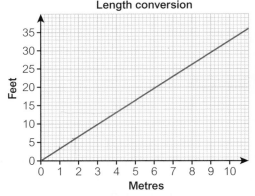

Length conversion

Key point

When two quantities are in **direct proportion**

- plotting them as a graph gives a straight line through (0,0)
- when one variable is zero, the other variable is also zero
- when one variable doubles, so does the other.

4 Are feet and metres in direct proportion? Explain.

Q4 hint Look at the graph in Q3.

5 **Problem-solving** Use the graph in Q3 to answer these questions.
   a Which is longer, 4 m or 12.5 feet?
   b Stuart is 6 feet tall. Dave is 1.6 m tall. Who is taller?
   c Chris needs 75 feet of wallpaper for her room. It is sold in 5 metre rolls. How many rolls will she need to buy to have enough wallpaper?

6 Which of these graphs show one variable in direct proportion to another?

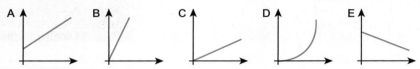

7 **Problem-solving** People buy and sell gold to make money.
   The graph shows the price of gold on one particular day.
   a What is the cost of 0 g?
   b What is the cost of
      i 1 g   **ii** 2 g
      iii 3 g   **iv** 4 g?
   c Complete this sentence: For every 1 g increase in weight of gold, the cost increases by £_____.
   d How much gold can you buy for £425?
   e Are the two quantities in direct proportion? Explain.
   f How can you use the graph to work out the cost of 30 g of gold?

Cost of buying gold

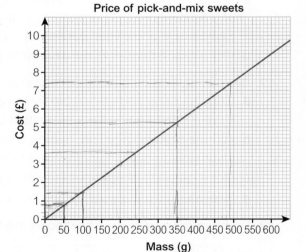

Price (£) vs Weight of gold (g)

Q7f hint The graph doesn't go to 30 g. Use values you know to work out larger values.

8 **Problem-solving** This graph shows the price of pick-and-mix sweets by mass.
   a How much does 100 g of sweets cost?
   b How many grams of sweets would you get for £7.50?
   c How much does 350 g of sweets cost?
   d How many grams of sweets would you get for £3.60?
   e Max is having a party for 30 people. He wants to buy sweets for everyone. He buys 50 g for each person. How much does that cost him?
   f How much does the price increase for every extra 100 g of sweets? Explain.
   g Are the two quantities in direct proportion? Explain.
   h Use the graph to work out the cost of 800 g of sweets.

Price of pick-and-mix sweets

Cost (£) vs Mass (g)

9 **Reasoning** A scientist gets these results in an experiment to test the resistance of different lengths of copper wire.

a Are resistance and length in direct proportion for this wire? Explain.

b Use the graph to work out the resistance of wire with length
  i 4 m   ii 10 m   iii 20 m

c Use the graph to work out the length of wire with resistance
  i 0.01 ohms   ii 0.20 ohms.

Q9c i hint

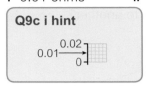

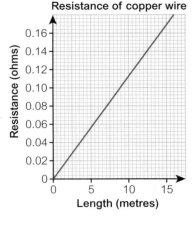

10 **Reasoning** The table shows some equivalent temperatures in Celsius and Fahrenheit.

Celsius (°C)	Fahrenheit (°F)
10	50
15	59
30	86

a Plot a graph for the points in the table.

The Government advises elderly people to keep their living rooms at 21 °C and their bedrooms at 18 °C.

b What are these temperatures in Fahrenheit?

c Are Celsius and Fahrenheit in direct proportion? Explain.

Q10a hint Plot Celsius (°C) on the horizontal axis up to at least 30 °C. Plot Fahrenheit (°F) on the vertical axis up to at least 86 °F.

11 **Reasoning** The table shows the amounts of CO_2 emitted from burning LPG (liquid petroleum gas).

LPG (litres)	0	6	12	18
CO_2 (kg)	0	4	8	12

a Without drawing a graph, decide whether CO_2 emissions and amount of LPG burned are in direct proportion. Explain and show your working.

b Plot a graph to check your answer to part a.

Q11a hint When the amount of LPG is 0 litres are CO_2 emissions 0 kg? When the amount of LPG doubles, do CO_2 emissions double? For example

LPG (litres) CO_2 (kg)

×2 (6 → ☐)(4 → ☐) ×2

12 **Reasoning** Posters are sold online for £7.50 each. The postage charge is £2.50 per order.

a Copy and complete this table for the price of buying different numbers of posters.

Number of posters	1	2	10
Price (£)			

b Without drawing a graph, decide whether number of posters and price are in direct proportion. Explain and show your working.

c Plot a graph to check your answer to part a.

d Use your graph to work out the price of 5 posters.

13 **Problem-solving** The table shows the temperatures at different heights on Mont Ventoux.

Height above sea level (m)	0	250	500	1000
Temperature drop (°C)	0	1.6	3.2	6.4

a Are height and temperature drop in direct proportion? Explain and show your working.

b Jay is at 400 m above sea level, and the temperature is 19.3 °C. He starts to cycle up the mountain. What is the predicted temperature at the summit (1900 m above sea level)?

14 **Problem-solving** The table shows the cost of perfume in different size bottles.
Are the price and volume in direct proportion?

Q14 hint Use working or plot a graph to show whether the quantities are in direct proportion.

Volume (ml)	30	50	120
Price (£)	45	75	140

15 **Problem-solving** The table shows the cost of hourly boat hire for different numbers of hours.

Number of hours	2	5	7
Cost (£)	£42	£105	£147

   a Are the number of hours and cost in direct proportion?

   b The Lomax family want to hire a boat for 6 hours. How much will it cost?

   It is also possible to hire boats for whole days. The table shows the cost of boat hire for different numbers of days.

Number of days	2	5	7
Cost (£)	£310	£775	£950

   c Are the number of days and cost in direct proportion?

   d **Reasoning** The Townsend family want to hire a boat for 6 days. Is it possible to work out how much it will cost? Explain.

16 Which of these are in direct proportion? Explain.
   A Inches and centimetres (1 inch ≈ 1.54 cm)
   B Temperature measured hourly over 24 hours
   C Pounds (£) and dollars ($)
   D The cost of a hotel phone call which is £1 plus 20p per minute

Challenge   Car A travels at a constant speed of 90 km/h.
   a Copy and complete this table for the distance travelled by car A.

Part a hint 'km/h' stands for kilometres per hour or kilometres travelled in every hour. This car travels 90 km every hour.

Time (hours)	0	1	2
Distance (km)			

   b Plot this journey on a distance–time graph.

   Car B travels for 1 hour at 100 km/h and then for two hours at 60 km/h.
   c Show this journey on your distance–time graph.
   d Which graph shows direct proportion?
   e When is distance travelled in direct proportion to time taken?

Part c hint Use different colours when you have two graphs on the same axes.

Reflect

   a List all the things you have to do to interpret graphs (as in Q7, Q8 and Q9). You may start your list, 'Read values'.
   b List all the things you have to do to draw graphs (as in Q10, Q11 and Q12). You may start your list, 'Draw a table of values'.
   c Which are you better at, interpreting or drawing graphs? Explain why.

9.2 Gradients

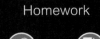
*Active*Learn
Homework

- Plot a straight-line graph and work out its gradient

Warm up

1   Fluency
    a   Complete these coordinate pairs for $y = 3x$.
        $(3, \Box)$, $(\Box, 24)$, $(10, \Box)$, $(\Box, 30)$, $(-2, \Box)$, $(\Box, -15)$
    b $y = 2x - 1$
        What is the value of y when
        i $x = 4$ ii $x = 0$ iii $x = -4$?

2   Order these distance–time graphs from the one showing the fastest speed to the one showing the slowest speed.

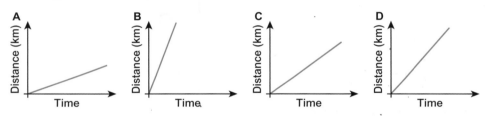

3   a   Copy and complete this table of values for the equation $y = 2x + 2$.

x	1	2	3	4	5
y	4				

   b   Complete these coordinate pairs from the table of values.
       $(1, 4)$, $(2, \Box)$, $(3, \Box)$, $(4, \Box)$, $(5, \Box)$
   c   i   Draw a coordinate grid from −3 to 5 on the x-axis and
           −12 to 12 on the y-axis, and plot the coordinates.
       ii   Draw a straight line that goes through all the points and
           extend the line to the edges of the grid.
      iii   Label the graph with its equation.
   d   What is the value of y when $x = -3$?

> **Q3c hint** If your points
> are not on a straight line,
> check the table of values.

4   a   Copy and complete this table of values for the equation $y = 2x - 5$.

x	−2	−1	0	1	2
y	−9				

   b   Use the same grid as for Q3 to plot the coordinates for $y = 2x - 5$.
       Join the points in a straight line and label the line.
   c   **Reasoning**   What do you notice about the two graphs you have drawn?

5 **a** Copy and complete the table of values for the equation $y = 3x$.

x	-2	0	2
y			

   b Draw a grid from -2 to 2 on the x-axis and -10 to 10 on the y-axis. Plot the graph of $y = 3x$.
Label the graph with its equation.

   c Copy and complete the table in part **a** for $y = 4x$.
On the same grid, plot the graph and label it.

   d Copy and complete the table in part **a** for $y = 5x$.
On the same grid, plot the graph and label it.

   e Which graph is steepest, $y = 3x$, $y = 4x$ or $y = 5x$?

   f **Reasoning**   Write a sentence describing what you think the graph of $y = 2x$ might look like.

   g Draw a table of values and plot the graph of $y = 2x$ to see if you were correct.

6 **a** Use the same grid as Q5 to plot the graph of $y = -2x$.

   b Compare your graphs of $y = 2x$ and $y = -2x$. What is the same? What is different?

   c **Reasoning**   Write a sentence describing what you think the graph of $y = -3x$ might look like.

   d Use the same grid as Q5 to plot the graph of $y = -3x$ to see if you were correct.

7 **a** How many squares does graph A go up for
   i every one square across to the right?
   ii every two squares across to the right?
   iii every three squares across to the right?

   b For each part, **ai, ii** and **iii**, divide the number of squares the graph goes up by the number of squares across to the right.

   c How many squares does graph B go down for
   i every one square across to the right?
   ii every two squares across to the right?
   iii every three squares across to the right?

Q7ai hint

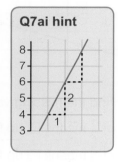

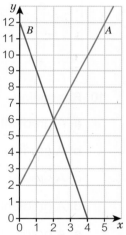

Worked example

Work out the gradient of each of these graphs.

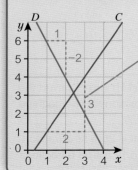

Divide the vertical distance by the horizontal distance.

Graph C goes 3 units up for every 2 units across to the right.

Gradient of graph $C = \dfrac{3}{2}$

Graph D goes 2 units down for every 1 unit across to the right.

Gradient of graph $D = \dfrac{-2}{1} = -2$

8   Write down the gradients of graph A and graph B in Q7.

9   a . Which of the line segments in the diagram have
        i a positive gradient   ii a negative gradient?
    b Work out the gradient of each line segment in the diagram.

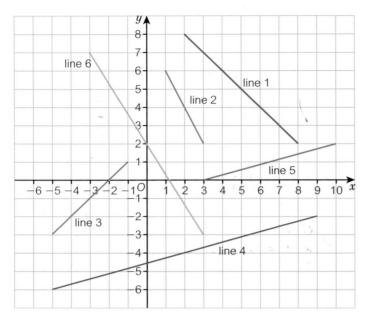

Q9b hint You will sometimes need to use the whole of the line segment to work out the gradient. A gradient can be a fraction. Write the fraction in its simplest form. 6 up with 8 across is $\frac{6}{8} = \frac{3}{4}$. Check whether each gradient is positive or negative.

10 **Reasoning**   Find the missing values.

    Q10 hint You could sketch these on squared paper.

    a A gradient of $\frac{1}{2}$ means ☐ up for every 2 across to the right.

    b A gradient of $\frac{3}{4}$ means ☐ up for every 4 across to the right.

    c A gradient of $\frac{1}{6}$ means ☐ up for every ☐ across to the right.

    d A gradient of $-\frac{1}{3}$ means ☐ down for every 3 across to the right.

    e A gradient of $-\frac{2}{5}$ means ☐ down for every ☐ across to the right.

    f Which of these gradients is the steepest? Explain.

11 **Problem-solving**   Here are some diagrams showing skateboard ramps.

    a Work out the gradient of each ramp.

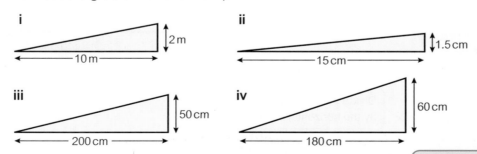

    b Write each gradient in part **a** as a percentage.

    Q11b hint Convert the fraction to a percentage.

    c Sketch these skateboard gradients on squared paper.
        i $\frac{1}{6}$ ii $\frac{2}{7}$

        iii 30%   iv 12.5%

    Q11c iv hint What is 25% as a fraction? Use this to work out 12.5% as a fraction.

12 Reasoning

a Draw a grid from −10 to 10 on both axes.
Complete the table of values for each graph.
Use the completed tables to plot each graph. Label each graph with its equation.

i $y = x - 1$

x	−2	−1	0	1	2	3
y	−3	−2	−1			

ii $y = 4x + 4$

x	−3	−2	−1	0	1
y			0	4	

iii $y = -2x + 3$

x	−2	−1	0	1	2	3
y	7					

b Work out the gradient of each graph.

c What is the connection between the gradient and the sequence of y values?

d What is the connection between the gradient and the coefficient of x?

> **Q12d hint** The **coefficient** is the number in front of the x.

Challenge   The graph shows the time trials results for four cyclists over a 10-mile course in 2013.

a Choose a point on each graph. Write down the distance and time at that point.

b Use your answers to part **a** to work out the average speed of each cyclist using
$$\text{speed} = \frac{\text{distance}}{\text{time}}$$

c Now work out the gradient of each graph.
What do you notice?

d Which graph shows the fastest speed?
What can you say about its gradient?

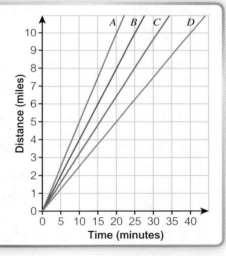

Reflect   Some people think of finding the gradient as 'rise over run' or 'upstairs above the corridor'.

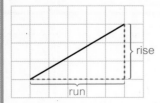

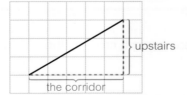

> **Hint** Think of rhymes, pictures, …

Do you like these ways of remembering how to find the gradient?
Can you think of your own way to remember it?
What else do you use to remember mathematics facts? Compare with your classmates.

9.3 Equations of straight lines

*Active*Learn
Homework

- Plot the graphs of linear equations
- Write the equations of straight-line graphs in the form $y = mx + c$

Warm up

1 Fluency What is the equation of
   a graph A **b** graph B?

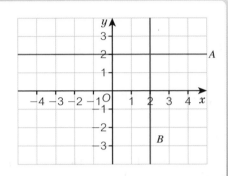

2 a Which of the line segments in the
      diagram have
      i a positive gradient
      ii a negative gradient?
   b Work out the gradient of each line
      segment in the diagram.

3 a Copy and complete the table of values
      for $y = 4x - 3$.

x	−1	0	1	2	3
y					

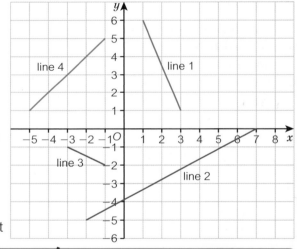

   b Choose a suitable pair of axes and plot
      the graph of
      $y = 4x - 3$.
   c Find the gradient of the graph.

> **Q3b hint** Draw a grid with an x-axis at least from the
> smallest to the largest x value in your table, and a y-axis at
> least from the smallest to the largest y value in your table.

Key point
The **y-intercept** is where a graph crosses the y-axis.

4 Reasoning
   a Draw tables of values for $y = 2x - 1$, $y = 2x + 5$ and $y = 2x - 6$.
      On the same grid, plot the graphs. Label each graph with its equation.
   b Work out the gradient of each graph.
   c Copy and complete these sentences.
      Graphs with the same gradient are _____.
      Parallel lines have the same _____.

5 For each graph you plotted in Q4
  a Write the coordinates of the y-intercept of each graph.
  b What do you notice about the equation of each graph and
     i its gradient   **ii** its y-intercept?
  c Where do you think the graph of $y = 2x + 3$ will be on your grid?
  d Draw a table of values for $y = 2x + 3$. Use this to check your answer to part **c**.

6 **a** Draw a table of values for $y = -3x$. Plot the graph.
  b Draw the graphs $y = -3x + 1$ and $y = -3x - 2$ on the same grid without working out the table of values.
  c Explain how you know the y-intercept from the equations of graphs.

7 Which of these graphs
  a are parallel   **b** have the same y-intercept?

$y = x + 7$	$y = 5x + 1$	$y = -2x + 7$	$y = x + 5$	$y = -2x + 1$	$y = 2x + 5$

Key point   A **linear equation** generates a straight-line (linear) graph.
The equation for a straight-line graph can be written as $y = mx + c$ where m is the gradient and c is the y-intercept.

Worked example

Write the equation of
a graph A
b graph B.

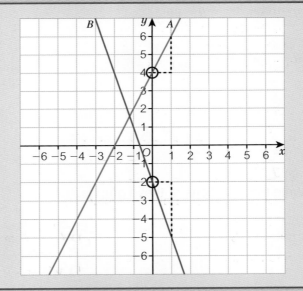

a $y = mx + c$
   gradient, $m = 2$
   y-intercept is (0, 4), so $c = 4$.
   Equation of line A is $y = 2x + 4$.

b $y = mx + c$
   gradient, $m = -3$
   y-intercept is (0, −2), so $c = -2$.
   Equation of line B is $y = -3x - 2$.

---

8 **Reasoning**
  a Work out the gradient and y-intercept for line A.
  b Use these to write the equation of line A.

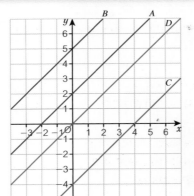

   $$y = \square x + \square$$
      ↑   ↑
   gradient y-intercept

  c What are the equations of lines B, C and D?

> **Q8a hint** $1x$ is always written as x.

> **Q8c hint** Use your equation for line A to help you find the equations of lines B, C and D.

9 Reasoning

a Match each graph to an equation.

$y = x$ $y = 2x + 4$

$y = 3x$ $y = 2x - 1$

b Which graphs pass through the origin?

c Which graph is the steepest?

d Write the equations of the two graphs that are parallel.

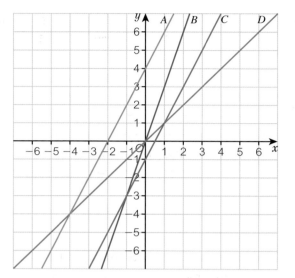

10 Match each graph to its equation.

$y = 5x + 5$ $y = \frac{1}{5}x + 5$

$y = -5x + 5$ $y = -\frac{1}{5}x + 5$

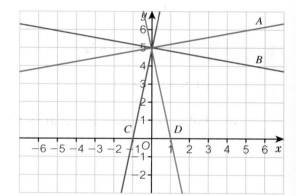

11 Write the equations of these graphs.

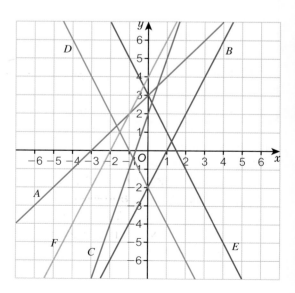

12 a Draw the graph of $y = 3$.

  b Reasoning Explain why there is no x term in this equation.

Q12 hint Use what you know about a linear equation, its gradient and its y-intercept.

13 Problem-solving Jayne carries out a science experiment. She puts different voltages across a wire and measures the current.

Here are her results.

Voltage, V (V)	2	4	6
Current, I (A)	1	2	3

  a Draw the graph of voltage against current.

  b Use your graph to work out the current when the voltage is 5 V.

  c Write an equation linking current (I) to voltage (V).

Q13c hint Write an equation in the from $y = mx + c$. Replace y with I and x with V.

14 Problem-solving A designer uses this graph to find the force exerted on a bicycle frame by people of different mass.

  a Are force and mass in direct proportion? Explain.

  b Write a formula linking force (F) and mass (M).

  c Use your formula to work out the force exerted by a person with mass

   i 30 kg   **ii** 60 kg   **iii** 90 kg.

  d What do you notice about the forces exerted by 30 kg, 60 kg, 90 kg?

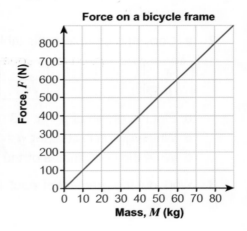

Force on a bicycle frame

Q14b hint Replace y with F and x with M.

Challenge A graph is steeper than the graph of $y = x - 3$ but not as steep as the graph of $y = 4x + 1$.

Its y-intercept lies between $(0, -2)$ and $(0, 1)$.

Draw two different possibilities for the graph and write their equations.

Reflect Write down what you think 'linear' means.

$y = mx + c$ is a linear equation.

Write, in your own words, what m and c stand for.

Write hints for how to remember what m and c stand for.

Hint Some say that m comes from the French word *monter*, meaning to climb. Others say it comes from the Latin word *modus*, meaning measure.

9 Check up

Straight-line graphs

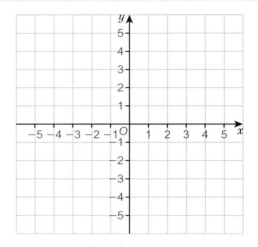

1   **a**   Copy and complete this table of values for the equation $y = 3x + 2$.

x	−2	−1	0	1	2
y					

     b   Plot the graph of $y = 3x + 2$ on a coordinate grid like this.

2   **a**   Copy and complete this table of values for the equation $y = x - 3$.

x	−2	−1	0	1	2
y					

     b   Plot the graph of $y = x - 3$ on your grid from Q1.
     c   Which graph is steeper, $y = 3x + 2$ or $y = x - 3$?
     d   Write the coordinates of the y-intercept of the line $y = x - 3$.

3   Work out the gradient of each line segment.

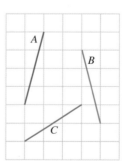

Finding equations of graphs

4   Write the equations of the graphs A, B and C.

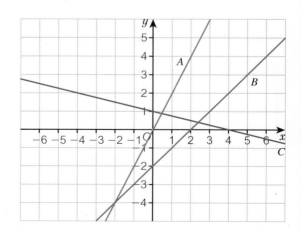

5 Match each graph to its equation.

a $y = -\frac{1}{2}x$

b $y = \frac{1}{2}x - 3$

c $y = 2x$

d $y = 2x + 3$

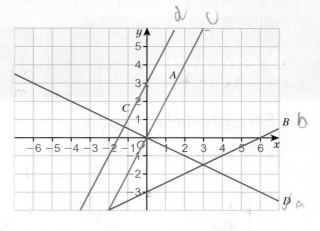

Direct proportion

6 A swimming pool is being filled.
The graph shows the depth of water in the pool over time.

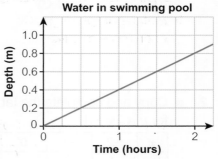

Water in swimming pool

a Is the depth of water directly proportional to the time? Explain.

b How deep is the water in the swimming pool after 1.5 hours of filling?

c How long does it take to fill the pool to a depth of

   i 0.5 m   **ii** 1.6 m?

7 The table shows the prices of different sized packets of rice.

Packet size	Price (p)
250 g	60
500 g	110
1 kg	180

a Draw a graph with size on the horizontal axis and price on the vertical axis.

b Are packet size and price in direct proportion? Explain.

8 In an experiment, different masses are hung on a spring. The amount the spring stretches is measured. Here are the results.

Mass (g)	0	10	15	20
Stretch (cm)	0	4.2	6.3	8.4

Are the mass and stretch in direct proportion? Explain.

Challenge Currency exchange rates change frequently. In 2018 the average exchange rate for pounds to euros was £1 = €1.18, but in the year 2000 it was £1 = €1.13.
If the exchange rate is shown as a line graph with £ on the vertical axis, how does the change in the rate affect the graph?
Which line will be steeper, 2018 or 2000?

Reflect How sure are you of your answers? Were you mostly

🙁 **Just guessing**   😐 **Feeling doubtful**   🙂 **Confident**

What next? Use your results to decide whether to strengthen or extend your learning.

9 Strengthen

Straight-line graphs

1 a Which hill is steepest?

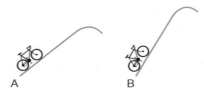

A   B   C

b Which graph is steepest?

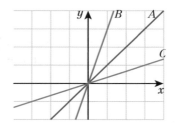

2 a Copy and complete the table of values for $y = 2x - 1$.

x	−2	−1	0	1	2
y	−5				

Q2a hint

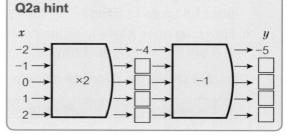

b Write the coordinate pairs for $y = 2x - 1$. The first one is done for you.

(−2, −5)

c i Draw a coordinate grid from −3 to 3 on the x-axis and −5 to 5 on the y-axis and plot the coordinates.

ii Draw a straight line that goes through all the points and extend the line to the edges of the grid.

iii Label the graph with its equation.

3 a Copy and complete the table of values in Q2 for $y = x - 1$.

b Write the coordinate pairs for $y = x - 1$.

c On the same grid as Q2, plot the graph of $y = x - 1$.

d Which graph is steeper, $y = 2x - 1$ or $y = x - 1$?

Q3d hint Imagine the graphs are hills and you are cycling up them. Which one is steeper?

4 Look at the diagram and then complete these sentences.

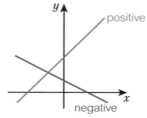

Q4 hint Use 'up' or 'down' in the last two sentences.

The steepness of the graph is called the _____.

A positive gradient goes _____ from left to right.

A negative gradient goes _____ from left to right.

5 a Are the gradients of these line segments positive or negative?

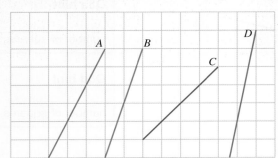

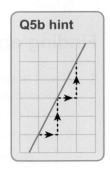

Q5b hint

b Choose a point on line segment A.
Move your finger one square across (to the right).
How many squares does your finger move up to meet line segment A again?

c Copy and complete.
Gradient of line segment $A = \dfrac{\text{number of squares up}}{\text{number of squares across}} = \dfrac{\square}{\square} = \square$

d Repeat parts **b** and **c** to work out the gradients of line segments B, C and D.

6 a Are the gradients of these line segments positive or negative?

b Choose a point on line segment E.
Move your finger one square across (to the right).
How many squares do you have to move your finger down to meet line segment E again?

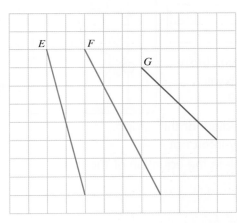

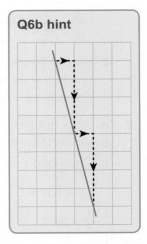

Q6b hint

Q6c hint The line segment goes down, so the number of squares up is a negative number.

c Copy and complete.

Gradient of line segment $E = -\dfrac{\text{number of squares up}}{\text{number of squares across}} = -\dfrac{\square}{\square} = -\square$

d Repeat parts **b** and **c** to work out the gradients of line segments F and G.

7 a Which of these graphs have
  i a positive gradient
  ii a negative gradient?

b Work out the gradients of these graphs by counting the squares up or down and dividing by the squares across.

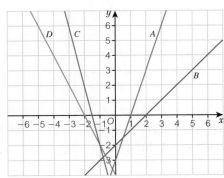

8 These lines have fraction gradients.

a

b

c

d

Write down the gradient of each line.

Q8a hint

$$\frac{1}{\text{number of squares across}}$$

Q8d hint

$$\frac{-1}{\text{number of squares across}}$$

Finding equations of graphs

1 These graphs are all parallel.
   a Work out their gradients.
      What do you notice?
   b Copy and complete this table.

Graph	y-intercept
$y = 3x + 3$	
$y = 3x + 1$	
$y = 3x$	
$y = 3x - 2$	

Q1b hint The y-intercept is the y value where the graph crosses the y-axis.

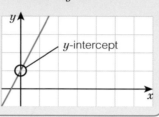

   c Where do you think the graph $y = 3x + 5$ will cross the y-axis?

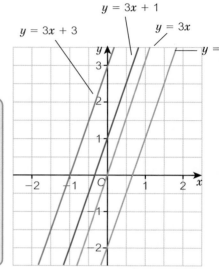

2 **a** Work out the gradient of this graph.
   b Write down the y-intercept.
   c Copy and complete the equation of the graph.

$$y = \square x + \square$$
   gradient y-intercept

3 Follow the steps in Q2 to write down the equations of these graphs.

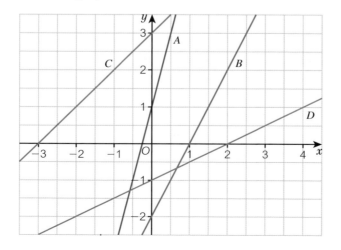

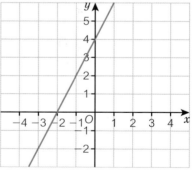

Q3 hint Write '$1x$' as 'x'.

239

4 Follow the steps in Q2 to write down the equations of these graphs.

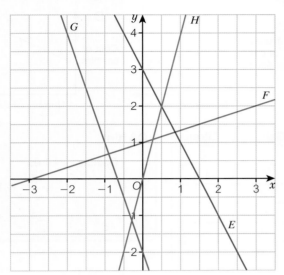

Q4 hint First decide if the gradient is positive or negative.

5 Follow these steps to match the graphs to their equations.

$y = -2x + 1$ $y = x + 3$

$y = -\frac{1}{2}x - 2$ $y = 3x + 3$

a Write down the two equations that have negative gradients.

b Use the y-intercept to match the two graphs to the equations in part **a**.

c Write down the two equations that have positive gradients.

d Can you use the y-intercept to tell which is which?

e Work out the gradient of one graph.

f Match the remaining graph and equation.

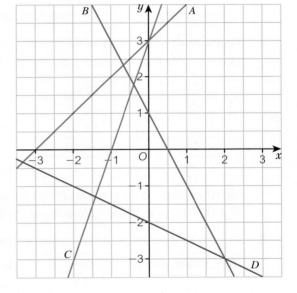

Direct proportion

1 **a** Draw a pair of axes like in the diagram.

b Draw any straight graph through the origin (0,0).

c Label your graph 'Direct proportion'.

d Underneath your graph, copy and complete:

When two quantities are in direct proportion their graph is a s_____ l_____ through _____.

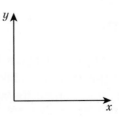

2 Which of these graphs show direct proportion?

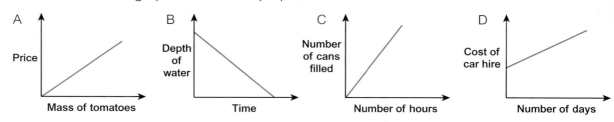

3 **Problem-solving**

a Copy and complete the conversion table to change gallons to litres.

b Plot a conversion graph to show this information.

c Use the graph to change these between gallons and litres.

   i 8 gallons   **ii** 18 litres

 iii 36 gallons   **iv** 76.5 litres

d Are gallons and litres in direct proportion? Explain.

Gallons	Litres
0	0
1	4.5
2	
5	
10	
20	

Q3 hint

Gallons   Litres

×☐ (1   4.5) ×☐
     2   ☐

×☐ (1   4.5) ×5
     5   ☐

4 **Reasoning** Here is a table showing the cost of sending a small parcel by first class post in the UK.

Mass	Cost
1 kg	£5.65
2 kg	£8.90
5 kg	£15.10
10 kg	£21.25

Plot the graph on a coordinate grid. How does the graph show that the mass and the cost are not in direct proportion?

Q4 hint Plot 'kg' on the x-axis and 'cost in £' on the y-axis.
Does the line go through (0, 0)?
Is it a straight line or are there different gradients?
Do the other points on the line, in between the plotted points, have any meaning?

5 Are these quantities in direct proportion?

a
Hours worked	Pay
0	£0
1	£16
2	£22
3	£28

b
Texts sent	Cost
0	£0
10	£7
50	£35
100	£70

Q5 hint When one value is zero, is the other value zero? When one value is doubled, is the other value doubled?

Challenge

Write a list of 10 items your family pays for each week. You could include groceries, electricity, gas or water, childcare, petrol etc.
Decide for each one if the amount bought is in direct proportion to the price.

Reflect   Look back at the questions you got wrong in the Check up test.
Now look back at the Strengthen questions you answered.
Write down one thing you now understand better.
Is there anything you still need help with? Ask a friend or your teacher to help you with it.

9 Extend

1 a Write down the gradient of this graph.
   b Work out the gradient using the formula

$$\text{gradient} = \frac{\text{change in } y}{\text{change in } x}$$

   Do you get the same answer?

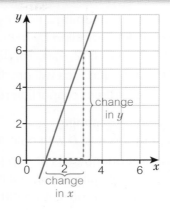

2 Use the formula to work out the gradients of these graphs.

$$\text{gradient} = \frac{\text{change in } y}{\text{change in } x}$$

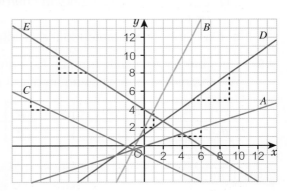

3 This graph converts centimetres to feet.
   a Are cm and feet in direct proportion? Explain.
   b Work out the gradient of the graph.
   c Write down the equation of the graph.
   d 1 foot = 30 cm.
      How does the equation show this relationship?

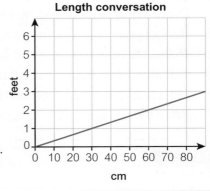

Length conversation

4 Write the equations of the graphs for these conversions.

	y	x
a	£1	€1
b	1 kg	2.2 lb
c	1 m	10 cm
d	1 mile	1.6 km

Q3c hint $y = \square x + \square$

Q4 hint Look back at Q3.

5 There is a link between how soon after a lightning flash you
   hear the thunder clap and how far away the thunderstorm is.
   Use the data to plot a graph to show the results. Is the distance of
   the thunderstorm in direct proportion to the number of seconds it
   takes to hear it?

Seconds	Miles
3	0.65
5	1.09
8	1.74

6 A laboratory measures a pair of variables.

    a Work out $y \div x$ for each pair.

    b Is $y \div x$ the same each time?

    c Are y and x in direct proportion?

x	3.5	4.5	8
y	21	27	48

7 **Problem-solving / Reasoning** Four cyclists are training for a competition.
The distances, in km, travelled by the cyclists each day are

    A 2, 7, 12, 17, 22, …   **B** 2, 4, 8, 16, 32, …   **C** 1, 4, 9, 16, 25, …   **D** 1, 4, 7, 10, 13, …

    a Which of these sequences will produce a straight-line graph?

    b Are any of these direct proportion relationships? Explain your answer.

8 **Problem-solving / Reasoning**

    a Match each graph A to D with calculations **i** to **iv**.

       i The cost of n phone calls at 40p per minute.

      ii The cost of n biscuits at 25p each.

     iii The cost of hiring a bike at £5 plus £2 for every hour of hire.

     iv Energy cost at £2 standing charge plus 50p per unit.

    b Explain how you matched the graphs.

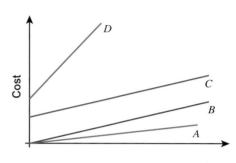

9 Here are some results from an experiment.
Which pairs of quantities are in direct proportion?

> **Q9 hint** Follow the steps in Q6.

c	4	6.5	7
d	12	19.5	21

p	2	5	6.5
q	13	25	31

r	2.1	4.5	8.1
s	7.35	15.75	31.59

Challenge

a Draw a coordinate grid from −10 to 10 on both axes.
Draw a graph in the first quadrant.

b Reflect your graph in the y-axis.

c Reflect both graphs in the x-axis.

d Do any of the graphs have the same gradient?

e Do any of the graphs intersect with each other?

f Write the equation of each graph.

> **Hint** The first quadrant is the top right quadrant, and has positive x and y coordinates.

Reflect   Larry enters pairs of coordinates in a spreadsheet like this.

	A	B
1	x	y
2	4	7
3	3	5
4		

> **Hint** What does 'slope' mean?
> What do you think B2:B3 means?
> What do you think A2:A3 means?

In cell B4, he types in the formula **=slope(B2:B3, A2:A3)**
Use what you know about gradients to explain what this spreadsheet formula does.
What answer does Larry get? Test it for yourself in a spreadsheet.

9 Unit test

1 Work out the gradient of this slide. Give your answer as
  a a fraction   **b** a percentage.

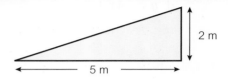

2 **a** Copy and complete this table of values for the equation $y = -2x + 5$.

x	−2	−1	0	1	2
y					

  b Plot the graph of $y = -2x + 5$ on a grid from −2 to 2 on the x-axis
     and −2 to 10 on the y-axis.
  c On the same grid, plot the graph of $y = -x + 4$.
  d Which graph is steeper, $y = -2x + 5$ or $y = -x + 4$?
  e Write down the coordinates of the y-intercept of the graph of $y = -x + 4$.

3 **a** Work out the gradient of each graph.
  b Write the equation of each graph.

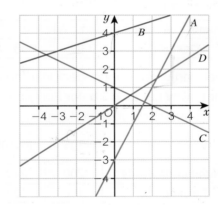

4 The table shows the prices of different masses of building sand.

Mass (tonnes)	1.5	2.1	2.6
Price (£)	45	63	78

  a Plot a graph of these values.
  b Are the price and mass in direct proportion?
     Explain.
  c What is the price for every 1 tonne of sand?

5 Are units of electricity used and cost in direct proportion?
  Show your working.

Units used	Cost (£)
50	19.25
100	21.50
200	26.00

6 Match each graph to its equation.

  a $y = 4x + 2$

  b $y = \frac{1}{4}x - 2$

  c $y = -x + 3$

  d $y = -4x + 2$

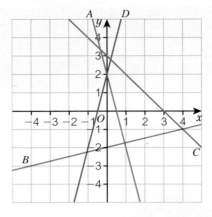

7 Two types of cat food are sold online.

   Pawsy is sold in packs of 12 and there is no delivery charge.
   Purry is sold as single packs and there is a delivery charge.

   The tables show the costs of ordering the different types of cat food.

   Pawsy cat food

Number of packs	12	24	36	48	60
Cost (£)	15.60	31.20	46.80	62.40	78

   Purry cat food

Number of packs	1	2	3	4	5	6
Cost (£)	3.99	4.98	5.97	6.96	7.95	8.94

   Without drawing graphs, decide if the cost is directly proportional to the number of packs
   a for Pawsy cat food **b** for Purry cat food.
   Explain and show your working.

8 The table shows the earnings of a journalist for writing articles with different numbers of words.

Number of words	200	240	320
Earnings (£)	100	120	160

   a Plot the points, with number of words on the horizontal axis and amount earned on the vertical axis. Join the points with a straight line.
   b Use your graph to work out how much the journalist earns for an article 300 words long.
   c Write an equation linking earnings (E) to number of words (N).

Challenge

a Plot these points on a coordinate grid and join them to make a triangle.
   A (1, 0) B (6, 5) C (−1, 12)
   What type of triangle is ABC?
b Extend any lines you need to so that they cross the y-axis.
   Write down the equations of the lines AB, BC, CA.

Reflect   How did you find the work in this unit on straight-line graphs?

   Easy   OK   Hard

   Explain why.

10 Percentages, decimals and fractions

Master   Check up p259   Strengthen p261   Extend p264   Unit test p266

10.1 Fractions and decimals

- Change time to decimal hours
- Recall equivalent fractions and decimals
- Recognise recurring and terminating decimals
- Order fractions by converting them to decimals or equivalent fractions

Active Learn
Homework

Warm up

1 **Fluency** Which of these numbers have the same value?

    3   3.033   3.0   3.33   3.00   3.330   3.000

2 Write each fraction as a decimal.

   a $\frac{2}{5}$ **b** $\frac{3}{10}$ **c** $\frac{23}{100}$ **d** $\frac{3}{100}$ **e** $\frac{2}{25}$ **f** $\frac{3}{20}$

3 Write each decimal as a fraction in its simplest form.
   a 0.2   **b** 0.22   **c** 0.02

4 Match these hours and minutes to the correct decimal hours.
   a 3 hours 15 minutes
   b 3 hours 30 minutes   A 3.5 hours   B 3.25 hours   C 3.75 hours
   c 3 hours 45 minutes

5 Write these hours and minutes as decimal hours.
   The first one is started for you.

   a 3 hours 12 minutes = $3\frac{12}{60}$ hours = $3\frac{\square}{10}$ hours = 3.$\square$ hours
   b 5 hours 36 minutes
   c 13 hours 42 minutes
   d 24 minutes

6 Write these decimal hours as hours and minutes.
   The first one is started for you.

   a 1.2 hours = $1\frac{2}{10}$ hours = $1\frac{\square}{60}$ hours = 1 hour $\square$ minutes
   b 4.3 hours
   c 9.1 hours
   d 8.9 hours

7 **Reasoning** Jayne spends 1 hour 48 minutes doing her homework one evening.
   She says, 'I have spent 1.48 hours doing homework this evening.'
   Is she correct? Explain your answer.

8 Write each fraction as a decimal.

a $\frac{7}{1000}$ **b** $\frac{71}{1000}$ **c** $\frac{471}{1000}$

9 Write each decimal as a fraction.
a 0.519   **b** 0.019
c 0.009   **d** 0.109

Q8a, b hint

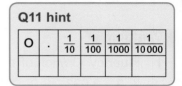

> **Key point**   A **terminating decimal** ends after a definite number of digits, for example 0.22 or 0.519.

10 Write these terminating decimals as fractions in their simplest form.
     a 0.035   **b** 0.362   **c** 0.256   **d** 7.125   **e** 63.025

11 Reasoning   Shelley converts 0.0675 to a fraction like this.

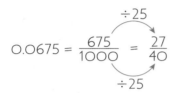

$$0.0675 = \frac{675}{1000} \overset{\div 25}{\underset{\div 25}{=}} \frac{27}{40}$$

Q11 hint

O	.	$\frac{1}{10}$	$\frac{1}{100}$	$\frac{1}{1000}$	$\frac{1}{10\,000}$

Explain the mistake that Shelley has made. Write the correct conversion.

> **Key point**   The line in a fraction means 'divide by'. You can use written division to write fractions as decimals. For example, to write $\frac{3}{8}$ as a decimal, work out $8\overline{)3}$

> **Worked example**
>
> Write $\frac{3}{8}$ as a decimal. $\frac{3}{8} = 8\overline{)3.^3 0 ^6 0 ^4 0}$ $\overset{0.\,3\,7\,5}{}$
>
> Rewrite as a written division.
>
> Keep putting zeros at the end of the decimal until there is no remainder when dividing by 8.

12 Use written division to write these fractions as decimals.
     a $\frac{5}{8}$ **b** $\frac{7}{8}$ **c** $\frac{5}{16}$

Q12a hint $8\overline{)5.0...}$ $\overset{0.\Box...}{}$

> **Key point**   A **recurring decimal** contains a digit, or sequence of digits, which repeats itself for ever.

13 Problem-solving / Reasoning   Jocelyn works out some divisions on her calculator and gets these answers.

0.333333333	0.8333333333	2.1666666667
0.666666667	0.1428571429	1.6666666667

a Why does a 7 appear at the end of three of the decimals?
b Match each decimal to one of these fractions.

     $\frac{1}{7}$ $\frac{1}{3}$ $\frac{5}{3}$ $\frac{2}{3}$ $\frac{5}{6}$ $\frac{13}{6}$

14 Write these recurring decimals using dot notation.
   a 0.8888...   b 0.363 636...   c 0.422 22...
   d 0.305 305 30...   e 0.1234 1234 12...   f 0.633 333...

15 A unit fraction has a numerator of 1, for example $\frac{1}{2}$, $\frac{1}{5}$, $\frac{1}{9}$.
   Which denominators of unit fractions up to $\frac{1}{15}$ give terminating decimals?
   Which give recurring decimals? Use a calculator to help.
   Write any recurring decimals using dot notation.

16 Match each of these fractions to the correct
   recurring decimal.
   Use a calculator to help.

   $\boxed{\dfrac{5}{9}}$ $\boxed{\dfrac{2}{11}}$ $\boxed{\dfrac{4}{15}}$ $\boxed{\dfrac{5}{12}}$

   $\boxed{0.\dot{1}\dot{8}}$ $\boxed{0.41\dot{6}}$ $\boxed{0.2\dot{6}}$ $\boxed{0.\dot{5}}$

17 Write these lengths of time as recurring decimals.
   a 5 hours 10 minutes   b 3 hours 20 minutes
   c 7 hours 40 minutes   d 6 hours 4 minutes

   Q17a hint 5 hr 10 min = $5\frac{10}{60}$ hours
   Simplify the fraction. Write it as a
   recurring decimal.

18 Which shape has the larger area?

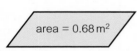

area = 0.68 m²

area = $\frac{2}{3}$ m²

19 By converting the fractions to decimals, write these in descending order.
   $\frac{1}{2}$ $\frac{3}{5}$ $\frac{5}{8}$ $\frac{1}{3}$ $\frac{5}{12}$

20 Write these numbers in descending order.
   $\frac{3}{5}$ $\frac{13}{20}$ 0.625 $\frac{8}{15}$ 0.76 $0.6\dot{3}$

Challenge

a Use the decimal equivalent of $\frac{1}{4}$ to work out these conversions.
   i $\frac{1}{8}$ as a decimal   ii $\frac{1}{16}$ as a decimal   iii $\frac{3}{16}$ as a decimal
b Use the decimal equivalent of $\frac{1}{9}$ to work out these conversions.
   i $\frac{2}{9}$ as a decimal   ii $\frac{3}{9}$ as a decimal   iii $\frac{4}{9}$ as a decimal
c Will all the multiples of $\frac{1}{16}$ be terminating decimals?
   Will all the multiples of $\frac{1}{9}$ be recurring decimals?
   Explain.

   Hint $\frac{1}{8}$ is half of $\frac{1}{4}$ $\frac{3}{16}$ is $\frac{1}{16} \times 3$

Reflect   Write a short definition, in your own words, for
   terminating decimals   recurring decimals
   unit fractions   equivalent fractions and decimals.
Give an example with each definition.

10.2 Equivalent proportions

- Recall equivalent fractions, decimals and percentages
- Use different methods to find equivalent fractions, decimals and percentages
- Use the equivalence of fractions, decimals and percentages to compare two proportions

Active Learn
Homework

Warm up

1 **Fluency** What are the missing numbers?
   a 200 × ☐ = 1000   b 250 × ☐ = 1000   c 12.5 ÷ 100 = ☐

2 Write these proportions as fractions in their simplest form and as decimals.
   Give your answers to 2 decimal places where needed.
   a 40 out of 100   b 35 out of 125
   c 2 out of 3   d 4 out of 30

   Q2d hint   0. 1 ☐ ☐ ☐
   30⟌4.⁴0¹⁰0 ☐ ☐

3 Copy and complete this table.

Fraction			$\frac{3}{5}$		$\frac{9}{50}$	
Decimal		0.2		0.7		
Percentage	75%				100%	

Key point   A positive mixed number is greater than 1, so the decimal equivalent is greater than 1 and the percentage equivalent is greater than 100%.
For example, $1\frac{3}{4}$ = 1.75 = 175%.

4 Copy and complete this table.

Mixed number	$1\frac{1}{2}$				
Decimal		1.7			1.05
Percentage			180%	110%	

5 Profits for a business increase by 200%.
   Write a sentence to explain what this means.

Key point   A **proportion** of a whole can be written as a fraction, decimal or percentage.

6 A magazine article states, 'The number of readers has gone up by 250%.'
   Write 250% as
   a a mixed number   b a decimal.

7 In a 25 g portion of cornflakes, 2 g is sugar.

   a Write the proportion of sugar in cornflakes as a fraction.

   b Write your fraction in part **a** as

     i a decimal   **ii** a percentage.

8 Here are the nutritional information panels from two brands of crisps.

Brand A	
Per 50 g	
Protein	5.0 g
Carbohydrate	26.1 g
Saturated fat	3.0 g
Unsaturated fat	12.5 g
Fibre	3.4 g

Brand B	
percentage content	
Protein	6.5%
Carbohydrate	53.4%
Saturated fat	13.1%
Unsaturated fat	20.7%
Fibre	6.3%

   a Write as a fraction, decimal and percentage the proportion of

     i protein   **ii** carbohydrate   **iii** fibre

   in Brand A.

   b Which brand has the higher proportion of saturated fat?

   c Which brand has the higher proportion of total fat?

> **Key point** Sometimes you might need to use a denominator of 1000 when you convert between fractions, decimals and percentages.

9 Write these fractions as decimals and percentages.
The first one is done for you.

   a

$$\frac{13}{40} \xrightarrow{\times 25} \frac{325}{1000} = 0.325 = 32.5\%$$

   b $\frac{19}{40}$ **c** $\frac{1}{8}$

   d $\frac{6}{125}$ **e** $\frac{17}{500}$ **f** $\frac{13}{250}$

> **Q9d hint** $8 \times 125 = 1000$

10 Write these proportions as percentages.

   a 120 out of 500 people are vegetarian.

   b 31 out of 250 students play a stringed instrument.

   c 30 out of 80 residents own their home.

   d 11 out of 125 items sold cost less than £35.

   e 40 out of 300 students drink coffee.

> **Q10e hint** Give your answer to 2 decimal places.

11 **Problem-solving** There are 287 students in Year 7 and 213 students in Year 8.
91 students in Years 7 and 8 attend an after-school club.
What percentage of Year 7 and Year 8 students attend an after-school club?

12 Problem-solving This yellow rectangle has had a triangle cut out of it.

Q12 hint Work out the areas of the rectangle and the triangle.

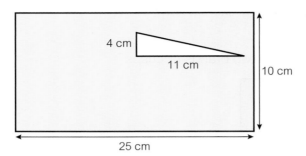

a What fraction of the yellow rectangle is left?

b What percentage of the yellow rectangle is left?

13 Problem-solving Geoff, Ishmael and Sumaya work as salespeople.
The table shows how many presentations they each made and how many won them deals.
Which person won the highest proportion of deals?

Person	Presentations	Won deals
Geoff	10	7
Ishmael	8	5
Sumaya	40	22

Q13 hint For each person, work out the percentage of presentations that won deals.

14 Reasoning Caroline and Greg are writing $\frac{35}{125}$ and $\frac{37}{200}$ as percentages.
Copy and complete their different methods.

a Caroline   Greg

b Caroline   Greg

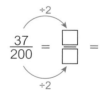

c Which method do you prefer for parts **a** and **b**? Explain.

15 The bar chart shows sales figures for one weekend.
a Work out the total sales for the weekend.
b What proportion of the total sales were
  i gloves   ii scarves
  iii boots and shoes?
  Give your answers as percentages.

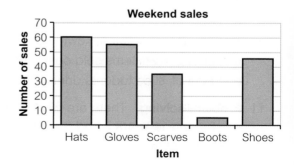

16 Problem-solving Sarah makes necklaces and bracelets.
She sells necklaces for £125 each.
They cost her £45 each to make.
She sells bracelets for £40 each.
They cost her £14 each to make.
Which makes her the greater percentage profit: necklaces or bracelets?

17 Problem-solving Ruth drives to see her sister. She has a choice of two routes.
Route A is 158 miles on the motorway and 42 miles on country roads.
Route B is 137 miles on the motorway and 113 miles on country roads.
Which route has the greater percentage of miles on country roads? Show how you know.

18 Problem-solving The pictogram shows the number of ice creams sold over a weekend.

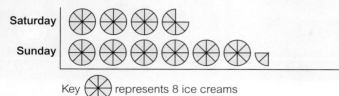

Key 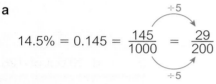 represents 8 ice creams

a What fraction of the ice creams sold over the weekend were sold on Saturday?

b What percentage of the ice creams sold over the weekend were sold on Saturday?

19 Write these percentages as decimals and fractions.
The first one is done for you.

a
$$14.5\% = 0.145 = \frac{145}{1000} \xrightarrow[\div 5]{\div 5} \frac{29}{200}$$

b 12.5%

c 9.5%

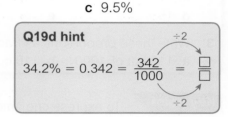

Q19d hint
$$34.2\% = 0.342 = \frac{342}{1000} \xrightarrow[\div 2]{\div 2} \frac{\square}{\square}$$

d 34.2%   e 62.4%   f 2.8%

20 Problem-solving Write these numbers in ascending order.

80% $\frac{7}{8}$ 0.885 $\frac{3}{4}$ 78.5%

Challenge You are given these cards.

Arrange all the cards to make two sets of numbers.
Each set of numbers must be an equivalent fraction, decimal and percentage.

Reflect Which is easier?
- Writing a fraction as a decimal and a percentage (as in Q9)
- Writing a percentage as a decimal and a fraction (as in Q19)

Look at the task you chose as easier. What made it easy?
Look at the task you chose as harder. What made it hard?
Write a hint to help you with the task you found harder.

10.3 Writing percentages

- Express one number as a percentage of another when the units are different
- Work out an amount increased or decreased by a percentage
- Use mental strategies to solve percentage problems

Active Learn
Homework

Warm up

1 **Fluency** How many
  a millilitres in 1 litre   b grams in 1 kg?

2 Find these percentages of £80.
  a 10%   b 20%   c 5%
  d 15%   e 1%   f 16%

3 Write these proportions as fractions and then percentages.
  a 110 out of 1000   b 110 out of 500   c 11 out of 250   d 10 out of 125

Key point   To express one amount as a fraction or percentage of another, they must be in the same units.

4 A $\frac{1}{2}$ litre bottle of mayonnaise contains 330 ml of fat.
  What percentage of the mayonnaise is fat?

5 A 10 km country walking route has a 280 m section along a road.
  What proportion of the route is walking on a road?
  Give your answer as a percentage.

6 A train journey is 4 hours and 10 minutes.
  20 minutes of the journey is spent at train stops, letting passengers on and off.
  What percentage of the journey is at train stops?

7 A 1 kg bag of mortar contains 250 g cement, 650 g sand and 100 g lime.
  What proportion of the bag is
  a cement   b lime   c sand and lime?
  Give your answers as percentages.

8 Write this saving as a percentage of the original selling price.

  > *save* **42p**
  > *originally* **£2.50**

9 Marc sells cakes for £1.25.
  He works out that each cake costs 30p to make.
  a What percentage of £1.25 is the cost?
  b What percentage of £1.25 is the profit?

  Q9b hint % profit = 100% − % cost

10 Sufjan buys some party lights. They cost £15 plus 20% VAT.
   a Work out 20% of £15.   b What is the total cost of the party lights?

11 In 2017 Renie's electricity bill was £876.
   In 2018 it increased by 10%.
   What was Renie's electricity bill in 2018?

12 **Problem-solving**   Leela gets a 2% pay rise.
   Her salary was £25000.
   What is her new salary?

> **Q12 hint** 1% of £25000 = ☐
> 2% = 1% × 2

13 Gary saves £500. He earns 5% simple interest per year.
   a How much interest does he earn in one year?
   b How much money does Gary have in his account after one year?

> **Q13 hint** Work out 5% of £500.

14 **Problem-solving**   Work out the amount of simple interest earned after one year for each of these investments.
   a £1000 at 5% per year
   b £300 at 2% per year
   c £5000 at 8% per year
   d £800 at 6% per year

> **Q14c hint** 1% of £5000 = ☐
> 8% = 1% × 8

15 **Problem-solving**   Jen buys a painting for £400.
   The artist becomes famous and the value increases by 35%.
   What is her painting worth now?

> **Q15 hint** 35% = 3 × 10% + 5%

16 **Problem-solving**   Rob buys £6500 worth of shares.
   The value of his shares increases by 2.5%.
   What is their value now?

> **Q16 hint** 2.5% = 5% ÷ 2

17 **Problem-solving**   Karen invests £400 for 3 years at 2.5% simple interest per year.
   Work out
   a the amount of interest she earns in 1 year
   b the amount of interest she earns in 3 years
   c the total amount her investment is worth at the end of the 3 years.

18 **Problem-solving**   A shirt costs £25. It is reduced in a sale by 10%.
   a Work out 10% of £25.
   b Work out the sale price of the shirt.

19 Problem-solving   A laptop costs £780. This weekend there is a special offer, reducing the price by 5%.
Work out the price of the laptop this weekend.

20 Problem-solving   A council has a housing budget of £240 000.
They have to decrease their budget by 3% next year.
What is their new budget?

21 Problem-solving   A company spends £1200 on office furniture and £1800 on computer equipment.
After 1 year the office furniture decreases in value by 15% and the computer equipment by 30%.
Work out the value after 1 year of
a the office furniture
b the computer equipment.

22 Problem-solving   The price of a smartphone was reduced by 40% in January.
Prices were further reduced by $\frac{1}{4}$ of the January price in February.
The original selling price of the smartphone was £250. What is the sale price in February?

23 Problem-solving   Ed spends £60 in a shop. He buys shoes which normally cost £32.50, but they have a 20% discount.
He spends £15.70 on a jumper.
He also buys a T-shirt.
How much did the T-shirt cost?

Challenge

1   Use these cards to solve this puzzle.

| 10% increase | | 20% decrease | | 15% decrease |

| 20% increase | | 40% increase | | 25% decrease |

You have £100.
Which cards can you use to end up with
a £88   **b** £90   **c** £119?

You can use each card only once.

2   The original price of an item is £100.
The price is decreased by 10% then increased by 10%.
Jen says, 'The new price will be £100 because a 10% increase will cancel out a 10% decrease.'
Is Jen correct? Explain your answer.

Reflect   What was the same and what was different about the way you worked out your answers to Q12 and Q20?

Write yourself three tips or hints for working out amounts increased or decreased by a percentage. Compare your hints and tips with others in your class.

10.4 Percentages of amounts

*Active*Learn
Homework

- Use a multiplier to calculate amounts increased or decreased by a percentage
- Use the unitary method to solve percentage problems

Warm up

1 **Fluency** The calculators show the results of measure calculations.
  Round each number to the required level of accuracy.

  a $\boxed{4.7368}$ metres to 3 significant figures

  b $\boxed{3087.2}$ pounds (£) to an appropriate number of decimal places

2 Write these percentages as decimals.
  a 30%   b 76%
  c 150%   d 265%
  e 5%   f 3.5%

3 Use a multiplier to calculate these percentages.
  a 20% of £34
  b 30% of 15 kg
  c 40% of 120 ml
  d 60% of 4 g

  > **Q3a hint** 20% = 0.2, so 0.2 is the multiplier.
  > 20% of £34 = 0.2 × £34

4 In year 1 a company makes a profit of £4000.
  In year 2 the profit goes up by 150%.
  a What multiplier would you use to calculate the profit at the end of year 2?
  b Work out the profit at the end of year 2.

  > **Q4a hint** Write 150% as a decimal.

5 A magazine article states, 'The number of readers has gone up by 250%.'
  They originally had 30 000 readers.
  How many do they have now?

6 **Problem-solving** Between 2004 and 2013 the price of gold went up by approximately 365%.
  In 2004, 1 ounce of gold cost $425.
  How much did it cost in 2013?

7 **Reasoning** A jacket costs £45. In a sale, the price of the jacket is reduced by 20%.
  a Work out 20% of £45.
  b Work out the sale price of the jacket.
  c Work out 80% of £45.
  d What do you notice about your answers to parts **b** and **c**? Explain.

> **Key point** To decrease an amount by a percentage, you can subtract the percentage from 100%, then work out the multiplier.

8 What multiplier would you use to find each of these percentage decreases?
  a 20%　　　　**b** 40%　　　　**c** 70%　　　　**d** 75%
  e 8%　　　　**f** 24%　　　　**g** 95%　　　　**h** 99%

9 Work out these percentage decreases.
  Use a multiplier for each one.
  a Decrease 6 litres by 20%　　　　**b** Decrease £150 by 70%
  c Decrease 60 ml by 35%　　　　**d** Decrease 800 m by 9%
  e Decrease 12 kg by 93%

10 A report states that the height of a hedge must be reduced by at least 15%.
  The hedge is currently 2.17 m tall.
  How tall will it be when the height is reduced?
  Give your answer to 3 significant figures.

11 A café increases the price of drinks by 20%.
  It originally charged £1.50 for a glass of fresh juice.
  a Work out 20% of £1.50.
  b Work out the new price of a glass of juice.
  c Work out 120% of £1.50.
  d What do you notice? Explain.

> **Key point** To increase an amount by a percentage, you can add the percentage to 100%, then work out the multiplier.

12 What multiplier would you use to find each of these percentage increases?
  a 20%　　　　**b** 30%　　　　**c** 88%　　　　**d** 2%

13 Work out these percentage increases.
  Use a multiplier for each one.
  a Increase 3 kg by 20%　　　　**b** Increase £2 by 88%
  c Increase 2.5 tonnes by 15%　　　　**d** Increase $7 by 11%
  e Increase 5 km by 6%　　　　**f** Increase 4 m by 6.5%

14 Sophie's broadband speed is 40 megabits per second.
  She upgrades it and is promised an increase in speed of 55%.
  a Write a calculation using a multiplier to work out the increased speed Sophie should get.
  b Work out Sophie's expected increased speed.

15 A village has a population of 2825.
  Some new houses are built in the village. This increases the population of the village by 4%.
  Use a multiplier to work out the new population of the village.

16 Miguel gets a 2.4% pay rise. His salary was £23 450.
  What is his new salary?

> **Q16 hint** Give your answer rounded to an appropriate degree of accuracy.

Worked example

20% of an amount is £40.
Work out the original amount.

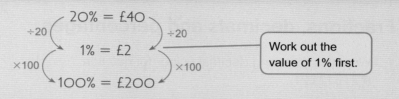

Work out the value of 1% first.

17 Work out the original amount for each of these.
   a 30% of an amount is £180.
   b 80% of an amount is 320 kg.
   c 15% of an amount is 45 litres.
   d 120% of an amount is 720 km.
   e 165% of an amount is 82.5 cm.

Q17d hint

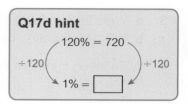

18 **Problem-solving** The cost of a DVD is reduced
   by 30%. It now costs £6.30.
   How much was it originally?

Q18 hint original amount − 30% = ☐%
☐% = £6.30

19 **Problem-solving** Sales of fair trade honey products in 2012 were 95% of what they
   were in 2011.
   In 2012 sales were £3.6 million.
   What were they in 2011?

Challenge The same computer is on sale in two different shops.

Computers 4 U!

PC LAND!

Cash Price £660
SPECIAL OFFER
15% Off Cash Price

How much more does it cost to buy the computer from PC Land?

Reflect

a Write a definition of a multiplier in your own words.
b Write the steps you take to use a multiplier to calculate
   i a percentage increase   ii a percentage decrease.
   Give examples.

10 Check up

Fractions, decimals and percentages

1 Write this recurring decimal using dot notation.
0.212 121 21...

2 Write these terminating decimals as fractions in their simplest form.
a 0.665   **b** 4.006   **c** 0.605

3 **a** Write 20 minutes as a decimal hour.
b Is it a terminating or recurring decimal?

4 Write these numbers in descending order.

$\frac{1}{4}$ 0.4 $\frac{3}{8}$ 4.5% $\frac{1}{3}$ $\frac{7}{20}$ 30%   0.75

5 The residents of three streets were surveyed to find out if they would like a skate park nearby. The table shows the results of the survey.

Street	Number of residents surveyed	Number of residents who said 'yes'
Elm Street	50	15
Oak Street	200	58
Ash Street	125	36

a For each street write the proportion of residents who said 'yes' as
  i a fraction of those surveyed
  ii a percentage of those surveyed.
b In which street did the greatest proportion of residents say 'yes'?

6 Copy and complete this table. Write the fractions in their simplest form.

Fraction	Decimal	Percentage
$\frac{9}{40}$		
	0.135	
		170%

Percentage problems

7 A $\frac{1}{2}$ kg box of cornflakes contains 490 g of corn.
What percentage of the contents of the box is corn?

8 A mirror costs £18 plus 20% VAT.
a Work out 20% of £18.
b What is the total cost of the mirror?

9 A tennis racket costs £30. It is reduced in a sale by 15%.
Work out the sale price of the tennis racket.

10 Work out these percentage increases and decreases.
   a Decrease 250 g by 28%   b Increase 45 kg by 11%
   c Increase £72 by 60%   d Decrease 420 ml by 2%

11 Mo invests £650 for 4 years at 3% simple interest per year.
    Work out
    a the amount of interest she earns in 1 year
    b the amount of interest she earns in 4 years
    c the total amount her investment is worth at the end of the 4 years.

12 Work out the original amount when
    a 60% of the amount is £2400   b 35% of the amount is 105 km.

13 The cost of a coat was reduced by 40%.
    It now costs £120.
    How much was the original price?

1   a Write one fraction with a denominator of 25, one with a denominator of 50 and one
       with a denominator of 200.
    b Write each of your fractions in part **a** as a decimal and a percentage.
    c Write your fractions in part **a** in order of size, starting with the smallest.

2   Fill in some possible percentages and amounts in this spider diagram.

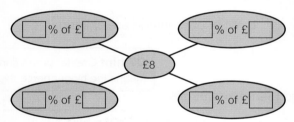

3   Part of the print on this sale sticker has been smudged.

    Give three examples of what the original price and percentage off could be.

10 Strengthen

1   Copy and complete to write these fractions as decimals.

a 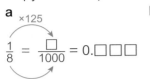 $\frac{1}{8} = \frac{\square}{1000} = 0.\square\square\square$

b $\frac{3}{8} = \frac{\square}{1000} = 0.\square\square\square$

c $\frac{1}{40} = \frac{\square}{1000} = 0.\square\square\square$

d $\frac{3}{40} = \frac{\square}{1000} = 0.\square\square\square$

2   Write each decimal answer in Q1 as a percentage by multiplying it by 100.

3   Copy and complete to write these percentages as decimals and as fractions in their simplest form.

   a $62\% = 0.\square\square = \frac{\square}{100} = \frac{\square}{50}$

   b $62.5\% = 0.\square\square\square = \frac{\square}{1000} = \frac{\square}{8}$

4   Write these numbers in descending order (from largest to smallest) by writing as decimals.
   $\frac{7}{40}$ 0.19   18.5%

 5   Nine out of 40 members of a knitting club are children.
   a What fraction are children?
   b What percentage are children?

> **Q5b hint** $\frac{\square}{40} \times 100$

6   21 out of 125 members of a gym are children.
   a What fraction are children?   **b** What percentage are children?

7   Is there a greater proportion of children in the knitting club in Q5 or the gym in Q6?

> **Q7 hint** Greater proportion means the bigger percentage.

8   Rewrite these statements as fractions and then percentages.
   a 12 out of 20 students like PE.
   b 13 out of 25 members of a judo club are girls.
   c 32 out of 50 members of a boxing club are boys.
   d 2 out of 10 students have a cat.
   e 4 out of 5 DVD purchases are made online.

> **Q8a hint**
>
> $\frac{12}{20} = \frac{\square}{100} = \square\%$

9   The members of three dog training clubs were surveyed to find out if they fed their dog a certain brand of food.

   The table shows the results of the survey.

   a How many in Cool K9s said 'yes'?

   b How many Perfect Pooches members were surveyed?

Club	Number of members surveyed	Number of members who said 'yes'
Perfect Pooches	200	16
Cool K9s	40	12
Delightful Dogs	125	21

   c For each club write the proportion of members who said 'yes' as
   i   a fraction of those surveyed
   ii a percentage of those surveyed.
   d In which club did the greatest proportion of members say 'yes'?

> **Q9c ii hint**
>
> $\dfrac{\text{number that said yes}}{\text{number surveyed}}$
>
> $= \frac{\square}{\square} \times \square = \square\%$

10 Write each of these terminating decimals as a fraction.

    a 0.007

    b 0.073

    c 0.173

    d 0.1073

> **Q10 hint** 3 digits after the decimal point means $\frac{\square}{1000}$.
> 4 digits after the decimal point means $\frac{\square}{10\,000}$.

11 Write each decimal under the heading 'terminating' or 'recurring'.

    1.6   0.1$\dot{6}$ 1.06   0.1$\dot{0}\dot{6}$ 0.166   1.0$\dot{6}$

> **Q11 hint** A dot over a digit shows it recurs and goes on for ever.

12 Write each recurring decimal in Q11 like this to show how the digits repeat.

    $\square$.$\square\square\square\square\square\square$ ...

> **Q12 hint** A single dot means only that digit repeats. Two dots mean the sequence of digits repeats.

13 Match each recurring decimal to a fraction.

> **Q13 hint** $\frac{1}{30} = 1 \div 30$

$\frac{1}{30}$	$\frac{1}{3}$	$\frac{2}{33}$	$\frac{2}{30}$	$\frac{2}{3}$	$\frac{1}{33}$
0.$\dot{6}$	0.0$\dot{3}$	0.$\dot{0}\dot{3}$	0.0$\dot{6}$	0.$\dot{3}$	0.$\dot{0}\dot{6}$

Percentage problems

1 For each of these, write the amounts in the same units.
Then write the first amount as a percentage of the second amount.

    a 48 cm out of 1 m

    b 15 mm out of 5 cm

    c 130 g out of 0.5 kg

    d 300 ml out of 2 litres

    e 750 m out of 3 km

> **Q1a hint** 1 m = $\square$ cm
> $\frac{48}{\square} = \square$%

> **Q1d hint** 2 litres = $\square$ ml
> $\frac{300}{\square} = \frac{\square}{100} = \square$%

2 Increase each amount by the given percentage.

    a £60 by 10%   **b** £60 by 20%   **c** £45 by 20%

    d £70 by 10%   **e** £70 by 5%   **f** £70 by 15%

> **Q2b and c hint** 10% × 2 = 20%

3 Ross invests £200 in a savings account that offers 1% simple interest per year.

    a Work out the amount of simple interest he earns in 1 year.

> **Q3a hint** Work out 1% of £200.

    b Work out the amount of simple interest he earns in 2 years.

> **Q3b hint** Amount of simple interest in 2 years = amount of simple interest in 1 year × 2

    c Work out the amount of simple interest he earns in 3 years.

    d Add the simple interest earned in 3 years to Ross's investment of £200 to work out how much money is in Ross's savings account after 3 years.

4 Decrease each amount by the given percentage.

    a £90 by 10%   **b** £90 by 20%   **c** £40 by 10%

    d £40 by 5%   **e** £40 by 15%   **f** £120 by 15%

> **Q4 hint** For a decrease, subtract from the original amount.

5 Copy and complete these percentage increases by using a multiplier.

  a Increase £35 by 12% = 112% of £35
                             = 1.12 × 35
                             = £☐

  b Increase 150 g by 41% = 141% of ☐
                            = ☐ × ☐
                            = ☐ g

  c Increase 55 m by 6% = 106% of ☐
                       = ☐ × ☐
                       = ☐ m

  d Increase 77 litres by 15% = 115% of ☐
                        = ☐ × ☐
                        = ☐ litres

6 Copy and complete these percentage decreases by using a multiplier.

  a Decrease £50 by 12% = 88% of £50
                          = 0.88 × 50
                          = £☐

> **Q6a hint** 100% minus 12% = 88%

  b Decrease 125 g by 40% = ☐% of 125 g
                            = ☐ × ☐
                            = ☐ g

  c Decrease 2000 km by 1% = ☐% of ☐
                       = ☐ × ☐
                       = ☐ km

7 10% of an amount is £12.
Copy and complete to work out 100%.

  ÷10 ⌒ 10% is £12 ⌒ ÷10
  ×100 ⌄ 1% is ☐ ⌄ ×100
           100% is ☐

8 5% of an amount is 30 g.
  a Work out 1% of the amount.
  b Work out the original amount.

9 The price of a computer is reduced by 10% in a sale.
  a What percentage of the original price does the computer cost now?

> **Q9a hint** 100% − 10%

  b The computer costs £1800 in the sale. Work out the original amount.

> **Q9b hint**
> ÷☐ ⌒ ☐% is £1800 ⌒ ÷☐
>   1% is ☐

Challenge   The value of a house could increase or decrease each year.

a Copy and complete the table to show the value of this house over a five-year period.

Year	Value at start of year	Percentage change	Value at end of year
1st	£120 000	10% increase	£132 000
2nd	£132 000	15% increase	
3rd		20% decrease	
4th		25% increase	
5th		15% decrease	

b What is the difference in the value of the house at the start of the 1st year and the end of the 5th year?

Reflect   Julie says, 'Working with fractions, decimals and percentages is all about multiplying and dividing.'

Look back at the questions you answered in this Strengthen lesson.
Write two questions where you had to multiply to find an answer.
Write two questions where you had to divide to find an answer.
Write two questions where you had to multiply *and* divide to find an answer.

10 Extend

1 A business is testing two different methods for delivering online shopping.
Method A has 24 dissatisfied customers out of 296.
1% of the Method B customers were dissatisfied. Which method is better?

2 Mark invests £12 500 for 4 years at 6.75% simple interest.
How much is his investment worth at the end of the 4 years?

3 Fatima invests £5000 for 5 years.
a Copy and complete the table showing the value of her investment at the end of each year.

Year	Value at start of year	Percentage change	Value at end of year
1st	£5000	20% increase	£6000
2nd	£6000	8% increase	
3rd		12% decrease	
4th		10% increase	
5th		3% decrease	

b Compare the value of her investment at the start of the 1st year and the end of the 5th year. Work out
i the actual increase in her investment
ii the percentage increase in her investment.

> **Q3b ii hint**
> Percentage increase
> $= \dfrac{\text{actual increase}}{\text{original amount}} \times 100$

4 **Problem-solving** The brown cube has a side length of 7 cm.
a Work out the surface area of the brown cube.
The surface area of the green cube is 85% greater than the surface area of the brown cube.
b Work out the side length of the green cube. Give your answer to the nearest millimetre.

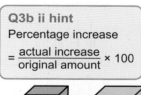
7 cm   ?

5 Harry carried out an experiment to measure the increase in the number of bacteria on food.
At 8 °C, he found that the number of bacteria increased by 40% every $\frac{1}{2}$ hour.
a Copy and complete this table to show the number of bacteria on the food between 10 00 and 13 00.
Write each answer to the nearest whole number.

> **Q5a hint**
> 100 × 1.4 = 140
> 140 × 1.4 = ☐

Time	10 00	10 30	11 00	11 30	12 00	12 30	13 00
Number of bacteria	100	140					

b Draw a graph to show the data in the table.
Plot 'Time' on the x-axis, and 'Number of bacteria' on the y-axis.
Plot your points and join them with a line.
c Use your graph to
i estimate the number of bacteria on the food at 10 45
ii estimate the time at which the number of bacteria reached 500.
d The food in a fridge should be kept at a temperature of 4 °C.
Do you think you could use the results from this experiment to model the bacteria growth on food in a faulty fridge?

6 Reasoning Your boss says you can either have a 1% pay rise this year and then a 2% pay rise next year, or a 1.6% pay rise this year. Which would you prefer?

7 Problem-solving Moira puts some money into low risk and high risk investments in the ratio 3 : 1.
a What fraction of her money does she put into
   i the low risk investments   **ii** the high risk investments?
The total amount she invests is £600.
b How much money does she put into
   i the low risk investments   **ii** the high risk investments?
Moira makes 4% on her low risk investments and 12% on her high risk investments.
c How much money does she make overall?

8 Problem-solving The volume of the larger cube is 20% more than the volume of the smaller cube.
Work out the side length of the larger cube.
Give your answer to 1 decimal place.

5 cm

9 Here is a sequence of numbers. 200, 160, 128, 102.4, …
Each term in the sequence is 80% of the previous term.
The term-to-term rule is 'multiply by 0.8'.
a Write the first four terms in each of these sequences.
   i First term is 400, each term in the sequence is 30% of the previous term.
   ii First term is 80, each term in the sequence is 120% of the previous term.
Look at this sequence of numbers. 300, 180, 108, 64.8, …
b Copy and complete these statements.
   i The term-to-term rule is 'multiply by ☐'.
   ii Each term in the sequence is ☐% of the previous term.
c Work out the term-to-term rule for each of these sequences.
   i 60, 30, 15, 7.5, …
   ii 800, 560, 392, 274.4, …
   iii 20, 32, 51.2, 81.92, …
   iv 60, 75, 93.75, …
d Problem-solving Work out the missing terms in this sequence.
   ☐, 550, 605, ☐, 732.05, …

> **Q9b i hint**
> 300 × ☐ = 180
> 180 ÷ 300 = ☐

Challenge Here are three ways of working out 20% of £150.
- Find 10% and double it.
- Work out 0.2 × £150.
- Find $\frac{2}{10}$ of £150.

Which is quickest?

Reflect Percentages can be used for
- assessing customer satisfaction (as in Q1)
- predicting the value of an investment (as in Q2, Q3 and Q7).

List three other ways that percentages can be used.

10 Unit test

1 Write the missing fractions, decimals and percentages in a copy of this table.

Fraction		$\frac{9}{10}$				$1\frac{3}{5}$
Decimal	0.75				1.3	
Percentage			25%	275%		

2 Write these terminating decimals as fractions in their simplest form.
   a 0.255   **b** 4.42

3 Three groups of students were surveyed to find out if they liked a new brand of milkshake. The table shows the results of the survey.

Group	Number of students surveyed	Number of students who liked the milkshake
A	125	72
B	50	37
C	200	142

   a For each group, write the proportion of students who liked the milkshake as
     i a fraction of those surveyed
     ii a percentage of those surveyed.
   b Which group had the greatest proportion of students who liked the milkshake?

4 A 1 litre carton of fruit drink contains 400 ml of orange juice.
   What percentage of the fruit drink is orange juice?

5 A kayak costs £320 plus 20% VAT.
   a Work out 20% of £320.
   b What is the total cost of the kayak?

6 Copy and complete this table. Write the fractions in their simplest form.

Fraction	Decimal	Percentage
$\frac{131}{200}$		
	0.525	
		2.5%

7 Write these fractions in descending order.
   $\frac{4}{5}$ $\frac{7}{8}$ $\frac{3}{4}$ $\frac{2}{3}$

8 Write $\frac{1}{22}$ as a decimal.

9 A CD player costs £60. It is reduced in a sale by 35%.
   Work out the sale price of the CD player.

10 Jatin gets a pay rise of 8%.
His old salary was £22 000.
What is his new salary?

11 **a** 10% of an amount is 6.2 kg.
Work out the original amount.
b 40% of an amount is 96 m.
Work out the original amount.

12 Serena invests £1800 for 5 years at 4% simple interest per year.
How much is her investment worth at the end of the 5 years?

13 This year's electricity bill is 105% of the amount it was last year.
This year it is £945.
How much was it last year? Show your working.

Challenge A surfboard in a shop has 20% off in a sale.

For one day only, the shop is advertising an extra 30% off all sale prices.
a Choose an original price for the surfboard. Reduce it by 20%.
Reduce the new price by 30%.
b Is 20% off, then 30% off, the same as 50% off? Explain.
c Explain how you can work out the combined discount of two discounts on the same item.

Reflect Look back at the tables you completed for Q1 and Q6 in this test.
How did you work out these types of conversions?
a You had a decimal and wanted to find its
   i equivalent fraction
   ii equivalent percentage.
b You had a fraction and wanted to find its
   i equivalent decimal
   ii equivalent percentage.
c You had a percentage and wanted to find its
   i equivalent fraction
   ii equivalent decimal.

Answers

UNIT 1 Number

1.1 Calculations

1 a 3 **b** 5

2 a 270 **b** 900 **c** 420 **d** 2500
e 620

3 a 861 **b** 1082 **c** 40.77 **d** 18.04

4 a 320 **b** 320
c 32 is 64 ÷ 2 and 10 is 5 × 2; the answers are the same.
d 400 **e** 400
f 4 is 8 ÷ 2 and 100 is 50 × 2; the answers are the same.

5 a 180 **b** 2300 **c** 440 **d** 3400
e 170 **f** 3600

6 a 280 **b** 270 **c** 180 **d** 40
e 49 **f** 45 **g** 99 **h** 39

7 It is better to halve 2.4; 2.4 × 50 = 1.2 × 100 = 120

8 a i 30 **ii** 8 **iii** 240
b i 120 **ii** 2200 **iii** 600

9 70 grams

10 a 606 **b** 594

11 a 808 **b** 792 **c** 714 **d** 686
e 3996 **f** 4004 **g** 1497 **h** 57
i 608

12 a £14.85 **b** 45p
c Students' own answers, e.g.
£1.02 = 99p + 3p, so the difference is 15 lots of 3p

13 £24.95

14 a 1770 **b** 1687 **c** 3086 **d** 3120
e 5603 **f** 52 009

15 18 155

16 a 25.64 **b** 103.83 **c** 6.31

17 a 401.33
b No, the subtractions need to be done separately.
ii 195.93 **iii** 121.51

18 0.37 m

19 7.15 mm

Challenge

a 10 471.9

b Students' own answers, e.g.
499 × 21 = 500 × 21 − 1 × 21 (rounding and adjusting)
= 500 × 20 + 500 × 1 − 21 (rounding and adjusting)
= 1000 × 10 + 500 − 21 (doubling and halving)
= 10 000 + 479
= 10 479
10 479 − 7.1 = 10 471.9

1.2 Divisibility and division

1 a Last digit is 0, 2, 4, 6 or 8 (even numbers)
b Last digit is 0
c Last digit is 0 or 5

2 a 21 **b** 212

3 Students' own answers, e.g.
a 12.0 = 12 + no tenths = 12
b 12.00 = 12 + no tenths + no hundredths = 12
c 12.40 = 12.4 + no hundredths = 12.4
d Putting a zero at the end of a whole number changes the place value, but putting a zero at the end of a decimal number does not.

4 2, 3, 4, 6, 8, 12

5 a 21, 24, 27, 30, 33, 36, 39, 42, 45, 48
b 3, 6, 9, 3, 6, 9, 12 → 3, 6, 9, 12 → 3
c The sum of their digits is 3 or a multiple of 3.
d All of the numbers are divisible by 3.

6 a 27, 36, 45, 54, 63, 72, 81, 99
b 9, 9, 9, 9, 9, 9, 9, 18 → 9
c The sum of their digits is 9 or a multiple of 9.
d i yes **ii** no **iii** yes
iv yes **v** no **vi** yes

7 Yes, Larry is correct.
Students' own examples

8 a, b 1<u>00</u>, 1<u>04</u>, 1<u>08</u>, 1<u>12</u>, 1<u>16</u>, 1<u>20</u>, 1<u>24</u>, 1<u>28</u>, 1<u>32</u>, 1<u>36</u>, 1<u>40</u>
c The underlined digits make numbers that are multiples of 4.
d i yes **ii** no **iii** yes **iv** yes
v yes **vi** yes **vii** no **viii** no

9 Kerry is correct.
a no **b** no **c** yes **d** yes
e no **f** yes **g** no **h** no

10 Yes, Sam is correct.
Students' own explanation, e.g.
Integers are whole numbers, or the counting numbers, and we counts in ones.

11 a £5.73 **b** £23.80 **c** £387.24 **d** 34p

12 a 3.6 **b** 6.45 **c** 3.45 **d** 46.75

13 £635.75

14 £50.75

15 a 3000 ÷ 30 = 100 and 11.5 is not close to 100.
b 101.5

Challenge

Students' own answers

1.3 Calculating with negative integers

1 a 9 **b** negative 3

2 a −2 **b** 3 **c** −5
d −7 **e** −9

3 a 36 **b** 80 **c** 5 **d** 10

4 a

Calculation	Answer
3 + 2	5
3 + 1	4
3 + 0	3
3 + −1	2
3 + −2	1
3 + −3	0
3 + −4	−1

Calculation	Answer
3 − 2	1
3 − 1	2
3 − 0	3
3 − −1	4
3 − −2	5
3 − −3	6
3 − −4	7

b i 3 − 5 **ii** 3 + 5
c i + − is the same as − **ii** − − is the same as +

5 a 3 **b** 5 **c** 2 **d** 6
e 1 **f** 7 **g** 0 **h** 8
i −1 **j** 9 **k** −2 **l** 10

6 a −2 **b** −2 **c** 12 **d** −4
e −4 **f** 16

7 a 7 **b** 9 **c** 10 **d** 14
e 2.5 **f** 10

8 Adam is correct.
Luke subtracted −12 from +10.
Jack subtracted 12 from +10.

9 a −8 **b** −72 **c** −72 **d** −72
e 8

10 a

Date in May	1	2	13	19	20	25	31
Deposit/ Withdrawal (£)	−145	+20	−37	+100	−12	+55	−25
Balance (£)	−25	−5	−42	58	46	101	76

b £101
c Balance, because it's positive

11 a −160 − 100 = −260 solid **b** 273 °C

12 a

Calculation	Answer
3 × 4	12
3 × 3	9
3 × 2	6
3 × 1	3
3 × 0	0
3 × −1	−3
3 × −2	−6

Calculation	Answer
4 × −3	−12
3 × −3	−9
2 × −3	−6
1 × −3	−3
0 × −3	0
−1 × −3	3
−2 × −3	6

b positive × positive = positive
positive × negative = negative
negative × positive = negative
negative × negative = positive

c Students' own answers, e.g.
If the signs are the same the answer is positive, if the signs are different the answer is negative.

13 a 8   **b** −24   **c** −36   **d** −45
   e 9   **f** −120   **g** 36   **h** −60
   i −5   **j** −10

14 a   **ii**   −3 × −4 = 12 so 12 ÷ −3 = −4 and 12 ÷ −4 = −3
      iii   −2 × 5 = −10 so −10 ÷ −2 = 5 and −10 ÷ 5 = −2

b positive ÷ positive = positive
positive ÷ negative = negative
negative ÷ positive = negative
negative ÷ negative = positive

15 a 4   **b** −5   **c** −3   **d** −4
   e −5   **f** 1   **g** 100   **h** −12
   i −8   **j** −0.4   **k** −6.2

16 a −4   **b** −7   **c** 4   **d** 100
   e −2   **f** −0.4   **g** −33   **h** 42

17 a 12 degrees   **b** −6 °C

18 a 32   **b** −15   **c** 14   **d** −55

19 a −13   **b** −1   **c** 5   **d** −10

Challenge

1 a positive   **b** negative

2 If the number of negative numbers is even, the answer is positive; if the number is odd, the answer is negative.

1.4 Powers and roots

1 a 81   **b** 3

2 a 1   **b** 4   **c** 16   **d** 25
   e 36   **f** 8   **g** 144   **h** 10000

3 a 10   **b** 18   **c** 12   **d** 32
   e 51

4 a 30   **b** 11   **c** 6
   d 8   **e** 8   **f** 25

5 a 51.84   **b** 11.56   **c** 46.24
   d 91.26   **e** 4.04   **f** 142.21

6 a 7.1   **b** 14.1   **c** 19.4   **d** 21.9
   e 94.6   **f** 1.0

7 a 2 and 3   **b** 3 and 4   **c** 6 and 7
   d 7 and 8   **e** 9 and 10   **f** 13 and 14

8 a between 7 cm and 8 cm
   b 7.75 cm (2 d.p.)

9 20 or 21 seats

10 a 1   **b** 8   **c** 27   **d** 64
   e 125   **f** 1000

11 a 5   **b** 1000   **c** 4   **d** 27
   e 1   **f** 125

12 a 7   **b** 9   **c** 1331   **d** 4096
   e 15

13 No; the cube roots of all the integers between 8 and 27, for example, are not integers.

14 a 4.6   **b** 166.4   **c** 753.6   **d** 3.9
   e 4.3   **f** 5.3

15 a 8   **b** 16   **c** 13   **d** 12
   e 0   **f** 52

16 a 4   **b** 9   **c** 16   **d** 25
   e 36   **f** 49   **g** 64   **h** 100

17 a The answer is positive.
   b No, because negative × negative = positive

18 a 5, −5   **b** 8, −8   **c** 9, −9   **d** 1, −1
   e 11, −11   **f** 12, −12

19 a −8   **b** −27   **c** −64   **d** −125
   e −1000   **f** −1
   g The cube is always negative.

20 a

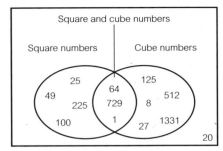

b 1, 64 and 729

Challenge

a No, e.g. $2^2 + 2^2 = 4 + 4 = 8$, which is not a square number.

b Yes, e.g. $x^2 \times y^2 = x \times x \times y \times y = xy \times xy = (xy)^2$

c Yes, e.g. $x^2 \times x^2 \times x^2 = x^6 = (x^3)^2$

1.5 Powers, roots and brackets

1 a 3, −3   **b** 81

2 a 11   **b** 3   **c** 10000   **d** 25
   e 10

3 a 2   **b** 5   **c** 66   **d** 16

4 a   **i** 36   **ii** 36
   b   **i** 64   **ii** 64
   c same answer
   d   **i** 100   **ii** 16

5 a   **i** $(2 \times 10)^2 = 2^2 \times 10^2 = 4 \times 100 = 400$
     ii $(4 \times 5)^2 = 4^2 \times 5^2 = 16 \times 25 = 400$

b Yes, both methods give the same answer.

6 a 225   **b** 900   **c** 2500   **d** 8100
   e 40000   **f** 250000   **g** 64000000

7 $49 = 7^2$, $4900 = 70^2$, $490000 = 700^2$

8 $1200^2 = 1440000 \, cm^2$

9 a 28   **b** 61   **c** 121   **d** 125
   e 6   **f** 117

10 a 16   **b** 7   **c** 5   **d** 2
   e 3   **f** 7   **g** 4   **h** 4

11 a 6, not the same answer
   b e.g. (1 2 + 2 0) ÷ (1 0 − 8) or use the fraction key

12 a 2   **b** 1.5   **c** 2   **d** 5
   e 2   **f** 4   **g** 5   **h** 2

13 a 6   **b** 5   **c** 10   **d** 9
   e 11

14 a 3   **b** 8   **c** 60

15 a,b Students' own answers

16 a 7   **b** 3   **c** 3   **d** 4
   e 6   **f** 13

17 a   **i** 6   **ii** 6
   b same answer
   c 24   **d** 99
   e No, $\sqrt{16} + \sqrt{9} = 4 + 3 = 7 \neq \sqrt{25}$
     $\sqrt{16} - \sqrt{9} = 4 - 3 = 1 \neq \sqrt{7}$

Challenge

1 a 2.236...   **b** 5
   c The answer is the original number.

2 a 2.24   **b** 5.0176
   c The answer is close to, but not exactly, 5.

3 i   **a** 2.23607
     b 5.000009045
   ii   **a** 2.236067977
     b 4.999999998
   c With more decimal places, the answers are increasingly close to exactly 5.

4 Yes, because squaring the calculator answer gives exactly 5.

1.6 More powers, multiples and factors

1 2, 3, 5, 7, 11

2 a 3×5 b 3×7 c 7×11

3 a **8:** 1, 2, 4, 8
   12: 1, 2, 3, 4, 6, 12
   b 24 c 4

4 a i 16 ii 32
   iii 100 000 iv 1 000 000

5 a 10^4 b $3^2 \times 4^3$ c $10^3 \times 2^5$
   d 2×3^4 e $2^3 \times 5^3$ f $2^2 \times 3^3 \times 7$

6 a $3 \times 6^2 + 8^2$ b $172\,m^2$

7 a 2 and 3 b 2 and 7 c 2 and 3 d 2
   e 13 f 2 and 23 g 2, 3 and 7 h 3, 11

8 a

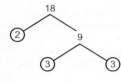 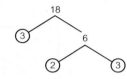

   b 2×3^2 c no

9 a Students' own factor trees
   i $2^2 \times 3$ ii 2^4 iii 2^5
   iv $2^2 \times 3^2$ v $2^4 \times 3$ vi $2^2 \times 3 \times 5$
   vii $2^4 \times 5$ vii $2^3 \times 3 \times 5$ ix $2^3 \times 5^2$
   x 2×13^2
   b Both products are a power of 2.

10 70

11 a $2 \times 2 \times 2 \times 3 \times 3 \times 5$ or $2^3 \times 3^2 \times 5$
    b $2 \times 2 \times 2 \times 3$ or $2^3 \times 3$
    c Yes, because $360 = 2 \times 2 \times 2 \times 3 \times 3 \times 5 = 24 \times 3 \times 5$, which is a multiple of 24.
    d i yes ii no iii yes

12 a,b $36 = 2 \times 2 \times 3 \times 3$
        $60 = 2 \times 2 \times 3 \times 5$
    c HCF = $2 \times 2 \times 3 = 12$

13 a 16 b 6 c 14 d 10

14 a,b $36 = 2 \times 2 \times 3 \times 3$
        $80 = 2 \times 2 \times 2 \times 2 \times 5$
    c LCM = $2 \times 2 \times 2 \times 2 \times 3 \times 3 \times 5 = 720$

15 a 96 b 60 c 140 d 900

16 a 3 packs of buns, 5 packs of sausages
    b 15 hotdogs
    c It is the lowest common multiple of 3 and 5.

17 a 126 hours b 9 pm on Saturday

18 £24

19 24 minutes; Adam 4 laps, Bertie 3 laps

Challenge

1 2, 3, 5, 7, 11, 13, 17 and 19 are all prime numbers.
   $4 = 2 \times 2$
   $6 = 2 \times 3$
   $8 = 2 \times 2 \times 2$
   $9 = 3 \times 3$
   $10 = 2 \times 5$
   $12 = 2 \times 2 \times 3$
   $14 = 2 \times 7$
   $15 = 3 \times 5$
   $16 = 2 \times 2 \times 2 \times 2$
   $18 = 2 \times 3 \times 3$
   $20 = 2 \times 2 \times 5$

2 e.g. Prime factorisation is the same as any other, so they are all unique.

1 Check up

1 a 90 b 60 c 1200 d 228

2 $4 + 0 + 9 + 5 = 18$, $1 + 8 = 9$

3 a £1275 b £106.25

4 a 24.95 b 30.22

5 a 48.6 b 2.15

6 a 8 b −1 c −4 d −114
   e −8 f −3 g −11 h 15

7 a 64 b 2 c 16 d 9
   e 13 f 3

8 8, −8

9 4 and 5

10 a 3 b 3 c 3600 d 3
    e 4 f 7

11 18

12 $2^3 \times 5$

13 $3^2 \times 5$

14 a 4 b 385

15 8

Challenge

1 a Students' own 3-digit multiple of 11
   b Students' own 4-digit multiple of 11
   c Students' own 5-digit multiple of 11
   d Students' own 6-digit multiple of 11

2 a i 4 ii yes
   b Students' own answers
   c Numbers that are far apart take the longest time, e.g. 4 and 94.

1 Strengthen: Calculating with positive and negative numbers

1 a i 9 ii 18 iii 12 iv 18
   b all of them
   c all of them

2 a 20 b 20 c 60 d 60
   e 400 f 400

3 a $3 \times 10 = 30$ b $8 \times 10 = 80$
   c $6 \times 100 = 600$ d $9 \times 100 = 900$
   e $10 \times 11 = 110$ f $100 \times 12 = 1200$

4 a i 5 ii 6 iii 30
   b i 160 ii 130 iii 27
   iv 40 v 84 vi 350

5 a i 300 ii 303 iii 297
   b i 500 ii 505 iii 495
   c i 1100 ii 1111 iii 1089

6 a 279 b 1755

7 a 4238 b 21840

8 £14 339

9 a 13.31 b 31.92

10 a 44.88 b £45.15

11 a 3.48 b 4.52 c 21.65 d 32.55

12 £6.25

13 a 5 b 12 c 6 d −7

14 a 48 b −48 c 5 d 5
    e 6 f 24 g −12

15 a −9 b −17 c −2 d 10
    e −12 f 5

1 Strengthen: Powers and roots

1 a 2 b 3
   $2^2 = 2 \times 2 = 4$ $3^2 = 3 \times 3 = 9$
   $2^3 = 2 \times 2 \times 2 = 8$ $3^3 = 3 \times 3 \times 3 = 27$
   c 10
   $10^2 = 10 \times 10 = 100$ $10^3 = 10 \times 10 \times 10 = 1000$

2 No, $4^3 = 64$, $4 \times 3 = 12$

3 a $2^2 = 4$ so $\sqrt{4} = 2$ b $3^2 = 9$ so $\sqrt{9} = 3$
   $2^3 = 8$ so $\sqrt[3]{8} = 2$ $3^3 = 27$ so $\sqrt[3]{27} = 3$
   c $4^2 = 16$ so $\sqrt{16} = 4$ d $5^2 = 25$ so $\sqrt{25} = 5$
   $4^3 = 64$ so $\sqrt[3]{64} = 4$ $5^3 = 125$ so $\sqrt[3]{125} = 5$

4 10

5 a

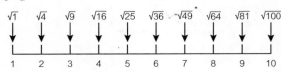

b ii 3 and 4 **iii** 7 and 8
iv 4 and 5 **v** 9 and 10
vi 5 and 6

6 a i 4 **ii** 100 **iii** 400
iv 20 **v** 400
b same answer

7 a 1600 **b** 8100 **c** 14 400 **d** 90 000
e 160 000 **f** 640 000

8 a i 4 **ii** 9 **iii** 100
b same answers

9 a The two square roots of 9 are 3 and −3.
b i 4 and −4 **ii** 10 and −10
iii 5 and −5 **iv** 7 and −7
v 11 and −11

10 a 6 **b** 20 **c** 7 **d** 12

11 a 20 **b** 5 **c** 4 **d** 3
e 5 **f** 3 **g** 2

12 a 12 **b** 16 **c** −4 **d** 20
e 1 **f** 9

13 a 15 **b** 32 **c** 35 **d** 8
e 2

14 a $4 \times 5 = 20$ **b** $2 \times 7 = 14$

15 $\sqrt{4 + 32} = \sqrt{36} = 6$ but $\sqrt{4} + \sqrt{32} = 7.656...$

16 a 5 **b** $\sqrt{16} = 4$ **c** 5 **d** 2
e 3

1 Strengthen: Factors and multiples

1 a 2, 3, 5, 7, 11, 13, 17, 19
b i 2 and 5 **ii** 3 and 7 **iii** 2 and 13
iv 5 and 11 **v** 2, 3 and 5

2 a i 4 **ii** $3 \times 3 \times 3 \times 3 = 3^4$
b i 4 **ii** 2
iii $3 \times 3 \times 3 \times 3 \times 5 \times 5 = 3^4 \times 5^2$
c $3^4 \times 5^2 \times 7$ **d** $2^3 \times 5^3$ **e** $2 \times 3^2 \times 5^3$
f $2^4 \times 3 \times 11$ **g** 2×3^5

3 a, b

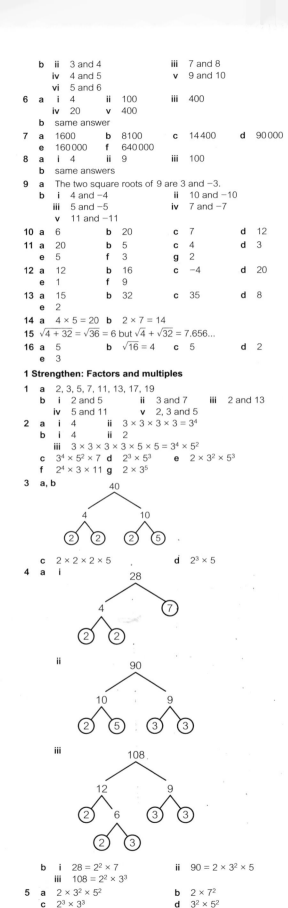

c $2 \times 2 \times 2 \times 5$ **d** $2^3 \times 5$

4 a i

ii

iii

b i $28 = 2^2 \times 7$ **ii** $90 = 2 \times 3^2 \times 5$
iii $108 = 2^2 \times 3^3$

5 a $2 \times 3^2 \times 5^2$ **b** 2×7^2
c $2^3 \times 3^3$ **d** $3^2 \times 5^2$

6 a i $30 = 2 \times 3 \times 5$
$48 = 2 \times 2 \times 2 \times 2 \times 3$
ii

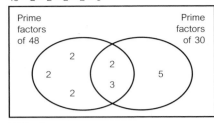

HCF = 6
iii 240

b i $24 = 2 \times 2 \times 2 \times 3$
$60 = 2 \times 2 \times 3 \times 5$
ii

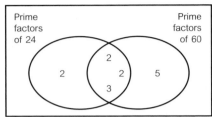

HCF = 12
iii 120

c i $42 = 2 \times 3 \times 7$
$70 = 2 \times 5 \times 7$
ii

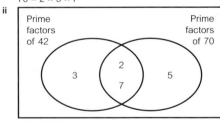

HCF = 14
iii 210

Challenge

1 a 8.23 pm
b 39 minutes

2 Students' own answers,
e.g. $210 = 2 \times 3 \times 5 \times 7$, $231 = 3 \times 7 \times 11$, $255 = 3 \times 5 \times 17$

1 Extend

1 a $28 \times 49 = 28 \times 50 - 28 \times 1 = 14 \times 100 - 28 \times 1 = 1372$
b $32 \times 49 = 32 \times 50 - 32 \times 1 = 16 \times 100 - 32 \times 1 = 1568$

2 a i 0.8 **ii** 1.2 **iii** 16
iv 22 **v** 30 **vi** 90
b i 15 **ii** 15 **iii** 50 **iv** 24

3 4 : 9

4 a A = 56 cm, B = 64 cm, C = 60 cm;
B has the greatest perimeter.
b A = 196 cm², B = 256 cm², C = 225 cm²;
A has the smallest area.

5 a, b

Pattern number	Calculation	Estimate
1	1980 × 198	400 000
2	1980 × 198 × 19.8	8 000 000
3	1980 × 198 × 19.8 × 1.98	16 000 000
4	1980 × 198 × 19.8 × 1.98 × 0.198	3 200 000
5	1980 × 198 × 19.8 × 1.98 × 0.198 × 0.0198	64 000
6	1980 × 198 × 19.8 × 1.98 × 0.198 × 0.0198 × 0.00198	128
7	1980 × 198 × 19.8 × 1.98 × 0.198 × 0.0198 × 0.00198 × 0.000198	0.0256

6 a 1.05 °C

  b 1.5 °C (rounding each temperature to the nearest whole number)

  c 18.5 °C

7 a It lowers the freezing point by 1.8 degrees.

  b −10.8 °C

8 *Students' answers may vary if different rounded values are used in their estimates.*

  a $50 + 6 \times 25 = 200$

  b $(350 + 250 + 1200) \div 3 = 1800 \div 3 = 600$

  c $\frac{1}{2} \times (7 + 9) \times 2 = 16$

  d No, only if rounding makes the calculation easier.

9 a **i** 12 544   **ii** 13 824

10 a **i** 4   **ii** 14

  b **i** 315   **ii** 144

  c HCF = $2^2 \times 3^4 = 324$; LCM = $2^3 \times 3^5 = 1944$

11 a 18 980 days   **b** 52 years   **c** about 99

12 12 floors

13 a 12   **b** 20   **c** $8000 = 2^3 \times 10^3$

Challenge

  a **i** 2 s   **ii** 2.4 s   **iii** 3.5 s

  b **i** 4.9 s   **ii** 6 s   **iii** 8.5 s

  c The stone falls faster on Earth because the gravitational force is stronger, so the acceleration due to gravity is greater.

  d 5 m

1 Unit test

1 a 10 °C

  b **i** −12 °C **ii** 4 °C

  c −10

2 $7 + 8 + 3 = 18$, $1 + 8 = 9$

3 a 20   **b** 7   **c** 4

4 8565 tonnes

5 £2.55

6 a 70   **b** 693   **c** 300   **d** 437

7 92.73

8 143.4

9 8 and 9

10 a 6   **b** 45   **c** 60 seconds

11 nearly 9 cm

12 a 6 and −6   **b** 4900   **c** 16

13 a 13   **b** −11   **c** −24   **d** −2

  e 50   **f** 1   **g** 36   **h** 72

  i −1

14 a **i** 24   **ii** $2^3 \times 3$

  b $180 = 2^2 \times 3^2 \times 5$

15 a 19   **b** 3

16 12.6

17 a 0   **b** 2

18 a 36   **b** 15

Challenge

A strategy to fill all of the squares is to start with a small number in the outside right square.

UNIT 2 Area and volume

2.1 Area of a triangle

1 a Perpendicular shapes are at right angles (90°) to each other
  b Congruent shapes are the same shape and size; corresponding angles and corresponding sides are equal.

2 a perimeter 20 cm, area 25 cm²
  b perimeter 17 cm, area 15 cm²
  c perimeter $2l + 2w$, area lw

3 a 48 cm   b 120 cm²

4 a 2 squares   b 8 squares   c 9 squares

5 a i Area A = 6 cm², Area B = 24 cm²
    ii 2
    iii Area A = 3 cm², Area B = 12 cm²
  b i 30 cm²
    ii half
  c e.g. Multiply the base by the perpendicular height and divide by 2.
  d $A = \frac{1}{2}bh$

6 a 48 cm²   b 100 cm²   c 45 cm²   d 88 cm²
  e 28 mm²   f 39 m²   g 6 cm²   h 14.07 mm²

7 27 000 cm² (or 2.7 m²) of each colour

8 72 cm²

9 a 2.1 m²   b £321.30

10 57 m²

Challenge

1a–d Scottish flag drawn accurately to scale

2 From scale drawing, two triangles have height ≈ 4.2 cm and base 11 cm, and two triangles have height ≈ 5.2 cm and base 8 cm.

Total blue area ≈ $\frac{1}{2} \times 4.2 \times 11 + \frac{1}{2} \times 5.2 \times 8 ≈ 87.8$ cm²

Area of flag = 12 × 15 = 180 cm²
87.8 cm² is less than half of 180 cm².

2.2 Area of a parallelogram and trapezium

1 Parallelograms: A, B, D,
  Trapezia: C, E
  Neither: F

2 a 15 cm²   b 120 mm²

3 a 45   b 14   c 56
  d 7   e 35

4 a 20 cm²   b 6 cm²   c 32 cm²

5 c 24 squares
  d area = base × perpendicular height
  e $A = bh$
  f,g Students' own checks

6 a 32 cm²   b 1875 mm²   c 7.5 cm²
  d The lengths of the sloping edges (5 cm, 32 mm and 2.7 m) were not used, because the area depends on the *perpendicular* height.

7 a 15 cm²   b 2640 mm²   c 26 cm²

8 £170.10

9 a i 80 cm²   ii 76 cm²
    iii 96 cm²   iv 90 cm²
  b any shape that has an area of 100 cm²

Challenge

a
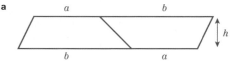

b $(a + b)h$

c $\frac{1}{2}(a + b)h$

2.3 Volume of cubes and cuboids

1 a 40   b 5   c 2

2 a 1, 8, 27, 64, 125   b 1000

3 a 8   b 15   c 30
  d 25   e 8

4 a 9   b 27 cm³   c 27
  d The numbers are the same.

5 a 8 cm³   b 64 cm³

6 a 343 cm³   b 0.512 m³   c 32 768 mm³

7 a 125 cm³   b 74.088 cm³
  c 1728 mm³   d 42.875 m³

8 a i 6   ii 3   iii 18 cm³
  b i 15   ii 2   iii 30 cm³

9 a area of top = length × width
  b volume = area of top × height = length × width × height

10 a 105 cm³   b 152 cm³   c 0.25 m³

11 a 7 500 000 m³
   b e.g. A lake is unlikely to have vertical sides, so a cuboid is not a good model.

12 a cube A = 216 cm³, cuboid B = 648 cm³
   b shape C = 1080 cm³, shape D = 1512 cm³

13 a 4 cm   b 48 cm³   c 120 cm³   d 168 cm³

14 a 190 cm³   b 76 m³

15 90 cm³

16 165 984 cm³

17 120

Challenge

a Students' own answers, e.g.
  C, because A is not big enough and there would be a lot of empty space in B.

b about 3.7 cm

c any sets of dimensions that multiply to give 50

2.4 2D representations of 3D solids

1 a 3   b 4   c 6

2 A sphere, B cube, C triangle-based pyramid, D square-based pyramid, E cuboid, F cylinder, G triangular prism

3 a 5 cm square drawn accurately
  b 6 cm by 4 cm rectangle drawn accurately

4 a e.g. A and I, or F and G, etc.
  b e.g. A and E, or L and K, etc.
  c e.g. A and H, or B and L, etc.
  d e.g. A, F and L; or D, E and K; etc.

5 a i 3 faces that are rectangles, 2 faces that are equilateral triangles
    ii 3 congruent rectangles, 2 congruent triangles
    iii 9 edges, 6 vertices
  b i 1 face that is a square, 4 faces that are isosceles (or equilateral) triangles
    ii 4 congruent triangles
    iii 8 edges, 5 vertices
  c i 2 faces that are circles, 1 faces that is a rectangle
    ii 2 congruent circles
    iii 2 edges, no vertices

6 a cuboid   b square-based pyramid

7 A, B, D and F are nets of an open cube.

8 C, D and F are nets of a square-based pyramid.
  A, B and E are not.
  A – triangles not big enough to meet.
  B – the bases of the triangles do not all touch the square.
  E – two of the bases of the triangles do not touch the square

9 Students' own sketches of nets of the solids, e.g.

a
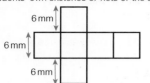

b
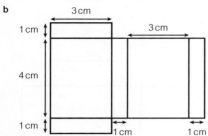

c
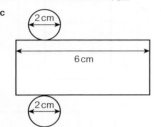

d
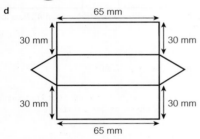

10 a,b Students' own sketch of nets of a dice, e.g.

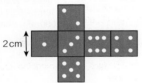

11
a **b**
c

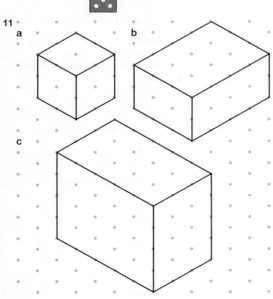

12 a

plan	front elevation	side elevation
6 cm / 4 cm	6 cm / 1 cm	4 cm / 1 cm

b

plan	front elevation	side elevation
8 cm / 2 cm	8 cm / 4 cm	2 cm / 4 cm

c

plan	front elevation	side elevation
3 cm / 3 cm	3 cm / 5 cm	3 cm / 5 cm

13 a cube, cuboid   **b** sphere, cylinder
   c triangular-based pyramid   **d** square-based pyramid

Challenge

a, b i

	Cube	Triangle-based pyramid	Triangular prism	Square-based pyramid
Faces	6	4	5	5
Vertices	8	4	6	5
Edges	12	6	9	8
Faces + Vertices	14	8	11	10

  ii Each number in the new row is 2 more than the number of edges for that shape.
  c number of edges + 2 = number of faces + number of vertices
  d Yes, e.g.
number of edges = 18, number of faces = 8 and number of vertices = 12; 18 + 2 = 8 + 12
  e No, e.g.
A cylinder has 3 faces, no vertices and 2 edges; $2 + 2 \neq 3 + 0$

2.5 Surface area of cubes and cuboids

1 a square   **b** rectangle (may be square)
2 a $21.2\,cm^2$ **b** $20.8\,cm^2$
3 a $64\,cm^2$ **b** 6   **c** $384\,cm^2$
4 a $49\,cm^2$ **b** $294\,cm^2$
5 $2000\,cm^2$
6 a $486\,cm^2$ **b** $54\,m^2$ **c** $3750\,cm^2$ **d** $1014\,mm^2$
7 a x^2 **b** $6x^2$
  c $A = 6x^2$
8 a $64\,cm^2$ **b** $8\,cm$
9 a

b All areas are in cm².

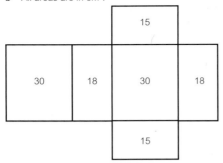

c 126 cm²
d The opposite faces are identical; they have the same area.
10 a 112 cm²   **b** 190 cm²   **c** 26 m²   **d** 4298 mm²
11 a 46 200 m²
b £5 913 600
Check: 50 000 m² × £100 = £5 000 000
12 4 packets
13 Students' own answers
Actual surface areas are **A** = 90 cm² and **B** = 94 cm², so **B** has the larger surface area
14 1868.5 cm²

Challenge

3 shelves

2.6 Measures

1 a 1 m = 100 cm   **b** 1 km = 1000 m
c 1 kg = 1000 g
2 a 650 cm = 6.5 m   **b** 4500 ml = 4.5 litres
c 0.8 kg = 800 g   **d** 1.6 km = 1600 m
e 0.25 litres = 250 ml   **f** 175 = 0.175 kg
3 a 1 m²   **b** 10 000 cm²
c 1 cm²   **d** 100 mm²
4 No. She needs 160 ml of medicine but the bottle only contains 150 ml.
5 a 6000 cm³ = 6000 ml   **b** 6000 cm³ = 6 litres
c 2 litres – 2000 ml   **d** 2 litres = 2000 cm³
e 3.5 litres = 3500 ml   **f** 3.5 litres = 3500 cm³
g 4200 cm³ = 4.2 litres   **h** 750 cm³ = 0.75 litres
i 0.35 litres = 350 cm³   **j** 9.2 litres = 9200 cm³
6 a length 5000 cm, width 2500 cm, depth 200 cm
b 2 500 000 000 cm³
c 2 500 000 litres
7 a >   **b** >   **c** =   **d** >
8 120 kg
9 a A 2.4   **b** B 2.04   **c** A 5.25   **d** B 0.95
10 a 600 000 m² or 0.6 km²   **b** 7200 cm² or 0.72 m²
c 6300 mm² or 63 cm²
11 a 1 cm²   **b** 100 mm²
c 1 cm² = 100 mm²   **d** 1 m² = 10 000 cm²
12 a 8 cm² = 8 × 100 = 800 mm²
b 9.5 m² = 9.5 × 10 000 = 95 000 cm²
c 700 mm² = 700 ÷ 100 = 7 cm²
d 940 mm² = 940 ÷ 100 = 9.4 cm²
e 30 000 cm² = 30 000 ÷ 10 000 = 3 m²
f 420 000 cm² = 420 000 ÷ 10 000 = 42 m²
13 2600 cm²
14 a 32 500 m²
b No, it should be 3.25 hectares. She has divided 32 500 by 1000 and not 10 000.
15 a 8 gallons = 36 litres
b 7 lb (pounds) = 3.18 kg
c 4 litres = 7 pints
d 15 litres = 3.3 gallons
e 6 kg = 13.2 lb
f 8 pints = 4.57 litres
16 Yes, 5 × 30 cm = 150 cm = 1.5 m, 1.5 m > 1.4 m
17 Earth to the Sun is approximately 148 800 000 km.

Mars to the Sun is approximately 227 000 000 km. Earth is closer to the Sun.

Challenge

1.4 kg Seville oranges, 2.6–3.4 litres water, juice of 2 lemons, 2.7 kg sugar

2 Check up

1 a 30 cm²   **b** 80 mm²   **c** 24 cm²
2 144 mm²
3 10.5 cm²
4 40 cm²
5 a

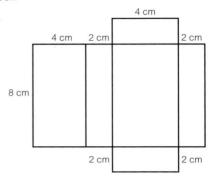

b

6 54 cm²
7 3.375 cm³
8 648 cm²
9 40
10 a 5 litres = 5000 cm³   **b** 2.7 litres = 2700 cm³
c 3600 cm³ = 3.6 litres   **d** 240 cm³ = 0.24 litres
e 2.4 tonnes = 2400 kg   **f** 30 000 m² = 3 ha
11 a 5 kg   **b** 12.8 km   **c** 200 gallons
d 5.1 litres   **e** 3 metres
12 2 400 000 cm³ or 2.4 m³

Challenge

Students' own shapes with area 32 cm²

2 Strengthen: Areas of shapes

1 a base length = 8 cm; perpendicular height = 6 cm
b base length = 24 mm; perpendicular height = 5 mm
2 a 24 cm²   **b** 60 mm²
3 area of rectangle = length × width
= 9 × 3
= 27 cm²
area of triangle = $\frac{1}{2}$ × base × height
= $\frac{1}{2}$ × 9 × 4
= 18 cm²

total area = area of rectangle + area of triangle
= 27 + 18
= 45 cm²
4 a 42.5 cm²   **b** 936 mm²
5 base length = 9 cm
perpendicular height = 5 cm
area = base × height
= 9 × 5
= 45 cm²
6 a 65.1 cm²   **b** 315 mm²

7 a $a = 4\,\text{cm}$, $b = 6\,\text{cm}$, $h = 3\,\text{cm}$

b Area $= \frac{1}{2}(a + b)h$

$\qquad = \frac{1}{2} \times (4 + 6) \times 3$

$\qquad = \frac{1}{2} \times 10 \times 3$

$\qquad = 5 \times 3$

$\qquad = 15\,\text{cm}^2$

8 a $70\,\text{cm}^2$ **b** $19.2\,\text{m}^2$

2 Strengthen: Surface area and volume

1 a C **b** B **c** A

2

Shape of face	Area of face	Number of faces	Total area
2 cm / 2 cm square	$2 \times 2 = 4\,\text{cm}^2$	6	$6 \times 4 = 24\,\text{cm}^2$

3 area of one face $= 8 \times 8 = 64\,\text{cm}^2$
surface area of cube $= 6 \times 64 = 384\,\text{cm}^2$

4 $864\,\text{mm}^2$

5

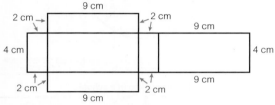

6 area of top face $= 8 \times 5 = 40\,\text{cm}^2$
total surface area $= 16 + 16 + 10 + 10 + 40 + 40 = 132\,\text{cm}^2$

7 a $358\,\text{cm}^2$ **b** $920\,\text{mm}^2$

8 a i $4\,\text{cm}$ **ii** $3\,\text{cm}$ **iii** $2\,\text{cm}$

b $24\,\text{cm}^3$

9 a $420\,\text{cm}^3$ **b** $1500\,\text{mm}^3$

10 a $2325\,\text{cm}^2$ **b** $7425\,\text{cm}^3$

2 Strengthen: Metric and imperial measures

1 a 3 litres $= 3000\,\text{cm}^3$ **b** 7 litres $= 7000\,\text{cm}^3$
c $4000\,\text{cm}^3 = 4$ litres **d** $9000\,\text{cm}^3 = 9$ litres
e 4.5 litres $= 4500\,\text{cm}^3$ **f** 8.7 litres $= 8700\,\text{cm}^3$
g $2600\,\text{cm}^3 = 2.6$ litres **h** $840\,\text{cm}^3 = 0.84$ litres

2 a 3 feet $\approx 90\,\text{cm}$ **b** $600\,\text{cm} \approx 20$ feet
c 2.5 feet $\approx 75\,\text{cm}$ **d** 4 litres ≈ 7 pints
e 7 pints ≈ 4 litres **f** 22.5 litres ≈ 5 gallons
g 6.2 gallons ≈ 27.9 litres **h** 7.2 miles $\approx 11.52\,\text{km}$
i $22.4\,\text{km} \approx 14$ miles **j** 11 pounds $\approx 5\,\text{kg}$
k $7.2\,\text{kg} \approx 15.84\,\text{lb}$

3 a $36\,\text{cm}^2$ **b** $9600\,\text{cm}^2$ **c** $975\,000\,\text{m}^2$

4 a $70.56\,\text{cm}^3$ **b** $1.1\,\text{m}^3$

Challenge

1 a i 9 squares **ii** each triangle 1 square
iii 5 squares
b 4×4 grid:
i 16 squares **ii** each triangle 1.5 squares
iii 10 squares
5×5 grid:
i 25 squares **ii** each triangle 2 squares
iii 17 squares

c

Grid size	Base of triangle	Height of triangle	Area of white square
3×3	2	1	5
4×4	3	1	10
5×5	4	1	17

d The sum of the square of the base and the square of the height of the triangle is equal to the area of the white square.

2 Extend

1 No, the base of the triangle is $8\,\text{cm}$, because half of 8 is 4, then $4 \times 4 = 16$

2 a $\frac{1}{2}bh$

b area of parallelogram, $A = 2 \times \frac{1}{2}bh = bh$

3 a $1.44\,\text{cm}^2$ **b** $1.2\,\text{cm}$

4 $585\,\text{mm}^2$

5 Students' own answers, e.g.

Area $= 10\,\text{cm}^2$ $\qquad$ Area $= 16\,\text{cm}^2$

$2 \times 10 \neq 16$

6 630 litres

7 a No, it will only hold another 936 litres.
b 806 litres **c** £565.81

8 175

9 a $90\,000\,\text{m}$ **b** 90 miles $\times 1.6 = 144\,\text{km}$. Her car battery may run out as 90 miles is about $144\,\text{km}$ and her car can do $140\,\text{km}$. However, she may make it. It depends on how she drives.

10 a 90 litres **b** 2166.75 litres

11 $64\,\text{cm}^2$

Challenge

a volume of iced cake $= 960\,\text{cm}^3$
volume of cake $= (8 - 2) \times (10 - 2) \times (12 - 2) = 480\,\text{cm}^3$
so volume of icing $= 960 - 480 = 480\,\text{cm}^3$

b about $9.7\,\text{cm}$ by $9.7\,\text{cm}$ by $9.7\,\text{cm}$

2 Unit test

1 a 9 litres $= 9000\,\text{cm}^3$ **b** 0.8 litres $= 800\,\text{cm}^3$
c $12\,000\,\text{cm}^3 = 12$ litres **d** $950\,\text{cm}^3 = 0.95$ litres

2 $216\,\text{cm}^2$

3 $172\,\text{m}^2$

4 $320\,\text{mm}^2$

5 8 faces, 18 edges, 12 vertices

6 $270\,\text{cm}^2$

7 a $850\,\text{mm}^2$ **b** $6\,\text{m}^2$ **c** 0.5 hectares **d** $25\,000\,\text{m}^2$

8 a $105\,\text{cm}^2$ **b** $230\,\text{mm}^2$

9 $5250\,\text{mm}^3$

10 a 1 foot (ft) $\approx 30\,\text{cm}$ **b** 1 mile $\approx 1.6\,\text{km}$
c 1 kg ≈ 2.2 pounds (lb) **d** 1 litre ≈ 1.75 pints
e 1 gallon ≈ 4.5 litres

11 about $19.2\,\text{km}$

12 about 2.3 litres

13 $46.656\,\text{cm}^3$

14 $519.86\,\text{cm}^2$

15 7875 litres

16 a 160 **b** $10\,240\,\text{cm}^3$

Challenge

a $320\,\text{cm}^3$ **b** $352\,\text{cm}^2$

UNIT 3 Statistics, graphs and charts

3.1 Pie charts

1   360°
2   circle and radius drawn
3   a   60° angle drawn accurately
    b   110° angle drawn accurately
4   a   90   b   60   c   180°   d   72°
5   a   Spanish; it is the biggest sector of the pie chart.
    b   i $\frac{1}{2}$ ii $\frac{1}{4}$ iii $\frac{1}{8}$ iv $\frac{1}{8}$
    c   140 Spanish, 70 German, 35 French, 35 Mandarin
6   a   80   b   20
7   a   natural gas   b   77%
8   a   insects   b   70 000   c   700 000
9   a   90
    b   90 students are 360°, 1 student is 4°
    c   cricket 144°, tennis 96°, rounders 120°
    d   **Student's sport choices**

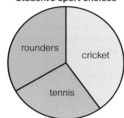

10   **Students' lunch choices**

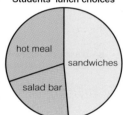

11   a   **Film genre**

     b $\frac{1}{4}$ c   Action   d   50%
12   a   i   180°   ii   36°   iii   72°
     b   **Percentage sales**

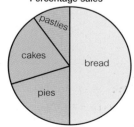

Challenge

a   **Languages spoken in a school**

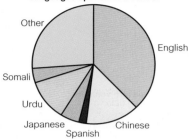

b   **Languages spoken in a school**

e.g. The pie chart in part **b** is easier to read as there are fewer sections.

c   **Languages spoken in a school**

e.g. It would depend on what you need to use the pie chart for and how many categories there are to start with. Combining categories loses information so this pie chart tells you less than the others.

3.2 Using tables

1   a   15   b   12   c   35
2   mean = 3.125, median = 3.5, mode = 4, range = 7
3   a   32   b   25   c   2   d   4
4   a   13   b   26   c   2
5   1.55
6   a   5   b   6   c   3.45
7   a   Mean is 3070 ÷ 97 = 31.65, or 32 if rounded up
        to a whole number
        Mode is 32
        So the label is accurate.
    b   In this case, there are no extreme values so use the mean.
8   a   37   b   27   c   72
9   a   42   b   24   c   96   d $\frac{24}{96} = \frac{1}{4}$
10   a

	Beginners	Intermediate	Advanced	Total
Men	33	36	21	90
Women	32	40	38	110
Total	65	76	59	200

     b   21   c   57   d   advanced
     e   19%
11   a   i   sandwiches   ii   cakes
     b   fish and chips
     c   He should cut salads as they make the lowest profit on Sundays.

12 a $2 \leqslant l < 4$

b

Length, l (cm)	Tally	Frequency
$0 \leqslant l < 2$		0
$2 \leqslant l < 4$	IIII	4
$4 \leqslant l < 6$	HHH II	7
$6 \leqslant l < 8$	HHH	5

c $4 \leqslant l < 6$
d $6.8 - 2.0 = 4.8$
e The estimate uses the limits of the highest and lowest class intervals not the exact data values.

13 a

Mass, m (kg)	Tally	Frequency
$3.0 \leqslant m < 3.5$	I	1
$3.5 \leqslant m < 4.0$	HHH	5
$4.0 \leqslant m < 4.5$	HHH	5
$4.5 \leqslant m < 5.0$	I	1
$5.0 \leqslant m < 5.5$	II	2

b $3.5 \leqslant m < 4.0$ and $4.0 \leqslant m < 4.5$
c 0.5 kg

14 a

Length, l (cm)	Tally	Frequency
$10 \leqslant l < 14$	II	2
$14 \leqslant l < 18$	HHH III	8
$18 \leqslant l < 22$	IIII	4

b $14 \leqslant l < 18$

15 a $3 \leqslant d < 6$ miles
b 6 miles   **c** 12 miles

Challenge

a For example
i

Time	Frequency
$55 \leqslant t < 70$	6
$70 \leqslant t < 85$	8
$85 \leqslant t < 100$	6

ii

Time	Frequency
$55 \leqslant t < 65$	3
$65 \leqslant t < 75$	5
$75 \leqslant t < 85$	6
$85 \leqslant t < 95$	4
$95 \leqslant t < 105$	2

iii

Time	Frequency
$55 \leqslant t < 60$	1
$60 \leqslant t < 65$	2
$65 \leqslant t < 70$	3
$70 \leqslant t < 75$	2
$75 \leqslant t < 80$	2
$80 \leqslant t < 85$	4
$85 \leqslant t < 90$	2
$90 \leqslant t < 95$	2
$95 \leqslant t < 100$	2
$100 \leqslant t < 105$	0

b For example, the table with 5 groups shows the data best because it shows the data clearly and you can use and interpret it.

3.3 Stem and leaf diagrams

1 median = 2.5, mode = 2, range = 4
2 No; the median is the 5.5th value (halfway between the 5th and 6th).
3 a   **i**   9   **ii**   5th   **iii**   8
   b   **i**   7   **ii**   4th   **iii**   10
   c   **i**   5   **ii**   3rd   **iii**   0
4 a   **i**   10   **ii**   5.5th   **iii**   10
   b   **i**   8   **ii**   4.5th   **iii**   7.5

5 a

```
1 | 4 8
2 | 2 3 7
3 | 1 8
4 | 5 9
5 | 1 3 6
```

Key: 1 | 4 means 1.4 kg

6 a

```
5 | 2 3 6
6 | 1 4 5 8
7 | 0 3 7 7 8 9
8 | 4 5 5 6 7
9 | 0 1 2
```

Key: 5 | 2 means 52 visitors
b   **i**   21   **ii**   13   **iii**   76%

7 a 155 and 165 cm   **b** $174 - 146 = 28$ cm
   c 22   **d** 162.5   **e** 162.5 cm
   f The leaves in the stem and leaf diagram are already in order.
   g 10 students

8 a 3.45 kg   **b** 4.2 kg
9 Before special offer, median = £2.95 and mean = £2.73
After special offer, median = £3.30 and mean = £3.04
So no, it has not increased the average spend by £1.

10 a

```
10 | 0 5 7
11 | 2 7 9
12 | 3 7
13 | 1 4
```

Key: 10 | 0 means 100 minutes
b 118 minutes

11 a Most of the scores are between 30 and 39.
   b   **i**   median = 44.5, range = 29
      ii   median = 33.5, range = 26

Challenge

a

Number of visitors	Frequency
50–59	3
60–69	4
70–79	6
80–89	5
90–99	3

b

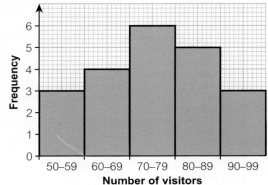

Number of visitors to a stately home each day

c For part **b**, can answer parts **i** and **ii**, but cannot answer part **iii**.
d Cannot find the median from a grouped bar chart.

e e.g.

Stem and leaf is better for	Bar chart is better for
Calculating exact values from the data	Colourful diagrams
Keeping all of the data points	Quick overview of the data
Quicker to draw	Large numbers of data points

3.4 Comparing data

1 a Set B   b Set A
2 a Team A median = 25, Team B = median is 25
   b Team A range = 14, Team B range = 4
   c Team A   d Team B
3 a Sprinter A range = 0.6, Sprinter B range = 0.3
   b Sprinter B   c Sprinter B
4 a Mean for Nathaniel = 14, mean for Caitlin = 16
   b Range for Nathaniel = 12, range for Caitlin = 2
   c Students' own answers, but should include:
     Nathaniel had a lower mean than Caitlin.
     Caitlin had a smaller range than Nathaniel so her times were more consistent.
5 a i Business A £8659, Business B £9258.25
     ii Business A £9641, Business B £1874
   b Business B has a higher mean quarterly profit.
     Business B has a lower range than Business A, so Business B's profits are more consistent.
6 a $6\frac{1}{2}$
   b $6\frac{1}{2}$; the mode
   c Students' own answers, e.g.
     The mean is less useful for this purpose than the mode.
   d Students' own answers, e.g.
     Probably order no shoes in sizes outside the range, as they are unlikely to be sold.
7 a Alex
   b Alex 4.66 m, Dan 5.09 m
   c Alex 5.23 m, Dan 5.10 m
   d median
   e 2.78 m. It did not affect the median because the median comes only from the middle value(s), and the 3rd jump was not one of these; it was the lowest value, but exactly how low makes no difference to the median.
   f Students' own answers, e.g.
     Alex has a higher median distance than Dan. (The median best represents his results.)
     Dan has a lower range so his results are more consistent. Dan may be better to represent the school as he jumps roughly the same distance each time.
     OR Alex may be better because he can jump further.
8 a line A (blue)
   b i week 6 (305 marks)
     ii week 5 (10 marks)
   c No, she is not correct; some losing scores are higher than winning ones, e.g. week 2 losing is higher than week 9 winning.
   d No, you can compare the data by looking at the positions of the lines on the graph.
9 a a £75 000
   b i £28 175 ii £21 350
   c 6   d 4   e median
   f i mean ii median

10 a

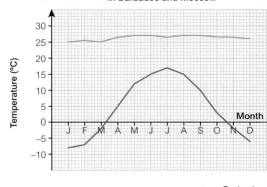

Mean monthly temperatures in Barbados and Moscow

— Barbados
— Moscow

   b Students' own answers, comparing temperature ranges and values
11 a i Loxley   ii Deerfield
   b i Deerfield   ii Loxley
12 a 2.78 m   b £75 000

Challenge

a i 3   ii 11.8   iii 4
b The data value of 100 has a large effect on the total (and hence the mean) but does not affect the middle value (the median).
c median
d i 3   ii 3   iii 4
e Students' own data sets, e.g.
   1, 1, 2, 3, 93
   6, 6, 7, 8, 323
f mean

3.5 Scatter graphs

1 a (4, 2)   b (5, 6)   c (0, 3)   d (9, 5)
2

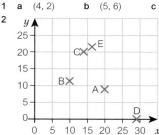

3 a 3   b 20   c 2, 4
   d negative correlation
   e The more lessons a student missed, the lower their test mark.
4 a i no correlation
     ii Class size and maths scores do not appear to be related.
   b i negative correlation
     ii As laptops get older, their price (or value) decreases (or falls).
5 a negative correlation
   b Yes; as alcoholic handrub use increases, the number of patient infections falls.
6 a

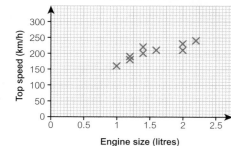

Top speeds of cars

b The larger the engine size, the faster the top speed.

7 a

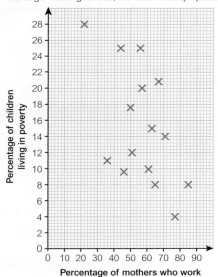

b negative correlation

c e.g. As the proportion of mothers who work increases, the proportion of children living in poverty falls (or decreases).

8 Lucy's graph is best; it has the same number of points on either side and it follows the shape of the data.

9 a Top speeds of cars

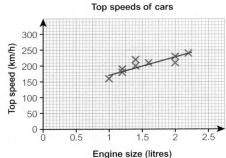

b

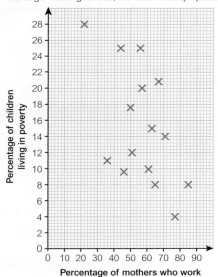

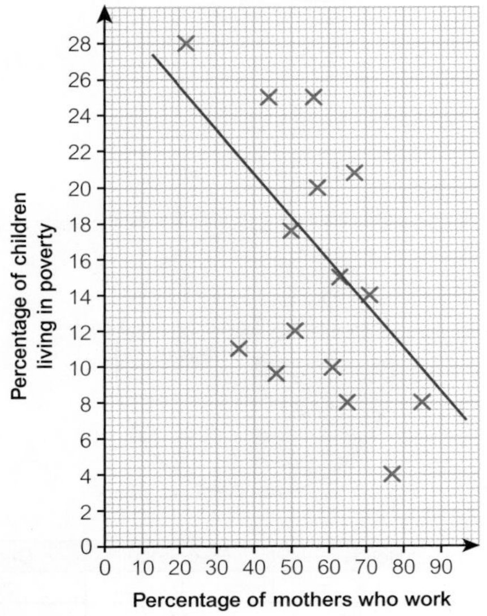

Challenge

Students' own answers, e.g.

The data shows a correlation between age and height. There is likely to be a real-life relationship between age and height as older children are likely to be taller.

3.6 Misleading graphs

1 There is no title, axes are not labelled, and there are no scales and categories on the axes.

2 a No; more people said that action films were their favourite (80 people) than romantic films (60 people).

b She has used different symbols, of different sizes, to represent different quantities.

c Favourite film genres

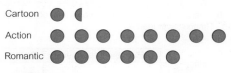

3 a The scale doubles for every square of graph paper, rather than going up by the same amount each time.

b Students' own predictions

Price of a loaf of white bread

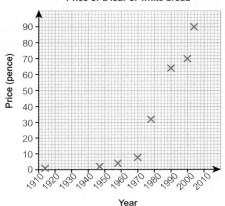

c the graph drawn in part **b**

4 a the left-hand graph

b The graph doesn't start at zero, so although it looks as though the cost has more than doubled, it has not.

c £7500

5 a the left-hand graph

b the right-hand graph

c £690

6 Students' own reasons, e.g.

The percentages do not add up to 100%.

The 40% sector looks far smaller than 40% of the pie chart.

The pie chart has no title.

The pie chart has no key.

7 a the right-hand graph

b the left-hand graph

The tablets' widths have been increased as well as their heights, which makes them look much bigger.

Challenge

1 10 to 49

2 a

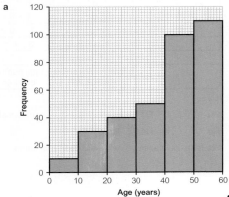

b $50 \leqslant a < 60$

c The 10–49 group on the first chart covers a 40-year age span, not 10.

3 Check up

1 a 2 merit points   **b** 4 merit points
c 1.83 (to 2 d.p.)

2 a e.g. Ali's mean was higher than Hetty's, so he got more merit points on average. Hetty's range was smaller than Ali's, so her numbers of points were more consistent.

b Hetty; her results are more consistent and her mean is not much lower than Ali's.

3 a 55   **b** 30
c

	Under 18s	18–40 years	Over 40	Total
Male	10	30	55	95
Female	30	38	37	105
Total	40	68	92	200

d 92   **e** 20%

4 a 41   **b** $40 \leqslant w < 50$
c $60 - 0 = 60\,g$
d No; the frequency of the $30 \leqslant w < 40$ class will increase to 14, but the frequency of the $40 \leqslant w < 50$ class will increase to 16, so the modal class will still be $40 \leqslant w < 50$.

5 a silver
b Yes; the silver sector is more than half, which is therefore larger than all the others put together.
c 72

6 a Vegetables Jan took from her allotment

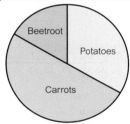

7 a 26   **b** 52   **c** 59   **d** 53
e 4

8 a positive correlation   **b** higher (or better)

9 a the left-hand graph
b It only shows 40–50 on the scale, so the increase looks much bigger than it does on the right-hand graph, which shows the full scale from 0 to 50.

Challenge

Students' own answers

3 Strengthen: Averages and range

1 a 2 children   **b** 5 children
c $1 + 3 + 5 + 2 + 3 + 2 + 0 + 2 + 2 + 3 = 23$ **d** 2.3

2 a 3   **b** 5   **c** 24
d 2 children   **e** 4
f

Number of children	Frequency	Total number of children
0	3	$0 \times 3 = 0$
1	6	$1 \times 6 = 6$
2	10	$2 \times 10 = 20$
3	4	$3 \times 4 = 12$
4	1	$4 \times 1 = 4$
	Total number of families 24	Total number of children 42

g 1.75

3 a Flo   **b** Flo 1, Jim 10   **c** smaller
d Flo   **e** Flo $6\frac{2}{3}$, Jim $4\frac{2}{3}$; Flo
f Students' own answers, with sensible explanation

4 9W had a larger median than 9R.
9R had a smaller range than 9W, so their results were more consistent.

5 a 59 minutes
b **i** 24 minutes   **ii** 27.3 minutes
    iii 40 minutes
c mode or median

3 Strengthen: Tables

1 a 13   **b** 12
c, f

	Flute	Violin	Trumpet	Total
Year 8	13	10	6	29
Year 9	12	8	4	24
Total	25	18	10	53

d 6 students in Year 8 play the trumpet.
e 18 students in Years 8 and 9 play the violin.
g 4   **h** 53

2 a 12   **b** 43   **c** 20   **d** 45

3 6 km, 6.5 km, 9 km, 5 km

4 a masses that are greater than or equal to 10 kg, but less than 12 kg
b

Mass, m (kg)	Tally	Frequency
$10 \leqslant m < 12$	III	3
$12 \leqslant m < 14$	I	1
$14 \leqslant m < 16$	IIII	4
$16 \leqslant m < 18$	II	2

c $14 \leqslant m < 16\,kg$ **d** 8 kg

3 Strengthen: Charts and graphs

1 a $\frac{1}{4}$
b–d

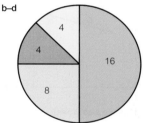

c 16
d **i** 4   **ii** 4
e 32

2 a 80   **b** $\frac{20}{80} = \frac{1}{4}$
c **i** $\frac{10}{80} = \frac{1}{8}$ **ii** $\frac{40}{80} = \frac{1}{2}$ **iii** $\frac{10}{80} = \frac{1}{8}$
d, e Different types of fish in a lake

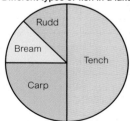

3 a 2°
b

Holiday	Frequency	Degrees
UK	100	200°
Spain	45	90°
India	20	40°
USA	15	30°
Total	180	360°

4 a age 40 **b** 5 **c** 5 **d** 22
  e age 51 **f** 25 **g** 13 **h** 51
5 a 20 minutes, 18 minutes, 5 minutes
  b As the students got older, they took less time to complete the puzzle.
6 A positive correlation
  B negative correlation
  C positive correlation
  D no correlation
  E negative correlation
7 a 120, 140
  b No; 120 × 2 = 240
  c the right-hand graph
  It looks as though sales have nearly doubled.

Challenge

a

Time, t (seconds)	Tally	Frequency
$4 \leqslant t < 6$	卌 I	6
$6 \leqslant t < 8$	卌 I	6
$8 \leqslant t < 10$	卌	5
$10 \leqslant t < 12$	IIII	4

b

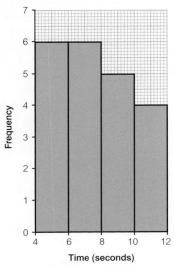

Rubik's cube World Record times 2005–2018

c 12 From the bar chart; because the data is in order

3 Extend

1 a Student's own answer, e.g.

	Comedy	Musical	Drama	Other	Total
Under 16					
16–25					
26–45					
Over 45					
Total					

b modal class for age, mode of theatre choices, median class for age

2 a Mark
b

Family member	Angle	Hours
Dad	45	2
Mum	45	2
Mark	135	6
Nathaniel	45	2
Gemma	90	4

c **i** 2 hours **ii** 2 hours **iii** 16 hours
3 4.9

4 a Joanne: mean = 3.3, range = 4
  Peter: mean = 3.5, range = 3
  b Peter did better. He had a higher mean and a smaller range.

5 a

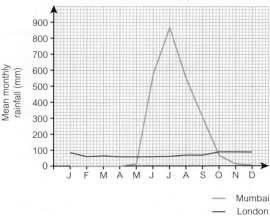

Mean monthly rainfall in Mumbai and London

— Mumbai
— London

b 8
c huge increase, maximum in July
d Mumbai: mean 200.1 mm, range 868.2 mm
  London: mean 71.2 mm (1 d.p.), range 33.3 mm
  e.g. The mean monthy rainfall in Mumbai is nearly three times higher than in London.
  The range for rainfall in Mumbai is much greater than for London – the rainfall in London is a lot more consistent (or less variable), whereas the rainfall in Mumbai is more extreme.

6

	Beginner	Intermediate	Advanced	Total
Girls	6	20	12	38
Boys	10	14	10	34
Women	2	10	13	25
Men	3	6	14	23
Total	21	50	49	120

a

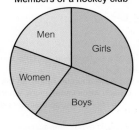

Members of a hockey club

b

Levels of players at a hockey club

7 a

1	25 37 96
2	00 56 94
3	16 27 58 67 76 82
4	12 20 46 64 88 96
5	17 34 62 78 84
6	27

Key: 1 | 25 means 125 pages

b

Number of pages, p	Frequency
$100 \leqslant p < 200$	3
$200 \leqslant p < 300$	3
$300 \leqslant p < 400$	6
$400 \leqslant p < 500$	6
$500 \leqslant p < 600$	5
$600 \leqslant p < 700$	1

c **i** 397 **ii** 394.25 **iii** 502
   iv $300 \leqslant p < 400$ and $400 \leqslant p < 500$ pages

Challenge

Students' own answers, e.g.
  a 1, 1, 1, 10, 10
  b 1, 1, 10, 10, 10
  c 1, 1, 1, 1, 10

3 Unit test

1 a brownie
  b Yes, as the proportion of brownies is larger than the other sectors.
  c 48

2 a 5 items   **b** 2.3 (1 d.p.)
  c **Number of items bought online**

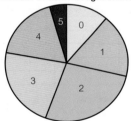

  d 2 items

3 a Students' own answers, e.g.
    The Smith family have a higher mean and median, so they spend more on average.
    The Smith family also have a higher range, so the amount they spend each week varies more, whereas the Jones family have a smaller range, so their spending is more consistent.
  b They are unlikely to spend exactly the same amount twice.

4 a mean £153.48 (nearest penny), median £118.95, no mode
  b Median, because the mean is higher than four of the five prices.

5

Mass, m (g)	Tally	Frequency
$45 \leqslant m < 50$	II	2
$50 \leqslant m < 55$		0
$55 \leqslant m < 60$	₩	5
$60 \leqslant m < 65$	III	3

6 a 3.8 seconds   **b** 12.9 seconds
7 a negative correlation
  b The price of a car decreases as it gets older.
8 The scale does not have equal intervals.

Challenge

About £86 400 000 per week

UNIT 4 Expressions and equations

4.1 Algebraic powers

1 a 16   b 8   c 81   d 27

2 a 20   b 18

3 a 2^5 b 10^2 c $3^3 \times 10$ d $5^2 \times 10^3$

4 a d^2 b m^3 c c^4 d t^6

5 a $10 \times 10 \times 10 \times 10$ b $2 \times 2 \times 2 \times 2 \times 2 \times 2$
   c $n \times n \times n$ d $x \times x$
   e $w \times w \times w \times w \times w$
   f $u \times u \times u \times u \times u \times u \times u \times u \times u \times u$

6 a $2st$ b $5st$ c $3st$ d $6ab$
   e $9ab$ f $6abc$ g $30abc$ h $40bcd$

7 a c^3d^2 b mn^2 c r^3s^2 d $3f^2$
   e $7e^3$ f $7e^2f$ g $7ef^2$ h $2n^2$
   i $5n^2$ j $5n^3$ k $30n^4$ l $24m^2n^2$
   m $24e^3fg^2$ n $30a^2b^3c$ o $-6e^2f$ p $6e^2f$

8 a 9   b 64   c 0.04   d 8
   e 1000   f 27

9 a s^2
   b i $3s^2$ ii ns^2 iii $2ns^2$
   c i $15s^2$ ii $5ns^2$

10 a $10\,800\,\text{cm}^2$ b $121\,500\,\text{cm}^2$

11 a $3x^2$ b $75\,\text{cm}^2$

12 a $A = 15m^2$, $B = 8a^3$, $C = 6t^3$ b $384\,\text{cm}^3$

13 $337.5\,\text{cm}^2$

Challenge

a

n	1	3	4	7	9	11	12	30
$2n$	2	6	8	14	18	22	24	60
n^2	1	9	16	49	81	121	144	900

b Yes; $2n$ means $2 \times n$ and n^2 means $n \times n$.

c Not in the table, but $2n = n^2$ when $n = 2$.

d Yes; $3n$ means $3 \times n$ and n^3 means $n \times n \times n$.

4.2 Expressions and brackets

1 a 2   b -2 c -15 d -15
   e 15

2 a $a + 2$ b $s + 6$ c $2m$ d $e - 4$
   e $b \div 2$ f $c \div 3$

3 a $7a + 4b$ b $7p + 3$ c $-3m$ d $-4d + 2$

4 a $2m - 14$ b $15s + 6$ c $6h + 6$ d $12e - 1$

5 a $\dfrac{m}{5}$ b $8 \div d$ c $\dfrac{2e}{3}$ d $(u - 3) \div 3$

6 a i $\dfrac{300}{100}$ or $300 \div 100$ ii $\dfrac{x}{100}$ or $x \div 100$
   iii $\dfrac{3x}{100}$ or $3x \div 100$
   b $\dfrac{600}{d}$ or $600 \div d$

7 a $\dfrac{n}{25}$ b $\dfrac{4n}{25}$ c $\dfrac{y}{125}$ d $\dfrac{4y}{125}$
   e $\dfrac{750}{x}$

8 a total weight of one tin of tomatoes
   b total weight of five tins of tomatoes

9 a $t + f$ b $4(t + f)$ c $n(t + f)$

10 a £$(m - 3)$ b £$8(m - 3)$

11 a $2(x + 3)$ b $y(y - 4)$
   c $z(z + 5)$ d $\dfrac{b}{2}(b - 5)$

12 a $T = 3x + 2$ b $T = 8x + 3$
   c $T = 2(3x + 2) = 6x + 4$
   d $T = 3(8x + 3) = 24x + 9$
   e $T = 2(3x + 2) + 3(8x + 3) = 30x + 13$

13 a $3c + 15$ b $-3c - 15$ c $-3c + 15$
   d $6c + 15$ e $-6c - 15$ f $-6c + 15$
   g $-8t - 6$ h $-8t + 6$ i $-10 - 5s$
   j $-10 + 5s$ k $-10 + 10x$ l $10 + 10x$
   m $y + 2$ n $-y - 2$ o $-y - 2$

   p $-3m + 5$

14 a $4 - 2c$ b $4 - 2b$ c $15 - 3n$
   d $5f + 6$ e $7u + 2$ f $p + 6$
   g $4b + 14$ h $3i - 15$

15 a $p^2 + 4p$ b $p^2 - 4p$ c $p^2 - 2p$
   d $3d^2 - 6d$ e $4d^2 - 8d$ f $8d^2 - 8d$
   g $8a^2 + 12a$ h $8a^2 - 12a$ i $-3g + 5g^2$
   j $-5g^2 - 3g$ k $-5g^2 + 3g$ l $-10g^2 + 6g$

Challenge

a i $P = 200$ ii $A = 100x - x^2$

b perimeter is always 200, so changing value of x does not affect the perimeter

c rectangles of side 20 and 80

d any pair of values that add to 100

e

x (cm)	10	20	30	40	50	60	70	80	90
Area (cm²)	900	1600	2100	2400	2500	2400	2100	1600	900

f No, you can use the fact that 10 and 90 give same rectangle, and so on.

g 50 cm

h square

4.3 Factorising expressions

1 a 1, 2, 5, 10   b 1, 2, 7, 14
   c 1, 2, 4, 5, 8, 10, 20, 40

2 a $6a + 6$ b $4b - 12$
   c $10y + 5$ d $d^2 + 4d$

3 a $6a = 3 \times 2a$ b $12p = 4 \times 3p$
   c $18u = 6 \times 3u$ d $100i = 4 \times 25i$
   e $-8m = -2 \times 4m$ f $-14w = 7 \times -2w$

4 a 3   b 4   c 10   d 6

5 a 7   b 5   c 3   d 2
   e 3   f 2

6 a $7y + 7 = 7(y + 1)$ b $5a + 10 = 5(a + 2)$
   c $6d - 3 = 3(2d - 1)$ d $12 + 15m = 3(4 + 5m)$
   e $8 + 10c = 2(4 + 5c)$ f $14 - 21a = 7(2 - 3a)$
   g $6 + 9w = 3(2 + 3w)$ h $20h - 10 = 10(2h - 1)$
   i $12n + 6 = 6(2n + 1)$ j $5a - 10 = 5(a - 2)$
   k $14u + 7v = 7(2u + v)$ l $16m + 24n = 8(2m + 3n)$

7 a $5(3 + 2h)$ b $3(i + 2)$ c $2(2c - 5)$
   d $2(3m - 4)$ e $3(d + 1)$ f $2(m - 1)$
   g $3(s - 3t)$ h $5(1 + k)$

8 a $5(e - 7)$ b the new monthly payment

9 a 6   b 10   c 4
   d 9   e 4   f 8
   g 15

10 a $6(1 + 2a)$ b $10(1 - 2b)$ c $9(p + 2)$
   d $4(3 + 4h)$ e $15(2m - 1)$ f $6(s + 3)$
   g $20(m - 5)$ h $9(3p + 4)$ i $4(2c + 3)$
   j $15(k - 3t)$ k $12(2r + 3s)$ l $40(n - 3p)$

11 a $5x + 35 = 5(x + 7)$ b $2m - 12 = 2(m - 6)$
   c $10n + 30 = 10(n + 3)$ d $15 - 9t = 3(5 - 3t)$

12 a x b y c n
   d n e 3, n, $3n$ f 2, b, $2b$

13 a $3n$ b $2a$ c $5b$
   d $2c$ e $3d$ f $2e$ g $3v$

14 a $p(p + 1)$ b $g(g - 1)$ c $h(1 + h)$
   d $f(1 - f)$ e $m(1 - 3m)$ f $m(3m - 1)$
   g $2d(2 + 3d)$ h $2d(2d - 3)$

15 a $(x + 4)$ and 2   b r and $(2r + 1)$

16 a 3 and 9 have a common factor of 3   b $3x(x + 3)$

Challenge

a $4(n + 3)$

b $n + 3$

c Inverse operation of $+3$ is -3, so need to subtract 3 from their answer

d Students' own answers

4.4 One-step equations

1 a i $+$ ii $-$
  b i $-$ ii $-$
  c i $\div$ ii $\div$
  d i $\times$ ii $\div$

2 a i -2 ii 7
  b i $\times 3$ ii 30
  c i -10 ii 90

3 a $\div 2$ b $+5$ c $\times 3$ d -3

4 a 5 b 2 c 30

5 a $x = 6$ b $y = 12$ c $z = 2$ d $n = 6$
  e $m = 10$ f $p = 16$

6 a $x = 4$ b $v = 8$ c $y = 7$ d $k = 3$
  e $p = 24$ f $u = 44$ g $x = 50$ h $m = 36$

7 £1350

8 a 4 b 12 c 11 d 6
  e 220

9 a $a = 4$ b $d = 0$ c $e = -2$ d $n = -5$
  e $r = 6$ f $h = -1.5$

10 a $t + 12$ b $t + 12 = 122$
   c $t = 110$, so the original length was 110 characters.

11 a $3h = 12$
   b $h = 4$, so a pair of hiking socks costs £4.

12 a $\frac{j}{8} = 150$ or $j \div 8 = 150$
   b $j = 1200$, so the total volume is 1200 ml.

13 a $m - 12 = 35$
   b $m = 47$, so the original collection was 47 CDs.

14 a $5d = 20$, $d = 4$ b $10a = 60$, $a = 6$
   c $8c = 16$, $c = 2$ d $4g = 18$, $g = 4.5$

15 a $3x = 15$, $x = 5$ b $8y = 40$, $y = 5$

16 a $6a = 180°$, $a = 30°$ b $12h = 24$, $h = 2$

Challenge

1 $3t = 360$ so $t = 120$
   $4s = 360$ so $s = 90$
   $5p = 360$ so $p = 72$
   hexagon 60, octagon 45, decagon 36

2 $10x = 360$, $x = 36$

3 $12x = 360$, $x = 30$
   assuming that the three hexagons are joined like this:

4 Students' own answers

4.5 Two-step equations

1 a 9 b 13 c -5

2 a $9, 23$ b $2, 9$ c $0, 15, 30$

3 a 26 b 4 c 28

4 a $-5, \div 2$ b $+1, \times 4,$ c $-5, \div 10$

5 a $x = 7$ b $x = 5$ c $b = 10$ d $b = 5$
  e $n = 7$ f $w = -4$ g $k = 8$ h $h = 3$

6 a $7f + 2$ b $7f + 2 = 30$
  c $f = 4$, so a rocket costs £4.

7 a $12c + 2 = 38$
  b $c = 3$, so the length of a plank is 3 m.

8 $2n + 12 = 28$, $n = 8$
  Marion first thought of the number 8.

9 $5n - 10 = 80$, $n = 18$
  18 bucketfuls were needed to fill the paddling pool.

10 a $5d + 8 = 23$, $d = 3$ b $6p + 4 = 28$, $p = 4$
   c $8a + 2 = 18$, $a = 2$ d $7b - 6 = 22$, $b = 4$

11 a $10n - 2 = 8$, $n = 1$ b $3n + 7 = 16$, $n = 3$
   c $7g - 8 = 34$, $g = 6$ d $8u + 25 = 65$, $u = 5$

Challenge

a i $6(a + 5)$
  ii $6(a + 5) = 48$, $a = 3$
  iii 8 m

b i $7b$
  ii $9(b + 2) - 7b = 2b + 18$
  iii $2b + 18 = 26$, $b = 4$

4.6 The balancing method

1 a $+ 3$ b $\div 4$ c $\times 7$ d $- 2$

2 a $8c + 3$ b $5z + 15$ c $4k - 12$

3 a -4 b -4 c 3 d -3

4 a $m = 2$ b $d = 14$ c $a = 7$ d $k = 4$
  e $g = -3$ f $n = 24$ g $t = 30$ h $s = -30$
  i $x = -30$ j $x = -200$

5 a $F = 15$ b $a = 5$ c $m = 6$

6 $5x - 4 = 6$, $5x = 10$, $x = 2$

7 a $m = 1$ b $n = 8$ c $t = 6$
  d $k = 20$ e $h = 7$ f $w = 9$

8 a $2n + 3 = 15$ b $n = 6$

9 a $m = 5$ b $t = 3$ c $x = 5$

10 a $-2u + 8 = 20$, $-2u = 12$, $u = -6$
   b $10 - 2d = 16$, $-2d = 6$, $d = -3$
   c $11 - 3d = 2$, $-3d = -9$, $d = 3$
   d $-5m - 7 = 3$, $-5m = 10$, $m = -2$

11 a $2(m + 3) = 8$, $2m + 6 = 8$, $2m = 2$, $m = 1$
   b $2(m + 3) = 8$, $m + 3 = 4$, $m = 1$

12 a $10s - 5 = 25$, $s = 3$ b $6w + 4 = 16$, $w = 2$
   c $20h - 12 = 48$, $h = 3$ d $2 + 6t = 32$, $t = 5$

Challenge

a i $50 = 6x + 8$
  ii $x = 7$, so there are 7 carriages.

b i 7
  ii $20 = 6x + 8$, $x = 2$

c 8 m, the engine, the number 8

d x carriages of length 6 m

4 Check up

1 a m^4 b $b \times b \times b \times b \times b \times b$
  c i a^3c^2 ii $24n^3$

2 a $10a^2$ b 160 cm^2

3 a A $27s^3$, B $15k^3$
  b 405 cm^3

4 a $V = w \div 15$ or $V = \frac{w}{15}$
  b $V = 30$ ml
  c $T = nV$

5 $120 \div n$ or $\frac{120}{n}$

6 a $2m + nm$ b $2b^2 - 6b$ c $-8t - 20$
  d $3u + 6$ e $2r - 8$

7 a 4 b $4(2n + 3)$

8 a $8(s - 1)$ b $4(3 + m)$ c $3(h + 3)$
  d $50(2 - t)$ e $9(6p + 2r)$ f $6(5j - 7q)$
  g $k(1 - k)$ h $4v(4v - 1)$ i $5a(3a + 5)$

9 a $h = 19$ b $w = 20$ c $m = -6$
  d $a = 6$ e $d = 1$ f $h = 3$

10 a $P = £44$ b $W = £46$

11 $t = 10$ seconds

12 $2n + 20 = 48$, $n = 14$

Challenge

a $2 + 2x$
b $2 + 8x$
c i $6x + 4$ ii $6x - 4$ iii $12x$
d i $8x + 4$ ii $8x - 4$ iii $16x$
e $P = 2nx$
f 1.5 m

4 Strengthen: Powers, expressions and formulae

1 a $u \times u \times u \times u \times u$ **b** $a \times a$ **c** $d \times d \times d$

2 a $4c$ **b** c^4 **c** $3h$ **d** h^3
  e m^5 **f** $5m$

3 a $4t^2$ **b** $5a^3$ **c** $2g^5$ **d** $6e^2$
  e $10m^3$ **f** $8n^2$ **g** $12d^3$ **h** $-15t^2$

4 a e^3d^2 **b** s^2t^3 **c** e^2f **d** p^4q

5 a $6x$ **b** $2x^2$ **c** $10y$ **d** $8y^2$

6 a $\dfrac{A}{2}$ **b** $\dfrac{A}{3}$ **c** $\dfrac{A}{4}$ **d** $\dfrac{A}{6}$

7 a £40 **b** £20 **c** £8 **d** $£\dfrac{80}{n}$

8 a hlw **b** $6x$ **c** $6x^2$ **d** $6x^3$

4 Strengthen: Brackets

1 a $9g - 15$ **b** $6g - 10$ **c** $-2n - 6$
  d $-2n + 6$ **e** $-12c - 8$ **f** $-12c + 8$
  g $-10p - 15$ **h** $-10p + 15$

2 a $8t + 6$ **b** $4t - 6$ **c** $8t - 6$
  d $4t + 6$ **e** $11m + 6$ **f** $11m - 6$
  g $5m - 6$ **h** $5m + 6$

3 a $8a + 13$ **b** $2a + 7$ **c** $2a - 2$
  d $2a + 10$ **e** $14m - 3$ **f** $-2m + 21$

4 a $a^2 + 5a$ **b** $a^2 - 5a$ **c** $2a^2 + 10a$
  d $2a^2 - 10a$ **e** $3p^2 - 12p$ **f** $3p^2 + 12p$
  g $6p^2 + 3p$ **h** $6p^2 - 3p$

5 $3c + 6 = 3(c + 2)$

6 a $4(b + 2)$ **b** $7(c - 2)$ **c** $2(a + 3)$
  d $5(m + 2)$ **e** $7(p - 1)$ **f** $3(w - 4)$
  g $10(t - 2)$ **h** $4(a - 3)$ **i** $2(5 + 2k)$
  j $4(3 + 4s)$ **k** $2(2a + 3b)$ **l** $2(3c + 5d)$

7 a $3m(2m + 5)$ **b** $2a(2a - 3)$ **c** $7u(u + 2)$
  d $3d(2d - 3)$

4 Strengthen: Equations

1 a $x = 5$ **b** $x = 8$ **c** $x = 4$ **d** $x = 15$

2 a $x = 8$ **b** $x = 9$ **c** $a = 5$ **d** $c = 6$
  e $p = 3$ **f** $t = 6$ **g** $m = 14$ **h** $e = 12$

3 a $x = 4$ **b** $y = 4$ **c** $a = 5$ **d** $c = 3$

4 a $t = 3$ **b** $x = 1$ **c** $d = 3$ **d** $m = 2$

Challenge

a $10n$

b $5n + 30$

c i $5n + 30 = 10n$
  ii $n = 6$, so they live on the 6th floor.

4 Extend

1

A	B	C	D	E
9	6	2	3	5

2 a $12h = 60, h = 5$
  b $8x = 24, x = 3$
  c $\dfrac{1}{2} \times 10h = 30, h = 6$
  d $\dfrac{1}{2}(5 + 3)h = 48, h = 12$

3 $3.5\,\text{cm}$

4 $180 = 20n$, $n = 9$, so 9 pencils can be bought.

5 a i $110 = 20x + 30$
  ii $x = 4$, so the repair took 4 hours.
  b i A $(110, 4)$ represents 4 hours costing £110, as in part **a**.
  ii $20x + 30 = 60$
  c $20x + 30 = 115$, $x = 4.25$, so the repair takes 4 hours 15 minutes. The calculation is more accurate.
  d £30 call-out fee
  e £20 hourly rate

6 a i £10 cost of one umbrella
  ii £5 postage and packing
  b i $35 = 10n + 5$
  ii $n = 3$, so he ordered 3 umbrellas.
  c i

n	0	2	4	6	8
C	5	25	45	65	85

ii

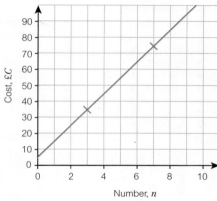

Online umbrellas

d i See graph.
  ii $(3, 35)$ represents 3 umbrellas costing £35 in total, as in part **b**.
e $(7, 75)$ marked on graph, $n = 7$

7 a $x = 1$ **b** $x = 5$ **c** $x = 2$

8 a $5(n + 20)$ or $5n + 100$
  b $5n + 100 = 125$, $n = 5$, so a nut weighs $5\,\text{g}$.

9 a $8(a + 3)$
  b $8(a + 3) = 180$, $a = 19.5$

10 a $3(4a + 2) = 12a + 6$
  b $12a + 6 = 2(6a + 3)$, so the length of the rectangle is $6a + 3$.

Challenge

$x = 7$

4 Unit test

1 a $t = 8$ **b** $y = 21$ **c** $a = -4$

2 $£P \div 4$ or $£\dfrac{P}{4}$

3 a $d = 10$ **b** $x = 7$ **c** $y = 4$

4 a $4t$ **b** $3(t + 1)$

5 a $A = 66$ **b** $I = 2.5$

6 a $2bc + 5c$ **b** $3u^2 + 3u$ **c** $-2t + 6$
  d $2m + 16$ **e** $3u^2 + 4u$ **f** $4a + 4b$

7 a $m = 5$ **b** $n = 7$

8 a i a^2 **ii** $3a^2$
  b $48\,\text{cm}^2$
  c i $A = 4a^2$ **ii** $A = 5a^2$ **iii** $A = na^2$

9 a c^5 **b** $m \times m \times m \times m$
  c i p^2t^3 **ii** $10a^3$ **iii** $24x^2y^3$

10 a i 8 **ii** $8(a + 2)$
  b i $4(3s + 2)$ **ii** $w(w - 1)$
  iii $2x(x + 4)$ **iv** $5y(3y - 2)$

11 a $\dfrac{36}{n}$ **b** $\dfrac{36}{n} = 2$, $n = 18$

12 a $\dfrac{x}{5}$
  b $\dfrac{x}{5} = 300$ so $x = 1500$

13 9 weeks

14 a $x = 50°$ **b** $50°, 100°, 30°$

15 $15\,\text{mm}$

Challenge

a i a^3 **ii** $8a^3$
b Volume of cube B $= 2^3 \times$ volume of cube A
c i $27a^3$
  ii Volume of cube C $= 3^3 \times$ volume of cube A
  iii $2460.375\,\text{cm}^3$
d i n^3a^3
  ii Volume of cube D $= n^3 \times$ volume of cube A
  iii $5359375\,\text{cm}^3$

UNIT 5 Real-life graphs

5.1 Conversion graphs

1 a 1 cm = 10 mm   **b** 1 kg = 1000 g
   c 1 litre = 1000 ml   **d** 1 km = 1000 m

2 a 400 g   **b** 0.5 litres or 500 ml
   c 0.25 m or 25 cm

3 a 24 km   **b** 9 litres

4 a 12 inches   **b** 16 inches   **c** 15 cm
   d about 27.5 cm   **e** 28 inches

5 a i $8   **ii** £2.50   **iii** £7.50
   b i £25   **ii** $24

6 **a, b**

Celsius/Fahrenheit conversion

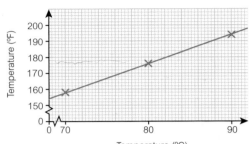

   c about 71 °C   **d**   about 182 °F   **e** nitric acid

7 **a**

Gallons	0	1	5
Litres	0	4.5	22.5

   b

Conversion graph for gallons and litres

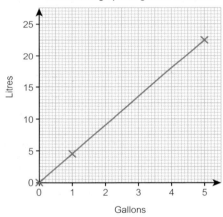

   c i 3.5 gallons ≈ 15.75 litres
     ii 0.2 gallons ≈ 0.9 litres
     iii 1 litre ≈ 0.2 gallons
     iv 12.5 litres ≈ 2.8 gallons

Challenge

   a i about 45 DKK   **ii** about £8.00
   b, c

£ to DKK currency conversion

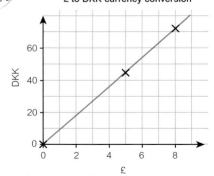

5.2 Distance–time graphs

1 a 30 minutes   **b** 20 minutes
   c 15 minutes   **d** 10 minutes

2 a 45 minutes   **b** 30 minutes
   c 75 minutes   **d** 45 minutes

3 a 20 km   **b** 1:30 pm   **c** 30 minutes
   d 1 hour 30 minutes   **e** 45 minutes
   f He drove faster on the way to the shops; it only took $\frac{1}{2}$ hour, compared with $\frac{3}{4}$ hour on the way back.

4 a 2.4 km   **b** 20 minutes   **c** 10 minutes
   d 20 minutes   **e** 45 minutes
   f on the way to the post office

5 a 800 m   **b** 1600 m   **c** 1 hour 30 minutes

6 a 140 km   **b** 7:45 and 8:15 am

7 **a**

Daya's journey

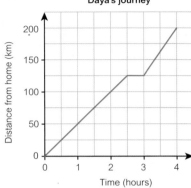

   b after her break (or between 3 and 4 hours)

8 **a**

Geoff's journey

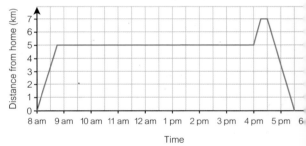

   b 1 hour

9 a line B (red)   **b** 45 miles
   c Bath to Newport arrives at 12:00;
     Newport to Bath arrives at 11:45
   d Newport to Bath

10 a 30 miles   **b** 4 hours   **c** 9:40 am
    d 2 hours   **e** 10:20 am

Challenge

e.g.

a 09:00 to 10:00   **b** 10:30 to 11:00
c 12:45 to 13:30   **d** 11:30 to 12:45
e 10:30   **f** 12:00 to 12:10

5.3 Line graphs

1 a 0.5   **b** 325   **c** 25

2 a 0–10   **b** 23 °C
   c 09:30 and 20:00   **d** every 2 hours

3 a increasing; the graph shows sales rising over time
   b between March and April, when the gradient is steepest

4 a $20 per ounce   **b** $5 per ounce
   c 2010 to 2012; steepest line
   d 2012 and 2016   **e** about $15.50

f The price increased from 2006 to 2012, then decreased until 2016, followed by a slight increase to 2018; the largest increase was from 2010 to 2012, and the smallest increase from 2016 to 2018.

5 a, b

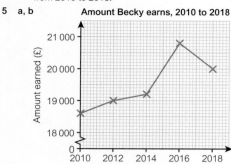

Amount Becky earns, 2010 to 2018

c about £20 400; the pattern of the graph is quite irregular, so the actual 2017 figure might have been higher or lower than the graph suggests.

d No; as the pattern is irregular, you cannot use it to make predictions.

6 a

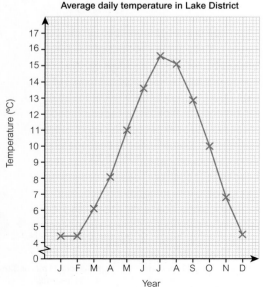

Theme park visitor numbers

b i August and September **ii** 14 000

c Students' own answers, e.g.
Visitor numbers increase each month from May to August, with a peak of about 28 000 in August, and then fall sharply in September and October.

Challenge

a

Average daily temperature in Lake District

b June, July and August

c May, June and July

d Students' own answers, e.g.
May; it is one of the driest months and the temperature won't be too cold or too hot for taking part in activities.

5.4 More line graphs

1 a Art **b** Maths **c** Computing

2 a 2000 **b** 2012 **c** 2004

d Students' own answers, e.g.
CD singles sales will stay near zero and digital singles sales will level off.

3 a An increasing trend

b A decreasing trend

4 a It shows the water level when the reservoir when full.

b 1 May

c i The overall trend is increasing.

ii The trend is decreasing.

5 a, b

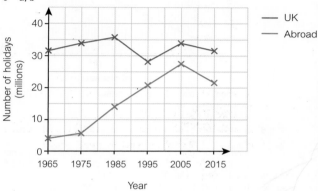

c Students' own answers, e.g.
The number of holidays taken abroad shows an increasing trend between 1960 and 2000; the number of holidays taken in the UK stays roughly constant.

6 a Students' own answers, e.g.
Bicycle – increased at first, but after 1980 has decreased and levelled off
Motorbike – has stayed fairly similar
Air – increased over the first 30 years, then levelled off
Rail – decreased slightly over the first 10 years, then increased after that (steep rise between 2000 and 2010)
Bus/coach – started as the type of transport with the greatest distance travelled, then overall has decreased over the years

b i 4 billion km **ii** 60 billion km

c 73.7%

d about 84%

e Students' own answers, e.g.
Between 1970 and 2010 the distance travelled by cars, vans and taxis more than doubled. The percentage of the total distance travelled, that is by cars, vans and taxis, increased by over 10%, showing that this type of transport became the type of transport with the greatest distance travelled.

7 a i 0.2 million cars **ii** 200 thousand cars

b i 27.5 million **ii** 28.5 million

c 2010

d 2008–2009; the line is horizontal.

e There are increasing numbers of cars.

Challenge

a July **b** May **c** 33 − 22 = 11 °C

d The weather will be quite hot (average 25 °C) and quite dry (average 100 mm rainfall).

5.5 Real-life graphs

1 graph B

2 a Naomi's times decreased over the 6-week period.

b Naomi took about 56 minutes to run 5 km in Week 1.

3 a No; the graph only shows the percentages.
  b The percentage of households with internet access is increasing.
  c No; if it increases to 100%, it cannot continue increasing beyond that.
4 a i 35% ii 81% iii 90%
  b The percentage of adults who use the internet every day is increasing and the percentage who never use it is decreasing.
  c Yes; the percentage has gone from 35% to 90%, which is more than double.
5 a

Number of hoodies	1	5	10	15	20
Cost (£)	60	100	150	200	250

  b

Cost of hoodies

  c the £50 cost to design the print
  d i 6 ii 12
  e £13 (or £12.95, nearest penny)
6 a £40 b £70 c £20 d £10
7 a i £46 ii £80
  b call-out fee (or students' own explanations of this concept)
  c £12 d £15 e £97 f £110.50
8 a i £45 ii £140
  b i £40 ii 45 minutes iii £20
9 A 3, B 5, C 1, D 6, E 2, F 4
10 a 35 newtons
  b about 0.57 cm
  c 2 cm
    The tension has changed to 0 indicating there is no tension, so the line has broken.
11 a the narrow part
  b steepest part of the graph
12 a A 2, B 4, C 3, E 1
  b container D

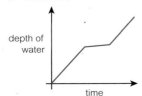

Challenge
a

Ice cube	Side length (mm)	Surface area (mm²)	Melt water (ml)
1	10	600	0.12
2	15	1350	0.27
3	20	2400	0.48
4	25	3750	0.75
5	30	5400	1.08

b

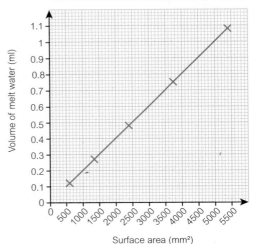

Ice cube surface area and melt water volume

  c i about 0.37 ml (accurate answer 0.39 ml, 2 d.p.)
    ii 27 mm

5.6 Curved graphs

1 The object is stationary (not moving).
2 a 2 am
  b Students' own answers, e.g.
    The cat is at home from midnight to 2 am, then sets off. It goes about 125 m away, then turns back for a little towards the house, then goes off further again, to about 440 m away by 6:30 am. Then the cat turns back towards the house, with a short stop on the way, arriving back about 8:30 am. It sleeps till just after 6 pm, when it goes out again, reaching its furthest point of 340 m from the house at about 11 pm. At about 11:45 pm it turns back in the direction of home.
3 a 10 °C
  b i 79 degrees ii 7 degrees
  c Students' own answers, e.g.
    The water cannot get any hotter than its boiling point.
4 a

Temperature (°C)	15	25	35	45
Number of lumens	2	4	8	16

  b

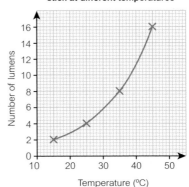

Number of lumens from a light stick at different temperatures

  c i about 5.6 lumens
    ii about 38 °C
5 a 90 cm³ b 60 cm³
  c i about 39 seconds
    ii about 24 seconds
    iii about 14 seconds
  d Increasing the temperature makes the reaction happen faster.
6 a about 29 seconds b about 31 m/s or 32 m/s
  c about 21 seconds d 54 seconds
  e 4 seconds

7 a i 11.3 m **ii** 9.4 m
b 12.6 m
c Fielder throws it and wicket keeper catches it at a height of 1.6 m (about their shoulder height).
d 1.15 and 1.85 seconds; on the way up and on the way down

Challenge

a 8 °C **b** 15 °C and 33 °C
c i It reaches 100%, which means it is growing as fast as it can.
ii It reaches 0%, which means it has stopped growing.
d The amount is increasing: even though the growth rate is decreasing, the yeast is still growing

5 Check up

1 a

Teaspoons	0	1	2	5
ml	0	5	10	25

b, c

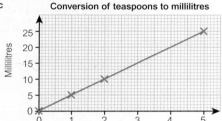

Conversion of teaspoons to millilitres

d i 17.5 ml **ii** 4.2 teaspoons
2 a 25 miles **b** about 5 minutes **c** 45 minutes
d 35 minutes **e** on her way home
3 a 218 million
b 2008 and 2013
c about 217 million
4 a No, she has misread the scale; about 70% were occupied.
b 2014 **c** 2009
d The trend is increasing: the percentage of international flight seats occupied is going up.

5 a

Length of call out (hours)	0	$\frac{1}{2}$	1	2	3
Total cost (£)	40	80	120	200	280

b

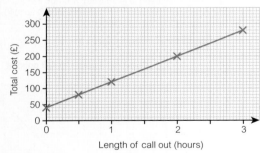

Cost of call out for a vet

c £260
6 a about 61 to 62 cm
b 12 months
c shorter than average
d 0–6 months; steepest part of the graph

Challenge

Students' own distance–time graphs

5 Strengthen: Conversion and distance–time graphs

1 a i 0.5 feet **ii** 0.5 metres

b i 3 feet ≈ 1 metre
ii 25 feet ≈ 8.3 to 8.5 metres
iii 12 metres ≈ 36 feet
iv 4.5 metres ≈ 13.5 feet

c 25 metres

2 a

£	0	5	10
Rand	0	75	150

b

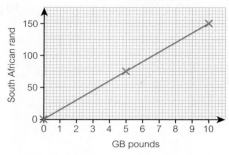

Conversion rate from GB pounds to South African rand

c i £4 = 60 rand **ii** 120 rand = £8
3 a The graph is flat; he's not moving away from or towards home.
b 10 minutes **c** 20 minutes
d 15 minutes **e** home to shop
f 10:45 am
4 a

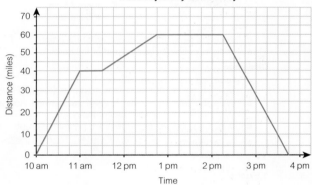

Nasim's journey on Saturday

b 120 miles **c** 3:45 pm

5 Strengthen: Line graphs

1 a 4 Sept **b** 25 Sept **c** about 6810
2 a week 5 to week 6
b week 7 to week 8
c No cars were sold.
3 a i 1 **ii** 400
b i 10 000 **ii** 21 000
c 2015
d 2013 to 2014; the graph is flat.
4 a i 1 **ii** 8000 km **iii** 200 km
b i 7800 km **ii** about 10 400 km
c 1972 to 1973 **d** 2005
5 a September **b** line A (red) **c** July
d January, February and December
e i 13 °C **ii** 6 °C
f December
6 a 62% **b** 5%
c 2008 and 2010
d The trend is increasing: more and more UK adults use internet shopping.
e 75% or 76%

7 a

Rental time (hours)	0	$\frac{1}{2}$	1	4
Cost (£)	0	6	12	48

b

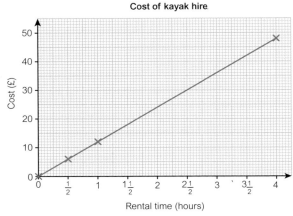

Cost of kayak hire

c i £36   **ii** £18

5 Strengthen: Curved graphs

1 a When the bean is just planted, the plant is just a seed in the ground so has 0 height above the ground.
b about 18.5 cm
c i about 3 cm   **ii** about 7.5 cm
iii about 8 cm   **iv** about 4 cm
v about 2 cm
d week 5 to week 6; least steep part of the graph
e week 3 to week 4; steepest part of the graph

Challenge

a False; it is just 10 more T-shirts.
b True; it is the highest part of the graph, showing 170 sold.
c False; the greatest increase in sales was between April and May, the steepest upward part of the graph.
d True; this is the steepest downward part of the graph.
e False; the mean is $\frac{120 + 130 + 150 + 140 + 170 + 150}{6} = \frac{860}{6} = 143$ (nearest whole number).

5 Extend

1 a £750   **b** 1.7 ounces
2 a   **i** Sayeed   **ii** Chan   **iii** Sayeed

b, c

	Distance (km)	Sayeed's time (minutes)	Chan's time (minutes)
Swim	1.5	20	25
Cycle	40	70	60
Run	10	30	40
Total	51.5	120	125

3 a

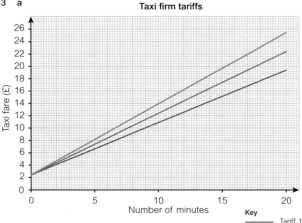

Taxi firm tariffs

Key
— Tariff 1
— Tariff 2
— Tariff 3

b £6.65   **c** £1.80
d from 15 minutes onwards

4 a The first day after the operation the patient is at pain level 9, the worst pain, where they can't do any activities because of the pain. The pain level drops to 8 on day 2 and stays there for day 3. It then drops to 7 on day 4 and stays there for days 5 and 6. The pain level drops to 6 on day 7 and stays there for day 8. It drops to 5 on day 9 and 4 on day 10, which is mild pain where they are unable to do some activities because of pain.
b Students' own answers, e.g.
Yes; the graph shows a decreasing trend: the pain is getting less, so their pain level should go down to 3 and then 2.
OR
No; the graph shows that the pain level might stay the same or go down to 3 or even 2, but it could also go up again if something unexpected happens.

5 Unit test

1 a i 8.9 million   **ii** 11.2 million
b 2006
c about 8.75 million

2 a

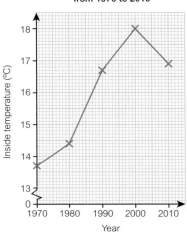

Average inside temperatures from 1970 to 2010

b The overall trend is increasing: average inside temperatures rose until 2000 and then dropped slightly in 2010.

3 a

£	0	5	10
Baht	0	250	500

b

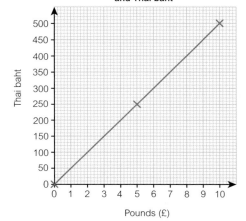

Conversion graph for GB pounds and Thai baht

c i 175 baht   **ii** £9.20

4 **a** 09 15   **b** 2 hours 30 minutes
     c 1 mile   **d** the cycle home
5 **a** about 600 g
     b between 10.5 and 11 weeks
     c less than average
     d 10 to 15 weeks; steepest part of the graph
6 **a**

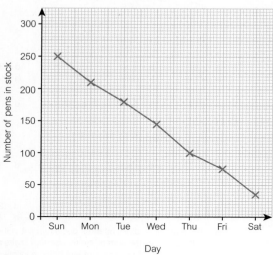

Number of pens in stock

     b 135 pens
     c No; they have 135 in stock ready for the next week, but this
        week they sold 215 altogether, so if they sell anywhere near
        the same number next week, they won't have enough.
7 **a**

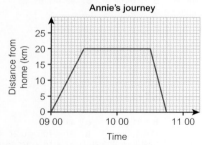

Annie's journey

     b start 09 30, end 10 30

Challenge

Students' own descriptions of the ride

UNIT 6 Decimals and ratio

6.1 Ordering decimals and rounding

1 **a** seven million, six hundred and two thousand, three hundred and eighty-five

  b seventeen million, four hundred thousand and thirty-nine

2 **a** **i** 7 tenths or 0.7   **ii** 7 hundredths or 0.07

   iii 7 thousandths or 0.007

  b neither

  c **i** 5.7   **ii** 6.0   **iii** 5.8

3 **a** 3 tenths   **b** 2 thousandths   **c** 1 hundredth

4 7.63 (2 d.p.)   12.041 (3 d.p.)

  37.3 (1 d.p.)   4.011 (3 d.p.)

  14.72 (2 d.p.)   9.00 (2 d.p.)

5 **a** 2.18   **b** 7.49   **c** 5.08   **d** 6.20

  e 45.16   **f** 23.01   **g** 0.86   **h** 9.00

6 **a** **i** 8.93   **ii** 8.932

  b **i** 69.09   **ii** 69.085

  c **i** 72.76   **ii** 72.758

  d **i** 3.26   **ii** 3.257

  e **i** 85.80   **ii** 85.801

  f **i** 29.80   **ii** 29.797

  g **i** 5.09   **ii** 5.087

  h **i** 34.06   **ii** 34.061

7 **a** £9.16

  b Need to round down, otherwise there will not be enough money for all the workers.

8 **a** 2.5 cm   **b** 6.1 cm (1 d.p.)

  c 3.4 m (1 d.p.)

9 Moscow   11.5 million

  London   8.2 million

  Berlin   3.5 million

  Madrid   3.2 million

  Rome   2.8 million

  Paris   2.3 million

  Budapest   1.7 million

  Vienna   1.6 million

  Prague   1.2 million

  Dublin   1.0 million

10 **a** 300   **b** 6000   **c** 20 000   **d** 0.6

11 **a** 60.25   **b** 0.006   **c** 360 000   **d** 3.14

12 **a** **i** 2.2   **ii** 7.5   **iii** 5.1   **iv** 6.2

   v 45   **vi** 23   **vii** 0.86   **viii** 9.00

  b If the number is between −1 and 1, the rounded numbers are the same, otherwise they are not.

13 **a** 4.3507 < 4.5307   **b** 0.2453 > 0.2435

  c 9.6271 < 9.671   **d** 21.029 > 21.021 11

  e 6.321 08 > 6.321 072

14 **a** 1.232, 1.093, 0.200 71, 0.1258, 0.086 66

  b 4.735, 4.23, 4.227, 4.051, 3.2924

  c 7.0932, 7.001, 0.749, 0.7113, 0.0732

  d 25.645, 25.62, 24.833, 24.4570, 22.964

15 **a** −0.2 > −0.3   **b** −0.3 < −0.29

  c −2.39 > −2.9   **d** −9.3 < −9.23

16 **a** −4.6, −4.2, 2.46, 2.6

  b −10.53, −10.5, −10.3, 10.35, 10.5

  c −0.77, −0.7, −0.07, 0.07, 0.7

  d −0.845, −0.149, −0.135, −0.125, -0.0122

  e −0.0342, −0.0325, −0.0309, 0.0324, 0.033

  f −5.5005, −5.055, −5.05, 5.0005, 5.0505

Challenge

Students' own answers, e.g.

a 0.112, 0.11, 0.109, 0.108, −0.112

b −6.007, −6.01, −6.1, −6.111, −6.7

6.2 Place-value calculations

1 **a** rectangle, 54 cm^2

  b triangle, 27 cm^2

  c parallelogram, 54 cm^2

2 **a** $1 \div 10 = 0.1$

  b $1 \div 100 = 0.01$

  c $1 \div 10 \div 10 = 0.01$

  d $1 \div 10 \div 100 = 0.001$

  e $34 \div 10 = 3.4$

  f $623 \div 100 = 6.23$

g $3461 \div 1000 = 3.461$

3 **a** 0.6   **b** 2.4   **c** 0.24   **d** 0.48

4 **a** 1335   **b** 1484   **c** 2784   **d** 4005

5 **a** **i** $29 \times 10 = 290$

     $29 \times 1 = 29$

     $29 \times 0.1 = 2.9$

     $29 \times 0.01 = 0.29$

   ii $107 \times 10 = 1070$

     $107 \times 1 = 107$

     $107 \times 0.1 = 10.7$

     $107 \times 0.01 = 1.07$

  b **i** ÷ 10   **ii** ÷ 100

6 **a** 0.86   **b** 1.16   **c** 0.053   **d** 36.21

  e 45.68   **f** 0.886   **g** 0.116   **h** 5.34

  i 6.83

7 **a** 0.021   **b** 0.024   **c** 0.012   **d** 0.072

8 685 (137 × 5)

  5480 (137 × 40)

  27 400 (137 × 200)

  33 565 (total)

9 **a** 35 787   **b** 78 302   **c** 180 336   **d** 419 965

10 222 976

11 **a** 2.04   **b** 30.26   **c** 9.89

12 **a** 8.14   **b** 10.75   **c** 78.12   **d** 22.382

  e 30.794   **f** 33.128   **g** 8.733   **h** 162.525

13 **a** The number of digits after the decimal point in the answer is the same as the sum of the numbers of digits after the decimal point in the two numbers being multiplied.

  b 16.6912

14 121.44 km

15 **a** 0.504   **b** 0.432   **c** 2.592   **d** 2.8608

16 **a** 0.018 m^2 **b** 2.04 m^2 **c** 52.14 cm^2

  d 503.88 cm^2 **e** 136.88 m^2

Challenge

3.0265 litres

6.3 Calculations with decimals

1 **a** 9   **b** 562   **c** 0.09

  d 3.7   **e** 4.23

2 **a** 53 108.917   **b** 14.81

  c 12.075   **d** 8.134

3 **a** 98   **b** 31.7   **c** 41

4 **a** **i** $143 \div 100 = 1.43$ **ii** $27 \div 100 = 0.27$

     $143 \div 10 = 14.3$ $27 \div 10 = 2.7$

     $143 \div 1 = 143$ $27 \div 1 = 27$

     $143 \div 0.1 = 1430$ $27 \div 0.1 = 270$

     $143 \div 0.01 = 14 300$ $27 \div 0.01 = 2700$

   iii $8 \div 100 = 0.08$

     $8 \div 10 = 0.8$

     $8 \div 1 = 8$

     $8 \div 0.1 = 80$

     $8 \div 0.01 = 800$

  b **i** × 10   **ii** × 100

5 **a** 150   **b** 26   **c** 8530

  d 57 200   **e** 760   **f** 3

6 **a** 3 and 3   **b** 9 and 9

  c 121 and 121   **d** 25 and 25

7 The answers to the calculations in each pair are the same.

  $8.1 \div 0.9 = 81 \div 9 = 9$

  $0.64 \div 0.08 = 64 \div 8 = 8$

8 **a** 9   **b** 8   **c** 11

  d 4   **e** 3   **f** 12

9 **a** 4

  b Larger; 0.02 is smaller than 0.2 so more 0.02s will 'fit into' 0.8 than 0.2s.

  c, d 40

10 **a** 50   **b** 70   **c** 70   **d** 110

11 **a** 21   **b** 36   **c** 52   **d** 356

  e 145   **f** 144.4   **g** 13.168

12 **a** 152.9   **b** 0.2   **c** 103.6

13 12 dishes (11.625 before rounding up)

14 a 8.853   **b** 12.68676   **c** 45.67266
   d 67.38208   **e** 2.933775

15 a 145.152 cm²   **b** 3.7 m

16 £546.80

17 a 34.535 ml   **b** 29.004 ml

18 a 12.86 m²   **b** 5.23 m²

Challenge

a The answer is larger than the starting number.

b The answer is smaller than the starting number.

c Students' own answers

6.4 Ratio and proportion with decimals

1 a 6 : 9, 14 : 21, 30 : 45

   b $\frac{6}{9}, \frac{14}{21}, \frac{30}{45}$

2 a 1 : 2

   b **i** $\frac{1}{3}$ **ii** $\frac{2}{3}$

3 a £8 and £12   **b** £16 and £20

   c 15 m and 9 m

4 a £1.40 and £2.10   **b** 2.8 m and 3.5 m

   c 12 kg and 7.2 kg   **d** $610.68 and $1424.92

5 a £24, £36, £48   **b** £54, £162, £270

   c £85, £170, £255   **d** £22, £44, £66, £110

   e 78 m, 117 m, 234 m

   f 49.25 km, 98.5 km, 197 km, 246.25 km

   g £182.12, £303.53, £546.35

   h 7.9 cm, 23.7 cm, 55.4 cm

6 a 5 : 3 : 2   **b** £150

   c **i** $\frac{3}{10}$ **ii** $\frac{1}{5}$

   d **i** 5 : 4 : 3   **ii** $\frac{1}{3}$ **iii** $\frac{1}{4}$

7 a 27 : 140   **b** 175 : 128   **c** 3 : 2

   d 7 : 1 : 5   **e** 572 : 103   **f** 5 : 8 : 100

8 a Sprint   3 : 80 : 20
     Olympic   3 : 80 : 20
     Half Ironman   19 : 900 : 211
     Ironman   19 : 901 : 211

   b **i** $\frac{3}{103}$ **ii** $\frac{80}{103}$ **iii** $\frac{10}{103}$

9 a £52 and £200   **b** 357 m and 291 m

   c 1054 km, 816 km, 170 km

   d 315 kg, 161 kg, 112 kg

10

Amount of mortar	Water (litres)	Cement (kg)	Sand (kg)
1.2 kg	0.2	0.4	0.6
3 kg	0.5	1.0	1.5
3.9 kg	0.65	1.3	1.95

11

Size	Blue	Green	Yellow
1 litre	625 ml	350 ml	25 ml
1.5 litre	937.5 ml	525 ml	37.5 ml
2.5 litre	1562.5 ml	875 ml	62.5 ml

12 a **i** 13.5 cm   **ii** 17.1 cm
     iii 23.46 cm   **iv** 24.92 cm

   b **i** 56 cm   **ii** 33.6 cm
     iii 46.93 cm   **iv** 62.58 cm

13 a 3.5 : 1   **b** 1 : 2.1   **c** 1.49 : 1

14 a 1.8 : 1   **b** 2.75 : 1   **c** 1 : 1.94   **d** 1 : 2.09

15 a **i** 1.67 : 1 **ii** 1.5 : 1   **iii** 1.6 : 1
     iv 1.33 : 1 **v** 1.85 : 1   **vi** 2.4 : 1

   b cinema widescreen

16

Front cog teeth	53	53	53	53	53
Gear	1	2	3	4	5
Rear cog teeth	32	25	19	14	11
Ratio of front teeth to rear teeth	53 : 32	53 : 25	53 : 19	53 : 14	53 : 11
Unit ratio	1.66 : 1	2.12 : 1	2.79 : 1	3.79 : 1	4.82 : 1
Number of rear wheel turns per turn of the pedals	1.66	2.12	2.79	3.79	4.82

Challenge

Students' own answers, e.g. 0.6 : 40, 0.3 : 20, 0.03 : 2

6 Check up

1 a 4.0531 > 4.0501   **b** 0.6091 < 0.6901
   c 32.49 > 32.3011

2 4.3 million   **c** 85.7 million

3 5.0982, 5.90113, 5.9281, 5.9408

4 0.59, 0.5691, −0.5, −0.563, −0.57

5 a **i** 7.134   **ii** 7.13
   b **i** 108.450 **ii** 108

6 a 453.6   **b** 4.536

7 a 70.8   **b** 0.37   **c** 0.41
   d 0.622   **e** 0.032

8 4.03 × 10

9 a 7340   **b** 17400   **c** 25300

10 a 80   **b** 6   **c** 0.7
   d 60

11 57.33

12 £64

13 7.54626

14 a 5 : 4   **b** 5 : 6

15 a 2.6 kg and 3.9 kg
   b 82 litres, 164 litres and 205 litres
   c £800 and £200

16 a 1 : 5 : 2   **b** $\frac{1}{4}$

17 a 4.5 : 1   **b** 1 : 1.9

Challenge

1 a 240 balls   **b** 1202 balls

2 1 ÷ 0.7 = 1.428571
   2 ÷ 0.7 = 2.857143
   3 ÷ 0.7 = 4.285714
   4 ÷ 0.7 = 5.714286
   The digits appear in the same order in the answers.
   1 ÷ 1.4 = 0.714286
   2 ÷ 1.4 = 1.428571
   A similar pattern emerges.

6 Strengthen: Ordering and rounding

1 a

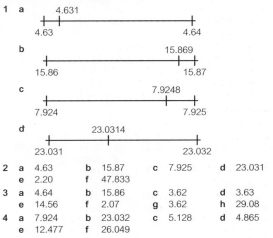

b

c

d

2 a 4.63   **b** 15.87   **c** 7.925   **d** 23.031
   e 2.20   **f** 47.833

3 a 4.64   **b** 15.86   **c** 3.62   **d** 3.63
   e 14.56   **f** 2.07   **g** 3.62   **h** 29.08

4 a 7.924   **b** 23.032   **c** 5.128   **d** 4.865
   e 12.477   **f** 26.049

5   **b**   8 million   **c**   12 million
    e   7.4 million   **f**   15.7 million

6   Downton Abbey   9.6 million
    By Any Means   3.5 million
    Countryfile   6.3 million
    The Crane Gang   0.9 million
    X Factor   9.5 million

7   **a**   ⑤6.882; value is 50 or 5 tens
    b   0.00④56; value is 4 thousandths
    c   ⑥73 500; value is 600 000 or 6 hundred thousands
    d   0.⑧834; value is 8 tenths

8   **a**   500   **b**   400   **c**   3000   **d**   200 000
    e   0.03   **f**   0.0005

9   **a**   5⑥8, 570   **b**   6③349, 63 000
    c   0.6⑤28, 0.65   **d**   0.004⑦81, 0.0048

10   **a**   70⑧4, 7080   **b**   47⑧901, 479 000
    c   0.73⑧19, 0.738   **d**   0.016③7, 0.0164

11   **a**   3.647   **b**   4.59   **c**   0.0618   **d**   0.003

12   7.2041, 7.2049, 7.3, 7.6011, 7.605

13   **a**   5.1   **b**   4.9   **c**   12.5   **d**   26.0

6 Strengthen: Decimal calculations

1   Centre **157**: 15.7, 15.7 (÷10, ×10) → 1570, 1570; ×0.1, ÷0.1, ÷100, ×100, ×0.01, ÷0.01; 1.57, 1.57 → 15 700, 15 700

2   **a**   Centre **57**: 5.7, 5.7 → 570, 570; 0.57, 0.57 → 5 700, 5 700
    b   Centre **101**: 10.1, 10.1 → 1010, 1010; 1.01, 1.01 → 10 100, 10 100
    c   Centre **45.2**: 4.52, 4.52 → 452, 452; 0.452, 0.452 → 4520, 4520
    d   Centre **2.8**: 0.28, 0.28 → 28, 28; 0.028, 0.028 → 280, 280

3   **a**   0.906   **b**   0.473   **c**   0.643   **d**   1.387

4   **a**   0.0342   **b**   0.0114   **c**   0.0736
    d   0.06214   **e**   0.57972   **f**   0.6103

5   **a**   0.528   **b**   0.975   **c**   75.1
    d   98   **e**   0.0043   **f**   256.5

6   **a**   936   **b**   13416   **c**   44616
    d   2008   **e**   9538   **f**   59738

7   **a** $3.12 \times 4.3 \approx 3 \times 4 = 12$
    b $25.1 \times 2.38 \approx 30 \times 2 = 60$

8   **a**   20.746   **b**   13.416   **c**   5.9738
    d   29.442   **e**   5.499

9   **a**   50   **b**   4   **c**   4   **d**   60

10   **a**   7   **b**   80   **c**   8   **d**   20

11   **a**   16.7   **b**   64.5   **c**   20.8

12   £41.98

6 Strengthen: Ratio and proportion with decimals

1   5.1 m and 3.4 m

2   92 cm, 69 cm and 23 cm

3   receptionists £76.80, porters £153.60, cleaners £192

4   **a**   13 : 6   **b**   17 : 6   **c**   12 : 5
    d   9 : 11   **e**   4 : 5   **f**   2 : 7

5   **a**   3 : 1   **b**   2 : 1   **c**   1.5 : 1   **d**   1.2 : 1

6   **a**   1 : 1.25   **b**   1 : 3.5   **c**   1.6 : 1   **d**   1.75 : 1

7   **a**   8.5 g   **b** $\frac{10}{17}$ **c** $\frac{2}{17}$ **d** $\frac{5}{17}$

Challenge

a   9 : 7 or 1.285... : 1

b   medium picture 5.14 cm, large picture 10.5 cm

c   15.75 cm², 20.57 cm² (or 20.56 cm² if rounded length used to calculate area), 141.75 cm²

d   9 times as big

6 Extend

1   **a**   **i**   72.17 minutes
       ii   72 minutes
       iii   1 hour 12 minutes and 10 seconds
    b   **i**   1 hour 12 minutes and 10 seconds; this answer is the exact value.
       ii   72 minutes; there is a difference of 10 seconds between this and the exact answer.

2   **a**   £47.40   **b**   No (£15.35)
    c   £4.74   **d**   £2.31   **e**   77p

3   **a**   increased steadily
    b   64 million
    c   2014 and 2015

4   **a**   any balance lower than −72.31
    b   any balance greater than −5.82 and lower than 0

5   **a**   0.6 g   **b**   1.8 g

6   **a**   21   **b**   21   **c**   85   **d**   85
    e   ÷5 is equivalent to ×0.2
       ÷0.2 is equivalent to ×5
       ÷2 is equivalent to ×0.5
       ÷4 is equivalent to ×0.25

7   **a**   100 m²   **b**   330 g

8   **a**   3880.8 cm³   **b**   1 : 8

9   **a**   0.625 miles   **b**   1.6 km

10   **a**   217   **b**   200   **c**   1908
    d   7023   **e**   7623   **f**   3050

11   7.13 m

12   **a**   6th is the fastest gear because it only takes 0.56 turns of the engine to turn the wheels once.
    b   280

Challenge

Students' own answers

6 Unit test

1   **a**   4.791   **b**   37.00   **c**   21.490

2   **a**   76 000   **b**   0.009   **c**   45.7

3   45.275, 45.33, 45.8, 66.0981, 66.39, 66.5

4   −9.9, −9.78, −9.57, −9.53, −9.511, −9.31, −9.3

5   **a**   0.57   **b**   0.92

6   **a**   360   **b**   41 900   **c**   8
    d   600   **e**   42   **f**   2.1

7   **a**   1.6014   **b**   16.014   **c**   1.6014   **d**   0.160 14

8   30 m

9   **a**   1 : 5   **b**   25 : 16

10   **a**   6.5 : 1   **b**   1 : 2.5

11   40 ml and 104 ml

12 800 ml, 640 ml and 60 ml

13 a 7 : 7 : 10 **b** $\frac{5}{12}$

14 £72 656

15 a 363.006 **b** 45.9

16 160.2 cm

Challenge

a Students' own answers, e.g.

$0.12 = 0.3 \times 0.4$
$0.86 = 6.2 \times 0.3 + 0.4 - 1.4$
$12.5 = 9.9 + 3.6 + 0.4 - 1.4$
$5.04 = 1.4 \times 3.6$
$0.7 = 5.7 - 3.6 - 1.4$
$9 = 5.7 + 3.6 - 0.3$
$11.3 = 9.9 + 1.4$
$6.3 = 6.2 + 0.4 - 0.3$
$0.1 = 0.4 - 0.3$
$51.3 = 5.7 \times 3.6 \div 0.4$
$2.97 = 9.9 \times 0.3$
$10.7 = 1.4 + 3.6 + 5.7$

b Students' own answers, e.g.

$17\,633.2464 = 1.4 \times 9.9 \times 3.6 \times 6.2 \times 5.7 \div (0.4 - 0.3)$
$-17\,633.2464 = 1.4 \times 9.9 \times 3.6 \times 6.2 \times 5.7 \div (0.3 - 0.4)$
$0.000\,0567... = (0.4 - 0.3) \div 1.4 \div 9.9 \div 3.6 \div 6.2 \div 5.7$

UNIT 7 Lines and angles

7.1 Quadrilaterals

1 a 360° **b** 180°

2 $AB = AD$, $BC = CD$

3

Quadrilateral	Square	Rectangle	Parallelogram	Rhombus	Kite	Trapezium	Isosceles trapezium
Number of lines of symmetry	4	2	0	2	1	0	1
Order of rotational symmetry	4	2	2	2	1	1	1

4 a square, rhombus
  b square, rectangle
  c kite, rectangle, parallelogram
  d trapezium
  e square, rhombus, rectangle, parallelogram
  f trapezium

5 a parallelogram
  b isosceles trapezium
  c kite
  d rectangle

6 Yes; it has one pair of parallel sides.

7 a (4, 6) **b** (6, –2) **c** (–4, 1)

8 a (–1, 0)
  b, c Any two of (–2, 0), (–1, 0), (0, 0), (1, 0), (2, 0), (3, 0)

9 $x = 130°$, $y = z = 50°$

10 $a = 110°$, $b = c = 70°$

11 $d = 100°$, $a = 110°$

12 a **i** Length AD is equal to length CD.
      ii Length AB is equal to length BC.
      iii $\angle BAD = \angle BCD$
      iv $ABCD$ has 1 line of symmetry and rotational symmetry of order 1.
  b **i** 40° **ii** 105° **iii** 150°

Challenge

a $c = 40°$ (opposite angles of a rhombus are equal)
  $a = b = 140°$ (angles in a quadrilateral add to 360° and opposite angles of a rhombus are equal)
  $f = 110°$ (opposite angles of a parallelogram are equal)
  $d = e = 70°$ (angles in a quadrilateral add to 360° and opposite angles of a parallelogram are equal)

b

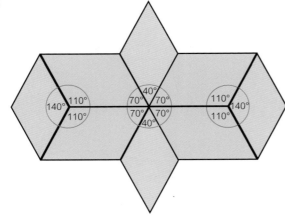

7.2 Alternate angles and proof

1 a 180° **b** 180°

2 a $y = 50°$
  b $s = 55°$, $t = 55°$, $u = 125°$
  c $x = 96°$
  d $a = 50°$, $b = 130°$

3 a $a = 60°$, $b = 120°$, $c = 120°$, $d = 60°$
  b a and d, b and c

4 u and y, x and v

5 a $a = 50°$ (alternate angles)
  b $c = 120°$ (alternate angles)
    $b = 60°$ (angles on a straight line)

6 a $a = 80°$ (alternate angles)
  b $b = 112°$ (alternate angles)
    $c = 68°$ (angles on a straight line)
  c $d = 72°$ (alternate angles)
  d $e = 115°$ (alternate angles)
    $f = 65°$ (angles on a straight line)
    $g = 65°$ (vertically opposite angles or angles on a straight line)

7 a Angle r and angle p are alternate angles.
  b Angle t and angle q are alternate angles.
  c Angle t is the same size as angle q because they are alternate angles.
  d Angle r is the same size as angle p because they are alternate angles.

8 a $e = 40°$ (alternate angles)
    $f = 50°$ (alternate angles)
  b $x = 38°$ (alternate angles)
    $y = 65°$ (alternate angles)
    $z = 77°$ (angles in a triangle/on a straight line)
  c $k = 60°$ (alternate angles)
    $l = 90°$ (angles in a triangle add up to 180°)
    $m = 30°$ (angles on a straight line or alternate angles)

9 a Angle x is equal to angle a because they are alternate angles.
  b Angle y is equal to angle c because they are alternate angles.
  c $x + b + y = 180°$ because they lie on a straight line.
  d Since $x = a$ and $y = c$
    $x + b + y = a + b + c$
    so $a + b + c = 180°$
  e This proves that the angles in a triangle add up to 180°.

10 $x + y + z = 180°$ because the angles in a triangle add up to 180°.
  $a + b + c = 180°$ because the angles in a triangle add up to 180°.
  $x + y + z + a + b + c = 360°$
  This proves that the angles in a quadrilateral add up to 360°.

Challenge

1 i a 130° **b** 120°
   ii a 50° **b** 60°
   iii a 130° **b** 120°

2 For each triangle, the answers are the same.

3 Yes; students' own explanations, e.g.
  $b = 180° - a$ (angles on a straight line)
  and $180° - a$ = sum of other two angles in the triangle
  so b = sum of other two angles

4 Students' own triangles

5 $b = c + d$

7.3 Angles in parallel lines

1 Alternate angles: $t = w$, $u = v$
  Vertically opposite angles: $r = u$, $s = t$, $v = y$, $w = x$

2 a $x = 25°$, $y = 155°$, $z = 155°$
  b $a = 72°$
  c $b = 105°$, $c = 105°$

3 a $x = 45°$, $y = 45°$, $z = 135°$
  b $a = 95°$, $b = 125°$
  c $c = 62°$, $d = 62°$, $e = 118°$, $f = 118°$

4 a $a = 105°$, $b = 75°$, $c = 105°$
  b $a = c$
  c a and b or b and c

5 **a** $a = 115°$ (corresponding angles)
  b $b = 95°$ (corresponding angles)
    $c = 85°$ (angles on a straight line)
  c $x = 95°$ (corresponding angles)
  d $d = 85°$ (corresponding angles)
    $e = 85°$ (vertically opposite angles)
  e $y = 60°$ (corresponding angles)
    $x = 60°$ (angles on a straight line)
  f $f = 112°$ (alternate angles)
    $g = 112°$ (corresponding angles)
    $h = 68°$ (angles on a straight line)
    $i = 112°$ (vertically opposite angles)
6 **a** $a = 110°$ **b** $b = 80°$ **c** $c = 105°$ **d** $d = 50°$
7 **a** $w = 42°$ (alternate angles)
    $x = 42°$ (vertically opposite angles)
    $y = 75°$ (corresponding angles)
  b $a = 132°$ (angles on a straight line)
    $b = 48°$ (corresponding angles)
    $c = 120°$ (corresponding angles)
    $d = 60°$ (angles on a straight line)
  c $c = 65°$ (corresponding angles)
    $d = 131°$ (alternate angles)
8 $c = 52°$ (alternate angles)
  $d = 52°$ (vertically opposite angles)
9 Angles 125° and 120° would be the same if the lines were parallel (or angles 60° and 55° would be the same).
10 **a** $x = 120°$ **b** $y = 60°$
11 $z = 270°$

Challenge

a Any two pairs of alternate angles, e.g. c and i; f and l
b Any two pairs of corresponding angles, e.g. a and m; b and n
c Any two pairs of angles that sum to 180°, e.g. d and e; d and i
d Any two sets of three angles that sum to 180°, e.g. a, b and c; b, c and h
e Any two sets of four angles that sum to 360°, e.g. k, l, p and q; d, e, i and j
f Any two sets of six angles that sum to 360°, e.g. a, b, c, f, g and h; m, n, o, r, s and t

7.4 Exterior and interior angles

1 All the side lengths are equal, and all the angles are the same size.
2 **a** 5 sides **b** 6 sides **c** 7 sides **d** 8 sides
  e 9 sides **f** 10 sides
3 **a** $y = 64°$, $z = 116°$
  b $d = 20°$, $e = 35°$, $f = 145°$
4 **a** $a = 62°$, $b = 68°$, $c = 79°$, $d = 79°$, $e = 72°$
  b 360°
  c The sum of the exterior angles is the same as the sum of the angles around a point.
5 **a** **i** $a = b = c = d = 90°$
      sum = 360°
    ii $e = 75°$, $f = 45°$, $g = 113°$, $h = 40°$, $i = 87°$
      sum = 360°
    iii $j = 60°$, $k = 85°$, $l = 53°$, $m = 38°$, $n = 109°$, $p = 15°$
      sum = 360°
    iv $q = 100°$, $r = s = 130°$
      sum = 360°
  b The sum is always the same.
6 **a** $v = 65°$ **b** $w = 118°$
7 **a** All the exterior angles are the same size.
  b Divide 360° (the sum of the exterior angles) by the number of sides.
  c $x = 72°$, $w = 60°$
  d $y = 108°$, $t = 120°$
8 **a** **i** 120° **ii** 60°
  b **i** 36° **ii** 144°
  c **i** 22.5° **ii** 157.5°
9 **a** Students' own diagrams
  b A pentagon divides into 3 triangles.
    The sum of the interior angles in a pentagon = 3 × 180° = 540°
  c 720°

d

Shape	triangle	quadrilateral	pentagon	hexagon
Number of sides	3	4	5	6
Number of triangles	1	2	3	4
Sum of interior angles	180°	360°	540°	720°

e subtract 2 **f** subtract 2 from the number of sides and multiply the answer by 180
10 **a** **i** 360° **ii** $x = 163°$
  b **i** 540° **ii** $y = 160°$
  c **i** 720° **ii** $z = 129°$
11 **a** 900°
  b 128.6° (1 d.p.)

Challenge

a $x = 90°$ (interior angle of a square)
    $- 60°$ (interior angle of an equilateral triangle)
  $= 30°$
b $y = 108°$ (interior angle of a regular pentagon)
    $- 90°$ (interior angle of a square)
  $= 18°$
c $z = 120°$ (interior angle of a regular hexagon)
    $- 108°$ (interior angle of a regular pentagon)
  $= 12°$

7.5 Solving geometric problems

1 **a** $a = b = 50°$ **b** $p = 72°$ **c** $m = 60°$
2 **a** $x = 30$ **b** $x = 50$
3 **a** $x = 63°$ **b** $y = 40°$ **c** $z = 45°$
4 **a** 135° **b** 50° **c** 102°
5 $\angle ADC = 112°$ (symmetry of kite)
  $112 + 112 + 36 + \angle BAD = 360°$ (angles in a quadrilateral)
  $\angle BAD = 100°$
  $\angle ABX = \angle ADX = y$ (ABD is isosceles triangle)
  $y + y + 100 = 180°$ (angles in a triangle)
  $y = 40°$
6 $\angle EBD = 90°$
  Students' own reasoning, e.g.
  $\angle ABE = 22°$ (angles in a triangle)
  $\angle DBC = 38°$ (angles in a triangle)
  $\angle EBD = 90 - 22 - 38 = 30°$ (90° in a right angle)
7 **a** $8x + 140 = 180$
    $x = 5°$
    Check: 8 × 5 = 40, 40 + 140 = 180
  b $5x + 90 = 180$
    $x = 18°$
    Check: 2 × 18 + 3 × 18 + 90 = 180
  c $3x + 21 = 180$
    $x = 53°$
    Check: 53 + 7 = 60, 3 × 60 = 180
  d $5x = 180$
    $x = 36°$
    Check: 2 × 36 + 2 × 36 + 36 = 180
  e Yes; $x + 7 = 60$
8 **a** $2x + 20 + x - 5 + x + 75 + 2x = 360$
  b $6x + 90 = 360$
  c $x = 45°$
  d 40°, 90°, 110°, 120°
9 $n = 360 ÷ 24 = 15$; 15 sides
10 **a, b**

  c $x = 45$
    $\angle ADC = \angle BCD = 45°$, $\angle BAD = \angle ABC = 135°$

Challenge

$a = 60°$ (opposite angles in a parallelogram)
$b = 75°$ (alternate angles)
$c = 105°$ (angles on a straight line)
$d = 120°$ (angles in a quadrilateral)

7 Check up

1 a $a = 55°$ (angles in a triangle)
$b = 125°$ (angles on a straight line)
b $c = 95°$ (angles on a straight line)
$d = 95°$ (angles in a quadrilateral)
c $e = 115°$ (opposite angles in a parallelogram are equal)
$f = 65°$ (angles in a quadrilateral)
d $g = 132°$ (angles in a quadrilateral)
e $h = 66°$ (angles in a quadrilateral)

2 a $2x + 3x + 4x = 180$ or $9x = 180$
b $x = 20°$
c $40°, 60°, 80°$

3 a $3x + x + 5 + 95 = 180$ or $4x + 100 = 180$
b $x = 20°$
c $25°, 60°, 95°$

4 $\angle DEA = 180 - 90 - 32 = 58°$ (angles in a triangle)
$\angle CEB = 180 - 86 - 58 = 36°$ (angles on a straight line)
$\angle BCE = 180 - 90 - 36 = 54°$ (angles in a triangle)

5 $a = 110°$ (angles in a isosceles triangle)
$b = 70°$ (angles on a straight line)
$c = 110°$ (angles in a quadrilateral)

6 a $x = 70°$ (alternate angles)
b $x = 125°$ (corresponding angles and angles on a straight line)
c $x = 142°$ (corresponding angles)
d $x = 95°$ (corresponding angles and angles on a straight line)

7 a $p = 82°$ (corresponding angles)
$q = 82°$ (vertically opposite angles)
b $r = 78°$ (alternate angles)
$s = 78°$ (vertically opposite angles)
c $a = 40°$ (alternate angles)
$b = 40°$ (vertically opposite angles)
$c = 75°$ (corresponding angles)
d $x = 60°$ (angles on a straight line)
$y = 60°$ (alternate angles)
$z = 125°$ (corresponding angles and angles on a straight line)
e $a = 110°$ (corresponding angles)
$b = 110°$ (vertically opposite angles)
$c = 30°$ (angles on a straight line)
$d = 150°$ (alternate angles)

8 $540°$

9 a $720°$ **b** $135°$

10 $x = 60°, y = 120°$

Challenge

Any three of:
exterior angle 80°, interior opposite angles 40° and 40°
exterior angle 100°, interior opposite angles 40° and 60°
exterior angle 120°, interior opposite angles 40° and 80°
exterior angle 120°, interior opposite angles 60° and 60°
exterior angle 140°, interior opposite angles 40° and 100°
exterior angle 140°, interior opposite angles 60° and 80°
exterior angle 140°, interior opposite angles 70° and 70°

7 Strengthen: Solving geometric problems

1 The angles in any quadrilateral add up to 360°.

2 a

i 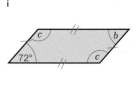 ii 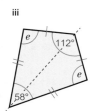 iii

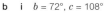

b i $b = 72°, c = 108°$
ii $d = 55°$
iii $e = 95°$

3

$q = 180 - 90 - 67 = 23°$

4 a LM and MN
b Isosceles and right-angled
c Angles p and r are the same size.
Their sum is $180 - 90 = 90°$
d $p = 45°$

5 a $a = 25°$ (angles on a straight line)
$b = 65°$ (angles in a triangle)
b $c = 40°$ (angles in a triangle)
$d = 140°$ (angles on a straight line)
c $e = 93°$ (angles in a quadrilateral)
$f = 83°$ (angles on a straight line)

6 $\angle BCA = 48°$ (angles in a triangle)
$\angle ECD = 42°$ (angles in a right angle)
$\angle CDE = 37°$ (angles in a right angle)
$\angle CED = 180 - 42 - 37 = 101°$ (angles in a triangle)

7 a, b

c $z + 20° + 20° + 90° = 180°$
d $z = 50°$

8 a $a + 140 = 180$
$a = 40°$
b $2b + 140 = 180$
$b = 20°$
c $4c + 100 = 180$
$c = 20°$
d $2d + 100 = 180$
$d = 40°$
e $3e + 120 = 180$
$e = 20°$
f $2f + 90 = 180$
$f = 45°$

9 a $6x + 60 = 180$ **b** $15x = 360$
$x = 20°$ $x = 24°$

10 a $2x + x - 10 + 135 + x + 15 = 360$
b $4x + 140 = 360$
c $x = 55°$
d $45°, 70°, 110°, 135°$

7 Strengthen: Parallel lines

1 a a and b are alternate angles.
b c and d are corresponding angles.

2 a a and b are vertically opposite angles.
b a and d are alternate angles.
c a and c are corresponding angles.
d b and d are corresponding angles.
e c and d are vertically opposite angles.

3 a $x = 118°$ (alternate angles)
b $x = 138°$ (corresponding angles)
c $x = 78°$ (corresponding angles)
d $x = 80°$ (alternate angles)
e $x = 85°$ (vertically opposite angles)
$y = 85°$ (corresponding angles)
f $x = 63°$ (angles on a straight line)
$y = 63°$ (alternate angles)
$z = 117°$ (angles on a straight line or corresponding angles)

4 a $c = 57°$ (alternate angles)
$d = 45°$ (alternate angles)
b $x = 45°$ (angles on a straight line)
$y = 45°$ (corresponding angles)
$z = 45°$ (vertically opposite angles)

7 Strengthen: Interior and exterior angles

1 a 360°

b The sum of the interior angles of a quadrilateral is $2 \times 180° = 360°$

c

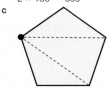

d The sum of the interior angles of a pentagon is $3 \times 180° = 540°$

e

f The sum of the interior angles of a hexagon is $4 \times 180° = 720°$

2 a **i** and **ii**   e.g.

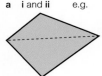

   iii   360°   **iv** $x = 86°$

b **i** and **ii**   e.g.

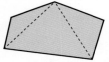

   iii   540°   **iv** $x = 119°$

c **i** and **ii**   e.g.

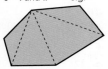

   iii   720°   **iv** $x = 85°$

3 $x = 102°$

4 c They add up to 360°

5 a 360°   **b** 5   **c** $x = 72°$ **d** $y = 108°$
   e 540°

6 a 60°
   b 120°
   c 720°

Challenge

a Sometimes true; e.g. a triangle could have the angles 60°, 60°, 60° (when it would be true) or 100°, 40° and 40° (when it would be untrue).

b Never true; if two angles are greater than 90° then the total is already greater than 180°, and the sum of the three angles in a triangle is 180°.

c Never true; if all four angles are less than 90°, then the total of the four angles is less than 360°, but the sum of the four angles in a quadrilateral is 360°.

7 Extend

1 $a = 65°$ (angles in quadrilateral = 360°, so
   $2a = 360 - 90 - 90 - 50 = 130°$)
   $b = 25°$ (angles in a triangle = 180°, so $b = 180 - 90 - 65$)
   $c = 65°$ ($b + c = 90°$)

2 20°

3 $\angle BAC = 30°$, $\angle ABC = 60°$, $\angle BCA = 90°$

---

4 a 540°
   b $y = 30°$
   c 45°, 120°, 95°, 30°, 250°

5 a, b

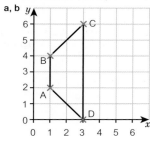

   c $\angle ADC = 45°$, $\angle DAB = 135°$

6 $a + b = 180°$ (angles on a straight line)
   $b = \frac{7}{12} \times 180° = 105°$
   $c = b = 105°$ (alternate angles)

7 a $x = 15°$ **b** $x = 50°$ **c** $x = 45°$

8 a $a = 42°$ **b** $b = 138°$ **c** $c = 42°$ **d** $d = 96°$

9 a $x = 35°$ **b** $y = 55°$ **c** $z = 110°$

10 a 30°   **b** 40°

11 a **i** 20 sides   **ii** 162°
   b 30 sides

12 $a = 80°$, $b = 100°$, $c = 40°$, $d = 80°$

Challenge

b About 53°

c Yes, angles stay the same in an enlargement.

d Students' own diagrams

e For each different ratio, the angle is always the same.

7 Unit test

1 a $y = 22°$ (angles on a straight line; angles in a triangle)
   b $y = 30°$ (angles on a straight line; angles in a triangle)

2 a $a = 35°$ (angles on a straight line)
      $b = 55°$ (angles in a triangle)
   b $a = 40°$ (angles on a straight line)
      $b = 75°$ (angles on a straight line)
      $c = 150°$ (angles in a quadrilateral)

3 a $a = 120°$ (opposite angles in a parallelogram)
      $b = 60°$ (angles in a quadrilateral)
   b $c = 75°$ (opposite angles in a parallelogram)
      $d = 105°$ (angles in a quadrilateral)
   c $e = 50°$ (isosceles trapezium has two pairs of equal angles)

4 $x = 15°$

5 a $x = 30°$ **b** 55°, 75°, 90°, 140°

6 $w = 140°$

7 a **i** The angles in a triangle add up to 180°.
      ii The angles in a quadrilateral add up to 360°.
      iii The angles in a pentagon add up to 540°.
      iv The angles in a hexagon add up to 720°.
   b $m = 60°$

8 a $a = 85°$ (alternate angles)
   b $b = 76°$ (corresponding angles)
   c $c = 100°$ (angles on a straight line and corresponding angles)
   d $d = 40°$ (vertically opposite angles)
      $e = 80°$ (corresponding angles)
      $f = 60°$ (angles in a triangle)

9 $\angle CDB = 90 - 68 = 22°$ (angles in a right angle)
   $\angle DBC = 180 - 22 - 36 = 122°$ (angles in a triangle)

10 a $x = 45°$ **b** $y = 135°$

11 a **i** 10 sides   **ii** 144°
   b 24 sides

Challenge

a Yes

b Yes

c Equilateral triangle, square, regular hexagon

d Regular octagons tessellate with squares.
   Regular dodecagons tessellate with equilateral triangles.

UNIT 8 Calculating with fractions

8.1 Ordering fractions

1 a $\frac{9}{12}$ b $\frac{13}{20}$ c $\frac{1}{2}$

   d $\frac{1}{5}$ e $\frac{1}{9}$

2 a $\frac{1}{2}=\frac{4}{8}$ b $\frac{1}{2}=\frac{5}{10}$ c $\frac{5}{6}=\frac{10}{12}$

   d $\frac{3}{4}=\frac{15}{20}$ e $\frac{1}{2}=\frac{3}{6}$ f $\frac{2}{5}=\frac{8}{20}$

3 a 12   b 20   c 10
   d 16   e 18   f 30

4 $\frac{3}{4},\frac{5}{6},\frac{4}{7},\frac{5}{8}$

5 More than $\frac{1}{2}$: $\frac{7}{10},\frac{5}{9},\frac{11}{20},\frac{6}{11}$

   Less than $\frac{1}{2}$: $\frac{2}{7},\frac{2}{5},\frac{9}{20},\frac{4}{11}$

6 Any fraction with denominator 17 and numerator 9 or greater

7 Any fraction with numerator 5 and denominator 11 or greater

8 Any denominator 27 or greater, so an infinite number of fractions

9 a $\frac{1}{4},\frac{1}{2},\frac{5}{8}$ b $\frac{2}{5},\frac{1}{2},\frac{7}{9}$

   c $-\frac{5}{8},-\frac{1}{2},-\frac{1}{4}$ d $-\frac{7}{9},-\frac{1}{2},-\frac{2}{5}$

10 a i $\frac{1}{6}=\frac{2}{12}$ ii $\frac{3}{4}=\frac{9}{12}$

      iii $\frac{2}{3}=\frac{8}{12}$

   b $\frac{1}{6},\frac{2}{3},\frac{3}{4}$

11 a i $\frac{30}{40}$ ii $\frac{28}{40}$

      iii $\frac{25}{40}$ iv $\frac{22}{40}$

   b $\frac{3}{4},\frac{7}{10},\frac{5}{8},\frac{11}{20}$

12 a $\frac{1}{6},\frac{2}{3},\frac{7}{9}$ b $\frac{13}{20},\frac{3}{4},\frac{4}{5}$

   c $\frac{1}{4},\frac{3}{8},\frac{9}{16}$ d $\frac{3}{10},\frac{1}{3},\frac{2}{5}$

   e $\frac{2}{3},\frac{7}{10},\frac{11}{15},\frac{4}{5}$ f $\frac{7}{12},\frac{5}{8},\frac{2}{3},\frac{5}{6}$

13 a $\frac{9}{14},\frac{1}{2},-\frac{5}{7},-\frac{3}{4},$

   b i Any fraction greater than $\frac{9}{14}$

      ii Any fraction less than $-\frac{3}{4}$

Challenge

$\frac{1}{2},\frac{2}{3},\frac{3}{4},\frac{4}{5},\frac{9}{10}$

8.2 Adding and subtracting fractions

1 a $\frac{4}{4}$ and $\frac{7}{7}$

   b $\frac{2}{5}$ and $\frac{4}{5}$, $\frac{6}{7}$ and $\frac{7}{7}$

2 a $\frac{1}{2}$ b $\frac{3}{4}$ c $\frac{2}{3}$ d $\frac{2}{5}$

3 a $3\frac{1}{2}$ b $1\frac{1}{9}$ c $4\frac{1}{25}$ d $2\frac{8}{9}$

   e $3\frac{3}{4}$

4 a $\frac{2}{8}$ and $\frac{1}{8}$ b $\frac{8}{10}$ and $\frac{7}{10}$

   c $\frac{1}{12}$ and $\frac{10}{12}$ d $\frac{3}{12}$ and $\frac{4}{12}$

5 a $\frac{3}{8}$ b $\frac{1}{2}$ c $\frac{11}{12}$ d $\frac{3}{4}$

   e $\frac{8}{15}$ f $\frac{1}{2}$ g 1   h $\frac{21}{25}$

6 a $1\frac{1}{9}$ b $1\frac{1}{3}$ c $1\frac{1}{2}$ d 2

7 a $\frac{1}{10}$ b $\frac{2}{5}$ c $\frac{1}{9}$ d $\frac{1}{6}$

8 a $\frac{5}{12}$ b Dom

9 a Kieran has made the mistake of adding the numerators together and the denominators together.

   b $1\frac{7}{12}$

10 a $\frac{5}{6}$ b $\frac{13}{15}$ c $\frac{9}{14}$ d $\frac{7}{12}$

   e $\frac{29}{30}$

11 a $\frac{1}{10}$ b $\frac{11}{40}$ c $\frac{31}{40}$

12 a $\frac{3}{4}$ b $\frac{2}{7}$ c $-\frac{2}{7}$ d 0

13 a $1\frac{7}{20}$ b $-1\frac{1}{10}$ c $7\frac{13}{28}$ d $8\frac{2}{5}$

   e Students' copy of their own calculator display

14 a $1\frac{1}{4}$ hours   b $\frac{11}{12}$ of an hour   c $2\frac{1}{6}$ hours

15 $\frac{1}{15}$

Challenge

1 a $\frac{2}{3}-\frac{1}{2}=\frac{1}{6}$ $\frac{3}{4}-\frac{2}{3}=\frac{1}{12}$

      $\frac{4}{5}-\frac{3}{4}=\frac{1}{20}$ $\frac{5}{6}-\frac{4}{5}=\frac{1}{30}$

   b $\frac{1}{9\times10}=\frac{1}{90}$

2 a $\frac{3}{4}-\frac{2}{4}=\frac{1}{4}$ $\frac{5}{6}-\frac{3}{4}=\frac{1}{12}$

      $\frac{6}{7}-\frac{4}{5}=\frac{2}{35}$

   b The answer is getting smaller; $\frac{2}{10\times8}=\frac{1}{40}$

8.3 Multiplying fractions

1 A and D, B and G, C and F, E and H

2 a 25 kg   b 75 kg   c 10 cm   d 40 cm

3 a $\frac{1}{3}$ b $\frac{2}{9}$ c $1\frac{3}{10}$ d $6\frac{1}{3}$

4 a 24   b 60   c 12   d 3

5 a 75   b 4   c 14   d 8

6 a yes (10)

   b $20\times\frac{3}{5}=20\times3\div5=60\div5=12$

      $20\times\frac{3}{5}=20\div5\times3=4\times3=12$

      The order does not matter.

7 a $3\frac{1}{3}$ m^2 b 5 cm^2 c $7\frac{1}{2}$ cm^2

8 a 4 m   b 2 m

9 18 litres

10 a $\frac{1}{4}$ b $\frac{1}{6}$ c $\frac{1}{12}$ d $\frac{3}{8}$

11 a $\frac{1}{2}$ b $\frac{1}{5}$ c $\frac{4}{15}$ d $\frac{9}{16}$

   e $\frac{9}{22}$ f $\frac{4}{21}$ g $\frac{7}{20}$ h $\frac{5}{16}$

12 a area = $\frac{1}{9}$ m^2, perimeter = $1\frac{1}{3}$ m

   b area = $\frac{9}{16}$ cm^2, perimeter = 3 cm

   c area = $\frac{1}{16}$ m^2, perimeter = 1 m

13 $\frac{1}{60}$

14 a $-\frac{1}{6}$ **b** $-\frac{5}{12}$ **c** $-\frac{3}{20}$ **d** $\frac{2}{7}$

15 a $\frac{5}{12} \times \frac{3}{10} = \frac{5 \times 3}{12 \times 10} = \frac{15}{120} = \frac{1}{8}$

   b Students' own answers and reasons

   c $\frac{1}{21}$

16 a $\frac{3}{4}$ **b** $\frac{1}{6}$ **c** $\frac{1}{2}$ **d** $\frac{1}{7}$

   e $\frac{1}{6}$ **f** $\frac{2}{7}$

17 $\frac{1}{3}$ litre

18 a $-\frac{7}{12}$ **b** $-\frac{1}{4}$ **c** $-\frac{8}{81}$ **d** $\frac{5}{27}$

Challenge

a $\frac{9}{11} \times \frac{2}{3} \times \frac{11}{20} = \frac{3}{10}$ **b** $\frac{9}{14} \times \frac{3}{18} \times \frac{7}{8} = \frac{3}{32}$

c $\frac{1}{3} \times \frac{5}{7} \times \frac{1}{2} = \frac{5}{42}$ **d** $\frac{1}{5} \times \frac{2}{9} \times \frac{1}{2} = \frac{1}{45}$

8.4 Dividing fractions

1 a 5   **b** 2   **c** 3   **d** 4

2 a $1\frac{1}{2}$ **b** $2\frac{1}{2}$ **c** $4\frac{1}{3}$ **d** $5\frac{3}{4}$

   e $22\frac{1}{2}$

3 a $\frac{1}{2}$ **b** $\frac{1}{6}$ **c** $\frac{6}{35}$ **d** $\frac{1}{2}$

   e $\frac{1}{6}$ **f** -2 **g** $\frac{2}{15}$ **h** $\frac{2}{15}$

4 a 1   **b** 1   **c** 1   **d** 1

   e Students' own answers, e.g.
     In each multiplication, one of the fractions is the same as the other one 'upside down'; all of the answers are 1.

5 Students' own answers, e.g. $\frac{7}{8} \times \frac{8}{7} = 1$

6 a $\frac{7}{2}$ **b** $\frac{5}{3}$ **c** $\frac{9}{8}$ **d** $\frac{3}{11}$

   e $\frac{7}{20}$

7 a $\frac{1}{4}$ **b** $\frac{1}{5}$ **c** $\frac{1}{7}$ **d** 10

   e 23   **f** 100

8 b $1 \div \frac{1}{4} = 4$ **c** $1 \div \frac{1}{3} = 3$

   d $3 \div \frac{1}{2} = 6$ **e** $2 \div \frac{1}{4} = 8$

9 a $3 \div \frac{1}{2} = 6 = 3 \times 2$ **b** $2 \div \frac{1}{4} = 8 = 2 \times 4$

   c $3 \div \frac{1}{5} = 15 = 3 \times 5$ **d** $4 \div \frac{1}{3} = 12 = 4 \times 3$

   e Students' own answers, e.g.
     To divide by a fraction, multiply by the reciprocal of the fraction.

10 a C, 2   **b** A, 2   **c** D, 6   **d** B, 3

   e yes

11 a 2   **b** 2   **c** 10   **d** 3

12 a $\frac{3}{5}$ **b** $\frac{8}{9}$ **c** $\frac{3}{5}$ **d** $\frac{14}{15}$

   e $\frac{2}{3}$ **f** $\frac{3}{4}$ **g** $\frac{4}{9}$ **h** $\frac{6}{7}$

13 a 9   **b** $3\frac{3}{4}$ **c** $5\frac{1}{3}$

   d 18   **e** 40   **f** 81

   g 30   **h** $22\frac{1}{2}$ **i** $17\frac{1}{2}$

14 12

15 6

16 a -50 **b** -45 **c** -36 **d** -50

   e $\frac{3}{8}$ **f** $-\frac{2}{3}$ **g** $-\frac{3}{4}$ **h** $-\frac{9}{10}$

17 a $4, 2, 1, \frac{1}{2}, \frac{1}{4}, \frac{1}{8}, \frac{1}{16}$

   b $\frac{1}{16}, \frac{1}{8}, \frac{1}{4}, \frac{1}{2}, 1, 2, 4$

   c Students' own answers, e.g.
     Each answer in part **a** is half of the previous answer.
     Each answer in part **b** is double the previous answer.

Challenge

a $\frac{5}{12}$ **b** 4   **c** $\frac{4}{11}$

d $1\frac{5}{7}$ or $\frac{12}{7}$ **e** $\frac{1}{4}$

f Students' own answers, e.g.
   If the second fraction is greater than 1, the answer will be smaller than the first fraction.

8.5 Calculating with mixed numbers

1 a 2 cm   **b** 0.5 cm

2 a 2   **b** $1\frac{3}{4}$ **c** 5   **d** $7\frac{1}{2}$

   e 3   **f** $1\frac{3}{7}$ **g** 6   **h** $1\frac{2}{3}$

3 a $\frac{7}{8}$ **b** $1\frac{1}{6}$ **c** $\frac{3}{20}$ **d** $7\frac{1}{2}$

   e $\frac{14}{27}$ **f** $\frac{2}{3}$ **g** $2\frac{2}{3}$ **h** $\frac{2}{33}$

4 a $5\frac{3}{4}$ **b** $6\frac{5}{6}$ **c** $7\frac{1}{2}$ **d** $8\frac{7}{15}$

   e $2\frac{43}{72}$ **f** $1\frac{1}{4}$ **g** $6\frac{1}{40}$

5 $6\frac{1}{4}$ hours or 6 hours 15 minutes

6 a $1\frac{1}{5}$ **b** $2\frac{1}{6}$ **c** $1\frac{1}{3}$ **d** $5\frac{1}{6}$

7 a $\frac{11}{2}$ **b** $\frac{55}{6}$ **c** $\frac{19}{8}$ **d** $\frac{43}{4}$

8 a $2\frac{3}{4}$ **b** $-\frac{1}{10}$ **c** $-2\frac{1}{2}$ **d** $-2\frac{2}{9}$

   e $3\frac{9}{10}$ **f** $\frac{11}{12}$ **g** $4\frac{1}{16}$ **h** $1\frac{2}{21}$

9 $9\frac{1}{21}$ miles

10 Students' own answers, e.g.

   a $7\frac{2}{3} + 6\frac{1}{9}$

   b $16\frac{2}{9} - 2\frac{2}{3}$

11 a $7\frac{1}{2}$ **b** $8\frac{1}{5}$ **c** 16   **d** $2\frac{1}{15}$

   e $1\frac{1}{35}$ **f** $6\frac{1}{4}$ **g** $5\frac{5}{12}$ **h** $7\frac{3}{7}$

12 $3\frac{2}{5}$ m

13 a $3\frac{1}{8}$ **b** $3\frac{2}{15}$ **c** $21\frac{1}{3}$ **d** $5\frac{5}{8}$

   e $4\frac{3}{8}$ **f** $5\frac{19}{25}$ **g** $2\frac{1}{5}$ **h** $1\frac{7}{13}$

14 $1\frac{3}{10}$ kg

15 $15\frac{5}{16}$ cm²

16 $\frac{5}{12}$ of a mile

17 104 cm

18 $\frac{7}{8}$ of a pint

19 25 seconds

20 a $8\frac{4}{9}$ m   **b** $7\frac{1}{3}$ m

21 a $24\frac{3}{5}$ **b** $3 \times 8\frac{1}{5}$

Students' own answers, e.g.

Group 1: $4\frac{2}{3} \times 1\frac{1}{5}$, $1\frac{1}{2} \times 8$, $1\frac{3}{7} \times 1\frac{1}{7}$

Group 2: $15\frac{1}{8} - 5\frac{1}{4}$, $6\frac{2}{5} + 20\frac{1}{2}$, $18\frac{3}{10} - 1\frac{4}{5}$

8 Check up

1   $\frac{2}{17}, \frac{1}{2}, \frac{7}{12}$

2   $\frac{7}{10}, \frac{18}{25}, \frac{4}{5}$

3   **a** $\frac{13}{16}$ **b** $\frac{1}{3}$ **c** $1\frac{1}{4}$ **d** $\frac{9}{10}$

   e $\frac{7}{24}$

4   $\frac{26}{63}$

5   **a** 5   **b** 21

6   **a** 12   **b** 25   **c** $8\frac{2}{5}$

7   **a** $\frac{1}{8}$ **b** $\frac{1}{2}$ **c** $-\frac{2}{11}$

8   **a** $\frac{1}{3}$ **b** 5   **c** $\frac{11}{2}$

9   **a** $\frac{1}{24}$ **b** $\frac{4}{27}$ **c** 10   **d** $2\frac{21}{52}$

   e $-\frac{1}{2}$ **f** $\frac{2}{7}$

10   **a** $2\frac{1}{5}$ m or $\frac{11}{5}$ m   **b** $\frac{6}{25}$ m²

11   $\frac{17}{5}$

12   **a** $3\frac{7}{10}$ **b** $8\frac{7}{12}$ **c** $6\frac{1}{4}$ **d** $\frac{13}{15}$

13   **a** $1\frac{2}{3}$ **b** $1\frac{1}{9}$ **c** 9   **d** 3

   e $16\frac{1}{2}$ **f** $1\frac{2}{5}$

14   $17\frac{1}{2}$

Challenge

1   Students' own answers, e.g. 20 and $\frac{1}{2}$

2   Students' own rectangles, e.g. $18\frac{1}{2}$ m by $\frac{1}{4}$ m, $9\frac{1}{4}$ m by $\frac{1}{2}$ m

8 Strengthen: Ordering fractions

1

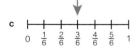

a   **b**

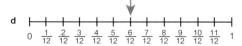

c

d

e

2   $\frac{3}{4}, \frac{5}{6}, \frac{7}{12}, \frac{11}{17}$

3   $\frac{5}{12}, \frac{7}{17}, \frac{3}{8}$

4   **a** $\frac{2}{5}, \frac{1}{2}, \frac{7}{12}$ **b** $\frac{5}{12}, \frac{1}{2}, \frac{4}{7}$

   c $\frac{6}{17}, \frac{1}{2}, \frac{6}{11}$ **d** $\frac{3}{8}, \frac{1}{2}, \frac{5}{8}$

   e $\frac{1}{8}, \frac{3}{8}, \frac{1}{2}, \frac{5}{6}$ **f** $\frac{1}{9}, \frac{4}{9}, \frac{1}{2}, \frac{5}{7}$

5   **a** 12   **b** $\frac{6}{12}, \frac{8}{12}, \frac{9}{12}$ **c** $\frac{3}{4}, \frac{2}{3}, \frac{1}{2}$

6   **a** 20   **b** $\frac{12}{20}, \frac{14}{20}, \frac{9}{20}$ **c** $\frac{7}{10}, \frac{3}{5}, \frac{9}{20}$

8 Strengthen: Calculating with fractions

1   **a** $\frac{3}{10}$ **b** $\frac{7}{10}$ **c** $\frac{9}{10}$

2   **a** $\frac{5}{9}$ **b** $\frac{7}{9}$ **c** $\frac{7}{9}$ **d** $\frac{8}{9}$

3   **a** $\frac{5}{9}$ **b** $\frac{2}{9}$ **c** $\frac{3}{10}$ **d** $\frac{1}{10}$

4   **a** $\frac{5}{15} + \frac{3}{15} = \frac{8}{15}$

   b $\frac{4}{12} + \frac{3}{12} = \frac{7}{12}$

   c LCM is 30; $\frac{9}{30} + \frac{20}{30} = \frac{29}{30}$

5   **a** $\frac{19}{24}$ **b** $\frac{19}{60}$ **c** $-\frac{4}{33}$

6   **a** Marie has made the mistake of adding the numerators together and the denominators together.

   b $\frac{3}{20}$

7   **a** $1\frac{2}{3}$ **b** $\frac{2}{7}$ **c** $2\frac{2}{5}$ **d** $1\frac{7}{11}$

   e $1\frac{3}{7}$ **f** $4\frac{1}{2}$ **g** 36

8   **a** $\frac{1 \times 1}{2 \times 2} = \frac{1}{4}$ **b** $\frac{2 \times 1}{3 \times 5} = \frac{2}{15}$

   c $\frac{9}{20}$ **d** $\frac{8}{21}$

9   **a** $\frac{1}{2}$ **b** $\frac{1}{2}$ **c** $\frac{1}{3}$ **d** 3

10   **a** $\frac{5 \times 3}{6 \times 10} = \frac{3 \times 5}{6 \times 10} = \frac{3}{6} \times \frac{5}{10} = \frac{1}{2} \times \frac{1}{2} = \frac{1}{4}$

   b $\frac{12 \times 11}{33 \times 4} = \frac{11 \times 12}{33 \times 4} = \frac{1}{3} \times \frac{3}{1} = 1$

   c $\frac{1}{9}$ **d** $\frac{4}{5}$ **e** $\frac{2}{7}$

11   **a** The reciprocal of $\frac{2}{5}$ is $\frac{5}{2}$

   b The reciprocal of $\frac{3}{5}$ is $\frac{5}{3}$

   c The reciprocal of $\frac{4}{5}$ is $\frac{5}{4}$

   d The reciprocal of $\frac{3}{4}$ is $\frac{4}{3}$

   e The reciprocal of $\frac{6}{7}$ is $\frac{7}{6}$

   f The reciprocal of $\frac{8}{7}$ is $\frac{7}{8}$

12   **a** $\frac{1}{2}$ **b** 4   **c** $\frac{1}{3}$ **d** $\frac{1}{6}$

   e $\frac{1}{11}$ **f** 5   **g** 7   **h** 12

13   **a** $\frac{2}{7} \times \frac{5}{3} = \frac{10}{21}$ **b** $\frac{1}{4} \times \frac{7}{6} = \frac{7}{24}$

   c $\frac{1}{6} \times \frac{5}{2} = \frac{5}{12}$ **d** $\frac{1}{3} \times \frac{7}{8} = \frac{7}{24}$

   e $\frac{1}{6} \times \frac{5}{3} = \frac{5}{18}$ **f** $\frac{2}{3} \times \frac{10}{7} = \frac{20}{21}$

14   **a** $\frac{2}{7} \times \frac{1}{4} = \frac{1}{14}$ **b** $\frac{1}{4} \times \frac{3}{1} = \frac{3}{4}$

   c $6 \times \frac{2}{1} = 12$ **d** $6 \times \frac{3}{2} = 9$

8 Strengthen: Calculating with mixed numbers

1 **a** 3   **b** 4   **c** 6   **d** 8
   e 5   **f** 10   **g** 8   **h** 16

2 **a** $\frac{5}{3}$ **b** $\frac{11}{4}$ **c** $\frac{6}{5}$ **d** $\frac{13}{5}$
   e $\frac{19}{8}$ **f** $\frac{11}{10}$ **g** $\frac{27}{10}$ **h** $\frac{93}{10}$

3 **a** 4   **b** $4\frac{3}{5}$ **c** 8

4 **a** $3\frac{5}{6}$ **b** $6\frac{9}{10}$ **c** $5\frac{7}{12}$ **d** $12\frac{19}{20}$

5 **a** $\frac{10}{2} - \frac{7}{2} = \frac{3}{2} = 1\frac{1}{2}$

   b $\frac{14}{3} - \frac{4}{3} = \frac{10}{3} = 3\frac{1}{3}$

   c $\frac{43}{4} - \frac{9}{4} = \frac{34}{4} = 8\frac{1}{2}$

   d $\frac{29}{5} - \frac{21}{10} = \frac{58}{10} - \frac{21}{10} = \frac{37}{10} = 3\frac{7}{10}$

   e $\frac{3}{2} - \frac{3}{4} = \frac{6}{4} - \frac{3}{4} = \frac{3}{4}$

   f $\frac{11}{4} - \frac{7}{6} = \frac{33}{12} - \frac{14}{12} = \frac{19}{12} = 1\frac{7}{12}$

6 **a** $\frac{4}{5} \times \frac{7}{3} = \frac{4 \times 7}{5 \times 3} = \frac{28}{15} = 1\frac{13}{15}$

   b $1\frac{1}{6}$ **c** $\frac{1}{6}$ **d** $\frac{35}{54}$

   e $\frac{13}{11} \times \frac{19}{3} = \frac{13 \times 19}{11 \times 3} = \frac{247}{33} = 7\frac{16}{33}$

7 **a** $\frac{11}{2} \times \frac{2}{1} = \frac{11 \times 2}{2 \times 1} = 11$

   b $\frac{35 \times 5}{11 \times 4} = \frac{175}{44} = 3\frac{43}{44}$

   c $6\frac{1}{6}$ **d** 50   **e** $3\frac{25}{33}$

8 **a** C   **b** $7\frac{1}{3}$ cm

Challenge

1 $\frac{9}{20}$

2 father 2 m, brother 1 m 20 cm

8 Extend

1 Students' own answers, e.g. $\frac{2}{3}, \frac{1}{2}, \frac{5}{12}, \frac{2}{5}, \frac{3}{8}$

2 $\frac{1}{18}$

3 **a** 10 cakes cut into sevenths gives 70 pieces, which is not enough for 75 people.
   b 8   **c** 5

4 **a** $\frac{1}{4}$ **b** $\frac{1}{16}$ **c** $\frac{4}{9}$ **d** $\frac{4}{5}$
   e $\frac{1}{8}$ **f** $\frac{3}{4}$

5 **a** $3\frac{17}{24}$ (or 3.708)   **b** $8\frac{19}{32}$ (or 8.59375)
   c $-\frac{8}{21}$ (or −0.381)   **d** $11\frac{9}{100}$ (or 11.09)
   e $11\frac{3}{8}$ (or 11.375)   **f** $6\frac{39}{100}$ (or 6.39)

6 **a**

$1\frac{1}{3}$	3	$\frac{2}{3}$
1	$1\frac{2}{3}$	$2\frac{1}{3}$
$2\frac{2}{3}$	$\frac{1}{3}$	2

   b Students' own answers

7 **a** 14 : 1   **b** 22 : 3   **c** 21 : 26

8 **a** $\frac{29}{75}$ **b** 2

9 20

10 $11\frac{1}{6}$ m

11 Students' own answers, e.g.
   a $5\frac{4}{5}$ and $6\frac{3}{5}$
   b $5\frac{3}{5}$ and $6\frac{4}{5}$

12 **a** $15\frac{5}{8}$ **b** $62\frac{1}{2}$

8 Unit test

1 $\frac{4}{9}, \frac{1}{2}, \frac{11}{18}, \frac{3}{4}, \frac{5}{6}$

2 **a** $\frac{1}{2}$ **b** $\frac{7}{8}$ **c** $\frac{3}{10}$ **d** $\frac{21}{40}$

3 **a** $8\frac{3}{4}$ **b** $7\frac{11}{15}$ **c** $13\frac{1}{2}$ **d** $\frac{7}{8}$

4 **a** 7   **b** 12   **c** $\frac{3}{20}$ **d** $-\frac{1}{5}$
   e $\frac{7}{15}$ **f** $\frac{1}{2}$

5 **a** $\frac{3}{5}$ **b** 3   **c** $\frac{2}{5}$ **d** $1\frac{1}{2}$

6 **a** $\frac{1}{5}$ **b** 2   **c** $\frac{11}{6}$

7 **a** 20   **b** 15   **c** $\frac{1}{20}$ **d** $5\frac{5}{8}$

8 **a** $\frac{2}{3}$ **b** $1\frac{3}{5}$ **c** $\frac{3}{4}$ **d** $\frac{3}{4}$
   e $-\frac{27}{28}$ **f** $1\frac{1}{24}$

9 **a** $5\frac{1}{60}$ **b** $2\frac{2}{11}$

10 65 minutes or 1 hour 5 minutes or $1\frac{1}{12}$ hours

11 $1\frac{4}{5}$ m

12 $7\frac{11}{14}$ miles

13 $\frac{19}{24}$ km

14 $1\frac{1}{8}$ cm

Challenge

a $\frac{1}{8}$

b Students' own answers

c 128

d Students' own answers, e.g.
Because 10 is not a power of 2 this can't be done by just folding in half and half again.

UNIT 9 Straight-line graphs

9.1 Direct proportion on graphs

1   A 1 kg, B £5.60

2   A and C

3   **a**   20 feet   **b**   9 m

4   Yes; straight line through (0, 0)

5   **a**   4 m (13 feet)   **b**   Stuart (6 feet ≈ 1.8 m)
    c   5 rolls (75 feet ≈ 23 m)

6   B and C

7   **a**   £0
    b   **i**   £20   **ii**   £40
        iii   £60   **iv**   £80
    c   £20
    d   21.25 g
    e   Yes; straight line through (0, 0)
    f   30 g = 2 × 15 g so the cost is 2 × £300 = £600

8   **a**   £1.50   **b**   500 g   **c**   £5.25   **d**   240 g
    e   £22.50   **f**   £1.50
    g   Yes; straight line through (0, 0)
    h   £12

9   **a**   Yes; straight line through (0, 0)
    b   **i**   0.044 ohms   **ii**   0.112 ohms
        iii   0.224 ohms
    c   **i**   1 m   **ii**   18 m

10   **a**

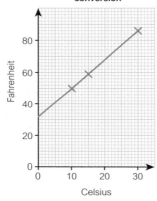

Temperature conversion

    b   70 °F; 64 °F
    c   No; the graph does not go through (0, 0).

11   **a**   Yes; when LPG is 0, amount of CO_2 is 0; when LPG
        doubles, amount of CO_2 doubles.
    b

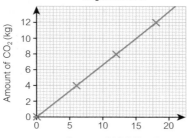

CO_2 emissions

12   **a**

Number of posters	1	2	10
Price (£)	10	17.50	77.50

    b   No; cost for 2 posters is not double the cost for 1 poster.

    c

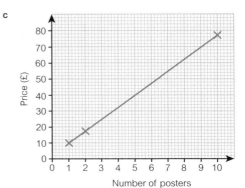

    d   £40

13   **a**   Yes; when height is 0, temperature drop is 0; when height
        doubles, temperature drop doubles.
    b   9.7 °C

14   No; cost for 120 ml is not 4 times the cost for 30 ml.

15   **a**   yes   **b**   6 × £21 = £126
    c   No   **d**   No; the cost of 5 days is directly
                     proportional to the cost of 2 days, but the
                     cost of 7 days is not; so don't know how 6
                     days would be calculated.

16   A and C

Challenge

a

Time (hours)	0	1	2
Distance (km)	0	90	180

b, c

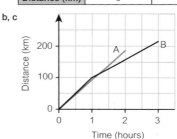

d   the graph for car A

e   Distance is proportional to time taken if the speed is constant.

9.2 Gradients

1   **a**   (3, 9), (8, 24), (10, 30), (10, 30), (−2, −6), (−5, −15)
    b   **i** $y = 7$ **ii** $y = -1$ **iii** $y = -9$

2   B, D, C, A

3   **a**

x	1	2	3	4	5
y	4	6	8	10	12

    b   (1, 4), (2, 6), (3, 8), (4, 10), (5, 12)
    c

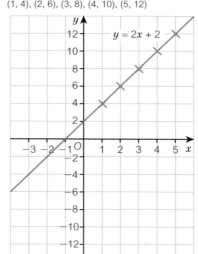

d $y = -4$

4 a

x	−2	−1	0	1	2
y	−9	−7	−5	−3	−1

b

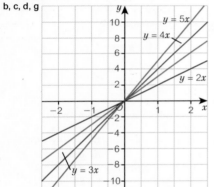

c The two lines are parallel.

5 a

x	−2	0	2
y	−6	0	6

b, c, d, g

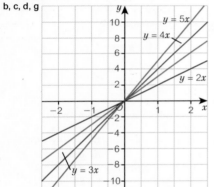

c

x	−2	0	2
y	−8	0	8

d

x	−2	0	2
y	−10	0	10

e $y = 5x$

f straight line through (0, 0) and less steep than $y = 3x$

g

x	−2	0	2
y	−4	0	4

6 a, d

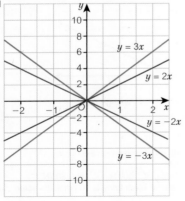

b Both graphs are straight lines through (0, 0) and are equally steep, but they slope in opposite directions.

c straight line through (0, 0) with the same steepness as $y = 3x$ but sloping downwards from left to right

7 a   i 2 squares   **ii** 4 squares
   iii 6 squares

b 2 squares

c   i 3 squares   **ii** 6 squares   **iii** 9 squares

8 A 2   **B** −3

9 a   i lines 3, 4 and 5   **ii** lines 1, 2 and 6

b line 1: −1   line 2: −2   line 3: 1

line 4: $\frac{2}{7}$ line 5: $\frac{2}{7}$ line 6: $-\frac{5}{3}$

10 a 1   **b** 3   **c** 1, 6   **d** 1

e 2, 5

f $\frac{3}{4}$, as it is the largest fraction.

11 a   i $\frac{1}{5}$ **ii** $\frac{1}{10}$

iii $\frac{1}{4}$ **iv** $\frac{1}{3}$

b   i 20%   **ii** 10%
   iii 25%   **iv** 33.3%

c   i

ii

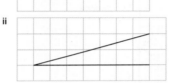

iii

iv

12 a   i

x	−2	−1	0	1	2	3
y	−3	−2	−1	0	1	2

ii

x	−3	−2	−1	0	1
y	−8	−4	0	4	8

iii

x	−2	−1	0	1	2	3
y	7	5	3	1	−1	−3

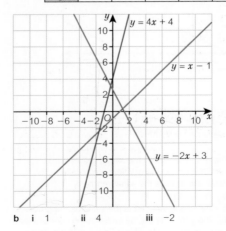

b   i 1   **ii** 4   **iii** −2

c Each gradient is the same as the difference between consecutive y values.

d The gradient is the same as the coefficient of x.

Challenge

a Students' own points from the graphs

b 30 mph, 24 mph, 19.2 mph, 15 mph

c Each line's gradient is the same as that cyclist's speed.

d line A (red); it has the most positive gradient.

9.3 Equations of straight lines

1 a $y = 2$ **b** $x = 2$

2 a i lines 2 and 4   **ii** lines 1 and 3

b line 1: $-2\frac{1}{2}$ line 2: $\frac{5}{9}$

line 3: $-\frac{1}{2}$ line 4: 1

3 a

x	−1	0	1	2	3
y	−7	−3	1	5	9

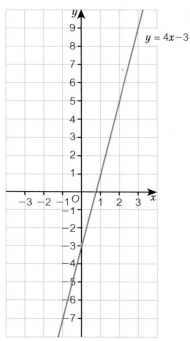

c gradient = 4

4 a

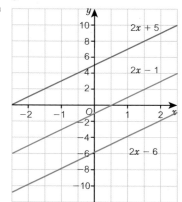

b The gradients are all the same; gradient = 2.

c Lines with the same gradient are parallel. Parallel lines have the same gradient.

5 a $(0, -1)$, $(0, 5)$, $(0, -6)$

b i The coefficient of x is the same as the gradient.

    ii The y-intercept is the same as the constant term.

c between the graphs of $y = 2x - 1$ and $y = 2x + 5$

d

x	−2	−1	0	1	2
$y = 2x + 3$	−1	1	3	5	7

6 a, b

x	−2	−1	0	1	2
y	6	3	0	−3	−6

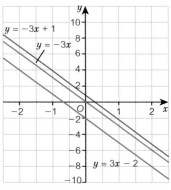

c The y-intercept is the same as the constant term in the equation.

7 a $y = x + 7$ and $y = x + 5$

    $y = -2x + 7$ and $y = -2x + 1$

b $y = x + 7$ and $y = -2x + 7$

    $y = 5x + 1$ and $y = -2x + 1$

    $y = x + 5$ and $y = 2x + 5$

8 a gradient = 1; y-intercept = 2

b $y = x + 2$

c B $y = x + 5$ C $y = x - 4$

    D $y = x$

9 a A $y = 2x + 4$ B $y = 3x$

    C $y = 2x - 1$ D $y = x$

b B and D

c B

d $y = 2x - 1$ (line C) and $y = 2x + 4$ (line A)

10 A $y = \frac{1}{5}x + 5$ B $y = -\frac{1}{5}x + 5$

     C $y = 5x + 5$ D $y = -5x + 5$

11 A $y = x + 3$ B $y = 2x - 2$

     C $y = 3x + 2$ D $y = -2x - 2$

     E $y = -2x + 3$ F $y = 2x + 4$

12 a

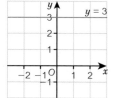

b The value of y is constant and does not depend on the value of x.

13 a

b 2.5 A

c $I = \frac{1}{2}V$

14 a Yes; straight line through the origin

b $F = 10M$

c i 300 N   **ii** 600 N   **iii** 900 N

d The value of each force is 10 times the value of the mass.

Challenge

Students' own graphs and equations, e.g.
$y = 2x$ and $y = 3x + 1$

9 Check up

1 a

x	−2	−1	0	1	2
y	−4	−1	2	5	8

b

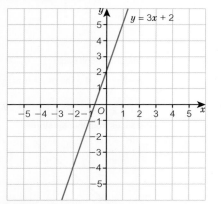

2 a

x	−2	−1	0	1	2
y	−5	−4	−3	−2	−1

b

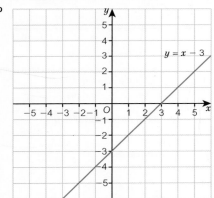

c $y = 3x + 2$ **d** $(0, -3)$

3 A 4 **B** −4 **C** $\frac{2}{3}$

4 A $y = 2x$ **B** $y = x - 2$ **C** $-\frac{1}{4}x + 1$

5 a D **b** B **c** A **d** C

6 a Yes; straight line through the origin
  b 0.6 m
  c **i** $1\frac{1}{4}$ hours **ii** 4 hours

7 a

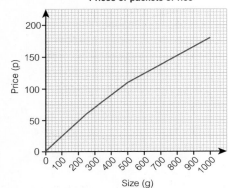

Prices of packets of rice

b No; the graph is not a straight line.

8 Yes; when mass is 0, stretch is 0; when mass doubles, stretch doubles.

Challenge

The higher the exchange rate, the less steep the graph. 2000 is steeper.

9 Strengthen: Straight-line graphs

1 a B **b** B

2 a

x	−2	−1	0	1	2
y	−5	−3	−1	1	3

b $(-2, -5)$, $(-1, -3)$, $(0, -1)$, $(1, 1)$, $(2, 3)$

c

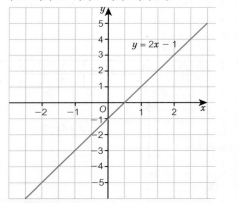

3 a

x	−2	−1	0	1	2
y	−3	−2	−1	0	1

b $(-2, -3)$, $(-1, -2)$, $(0, -1)$, $(1, 0)$, $(2, 1)$

c

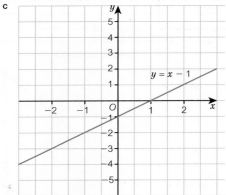

d $y = 2x - 1$

4 The steepness of the graph is called the gradient.
A positive gradient goes up from left to right.
A negative gradient goes down from left to right.

5 a positive **b** 2
  c Gradient of line segment A $= \frac{2}{1} = 2$
  d B 3 C 1 D 5

6 a negative **b** 4
  c Gradient of line segment E $= -\frac{4}{1} = -4$
  d F −2 G −1

7 a i A and B **ii** C and D
  b A 3 B 1 C −4
    D −2

8 a $\frac{1}{2}$ **b** $\frac{1}{4}$ **c** $\frac{1}{3}$ **d** $-\frac{1}{2}$

9 Strengthen: Finding equations of graphs

1 a The gradients are all the same; gradient = 3.

   b

Line	y-intercept
$y = 3x + 3$	3
$y = 3x + 1$	1
$y = 3x$	0
$y = 3x - 2$	-2

   c (0, 5)

2 a 2   b 4   c $y = 2x + 4$

3 A $y = 4x + 1$ B $y = 2x - 2$
   C $y = x + 3$ D $y = \frac{1}{2}x - 1$

4 E $y = -2x + 3$ F $y = \frac{1}{3}x + 1$
   G $y = -3x - 2$ H $y = 4x$

5 a $y = -2x + 1$ and $y = -\frac{1}{2}x - 2$

   b B $y = -2x + 1$ D $y = -\frac{1}{2}x - 2$

   c $y = x + 3$ and $y = 3x + 3$
   d No; both have the same y-intercept.
   e, f A $y = x + 3$ C $y = 3x + 3$

9 Strengthen: Direct proportion

1 d When two quantities are in direct proportion their graph is a straight line through (0, 0).

2 A and C

3 a

Gallons	Litres
0	0
1	4.5
2	9.0
5	22.5
10	45.0
20	90.0

   b

Volume conversion

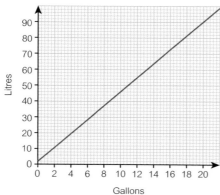

   c i 36 litres   ii 4 gallons
      iii 162 litres   iv 17 gallons
   d Yes; straight line through the origin

4

Cost of 1st class post

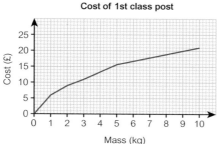

Gradient of line is not constant; cost for 2 kg is not double cost for 1 kg.

5 a No; cost for 2 hours is not double the cost for 1 hour
   b Yes; texts sent is zero, cost is zero; when texts sent multiplies by 10, cost multiplies by 10.

Challenge

Students' own answers

1 a 3   b 3, same answer

2 A $\frac{1}{3}$ B 2   C $-\frac{1}{2}$
   D $\frac{3}{4}$ E $-\frac{2}{3}$

3 a yes, straight line graph through origin
   b $\frac{1}{30}$ c $y = \frac{1}{30}x$ d The gradient is $\frac{1}{30}$

4 a $y = x$ b $y = \frac{x}{2.2}$ c $y = \frac{x}{10}$ d $y = \frac{x}{1.6}$

5

Distances from thunderstorm

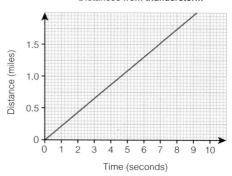

Yes, the distance is in direct proportion to the time (within the bounds of accuracy of the measurements).

6 a 6   b yes   c yes

7 a A and D
   b No; the sequences do not start at zero.

8 a i B   ii A
      iii D   iv C
   b Students' own explanations

9 quantities C and D

Challenge

Students' own answers

9 Unit test

1 a $\frac{2}{5}$ b 40%

2 a

x	-2	-1	0	1	2
y	9	7	5	3	1

   b, c

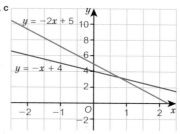

   d $y = -2x + 5$ e (0, 4)

3 a A 2   B $\frac{1}{3}$ C $-\frac{1}{2}$ D $\frac{2}{3}$
   b A $y = 2x - 3$ B $y = \frac{1}{3}x + 4$
      C $-\frac{1}{2}x + 1$ D $y = \frac{2}{3}x$

4 a

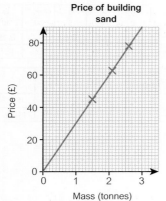

Price of building sand

b Yes; straight line through the origin

c £30

5 No; when the units used doubles from 50 to 100, the cost does not double. £21.50 is not double £19.25.

6 a *D*   **b** *B*   **c** *C*   **d** *A*

7 a Yes; when the number of tins doubles, the cost doubles.

b No; when the number of tins doubles from 1 to 2, the cost does not double. £4.98 is not double £3.99.

8 a

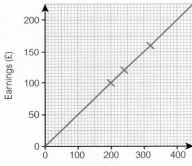

Journalist's earnings

b £150   **c** $E = \dfrac{N}{2}$

Challenge

a

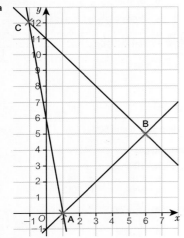

right angled

b *AB*: $y = x - 1$
BC: $y = -x + 11$
CA: $y = -6x + 6$

UNIT 10 Percentages, decimals and fractions

10.1 Fractions and decimals

1   3, 3.0, 3.00 and 3.000; 3.33 and 3.330

2   **a**   0.4   **b**   0.3   **c**   0.23   **d**   0.03
   e   0.08   **f**   0.15

3   **a** $\frac{1}{5}$ **b** $\frac{11}{50}$ **c** $\frac{1}{50}$

4   **a**   3.25 hours (B)   **b**   3.5 hours (A)
   c   3.75 hours (C)

5   **a** $3\frac{2}{10}$ hours = 3.2 hours

   b   5.6 hours   **c**   13.7 hours
   d   0.4 hours

6   **a** $1\frac{12}{60}$ hours = 1 hour 12 minutes

   b   4 hours 18 minutes   **c**   9 hours 6 minutes
   d   8 hours 54 minutes

7   Jayne is not correct because 48 minutes is not 0.48 hours;
   it is 0.8 hours.

8   **a**   0.007   **b**   0.071   **c**   0.471

9   **a** $\frac{519}{1000}$ **b** $\frac{19}{1000}$ **c** $\frac{9}{1000}$ **d** $\frac{109}{1000}$

10   **a** $\frac{7}{200}$ **b** $\frac{181}{500}$ **c** $\frac{32}{125}$ **d** $7\frac{1}{8}$

   e $63\frac{1}{40}$

11   Shelly has put the denominator as 1000 when it should
   be 10000. You can divide Shelly's answer by 10 to get the
   correct conversion.

12   **a**   0.625   **b**   0.875   **c**   0.3125

13   **a**   The 6 recurs but the calculator rounds the last digit up to 7.

   b $0.333333333 = \frac{1}{3}$ $0.8333333333 = \frac{5}{6}$

     $2.1666666667 = \frac{13}{6}$ $0.6666666667 = \frac{2}{3}$

     $0.1428571429 = \frac{1}{7}$ $1.6666666667 = \frac{5}{3}$

14   **a** $0.\dot{8}$ **b** $0.\dot{3}\dot{6}$ **c** $0.4\dot{2}$ **d** $0.3\dot{0}\dot{5}$
   e $0.\dot{1}23\dot{4}$ **f** $0.6\dot{3}$

15   Terminating: 2, 4, 5, 8, 10
   Recurring: 3, 6, 7, 9, 11, 12, 13, 14, 15

   $\frac{1}{3} = 0.\dot{3}, \frac{1}{6} = 0.1\dot{6}, \frac{1}{7} = 0.\dot{1}4285\dot{7}, \frac{1}{9} = 0.\dot{1}, \frac{1}{11} = 0.\dot{0}\dot{9},$

   $\frac{1}{12} = 0.08\dot{3}, \frac{1}{13} = 0.\dot{0}7692\dot{3}, \frac{1}{14} = 0.0\dot{7}1428\dot{5}, \frac{1}{15} = 0.0\dot{6}$

16   $\frac{5}{9} = 0.\dot{5}, \frac{2}{11} = 0.\dot{1}\dot{8}, \frac{4}{15} = 0.2\dot{6}, \frac{5}{12} = 0.41\dot{6}$

17   **a** $5.1\dot{6}$ hours   **b** $3.\dot{3}$ hours
   c $7.\dot{6}$ hours   **d** $6.0\dot{6}$ hours

18   the parallelogram

19   $\frac{5}{8}, \frac{3}{5}, \frac{1}{2}, \frac{5}{12}, \frac{1}{3}$

20   $0.76, \frac{13}{20}, 0.\dot{6}\dot{3}, 0.625, \frac{3}{5}, \frac{8}{15}$

Challenge

a   **i**   0.125   **ii**   0.0625   **iii**   0.1875
b   **i** $0.\dot{2}$ **ii** $0.\dot{3}$ **iii** $0.\dot{4}$

c   Multiples of $\frac{1}{16}$ will be terminating decimals as the unit fraction
   $\frac{1}{16}$ is a terminating decimal.

   Multiples of $\frac{1}{9}$ in the 9 times table will give whole numbers.
   Other multiples of $\frac{1}{9}$ will give recurring decimals as the unit
   fraction $\frac{1}{9}$ is a recurring decimal.

10.2 Equivalent proportions

1   **a**   200 × 5 = 1000   **b**   250 × 4 = 1000

   c $12.5 \div 100 = \frac{1}{8}$

2   **a** $\frac{2}{5}$, 0.4   **b** $\frac{7}{25}$, 0.28

   c $\frac{2}{3}$, 0.67 (2 d.p.)   **d** $\frac{2}{15}$, 0.13 (2 d.p.)

3
Fraction	$\frac{3}{4}$	$\frac{1}{5}$	$\frac{3}{5}$	$\frac{7}{10}$	$\frac{9}{50}$	1
Decimal	0.75	0.2	0.6	0.7	0.18	1
Percentage	75%	20%	60%	70%	18%	100%

4
Mixed number	$1\frac{1}{2}$	$1\frac{7}{10}$	$1\frac{4}{5}$	$1\frac{1}{10}$	$1\frac{1}{20}$
Decimal	1.5	1.7	1.8	1.1	1.05
Percentage	150%	170%	180%	110%	105%

5   Students' own explanations, e.g.
   The profits are 2 times what they were before.

6   **a** $2\frac{1}{2}$ **b**   2.5

7   **a** $\frac{2}{25}$

   b   **i**   0.08   **ii**   8%

8   **a**   **i** $\frac{1}{10}$, 0.1, 10%   **ii** $\frac{261}{500}$, 0.522, 52.2%

     iii $\frac{17}{250}$, 0.068, 6.8%

   b   Brand B   **c**   Brand B

9   **b**   0.475 = 47.5%   **c**   0.125 = 12.5%
   d   0.048 = 4.8%   **e**   0.034 = 3.4%
   f   0.052 = 5.2%

10   **a**   24%   **b**   12.4%   **c**   37.5%   **d**   8.8%
   e   13.33%

11   91/(287 + 213) × 100 = 18.2%

12   **a** $\frac{114}{125}$ **b**   91.2%

13   Geoff

14   **a**   Caroline: $\frac{280}{1000} = \frac{28}{100} = 28\%$

     Greg: $\frac{7}{25} = \frac{28}{100} = 28\%$

   b   Caroline: $\frac{185}{1000} = 18.5\%$

     Greg: $\frac{18.5}{100} = 18.5\%$

   c   Students' own answers

15   **a**   200
   b   **i**   27.5%   **ii**   17.5%   **iii**   25%

16   bracelets

17   Route B

18   **a** $\frac{3}{8}$ **b**   37.5%

19   **b** $0.125 = \frac{1}{8}$ **c** $0.095 = \frac{19}{200}$ **d** $0.342 = \frac{171}{500}$

   e $0.624 = \frac{78}{125}$ **f** $0.028 = \frac{7}{250}$

20   $\frac{3}{4}$, 78.5%, 80%, $\frac{7}{8}$, 0.885

Challenge

Students' own answers,

e.g. $\frac{4}{5}$, 0.8, 80% and $\frac{12}{24}$, 0.5 and 50%

10.3 Writing percentages

1   **a**   1000   **b**   1000

2   **a**   £8   **b**   £16   **c**   £4
   d   £12   **e**   80p   **f**   £12.80

3   **a** $\frac{11}{100}$, 11%   **b** $\frac{11}{50}$, 22%

   c $\frac{11}{250}$, 4.4%   **d** $\frac{2}{25}$, 8%

4   66%

5   2.8%

6   8%

7   **a**   25%   **b**   10%   **c**   75%

8   16.8%

9   **a**   24%   **b**   76%

10   **a**   £3   **b**   £18

11 £963.60

12 £25 500

13 a £25   b £525

14 a £50   b £6   c £400   d £48

15 £540

16 £8125

17 a £10   b £30   c £430

18 a £2.50   b £22.50

19 £741

20 £232 800

21 a £1020   b £1260

22 £112.50

23 £18.30

Challenge

1 a 10% increase, 20% decrease
   b 20% increase, 25% decrease
   c 40% increase, 15% decrease

2 No; the final price is £99 not £100.

10.4 Percentages of amounts

1 a 4.74 m
   b £3087.20

2 a 0.3   b 0.76   c 1.5   d 2.65
   e 0.05   f 0.035

3 a £6.80   b 4.5 kg   c 48 ml   d 2.4 g

4 a 1.5   b £10 000

5 105 000

6 $1976.25

7 a £9   b £36   c £36
   d The answers are the same.
     100% − 20% is the same as 80%.

8 a 0.8   b 0.6   c 0.3   d 0.25
   e 0.92   f 0.76   g 0.05   h 0.01

9 a 4.8 litres   b £45   c 39 ml   d 728 m
   e 0.84 kg

10 1.84 m

11 a 30p   b £1.80   c £1.80
   d The answers are the same.
     100% + 20% is the same as 120%.

12 a 1.2   b 1.3   c 1.88   d 1.02

13 a 3.6 kg   b £3.76   c 2.875 tonnes
   d $7.77   e 5.3 km   f 4.26 m

14 a 40 × 1.55
   b 62 megabits per second

15 2938 people

16 £24 012.80 or £24 013 or £24 000

17 a £600   b 400 kg   c 300 litres
   d 600 km   e 50 cm

18 £9

19 £3.79 million (2 d.p.)

Challenge

£561 − £550 = £11

10 Check up

1 $0.2\dot{1}$

2 a $\frac{133}{200}$ b $4\frac{3}{500}$ c $\frac{121}{200}$

3 a 0.333... hour or $0.\dot{3}$ hour
   b recurring

4 0.75, 0.4, $\frac{3}{8}$, $\frac{7}{20}$, $\frac{1}{3}$, 30%, $\frac{1}{4}$, 4.5%

5 a i Elm Street $\frac{3}{10}$

      Oak Street $\frac{29}{100}$

      Ash Street $\frac{36}{125}$

   ii Elm Street 30%
      Oak Street 29%
      Ash Street 28.8%
   b Elm Street

6

Fraction	Decimal	Percentage
$\frac{9}{40}$	0.225	22.5%
$\frac{27}{200}$	0.135	13.5%
$\frac{17}{10}$	1.7	170%

7 98%

8 a £3.60   b £21.60

9 £25.50

10 a 180 g   b 49.95 kg   c £115.20   d 411.6 ml

11 a £19.50   b £78   c £728

12 a £4000   b 300 km

13 £200

Challenge

1 Students' own answers, e.g.
   a $\frac{3}{25}$, $\frac{7}{50}$, $\frac{17}{200}$
   b 0.12, 12%; 0.14, 14%; 0.085, 8.5%
   c $\frac{17}{200}$, $\frac{3}{25}$, $\frac{7}{50}$

2 Students' own answers e.g.
   10% of £80, 20% of £40, 40% of £20, 80% of £10

3 Students' own answers, e.g.
   20% off £30, 50% off £48, 40% off £40

10 Strengthen: Fractions, decimals and percentages

1 a $\frac{125}{1000} = 0.125$ b $\frac{375}{1000} = 0.375$
   c $\frac{25}{1000} = 0.025$ d $\frac{75}{1000} = 0.075$

2 a 12.5%   b 37.5%   c 2.5%   d 7.5%

3 a $0.62 = \frac{62}{100} = \frac{31}{50}$ b $0.625 = \frac{625}{1000} = \frac{5}{8}$

4 0.19, 18.5%, $\frac{7}{40}$

5 a $\frac{9}{40}$ b 22.5%

6 a $\frac{21}{125}$ b 16.8%

7 the knitting club

8 a $\frac{3}{5}$ = 60% of students like PE.

   b $\frac{13}{25}$ = 52% of members of a judo club are girls.

   c $\frac{16}{25}$ = 64% of members of a boxing club are boys.

   d $\frac{1}{5}$ = 20% of students have a cat.

   e $\frac{4}{5}$ = 80% of DVD purchases are made online.

9 a 12   b 200
   c i Perfect Pooches $\frac{2}{25}$
      Cool K9s $\frac{3}{10}$

      Delightful Dogs $\frac{21}{125}$

    ii Perfect Pooches 8%
      Cool K9s 30%
      Delightful Dogs 16.8%
   d Cool K9s

10 a $\frac{7}{1000}$ b $\frac{73}{1000}$ c $\frac{173}{1000}$ d $\frac{1073}{10000}$

11 Terminating: 1.6, 1.06, 0.166,
   Recurring: $0.1\dot{6}$, $0.10\dot{6}$, $1.0\dot{6}$

12 $0.1\dot{6} = 0.166666...$
   $0.10\dot{6} = 0.106106...$
   $1.0\dot{6} = 1.060606...$

13 $\frac{1}{30} = 0.0\dot{3}$ $\frac{1}{3} = 0.\dot{3}$ $\frac{2}{33} = 0.\dot{0}\dot{6}$

$\frac{2}{30} = 0.0\dot{6}$ $\frac{2}{3} = 0.\dot{6}$ $\frac{1}{33} = 0.\dot{0}\dot{3}$

10 Strengthen: Percentage problems

1 a 0.48 m, 48% b 1.5 cm, 30%
   c 0.13 kg, 26% d 0.3 litres, 15%
   e 0.75 km, 25%

2 a £66 b £72 c £54 d £77
   e £73.50 f £80.50

3 a £2 b £4 c £6 d £206

4 a £81 b £72 c £36 d £38
   e £34 f £102

5 a £39.20
   b 141% of 150 g = 1.41 × 150 = 211.50 g
   c 106% of 55 m = 1.06 × 55 = 58.3 m
   d 115% of 77 litres = 1.15 × 77 = 88.55 litres

6 a £44
   b 60% of 125 g = 0.6 × 125 = 75 g
   c 99% of 2000 km = 0.99 × 2000 = 1980 km

7 1% is £1.20, 100% is £120

8 a 6 g b 600 g

9 a 90% b £2000

Challenge

a

Year	Value at start of year	Percentage change	Value at end of year
1st	£120 000	10% increase	£132 000
2nd	£132 000	15% increase	£151 800
3rd	£151 800	20% decrease	£121 440
4th	£121 440	25% increase	£151 800
5th	£151 800	15% decrease	£129 030

b £9030

10 Extend

1 Method A

2 £15 875

3 a

Year	Value at start of year	Percentage change	Value at end of year
1st	£5000	20% increase	£6000
2nd	£6000	8% increase	£6480
3rd	£6480	12% decrease	£5702.40
4th	£5702.40	10% increase	£6272.64
5th	£6272.64	3% decrease	£6084.46

b i £1084.46 ii 21.7% (1 d.p.)

4 a 294 cm² b 95 mm

5 a

Time	10 00	10 30	11 00	11 30	12 00	12 30	13 00
Number of bacteria	100	140	196	274	384	538	753

b

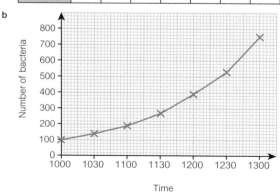

c i between 160 and 180
   ii between 12 20 and 12 25
   d It might not be accurate as a faulty fridge might slowly increase in temperature until it reached room temperature.

6 1.6% this year

7 a i $\frac{3}{4}$ ii $\frac{1}{4}$
   b i £450 ii £150
   c £36

8 5.3 cm

9 a i 400, 120, 36, 10.8
       ii 80, 96, 115.2, 138.24
   b i The term-by-term rule is 'multiply by 0.6'.
      ii Each term in the sequence is 60% of the previous term.
   c i multiply by 0.5
      ii multiply by 0.7
      iii multiply by 1.6
      iv multiply by 1.25
   d 500, 550, 605, 665.5, 732.05, ...

Challenge

Students' own answers

10 Unit test

1

Fraction	$\frac{3}{4}$	$\frac{9}{10}$	$\frac{1}{4}$	$2\frac{3}{4}$	$1\frac{3}{10}$	$1\frac{3}{5}$
Decimal	0.75	0.9	0.25	2.75	1.3	1.6
Percentage	75%	90%	25%	275%	130%	160%

2 a $\frac{51}{200}$ b $4\frac{21}{50}$

3 a i Group A $\frac{72}{125}$
         Group B $\frac{37}{50}$
         Group C $\frac{71}{100}$
      ii Group A 57.6%
         Group B 74%
         Group C 71%
   b Group B

4 40%

5 a £64 b £384

6

Fraction	Decimal	Percentage
$\frac{131}{200}$	0.655	65.5%
$\frac{21}{40}$	0.525	52.5%
$\frac{1}{40}$	0.025	2.5%

7 $\frac{7}{8}, \frac{4}{5}, \frac{3}{4}, \frac{2}{3}$

8 $0.0\dot{4}\dot{5}$

9 £39

10 £23 760

11 a 62 kg b 240 m

12 £2160

13 £900

Challenge

a Students' own answers

b No; the price after the combined discount is 56% of the original price, not 50%.

c Students' own answers, e.g.
   Work out the multiplier for each discount separately, and multiply them to find the multiplier for the combined discount.

Index